STUDIO OF THE SOUTH

MARTIN BAILEY

STUDIO OF THE SOUTH

VAN GOGH IN PROVENCE

FRANCES LINCOLN

First published in 2016 by Frances Lincoln Publishing
an imprint of the Quarto Group
The Old Brewery, 6 Blundell Street, London, N7 9BH, United Kingdom
www.QuartoKnows.com

Studio of the South: Van Gogh in Provence
Text copyright © Martin Bailey 2016
Illustrations copyright © as listed on page 223–4

Paperpack edition published in 2021 by Frances Lincoln Publishing

A catalogue record for this book is available from the British Library.

978-0-7112-6818-0

Printed and bound in China

1 2 3 4 5 6 7 8 9

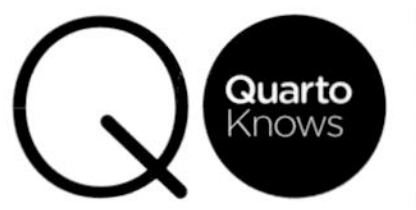

Quarto is the authority on a wide range of topics.
Quarto educates, entertains and enriches the lives of
our readers – enthusiasts and lovers of hands-on living.
www.QuartoKnows.com

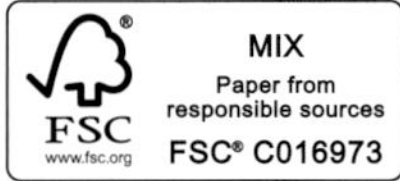

CONTENTS

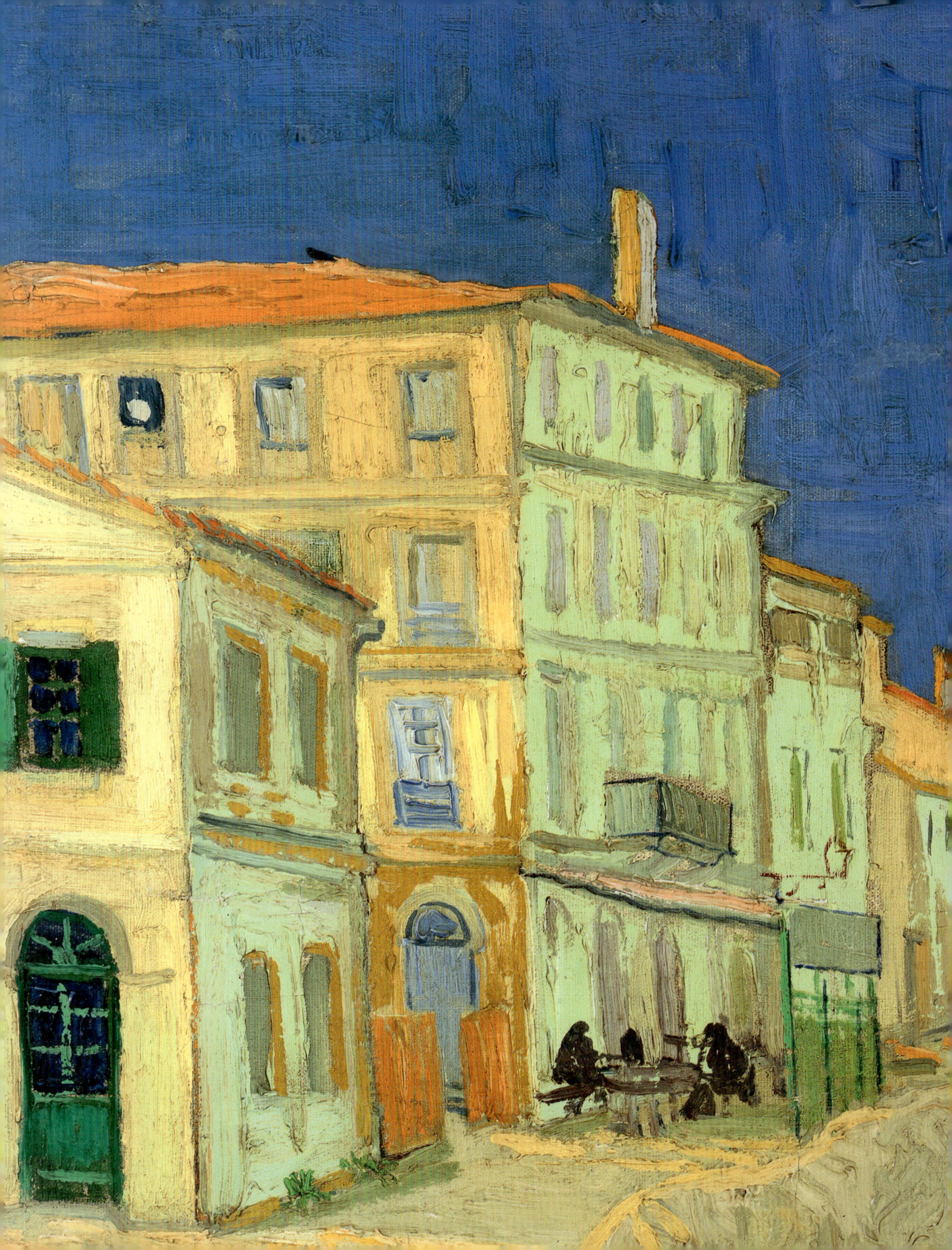

PREFACE

Vincent van Gogh created his most exuberant works in Arles, under the strong sun of Provence. During his fifteen-month stay in 1888–89 he completed around 200 paintings, at the impressive rate of over three a week. These include many of his finest works: blossoming orchards, golden wheatfields, Mediterranean seascapes, portraits of the postman and flower still lifes. This book reproduces a third of his Arles paintings – most of his iconic works, along with lesser known pictures such as his recently accepted portrait of Gauguin (fig. 97).[1]

Van Gogh's home and studio was the Yellow House, which he rented two months after his arrival in Arles. It provided his own personal space to sleep and paint – a welcome change from a cramped hotel room. Van Gogh immediately dreamed of sharing his new home with a fellow artist from Paris. Life would be cheaper, but more importantly it would be stimulating to live and work with a companion. He described it as the 'studio in the south'. Vincent first used this expression in a letter to his brother Theo. Asking for money to buy beds and other furniture, he exclaimed: 'How I'd like to set myself up so that I could have a home of my own!'[2] Once furnished, 'we'd have a studio in the south where we could put someone up'. He regarded his beloved Yellow House as not simply a physical space, but a 'living studio'.[3]

The Yellow House gives a vivid impression of his home and its setting, the bright yellows contrasting dramatically with the deep blue sky (fig. 1). Located on Place Lamartine, half way between the railway station and the ramparts of Arles, the house was 'painted outside in the yellow of fresh butter, with garish green shutters'.[4] Van Gogh's half of the building had just been repainted and its exterior stands out brighter than the neighbouring part with the pink awning.

Detail of fig. 1 *The Yellow House*, Van Gogh Museum, Amsterdam (Vincent van Gogh Foundation)

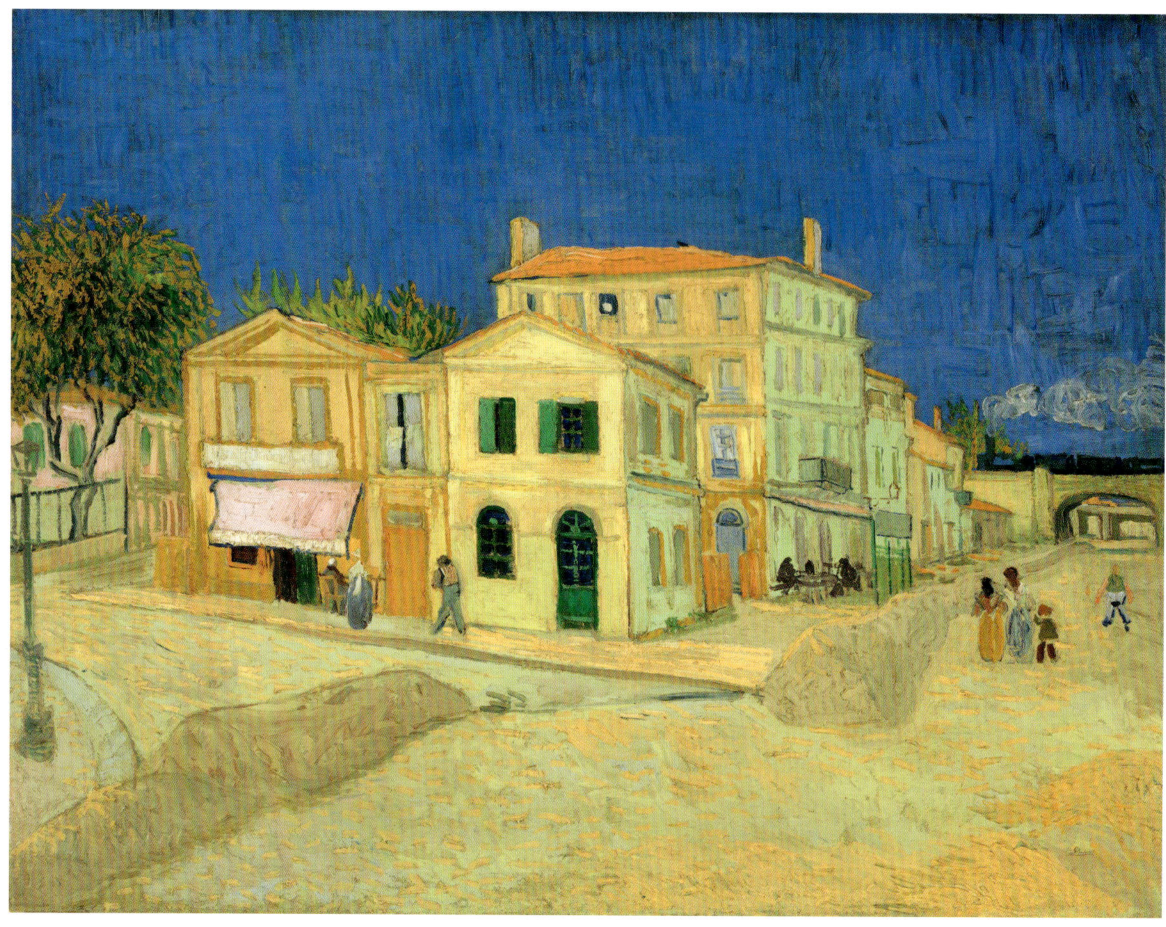

The green front door with window panes opened into the lounge, which served as his studio. Beyond lay the kitchen. Upstairs there were two bedrooms, one for Van Gogh (with closed shutters in the painting) and a smaller guest room. When Van Gogh talked of his 'studio', he usually meant the entire house. Art was his life and took up most of his waking hours. Although there was no toilet, he had access to one in the larger building just behind the Yellow House, which included a café (in the painting, drinkers are seated outside, see detail, p. 6).

The other half of the building with the Yellow House housed a grocery shop (with the pink awning) on the ground floor, and the tiny figure with a white bonnet seated on the pavement could well be its proprietor, Marguerite Crevoulin. Outside the central window on the upper floor, above the main door, both households could hamg up their washing to dry (as can be seen in

ABOVE fig. 1 *The Yellow House*, September 1888, oil on canvas, 72 x 92 cm, Van Gogh Museum, Amsterdam (Vincent van Gogh Foundation) (F464)

RIGHT fig. 2 The Yellow House and Avenue de Montmajour, c.1905, postcard (detail)[5]

the painting, see detail on p. 34). The rooms of Marguerite and her husband François Damase Crevoulin were upstairs. I was in touch with the grandson of the family who lived in the building in the early 1920s, and he confirms that the staircase which lay in the centre of the building (behind the orange-brown door in the painting) gave access to the rooms of both Van Gogh and the Crevoulins.[6] The two households would therefore sometimes encounter each other in the evenings. It has not been appreciated that this easy access to each other's rooms understandably terrified Madame Crevoulin after the ear incident – and ultimately forced Van Gogh to vacate the Yellow House.

The earliest surviving photograph showing the exterior of the Yellow House dates from around 1905 (fig. 2). The building looks rather as it did in Van Gogh's time, although the yellow has become dirty and the lower facade of the grocery shop has been whitewashed. As for the interior of the Yellow House, this book is the first to include a photograph of what had once been the artist's bedroom with its later owner (fig. 119). Sadly, the Yellow House was bombed during the Second World War and then demolished.

For Van Gogh, the countryside around Arles represented an extension of his 'studio'. He relished working outdoors in the landscapes that had enticed him from Paris. Provence would quickly make a deep impact on Van Gogh's art and his palette was transformed by the heightened colours he encountered under its powerful sun. As he wrote in June, four months after his arrival: 'When the vegetation is fresh it's a rich green the like of which we seldom see in the north, calm. When it gets scorched and dusty it doesn't become ugly, but then a landscape takes on tones of gold of

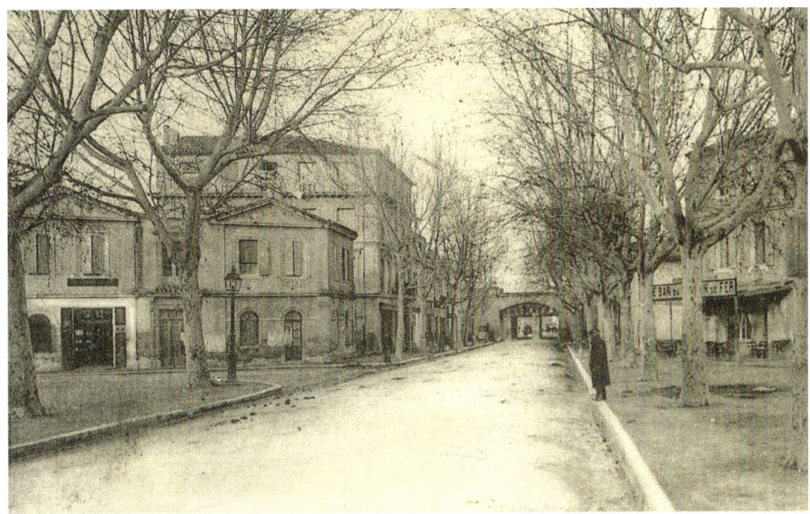

every shade.'[7] It was in Arles that Van Gogh first described himself as a 'landscape painter'.[8]

* * *

Van Gogh's stay in Provence produced the artist we know and love today. Yet this is the first comprehensive book covering the art of his 444 days in Arles.[9] I should emphasise that this book does not deal with his subsequent year in the asylum at Saint-Rémy, 20 kilometres to the north-east, where he stayed from May 1889 to May 1890.

Researching the Arles story became a quest of discovery. I spent many days exploring the narrow streets of the city's historic centre. I imagined Van Gogh shopping in the market, patronising modest restaurants, arguing about art with friends in the cafés, attending bullfights, buying paint and canvas, posting letters to his brother and indulging in his fortnightly visits to the brothel.

I searched for accounts of witnesses who had encountered Van Gogh in Arles. Nearly all were dead by the Second World War, but a few had been interviewed by early Van Gogh specialists.[10] Scant attention has been paid to many of these recollections and I unearthed memories which shed fresh light on the artist's stay.

It was much too late to meet anyone who had known Van Gogh, with one notable exception, Jeanne Calment. She would have been 13 when, she claims, Van Gogh bought canvas from her family's textile shop. On her death, aged 122, she was the oldest person who has ever lived. By the time I interviewed Madame Calment her stories were well honed. Van Gogh, she told me, was an ugly man, 'more interested in drinking than painting'. The local children teased him, although they were frightened by his unkempt appearance. 'Most of the girls were afraid of him, but the prostitutes liked him because he paid them well,' she explained. Van Gogh eventually went mad and 'sliced off his ear like a piece of cheese'.[11]

I found Pauline Mourard, daughter of Dr Félix Rey (who treated Van Gogh), somewhat more reliable. She was a sprightly 90 when I met her, still living close to the Trinquetaille Bridge, where Van Gogh would visit her father. Pauline had been born eight years after the artist's departure, but she vividly recalled family stories about him. When we met, she had never seen the original of the famous portrait of her father (fig. 109), since it was at Moscow's Pushkin Museum in the Soviet Union. 'I want to see it before I die,' she told me. Her wish was granted in 1989, when the portrait came on loan to an exhibition in Arles, and she passed away later that year.[12]

It is now unusual to hear fresh (and authentic-sounding) memories about people who had encountered Van Gogh. I was therefore delighted to make contact with a family who owned land around Montmajour. In his letters, Van Gogh writes about sketching there, deep in the countryside five kilometres from Arles. For refreshments, he had to make do with 'a bit of bread and some milk, it being too far to be going back to town'.[13] But this may not have been the full story. A descendant of the family who then owned the local vineyards told me that her great-grandmother had recalled regularly giving Van Gogh wine to keep him going.[14]

Most writers have assumed that in Arles Van Gogh was relatively isolated from other artists – with the notable exception of Gauguin. Van Gogh's situation was certainly very different from that in Paris, where he moved in avant-garde circles and met many of the leading Impressionists. There were, however, a surprising number of artists in and around Arles, many of whom were also foreign visitors.[15] This book illustrates some of their pictures, providing revealing comparisons with the paintings of Van Gogh and emphasising how his work stands out. We reproduce an article from an 1888 newspaper which names several painters working in Arles, including 'Mr Vincent, an impressionist artist' (fig. 70). Comparing Van Gogh's paintings with early photographs of his motifs (such as postcard views) is also interesting, showing how he would modify the landscape for artistic effect.

* * *

The tragic end of the Studio of the South came with Van Gogh's self-mutilation. Why did he cut off his ear – and then present it to a prostitute? Behind this sensationalist query lies a more serious conundrum: what made such a creative artist become so self-destructive? As Claude Monet put it so well, 'how could a man who has loved flowers and light so much and has rendered them so well, how could he have managed to be so unhappy'?[16]

The trigger for the self-mutilation, I believe, has largely been overlooked.[17] Just a few hours before Van Gogh cut his ear he received a letter from Paris. This brought news that his brother had met Johanna (Jo) Bonger, a young Dutch woman visiting Paris, and within days they had decided to marry. Vincent feared that he would then 'lose' Theo, his closest companion. He was equally worried that his brother might withdraw the financial support which had enabled him to devote his life to art. All this was threatened by the unexpected appearance of a fiancée.

Had Van Gogh been elated by the engagement, it is virtually inconceivable that he would have sliced off part of his ear a few hours after receiving Theo's news, whatever other difficulties he was facing – even his deteriorating relations with Gauguin. The engagement may not have been the fundamental cause, but it sparked off this destructive act. Medical specialists and psychiatrists have endlessly debated Van Gogh's underlying medical and mental problems, with little consensus.

I also discovered more about the brothel which Van Gogh visited on that fateful night. For many years I had asked to see the municipality's nineteenth-century file on registered brothels, but the papers remained closed on grounds of confidentiality. Eventually I was allowed access.[18] By coincidence, the archive is now located in the town's former hospital, so I ended up consulting the file in what had been part of one of the wards on the floor where the artist had been treated. Although the papers contained no direct references to Van Gogh, it did help to confirm the place where he delivered his gruesome package: 1 Rue du Bout d'Arles.[19]

The location is also confirmed in an extremely rare international directory of brothels. Entitled the *Annuaire Reirum* (named after its publisher, Murier, spelt backwards), it lists addresses in countries ranging from Algeria to the Netherlands. No copies of the 1890 edition survive in any library, but fortuitously the first page of the alphabetical directory (which covers Arles) was reprinted two years later in a treatise on prostitution.[20]

The brothel can be spotted in the balloon view of the town (fig. 9). It is the last house in the bottom right corner, close to the ramparts and the canal. Rue du Bout d'Arles is the narrow street that runs towards the right from the middle of the church tower.

The original register of the Arles hospital disappeared long ago, but Van Gogh's admission entry had been seen by the poet Alfred Massebieau, who transcribed it in a letter written in 1893. Although Massebieau's letter was first published in a literary journal half a century later, it has escaped the attention of Van Gogh scholars.[21] I also discovered the earliest newspaper report on the ear incident, published on Christmas Day 1888, the day after Van Gogh was admitted to hospital (fig. 106).

My research threw up other surprises. Dr Rey, who treated Van Gogh in hospital, is known to have been curious about his art, but so too were other colleagues at the hospital. Just a week after Van Gogh had been deemed dangerous enough to be locked up in an isolation cell (on a bed with leather wrist-straps), he convinced three busy senior staff to return with him to his home in order to view his pictures.

It is widely known that Van Gogh failed to sell his paintings and was virtually ignored by the art establishment during his lifetime. Although largely true, it was while he was in Arles that the first signs of appreciation began to emerge.[22] But most Van Gogh specialists have failed to notice that one of his orchard scenes was admired by Jozef Israëls – then revered as the greatest living Dutch artist. On seeing *Pink Peach Trees* (fig. 12), the elderly Israëls described Van Gogh as 'a clever lad!'[23]

I was struck by the way that Van Gogh's still-life paintings are so revealing – because of the very personal reasons he has for selecting the objects he chooses to depict. In *Still Life with Coffee Pot* (fig. 18) he celebrates his newly-found domestic bliss (and his love of coffee). *The Bedroom* (fig. 21) represents a moment just after he had furnished the room where he sought utter peace and a place to dream of the pictures he would paint. *Van Gogh's Chair* (fig. 98) is a sort of self-portrait, depicting his trusty pipe and tobacco (he smoked incessantly and this represented a constant source of solace). *Still Life with Onions and Letter* (fig. 111) includes the envelope of the most important letter which he ever received.

* * *

Separating Van Gogh's life from his art is difficult; both are so closely intertwined. It is the art which has lasting importance and which is the primary focus of this book, but an understanding of the personal challenges he faced lends an added dimension to his achievements. I have set out to tell both stories, covering his fifteen months in Arles (after setting the scene with an introductory prologue on Paris, where he lived for two years before heading south).

My aim has been to look afresh at Van Gogh, using new sources and images to illuminate his period of greatest creativity. Some 20 of the illustrations reproduced here have never previously appeared in the Van Gogh literature. The unfolding story of Van Gogh in Arles is presented more or less chronologically, but in chapters focusing on different aspects of his art or life. Where possible, I have used his own eloquent words about pictures, places and people. Van Gogh's art and his letters allow us the privilege of looking at Provence through his own eyes – the flowering fruit trees, golden wheatfields, luxuriant vineyards and gnarled olive trees. His exploration of the Provençal landscape played a key role in leading the way to a transformation of modern painting. I hope you, the reader, will enjoy following Van Gogh on this journey of discovery.

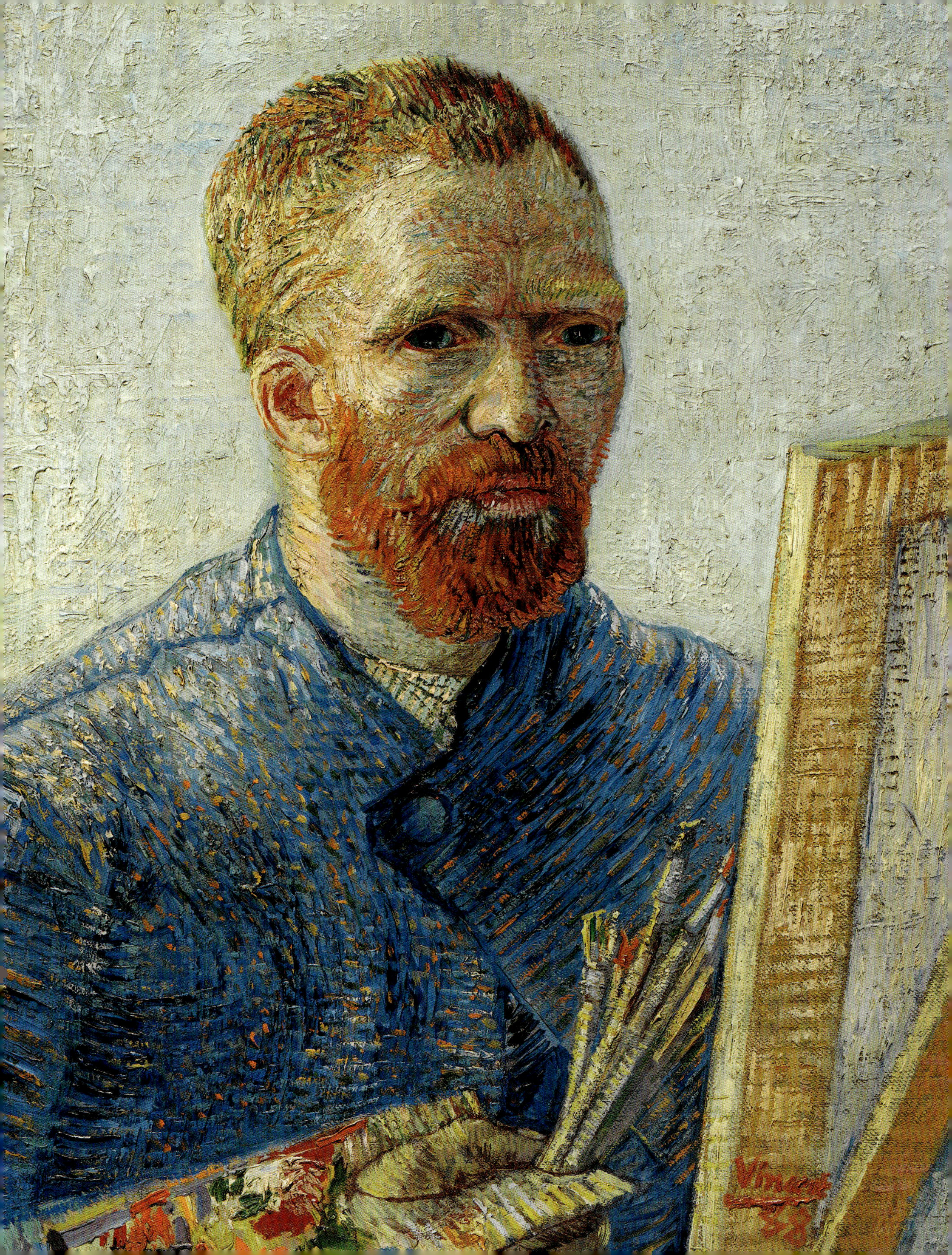

Vincent
88

PARIS

'It seems to be almost impossible to be able to work in Paris, unless you have a refuge in which to recover and regain your peace of mind'[1]

Self-portrait as an Artist (fig. 3) was probably the last picture which Van Gogh completed while living in Paris, before his departure for Arles. The artist is working on a canvas which is hidden from our view. He holds his palette, with two little pots for oil and turpentine, along with seven brushes – ready for use. Most of Van Gogh's numerous self-portraits are simple head-and-shoulders compositions, but here he depicts himself in the act of painting. He stares out beyond his easel.

Van Gogh described this self-portrait as showing him with 'a very red beard, quite unkempt'.[2] His pursed lips and sunken, darkened eyes suggest a certain melancholy. Most striking is the determined gaze of the man, focused on the task of expanding the boundaries of modern art. He worked on this picture intermittently for several weeks in February 1888, a long time for someone who could complete a work in a single day. Pleased with the final result, he proudly signed it in red on the back of the stretcher frame in the painting.

Vincent left the self-portrait behind in Paris as a parting gift to his brother Theo – and as a reminder of his presence during the previous two years. In this picture, he later wrote, he had been seeking 'a deeper likeness than that of the photographer'.[3] Theo's wife Jo later agreed, praising it as the self-portrait which was 'most like him'.[4]

Detail of fig. 3 *Self-portrait as an Artist*, Van Gogh Museum, Amsterdam (Vincent van Gogh Foundation)

This self-portrait vividly demonstrates the enormous strides Van Gogh had made during his stay in Paris. He had turned to art fairly late in life and it was not until he was 27, and living in Brussels, that he seriously began to draw. He returned to his native Netherlands in 1881, where he spent four years developing his skills, essentially by himself – in Etten, The Hague, Drenthe and Nuenen. After a short stay in Antwerp during the winter of 1885–86 he arrived in Paris in February 1886, to immerse himself in the excitement of its highly creative art scene. Paris was the hub of the Impressionists, whose light-infused scenes were taking painting into new realms.

Vincent had come to Paris so that he could stay with Theo, who had been supporting him financially and emotionally. Theo, four years younger than Vincent, was working for the Parisian art dealer Boussod & Valadon, formerly known as Goupil. He lived in a small apartment just below Montmartre, but needing more space after Vincent's arrival, the brothers moved nearer the brow of the hill, to 52 Rue Lepic.

Until recently it seemed that Vincent had never painted a portrait of his brother. However, Van Gogh specialist Louis van Tilborgh believes that a picture long assumed to be a self-portrait really portrays Theo (fig. 5, reproduced here at actual size). Van Tilborgh realised that two small 'self-portraits' done in the same style apparently depict different individuals, although their faces are similar. After comparing the features in the two paintings with photographs (such as fig. 4) and other self-portraits, Van Tilborgh concluded that one must be Vincent and the other – the man with a straw hat – is Theo.[5]

Soon after his arrival in Paris in February 1886 Van Gogh had begun training at the art school run by Fernand Cormon, a successful artist of dramatic historical scenes. Among Van Gogh's fellow students was 17-year-old Emile Bernard, with whom he quickly struck up a friendship. Together, they painted and enjoyed the Bohemian nightlife. Astonishingly, an unknown sketch depicting Van Gogh was recently identified in a

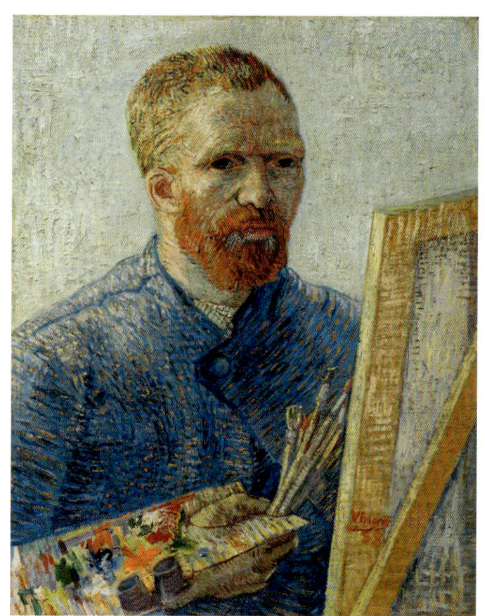

ABOVE fig. 3 *Self-portrait as an Artist*, February 1888, oil on canvas, 65 x 50 cm, Van Gogh Museum, Amsterdam (Vincent van Gogh Foundation) (F522)

BELOW fig. 4 Theo van Gogh, January 1889, photograph by Frederik van Rosmalen Jr, Van Gogh Museum, Amsterdam (Vincent van Gogh Foundation)[6]

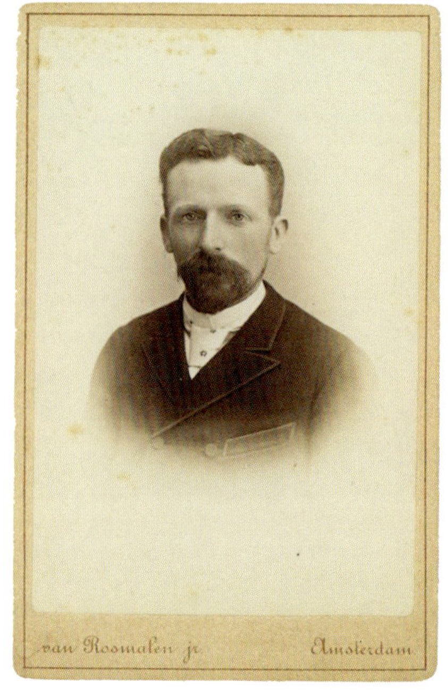

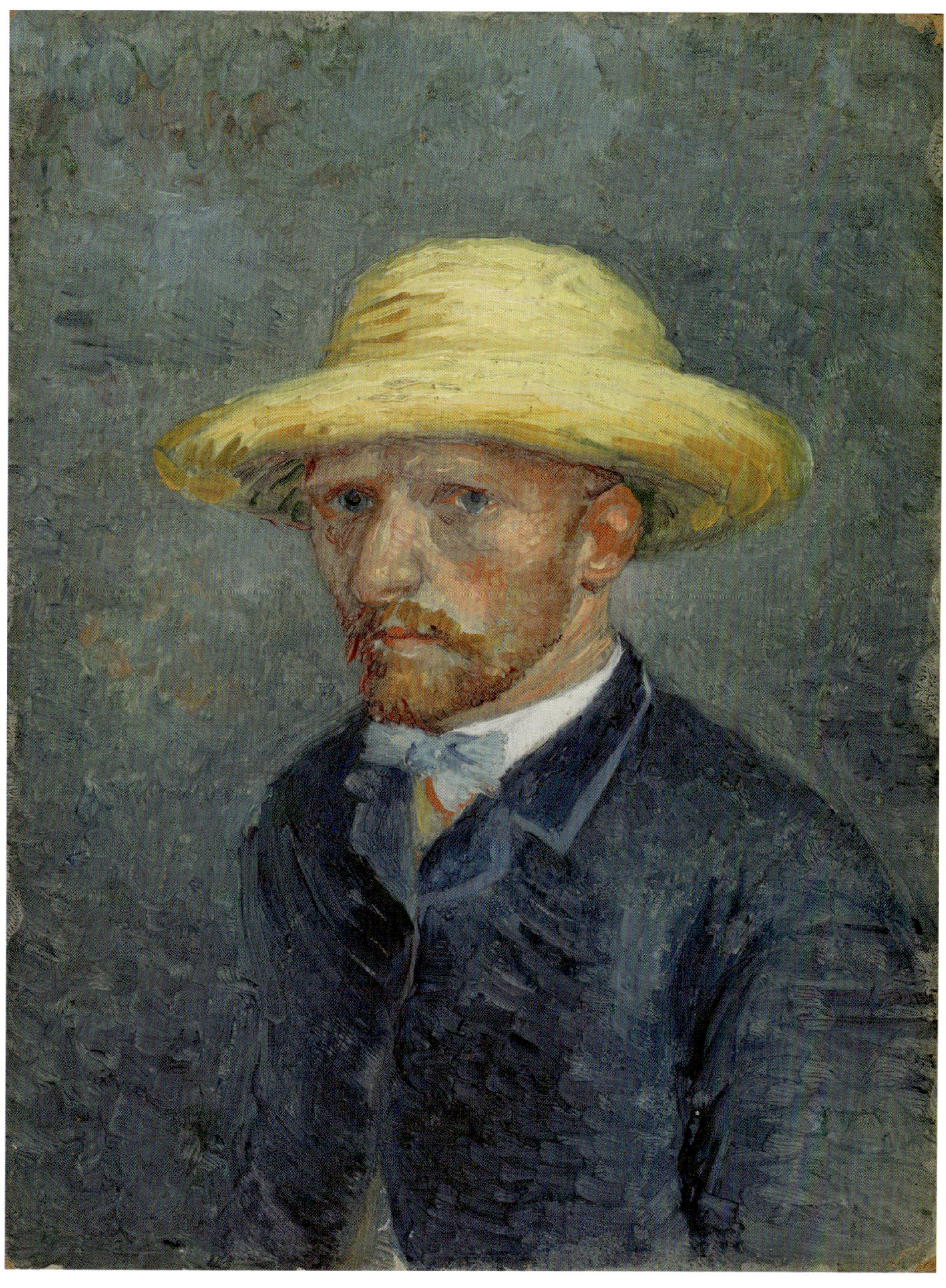

fig. 5 *Theo van Gogh*, summer 1887, oil on carton, 19 x 14 cm, Van Gogh Museum, Amsterdam (Vincent van Gogh Foundation) (F294)

large album containing over 800 drawings by Bernard. This discovery was announced in 2015 and the drawing is reproduced here for the first time in the Van Gogh literature and also at its actual size (fig. 6).[7]

Sketched quickly and spontaneously, it captures Van Gogh drinking in a Parisian café, most likely in Montmartre. Two bottles sit prominently in front of him, while behind him are a pair of women, probably prostitutes. Van Gogh appears uninterested in either the drink or his companions, gazing out and looking slightly ill at ease. Most noticeable are his sunken, piercing eyes, similar to those captured in his final Paris self-portrait.

Van Gogh became increasingly frustrated with studying at Cormon's studio and left after only three months, wanting to develop in his own way. He soon discovered Impressionism and met many of the key modern artists of his time – including Camille Pissarro, Edgar Degas, Georges Seurat, Paul Signac, Henri de Toulouse-Lautrec and, most importantly, Paul Gauguin.

It was in Paris that Van Gogh developed his palette, abandoning the dark and muted tones he had used in his Dutch paintings. He soon discovered how to apply colour in bold, lively strokes, as in his *Self-portrait as an Artist*. Conservators have recently confirmed that the pigments on the palette in the self-portrait represent those he used to make the rest of the picture. Along with white, the main blobs are the three primary (red, yellow and blue) and secondary (orange, purple and green) colours. Van Gogh was indulging in his newly-acquired love of complementary colours. Setting his orangey beard against the blue of his smock, the bright hues sing out.[8]

After two years in Paris, Van Gogh began to hanker for change. Life in the capital was pressurised and he drank too much, so he cast around for a more peaceful environment. Although he was close to his brother, tensions often erupted between them, making life in Theo's apartment difficult. Vincent also realised that the warmer climate would make it feasible to do more work outdoors. He opted for Arles, the last town before Marseille on the rail route to the Mediterranean. Although the two brothers were to be 600 kilometres apart, Theo would continue to play a vital part in Vincent's life in Arles – sending a regular allowance, corresponding frequently and providing moral support.

On Sunday 19 February 1888, Vincent's final day in Paris, he and Theo visited Seurat's studio, just below Montmartre. This made a deep impression on the brothers, with Vincent recalling more than two years later how they had been 'so struck by Seurat's canvases'. Later on in Arles he thought about exchanging self-portraits with Seurat – and even tentatively suggested that Seurat might join Gauguin and himself in the Yellow House.[9]

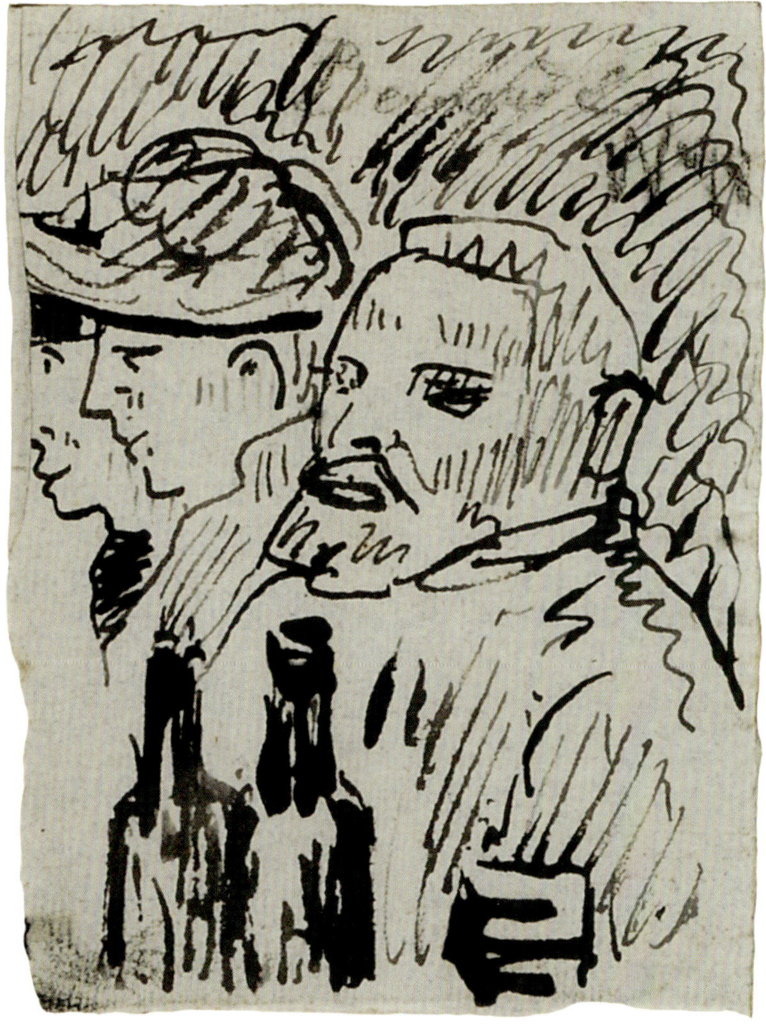

That last evening Vincent and Bernard decorated Theo's apartment. Bernard later recalled Vincent's suggestion: 'I am leaving tomorrow, let's arrange the studio together, in such a way that my brother still thinks I am there.' The two painters, who greatly admired the art of Japan, pinned Japanese prints to the wall. They placed some of Van Gogh's paintings on easels (probably including the latest self-portrait, depicting him at his easel). Dozens of other canvases remained piled in heaps, the result of his two years' work in Paris. Vincent's parting words to Bernard were an invitation to join him in Arles: 'It is in the South that one should now establish the studio of the future.'[10]

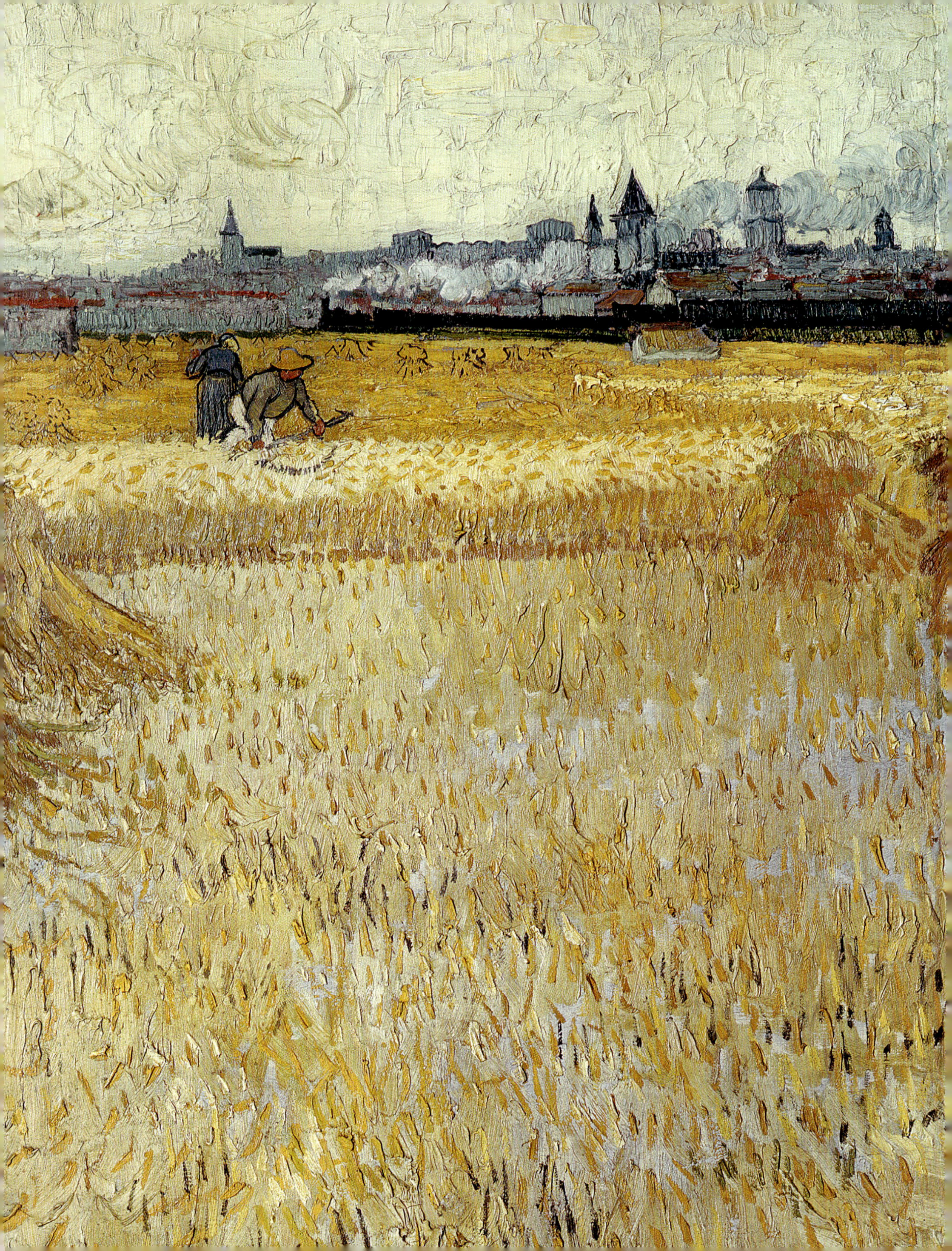

CHAPTER ONE

DISCOVERING ARLES

'The coquettish little town of pretty women'[1]

Van Gogh arrived in Provence at an extraordinary moment. Having taken the overnight train from Paris he awoke on the morning of 20 February 1888 to find the countryside blanketed with snow, although Arles normally enjoys mild Mediterranean winters. He described the scene to Theo: 'The landscape under the snow with the white peaks against a sky as bright as the snow was just like the winter landscapes the Japanese did.'[2] The white hills were the Alpilles (the Little Alps), a chain with craggy peaks which begins just north of Arles – and which would soon appear in the background of many of his landscapes. A local newspaper reported that the snow was 45 centimetres deep, 'enormous for the land of the sun'.[3]

In Arles the station lies just to the north of the centre so Van Gogh would have needed a porter to help him with his luggage (see the upper right corner of the map, fig. 10). He soon reached Place Lamartine, which was named after Alphonse de Lamartine, the poet and politician who had campaigned for the construction of the Paris-Marseille railway. After crossing the public garden (Jardin de la Cavalerie) Van Gogh reached the Porte de la Cavalerie, a gateway with its pair of sixteenth-century circular towers, part of the ramparts which once surrounded Arles. He then entered the historic centre of the town, which dates back to Roman times.

Van Gogh found a room at the Hotel Carrel at 30 Rue Amédée Pichot (fig. 7).[4] Run by Albert and Cathérine Carrel, it was a middle-range establishment, with a restaurant on the ground floor and bedrooms on two upper levels. Having checked in, Van Gogh set off to explore the town. To a northerner who had never ventured south of Paris, Provence must have seemed exotic, even in the melting snow.

With 23,500 inhabitants, Arles was then a market town. Its compact size meant that the facilities Van Gogh needed were conveniently close at hand. The shops, cafés and restaurants were all around and the riverside promenade was only two minutes' away. However, the medieval labyrinth of narrow, cobbled alleys seemed dark in winter and shabby. 'It's dirty, this town, with its old streets', Vincent wrote back to Theo. But although appearing 'sickly and faded', once one got to know it, 'the old charm reveals itself.'[5]

Detail of fig. 40 *Arles seen from the Wheatfields,* Musée Rodin, Paris

The best overall visual impression of nineteenth-century Arles is captured in a print showing the view from a balloon, from the east (fig. 9). The Roman arena dominates the town and the ramparts still delineate the urban area. The Rhône's importance as a shipping route is emphasised by the boats plying their trade, although the new railway line in the foreground would soon take most of the traffic. The station lies just off the right edge of the print, and the green area on the right side is the public garden in Place Lamartine.

Arles had two main claims to fame, its classical antiquities and the renowned beauty of its women. The town had been the largest Roman settlement in southern France and three important sites survived: the arena, the theatre and the Alyscamps. Surprisingly, in view of his cultured background, Van Gogh was uninterested in them, although they attracted the attention of many artists. He never painted the impressive ruins of the Roman theatre or mentioned them in his letters, although he did once refer to the famous Venus of Arles sculpture which had been excavated there.[6] The arena, the largest outside Rome, had been brought back into use for bullfights. It was the bulls and the excited crowds which eventually caught his imagination, not its ancient origins or weathered stones. The burial ground of the Alyscamps was lined with sarcophagi, but when Van Gogh eventually painted there, he focused not on the tombs, but the avenue of trees.

Van Gogh was far more interested in the women of Arles, the famed Arlésiennes renowned for their striking looks and distinctive costume. Celebrated in Alphonse Daudet's 1869 short story *L'Arlésienne*, they too were a favourite subject for artists. Soon after his arrival Van Gogh began searching for an Arlésienne to portray, but models were disinclined to pose for him and finding one would take months.

One of Van Gogh's first outings was to visit the town's two museums. Paintings were displayed at the Musée Réattu, established in 1868 with works acquired from the daughter of the Arles artist Jacques Réattu. Set in a Renaissance mansion, the museum housed Réattu's

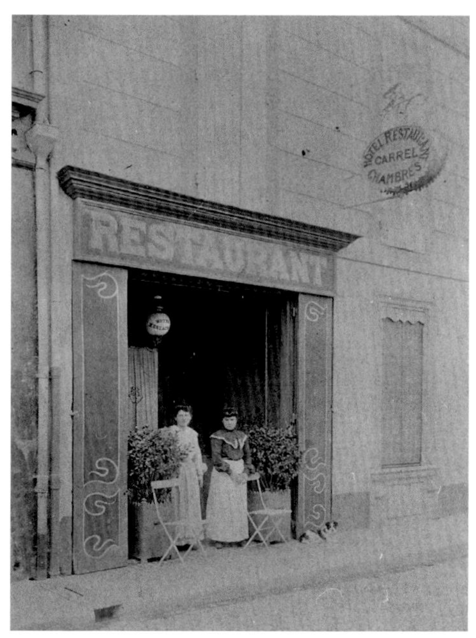

ABOVE fig. 7 Hotel Carrel, c.1920s, photograph[7]

RIGHT fig. 8 *View of a Butcher's Shop*, February 1888, oil on canvas, 40 x 32 cm, Van Gogh Museum, Amsterdam (Vincent van Gogh Foundation) (F389)

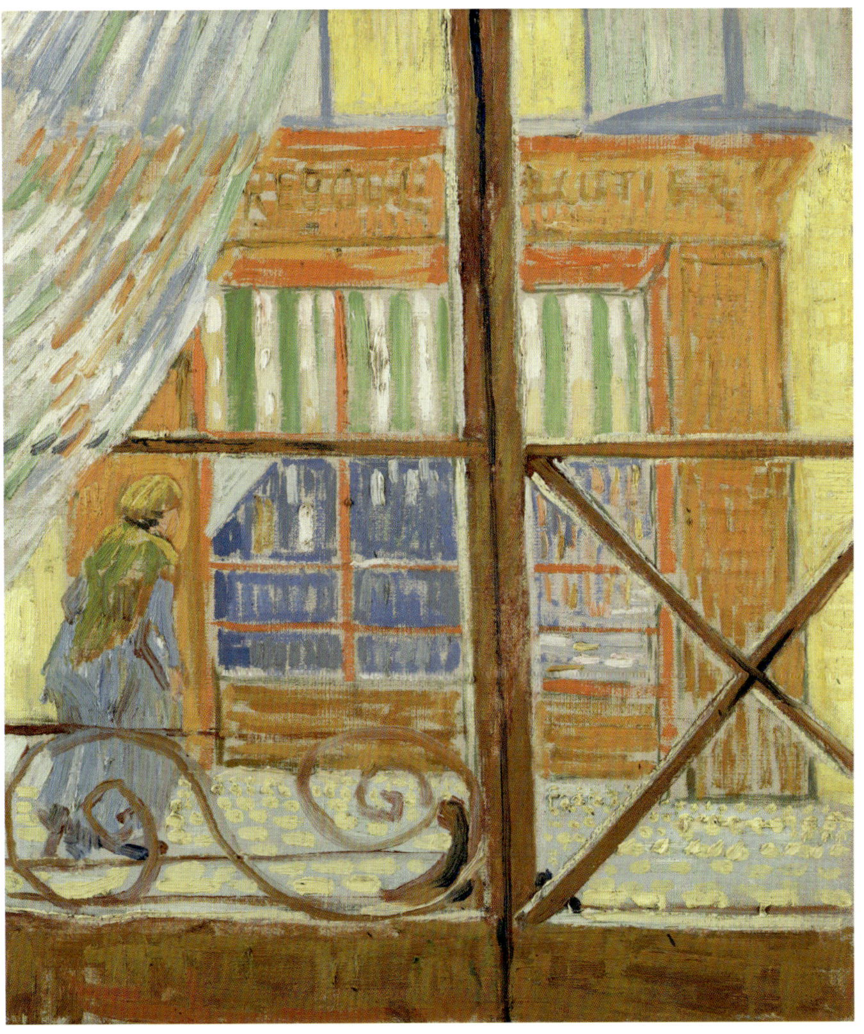

own work and other pictures he had owned. The collection soon came to be poorly regarded, with many paintings being dismissed as copies of the masters. Van Gogh concurred, describing the museum 'dreadful and a joke'.[8]

Van Gogh was rather more enthusiastic about the Musée Lapidaire, with antiquities he described as 'genuine'. It held one of France's finest collections of Roman sculptures and stone inscriptions. These were displayed in the deconsecrated Church of St Anne in Place de la République. Just across the square lies the Church (and former cathedral) of St Trophime, famed for its magnificent portal with figures of apostles, saints and bizarre creatures. Van Gogh described its twelfth-century facade as 'admirable', although the figures were 'so cruel, so monstrous'.[9]

fig. 9 Alfred Guesdon,
Balloon View of Arles,
c.1850, coloured
lithograph, 29 x 44 cm[10]

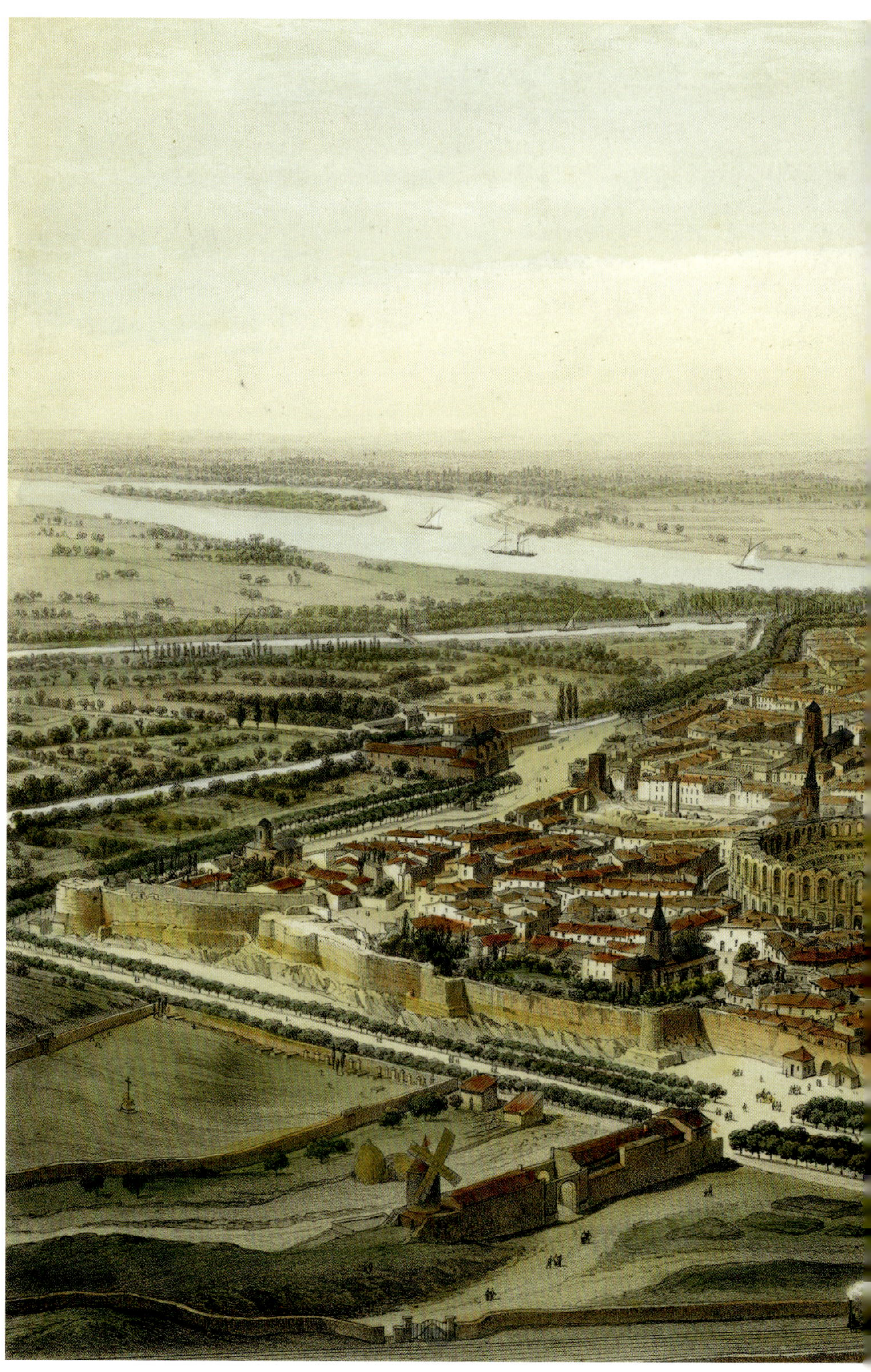

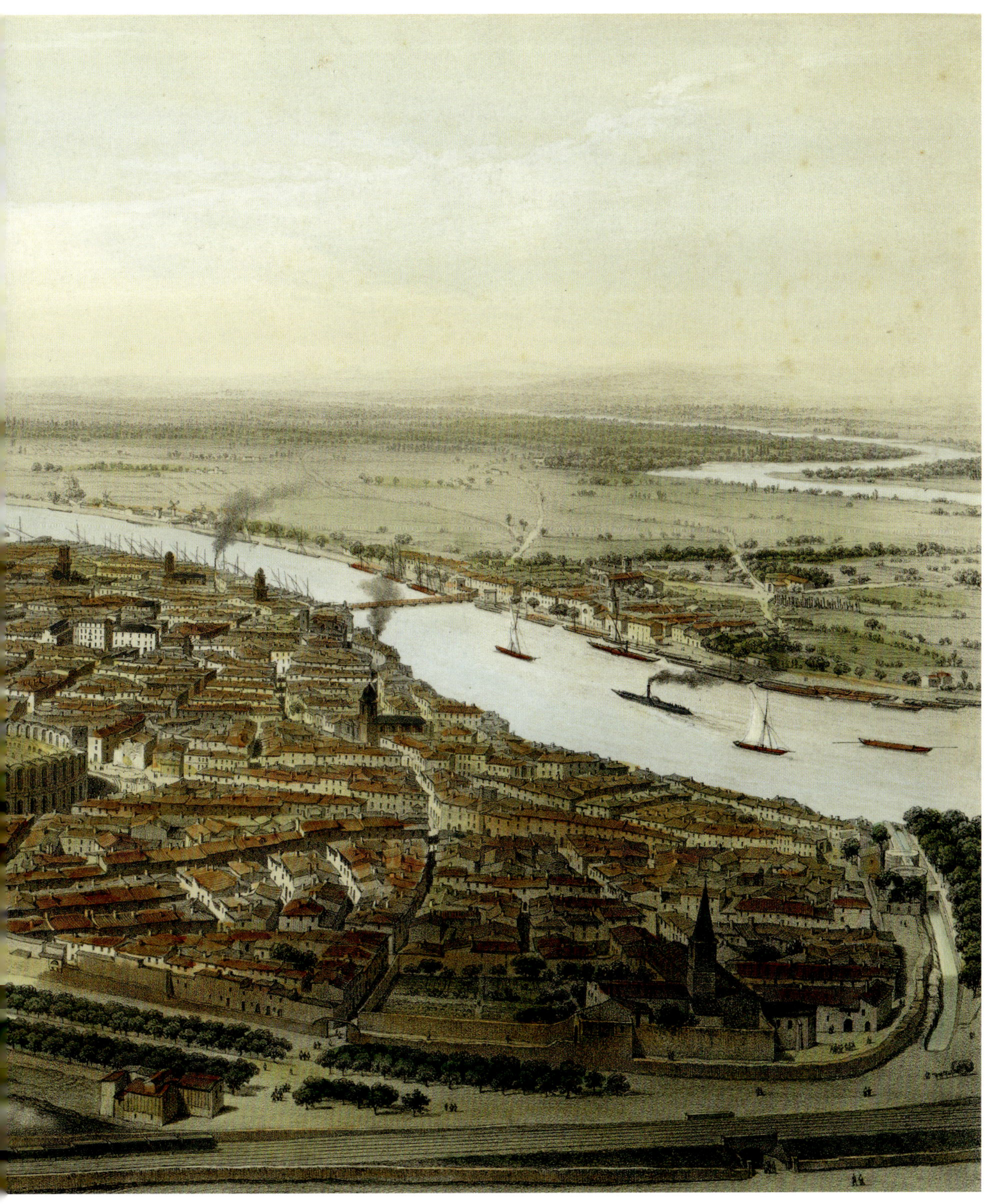

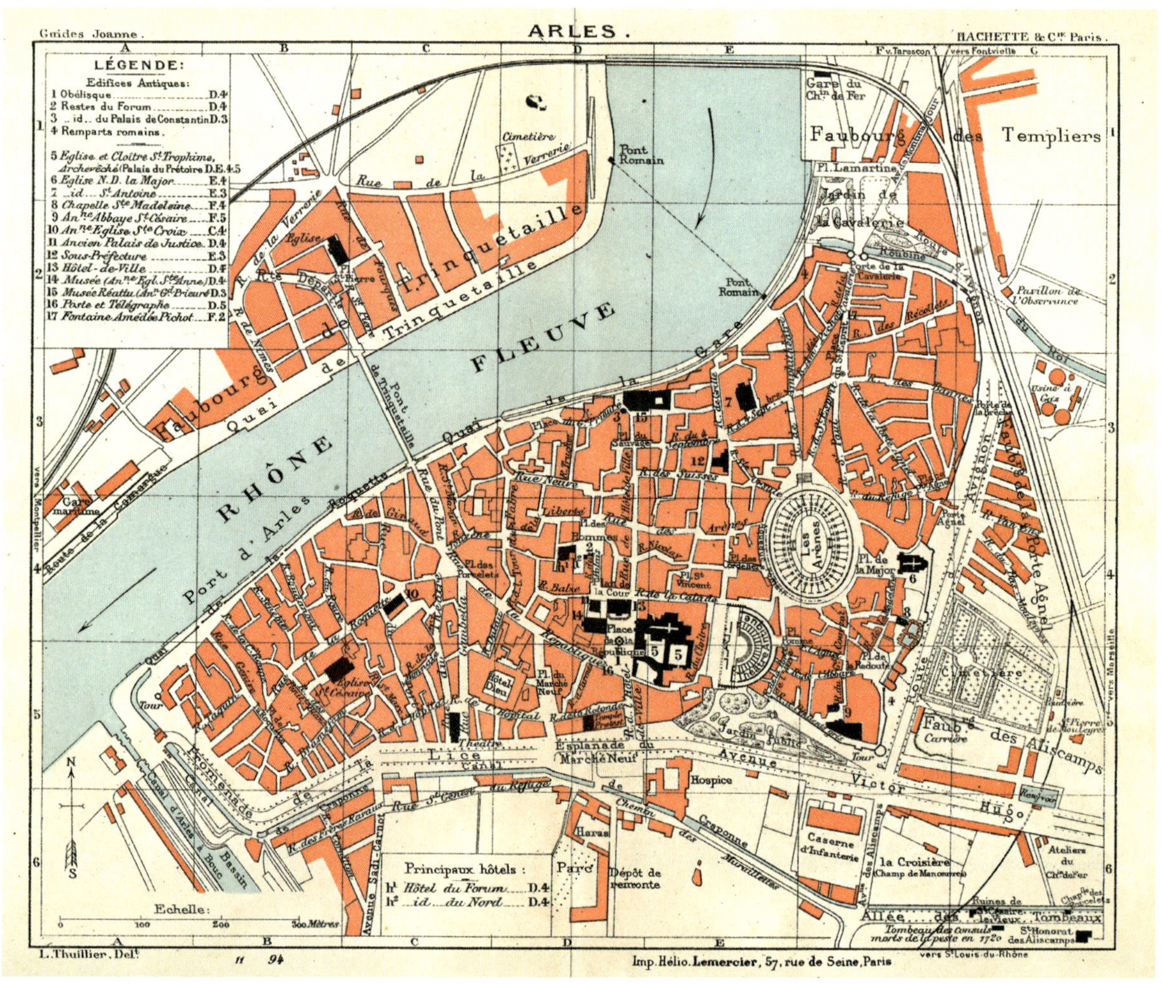

Although Van Gogh had brought art supplies from Paris, he was immediately anxious to find where he could buy more paint and canvas. He quickly discovered he could get them from 'either a grocer or a bookseller'.[11] The grocer (and hardware merchant), Jules Armand, had his shop conveniently close to the Hotel Carrel. Armand was also a talented amateur artist, and during the period Van Gogh was in town he painted at least three subjects which the Dutchman also tackled: the Alyscamps, the Abbey of Montmajour and an Arlésienne.[12] Decades later Armand's wife Joséphine Ronin recalled Van Gogh as 'a very original man, suspicious . . . with blue eyes and a small red beard'.[13]

Among Van Gogh's first Arles paintings was one he prosaically described as of 'a stretch of pavement with a butcher's shop' (fig. 8).[14] The name

RIGHT fig. 11 *Tiled Roof with Chimneys and Church Tower,* April 1888, ink on paper, 26 x 35 cm, private collection (F1480a)

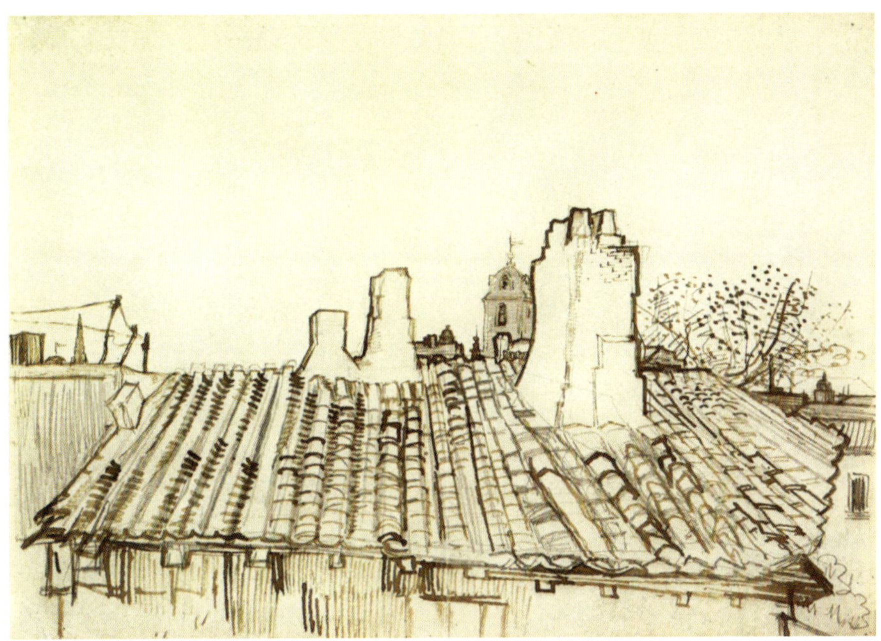

'Reboul . . . rcutier' can just be made out above the shop window in the picture. Paul Reboul, a *charcutier*, was just opposite the Hotel Carrel. Van Gogh presumably painted the scene through the hotel's glass door, while he stayed snug inside. His striking composition makes use of the stark grid of the door, calling to mind certain Japanese prints.

Van Gogh also drew a sketch from the hotel's third-floor roof terrace, which overlooked the town (fig. 11). This may well date from mid-April, when he rented a small covered part of the terrace to provide space for drying his paintings. The composition is dominated by terracotta roof tiles, looking south-west. The church tower near the centre is St Julien; on the far left one of the towers of the Roman arena and the spire of the Convent of the Cordeliers are just visible.

The Hotel Carrel was a convenient base, but two months after his arrival Van Gogh had a series of arguments with the owners. This, he explained, was partly because he took up 'a little more room with my paintings than their other customers who aren't painters' (their lodgers were often shepherds from the Camargue). Van Gogh also disliked their restaurant, complaining that they couldn't even boil potatoes properly and the wine was 'real poison'.[16] Many years later Cathérine Carrel vividly recalled their guest: 'He did nothing except for work. Even when eating he looked at his canvasses, which he retouched. He worked very fast.'[17]

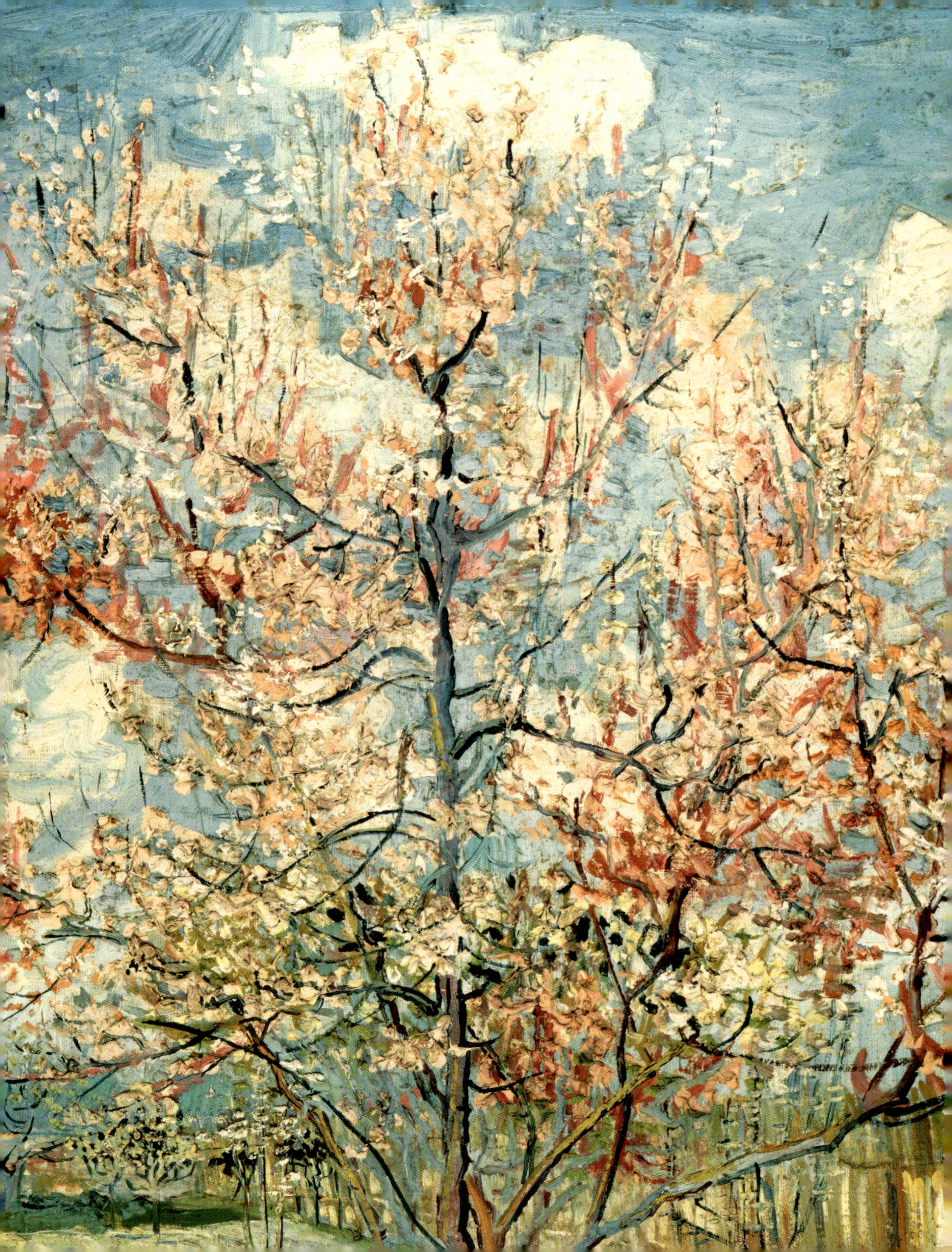

CHAPTER TWO

BLOSSOMING ORCHARDS

'I wanted to do a Provence orchard of tremendous gaiety'[1]

Spring was on the way. By the end of Van Gogh's second week in Arles he had completed two small paintings of 'a branch of an almond tree that's already in flower despite everything', a reference to the snow.[2] He spotted the blossom on a walk discovering the countryside. It was too cold to work outdoors, so he had snapped off a short branch and brought it back to his cramped hotel room. This pair of modest still lifes, sent to Theo and their sister Willemien (Wil), would soon lead to a much more ambitious project outdoors in the orchards.

In late March 1888 Van Gogh started feverish work on a series of blossoming fruit trees – apricot, cherry, peach, pear and plum. He described his amazement as the fresh pastel hues burst out of the drab winter landscape. Ever since his childhood in the Brabant countryside Van Gogh had been acutely aware of the changing seasons, but Mediterranean Provence was altogether different. The early blossoms represented for him a symbol of rebirth. Embarking on his new life in the south, Van Gogh was full of enthusiasm for what lay ahead.

The blossoms also called to mind Japan, whose art he had fallen in love with in Paris. Like many other avant-garde artists, Van Gogh was greatly attracted to Japanese prints, which must have appeared bewitchingly exotic, with their strong designs and bold colours. While working in Paris he had bought hundreds of prints, many of which included flowering fruit trees, a favourite motif of artists in Japan.[3] There were also pragmatic reasons for painting flowering fruit trees. 'Orchards in blossom are subjects we have a chance of selling or exchanging', Vincent wrote to Theo.[4] Van Gogh painted in several orchards just east and south of the town, working outside, but then adding finishing touches or making other versions back in his hotel. He worked quickly, using thick impasto paint to catch the light and colour – creating scenes redolent with freshness and immediacy.

Detail of fig. 12 *Pink Peach Trees*, Kröller-Müller Museum, Otterlo

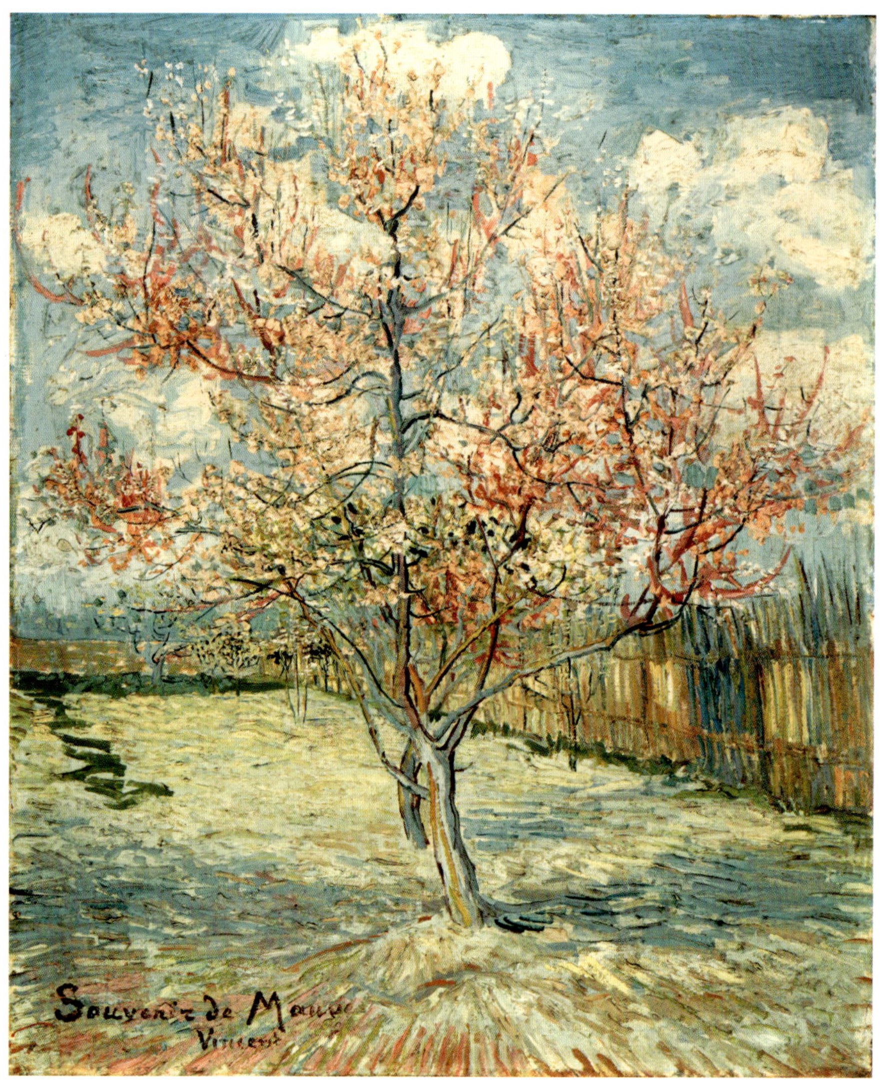

Among the first of the series was *Pink Peach Trees* (fig. 12), 'two peach trees in full bloom, pink against a sparkling blue sky with white clouds and in sunshine' (one of the trees is almost hidden behind the front one).[5] Van Gogh finished *Pink Peach Trees* on 30 March, his 35th birthday.

On his return to the hotel, he found a letter from his sister Wil enclosing an obituary of the Dutch landscape artist Anton Mauve, the husband of their cousin Jet. Vincent had a special link with Mauve, since it was he who had helped him learn to paint seven years earlier while living in The Hague. On reading the obituary, 'something or other grabbed hold of me and made my throat tight with emotion', he wrote to Theo. He then prominently inscribed the painting 'Souvenir de Mauve' (In memory of Mauve), to present it to Jet. He wanted her to have a picture which would be 'both tender and very cheerful'.[6]

Van Gogh's gift may also have had something of an ulterior motive, since he hoped that it would be seen by artlovers in Jet's home. This came true in a way that he could hardly have anticipated. Later that year *Pink Peach Trees* was spotted there by Jozef Israëls, the most successful Dutch artist of the late nineteenth century. Israëls reacted by saying that Van Gogh was 'a clever lad!'[7] Wil passed on this astonishing compliment in a letter to Theo on 23 December 1888, the very day that Vincent slashed his ear. Had Vincent heard this accolade from his country's most distinguished painter (whom he had long admired), he might never have picked up the razor.

Van Gogh had painted *Pink Peach Trees* alongside a friend, Christian Mourier-Petersen (fig. 13). The Danish artist worked a few metres to Van Gogh's right, since he has shown more space between the two main trees. Both painters captured the blossom differently, with Mourier-Petersen giving it a more ethereal feel than Van Gogh's pointillist effect.

Mourier-Petersen had also come from Paris, arriving in Arles some months before Van Gogh. The Dane wrote about their early meetings to a friend in Copenhagen, saying that he had encountered 'a Dutch painter, an Impressionist . . . I thought he was "mad" at first, yet I am finding out gradually that there is method in his madness.'[8] Mourier-Petersen remained in Arles until late May and Van Gogh said that until then they saw each other 'every day'.[9] They enjoyed each other's company and the Dane later reminisced about their discussions in the cafés.[10] However, Van Gogh was unimpressed by his friend's artistic technique, describing it as 'dry, correct and timid'.[11]

A week or so after tackling the peach blossom Van Gogh moved on to pear trees in *Orchard bordered by Cypresses* (fig. 14), probably on the same farm. The cypresses on the windy side of the field protected the fruit

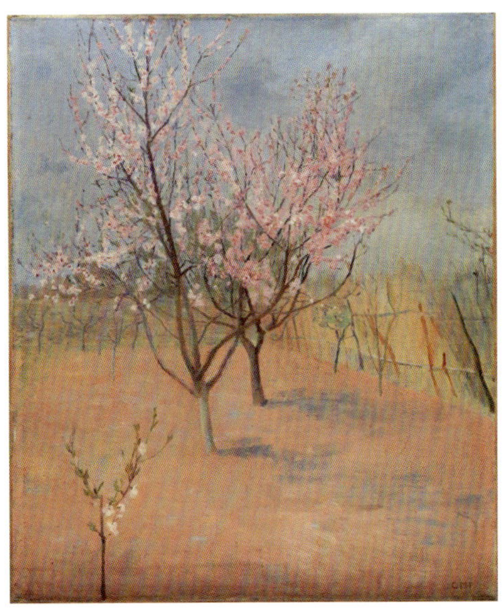

ABOVE fig. 13 Christian Mourier-Petersen, *Peach Trees in Bloom*, March 1888, oil on canvas, 55 x 45 cm, Hirschsprung Collection, Copenhagen

OPPOSITE fig. 12 *Pink Peach Trees*, March 1888, oil on canvas, 73 x 60 cm, Kröller-Müller Museum, Otterlo (F394)

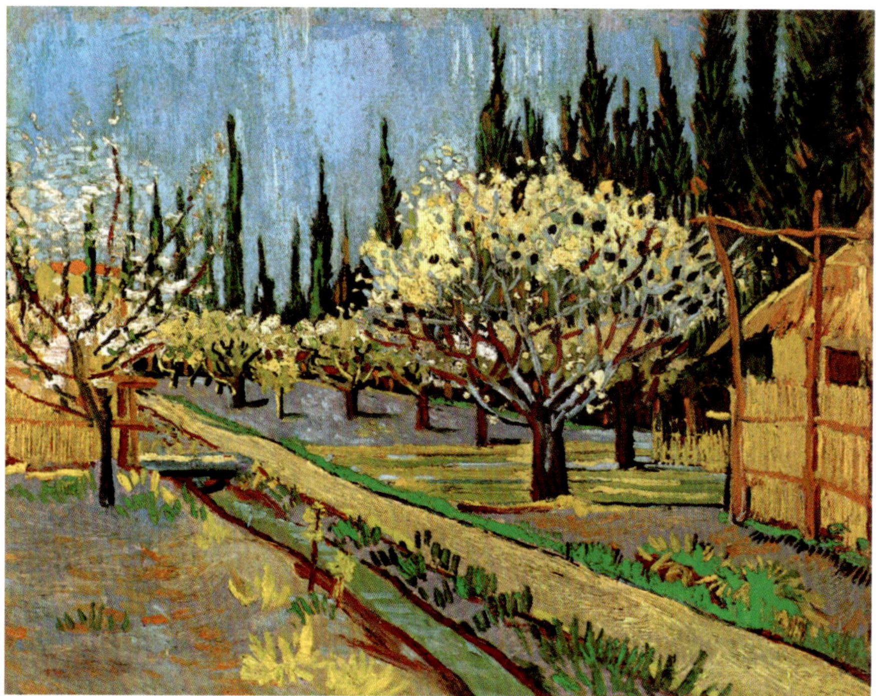

from the cold mistral which blows down the Rhône valley. The mistral often caused difficulties for Van Gogh: 'I have a lot of trouble painting because of the wind, but I fix my easel to pegs stuck in the ground and work anyway, it's too beautiful.'[12]

Writing to Bernard, Van Gogh described *Orchard bordered by Cypresses* as 'the entrance to a Provençal orchard with its yellow reed fences, with its shelter (against the mistral), black cypresses, with its typical vegetables of various greens, yellow lettuces, onions and garlic and emerald leeks'. He commented on his rough and rapid technique: 'I hit the canvas with irregular strokes which I leave as they are, impastos, uncovered spots of canvas – corners here and there left inevitably unfinished – reworkings, roughnesses.'[13]

Van Gogh worked at frenetic speed, only too aware of the brief life of the blossom. On 5 April he impatiently asked Theo for more paint: 'I have another new orchard for you – but for Christ's sake get the paint to me without delay. The season of orchards in blossom is short, and you know these subjects are among the ones that cheer everyone up.' His order was enormous: 107 tubes of paint and 10 metres of canvas. Four days later he was even more agitated: 'This rage to paint orchards won't last forever . . . I can't do anything but strike while the iron's hot. Will be worn out after the orchards.'[14]

A few days afterwards Van Gogh was already working on 'some yellow-white plum trees with thousands of black branches' – *The White Orchard* (fig. 15). Yet another mistral blew up, but between the periods of 'tremendous wind' there was 'sunshine that made all the little white flowers sparkle'. Mourier-Petersen showed up while he was painting, another indication of their close working relationship. Van Gogh was pleased with his picture, advising Theo it would look best in a 'raw white frame'.[15]

The orchard series had taken nearly four weeks, from 24 March to 20 April. During this time Van Gogh completed fifteen paintings.[16] He regarded the orchards as a 'series'[17], an idea recently adopted by avant-garde artists such as Monet and Paul Cézanne. He was also following the practice of Japanese artists such as Katsushika Hokusai, who produced sets of prints on a theme. The springtime blossoms represented Van Gogh's first exploration of the Provençal countryside, an exuberant taster for what was to come.

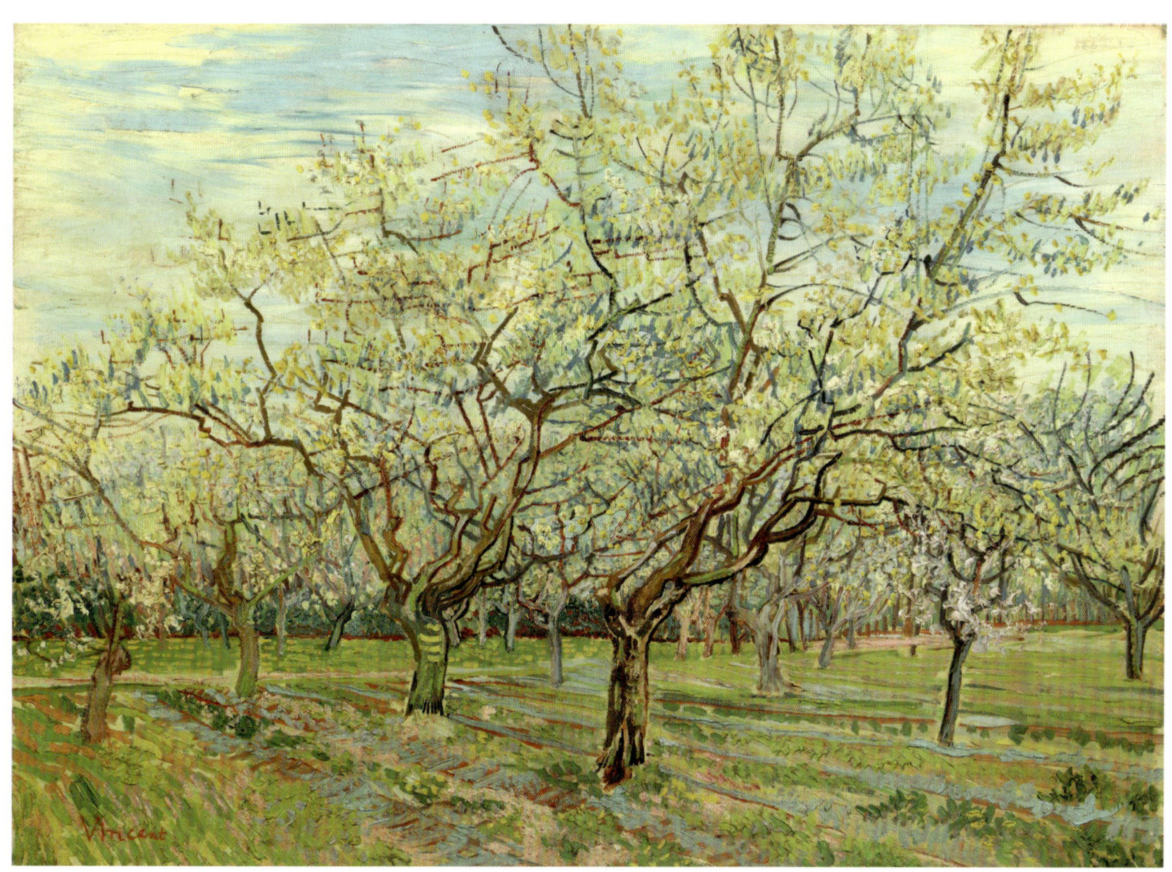

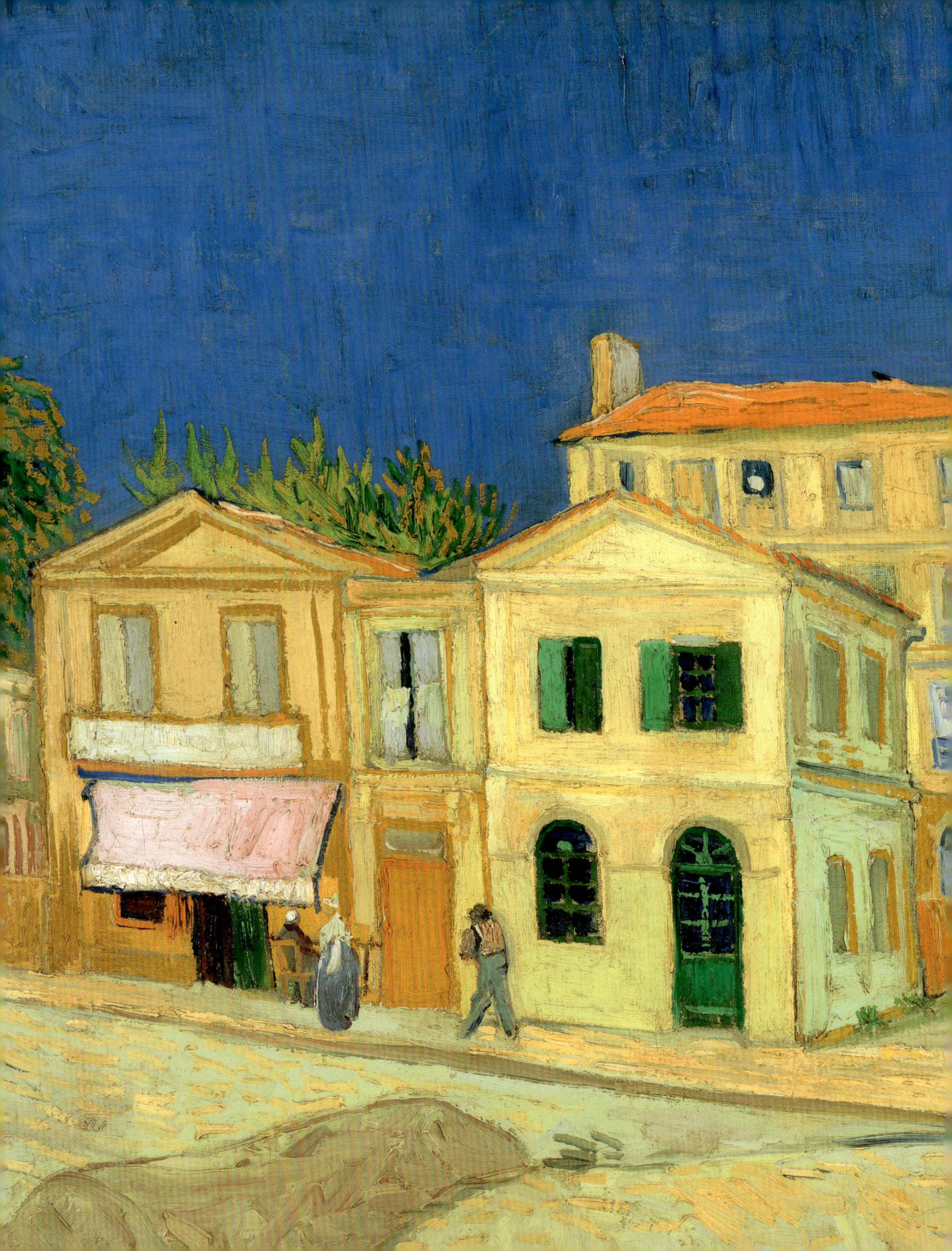

CHAPTER THREE

AN ARTIST'S HOUSE

'I live in a little yellow house with green door and shutters, whitewashed inside'[1]

On 1 May 1888 Vincent told Theo that he had rented what he would soon call his 'little yellow house', at 2 Place Lamartine. Theo would effectively be paying the rent and buying furniture, so it was rather sensitive news and Vincent broke it in a roundabout way. He began his letter by saying that he had just posted a dozen drawings, including one he singled out for special mention: a public garden with a pair of small buildings with pediments (fig. 16). Vincent then casually added in his letter, 'ah, well – today I rented the right hand wing of this building . . . it's painted yellow outside, whitewashed inside.'[2]

Van Gogh's drawing gives the impression that the Yellow House was favourably located, facing parkland. It was actually in a slightly insalubrious part of town, half way between the railway station and the brothels, and very close to several all-night cafés and the main police station. Two railway viaducts were nearby, with trains running throughout the night. Place Lamartine would have been noisy at all hours.

Vincent must have realised that Theo would find it difficult to spot his new home in the enclosed drawing, so in his letter he made a very rough sketch showing a detail. The Yellow House is the one with three windows, although he managed to depict the door on the wrong side (fig. 17). In both the enclosed drawing and the letter sketch Van Gogh also made another inexplicable mistake: he drew a pair of separate small houses – whereas it was actually a single building divided into two. The left half was the grocery shop run by François and Marguerite Crevoulin and the right half was the Yellow House. It is astonishing that a skilled artist who had just made a momentous decision about renting a house should have introduced two fundamental errors in depicting its architecture.

Although Van Gogh immediately set up his studio in the building, he did not sleep there. Dating from the early 1860s, the Yellow House had lain unoccupied for some time and its condition had deteriorated. This helps to explain why the rent was a very modest 15 francs a month.[3] Van Gogh and his

Detail of fig. 1 *The Yellow House*, Van Gogh Museum, Amsterdam (Vincent van Gogh Foundation)

landlord arranged some immediate repairs and redecoration, with the faded exterior yellow being repainted later that month. It then became the 'butter' yellow which led the artist to give his house its very personal name.[4]

As the house was unfurnished, Van Gogh needed a bed and other furniture, but he lacked the necessary funds. For the first few days in early May he continued to sleep at the Hotel Carrel, but his new rental agreement meant he became more assertive over problems with the hotel proprietors. After a row with the Carrels, he moved out and took a room at the Café de la Gare, just a couple of doors from the Yellow House. This establishment was run by Joseph and Marie Ginoux, with whom he had struck up a friendly rapport.

Vincent enjoyed settling in to work at the Yellow House, which offered plenty of space to spread out his materials. He reported to Theo that he had bought 'what I need to make a little coffee or broth at home, and two chairs and a table'.[5] A week later he had completed *Still Life with Coffee Pot*, an image of contented domesticity (fig. 18). The painting is centred around his newly acquired enamel coffee pot, with a royal blue cup and saucer. A milk jug with a chequerboard design, a large majolica jug and cup, a small plate, two oranges and three lemons complete the composition. Everything sits on a light blue tablecloth, set against a contrasting yellow background.

Although the choice of objects was partly aesthetic, the selection of the mundane possessions symbolised his new domestic life. Unusually, the entire picture has a narrow red painted border and then a wide white one, representing a *trompe l'oeil* white wooden frame (Van Gogh's occasional painted borders are usually, quite wrongly, cropped out of reproductions).[6] Pleased with the picture, he signed it in red and may well have hung it in his kitchen.

The small cluster of buildings on the north side of Place Lamartine now became the centre of Van Gogh's world, as shown in his vibrant September painting of *The Yellow House* (fig. 1). Next door was the Crevoulins' grocery shop, a convenient place to buy necessities (no doubt Van Gogh tried to get items on credit while he was awaiting his allowance from Theo). Further to the left, in the pink building beneath a tree, was the restaurant run by 70-year-old Marguerite Vénissac where Van Gogh usually took his supper. Beyond that to the left (but just outside the painting) was the Café de la Gare, where he slept.[7]

The road at the side of the Yellow House was the Avenue de Montmajour (or the Route de Tarascon), which then runs below two railway viaducts. Van Gogh's side windows in his studio and kitchen overlooked this street and passers-by would sometimes peek into his strange household, curious about his work. The artist probably tried to discourage this by planting oleanders in tubs outdoors, as can be seen in *The Yellow House* (under the two side windows).[8]

Vincent wrote enthusiastically to Theo saying that 'the delightful thing

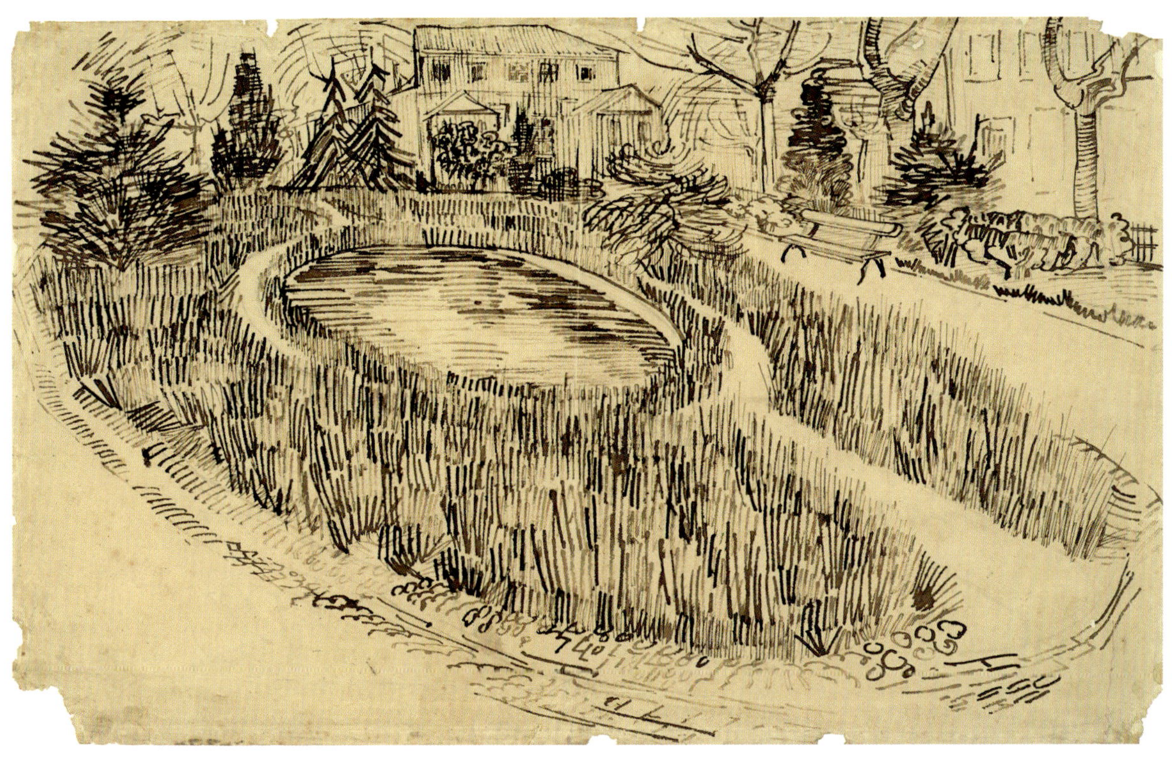

travailler   Tu y trouveras un croquis
hatif sur papier jaune
une pelouse dans lesquare
qui se trouve au à l'entrée
de la ville. et au fond
d'une bâtisse à peu
près comme ceci —
Eh bien - j'ai aujourd'hui
loué l'aile droite »
de cette construction qui contient 4 pièces
ou plutôt deux avec deux cabinets
C'est peint en jaune dehors blanchi à la

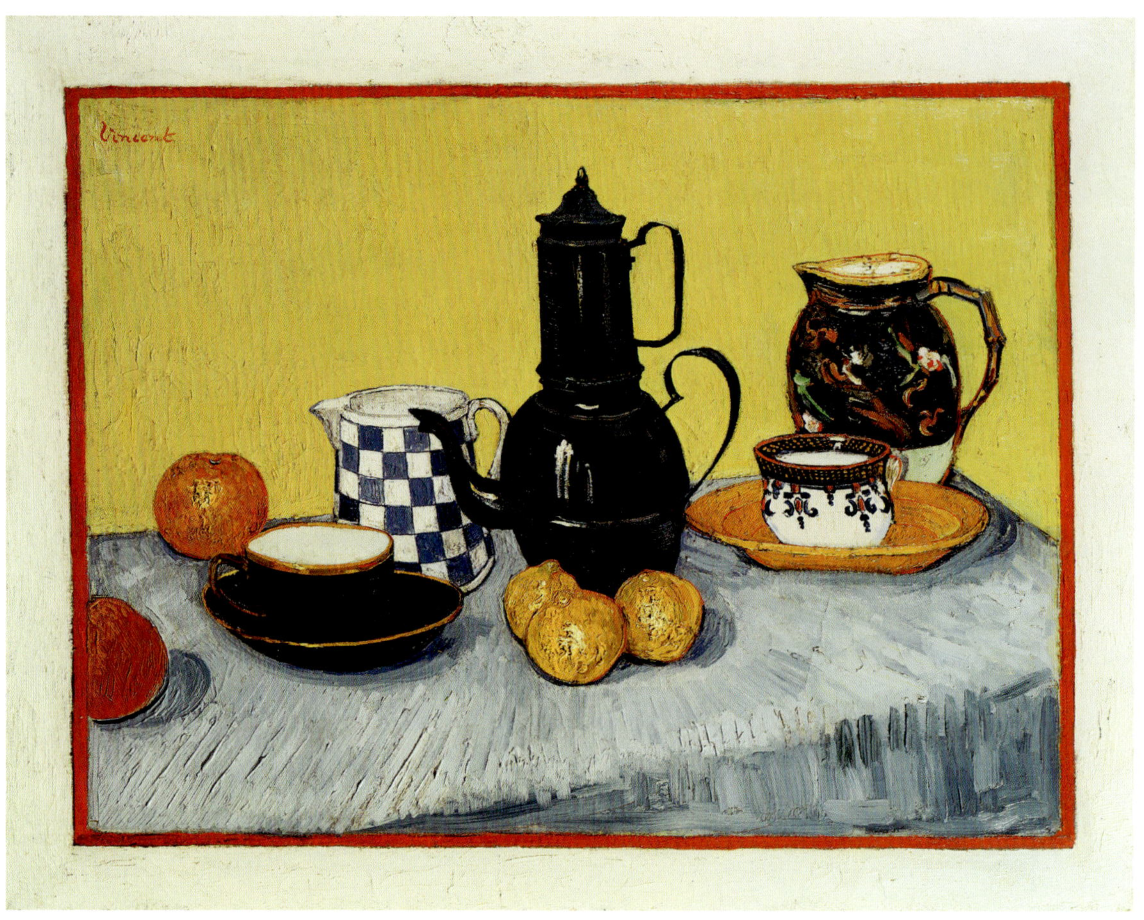

about this studio is the gardens opposite' – which must have been looking their best in spring after he took on the lease.[10] Place Lamartine had been remodelled in the early 1870s and turned into three small public gardens, with the largest one just opposite the Yellow House. In the early autumn Van Gogh made a series of paintings of these gardens, which were to form part of his *décoration* – a term he invented for the large pictures he hung in the whitewashed interior of the Yellow House. Van Gogh described *The Public Garden with a Couple Strolling* (fig. 19) as 'a huge green-blue fir tree spreading its horizontal branches over a very green lawn and sand [path] dappled with light and shade', with 'two figures of lovers'.[11] The figure in the straw hat could well be a self-portrait, with Van Gogh imagining himself strolling with a female companion.

It was not until mid-September, after Van Gogh had eventually bought a bed, that he began to sleep in the Yellow House. This brought great satisfaction. In the newly-furnished home, 'I can live and breathe, and think and paint', he

ABOVE fig. 18 *Still Life with Coffee Pot*, May 1888, oil on canvas, 65 x 81 cm (including white and red borders), private collection (F410)

RIGHT fig. 19 *The Public Garden with a Couple Strolling*, October 1888, oil on canvas, 73 x 92 cm, private collection (F479)

wrote to Wil. A month later he made a painting of his new bedroom, a scene capturing his delight in having a home of his own. He began work on the subject after having had a very long sleep, following a week of intensive work. 'I've just slept for 16 hours', he wrote to Theo.[12] The day before finishing the bedroom picture, he posted a sketch to his brother (fig. 20).[13] In the final painting he made several changes, moving his straw hat along the pegs and taking away the basin from beneath the dressing-table. He also added two more framed pictures just above the bed. Most significantly, he changed the image hanging above his pillow – a portrait of his mother Anna, which he had completed a week earlier (fig. 56), was replaced with a landscape, probably an imaginary one (rather than a copy of a lost picture).

The final painting of *The Bedroom* (fig. 21) shows five pictures hanging above the bed – a mini-gallery. In addition to the landscape above the bedhead, there are portraits of two of his closest Arles friends, the Belgian artist Eugène Boch (fig. 55) and the Zouave soldier Paul-Eugène Milliet (fig. 58). Beneath these, the pictures with large white borders may well be two of his favourite Japanese prints. Above the table is a mirror, bought in early September, which he used when shaving and for painting self-portraits. There are two 'empty chairs', prefiguring the astonishingly bold painting that he was to do a few weeks later (fig. 98).

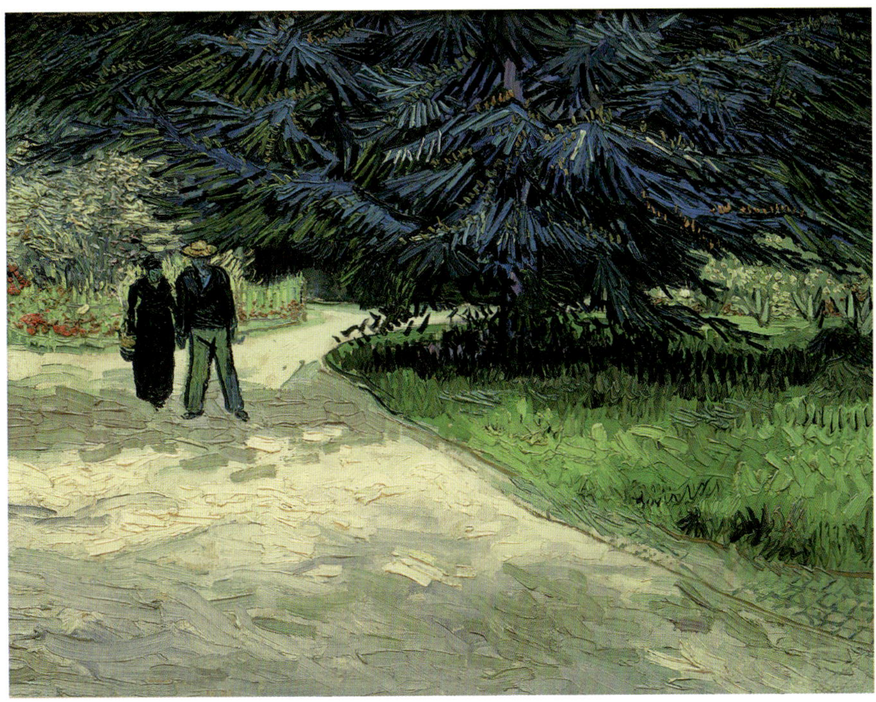

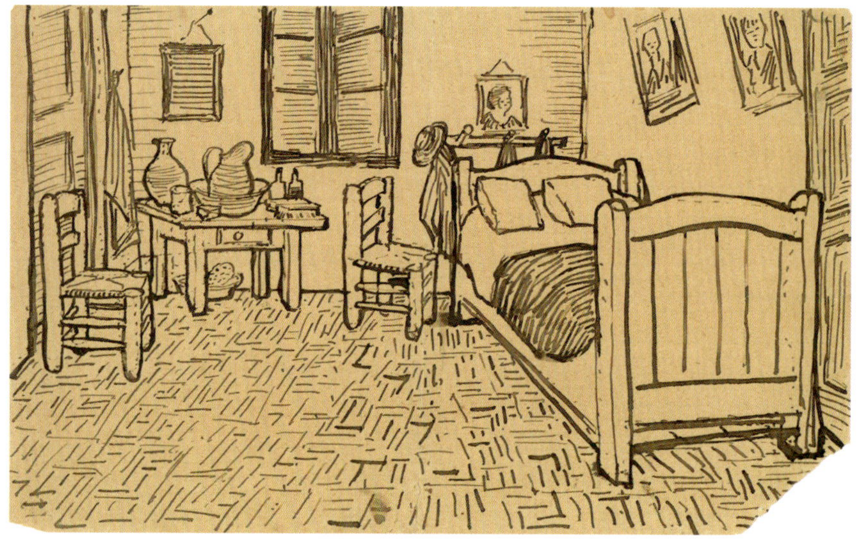

In Van Gogh's comments on *The Bedroom* he focused on the colours: 'The walls are of a pale violet. The floor – is of red tiles. The bedstead and the chairs are fresh butter yellow. The sheet and the pillows are very bright lemon green. The blanket scarlet red. The window green. The dressing table orange, the basin blue. The doors lilac . . . The solidity of the furniture should also now express unshakeable repose.' The painting was 'coloured in flat, plain tints like Japanese prints'.[14] As in the art of Japan, there are no shadows.

Van Gogh's description of the colours has now assumed a greater importance, because his pigments have now deteriorated (unfortunately a common problem with many of his paintings). Although he describes the walls as 'pale violet', the cochineal red in the blended violet has faded, leaving it bluish. Conservators at the Van Gogh Museum recently examined microscopic samples of the paint using modern scientific techniques to confirm these changes.[15]

It is ambiguous whether the room is a daytime or nighttime scene, since the shutters appear closed (in October they would not be needed against the Provençal sun). Van Gogh depicts a sheltered environment, protected from the pressures of everyday life and the bustle of Place Lamartine. He set out to evoke a peaceful atmosphere; 'looking at the painting should *rest* the mind, or rather, the imagination.'[16]

The view in the painting appears clumsy and the bedroom almost seems to sway, as in a dream – but this is partly because of the room's unusual trapezoid shape. The house had a diagonal front where it met Place Lamartine, slicing off the room at an angle near the table. Although the painting's apparently distorted

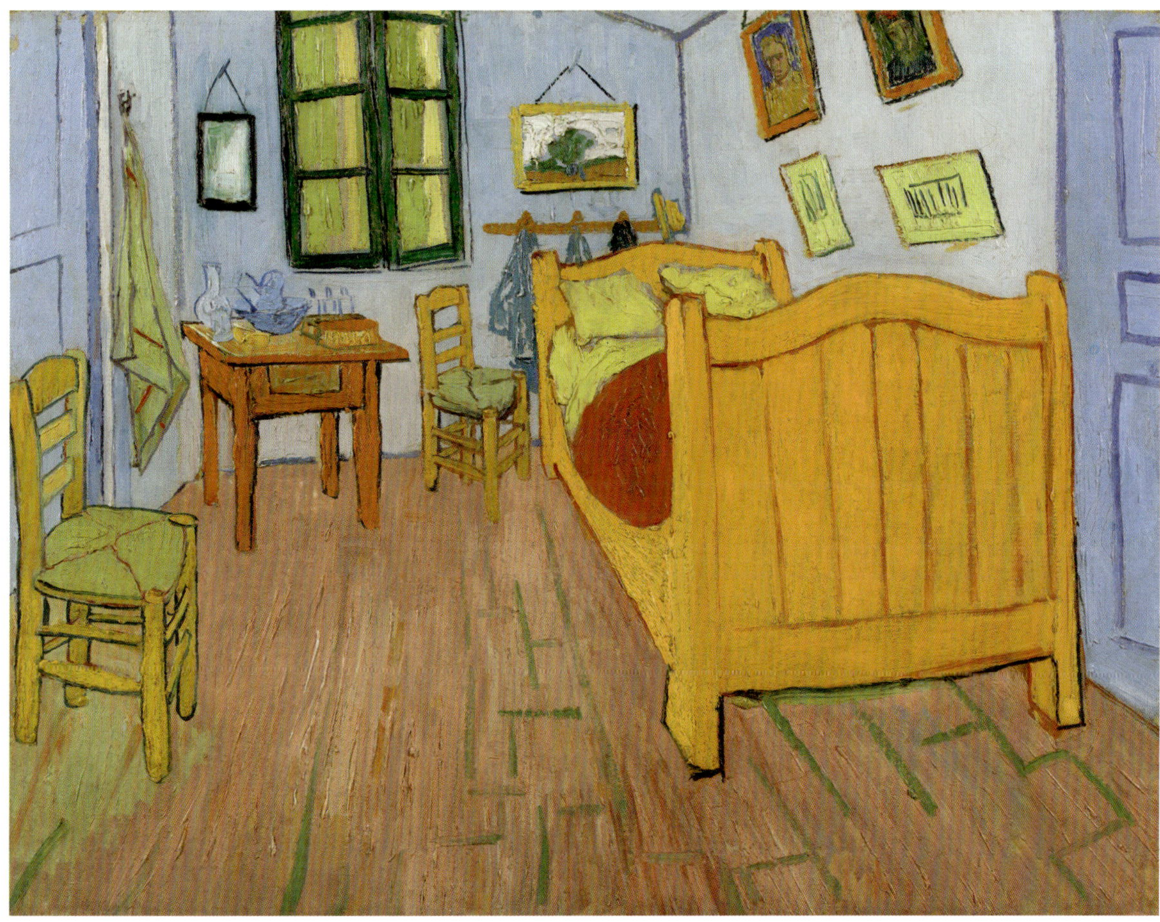

perspective can be partly ascribed to the room's physical configuration, this has been exaggerated and the proportions of the bed are most curious. The foot of the bed seems just as high as the head.

Van Gogh was pleased with the picture, believing that it was one of his most successful.[17] Vincent promised Theo that he would make paintings of his other rooms, but sadly he never did so.[18] How marvellous it would have been to have a depiction of his studio, packed with the jumble of his equipment and with his favourite works hanging on its walls – the best of his own Arles paintings, re-productions of other artworks he admired and his much-loved Japanese prints.

In the late nineteenth century successful Parisian artists often turned their studios into elegant interiors with exotic furnishings, to demonstrate their sophisticated tastes and impress potential customers. Van Gogh had a quite different ambition. He wanted the Yellow House to become 'an artist's house – but a *practical* one and not the usual studio full of curios'.[19]

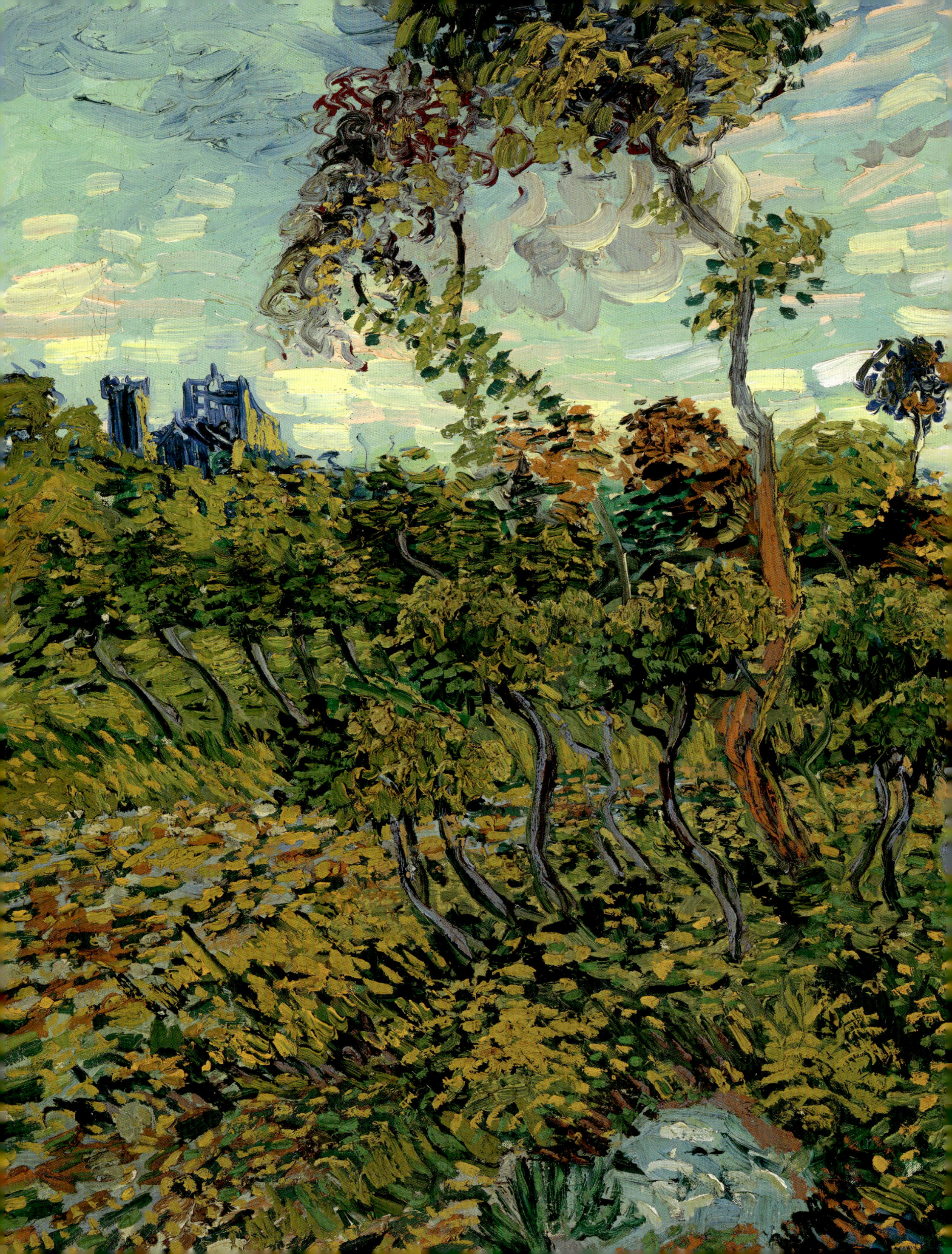

CHAPTER FOUR

HEIGHTS OF MONTMAJOUR

'A really beautiful corner of Provence'[1]

Detail of fig. 24 *Sunset at Montmajour,* private collection

Van Gogh frequently set off along the tree-lined avenue that left Place Lamartine for the 'wild and romantic' abbey of Montmajour. The ruins are set on a 40-metre craggy hill near the western end of the Alpilles, rising above the flat farmland of the Rhône plain. Crowning its limestone summit are the sprawling remains of the fortified Benedictine abbey, a landmark easily visible from Arles, five kilometres away. Partly dating back to the eleventh century, the abbey later fell into decay, although restoration work had begun in the 1860s. By July 1888 Van Gogh had been there no fewer than fifty times.[2]

Vincent first discovered Montmajour two weeks after his arrival in Arles. He wrote enthusiastically to Theo of a walk to 'a ruined abbey on a hill planted with hollies, pines and grey olive trees'.[3] The trip there represented a pilgrimage into the Provençal landscape, as captured in his slightly later drawing of *The Route de Tarascon with a Man Walking* (fig. 22).[4] The fresh leaves sprouting on the trees suggest spring. Most of the drawing was done by the roadside, but back in his studio Van Gogh partially erased and adjusted the striding walker. This figure may well represent a self-portrait, showing the artist setting off for a day's work.

In mid-May Van Gogh concentrated his efforts on Montmajour, hoping to do a set of drawings for exhibition or even for sale.[5] By the end of the month he had sent Theo eight drawings done around the abbey.[6] The finest is *View of Arles from a Hill* (fig. 23), 'a vista of meadows, a road with poplars and, right in the distance, the town'.[7] It depicts the distant buildings of Arles on the horizon, with the church towers and the chimneys of the railway workshops on the left. The distant track which diagonally bisects the drawing is the turn-off from the Route de Tarascon which climbs up to Montmajour. Van Gogh mainly used a thick reed pen, deploying it with great skill to render the landscape, and with a quill he added the fine lines which delineate the horizon.

Two months later Vincent returned to Montmajour for an even more ambitious bout of work. On 5 July he described an impressive sunset to Theo: 'I was on a stony heath where very small, twisted oaks grow, in the background a ruin on the hill ... the sun was pouring its very yellow rays over

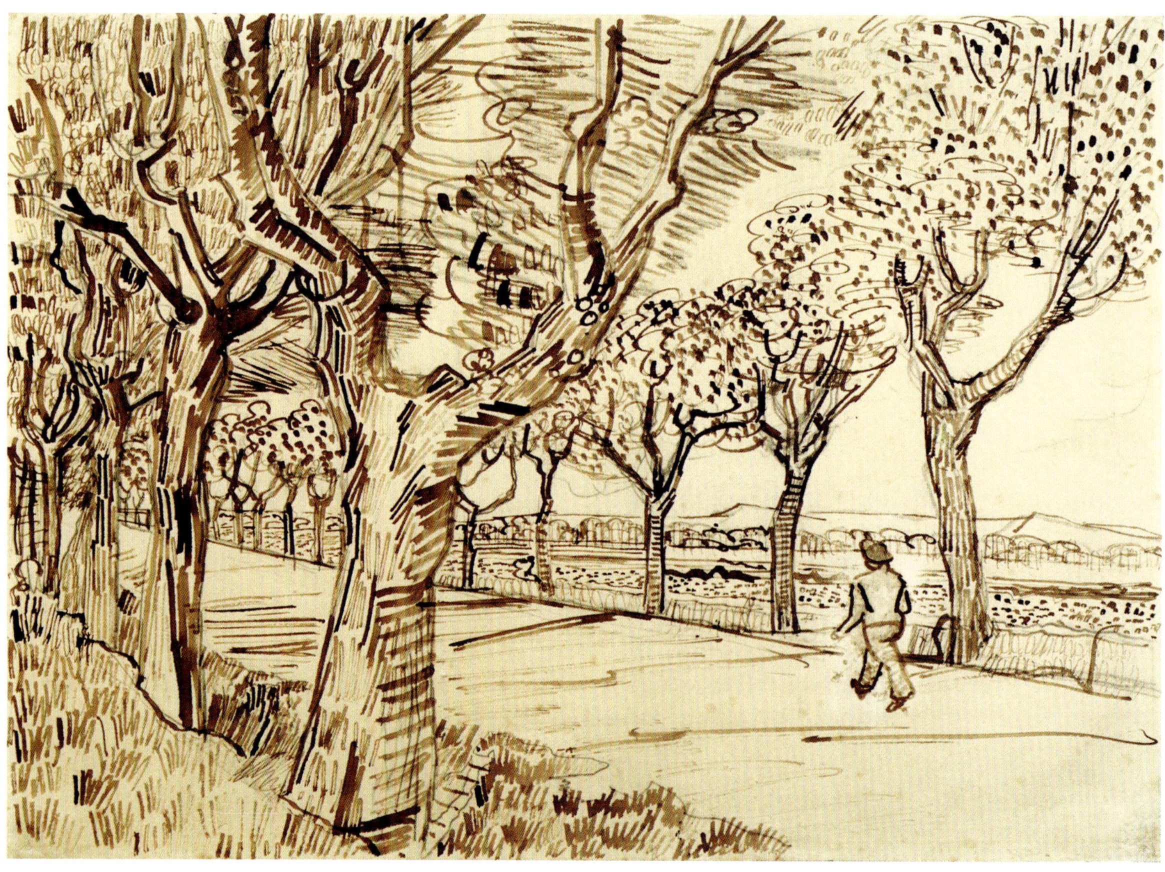

the bushes and the ground, absolutely a shower of gold.'[8] He then mentions having completed a painting, but until recently this was assumed to be lost.

Sunset at Montmajour (fig. 24) represents a stunning rediscovery. In 1908 the picture had been bought by Christian Mustad, a Norwegian industrialist. Soon afterwards a knowledgeable friend advised him that the painting was a fake and Mustad promptly banished it to the attic. It remained in store until his death in 1970. Twenty-one years later his descendants showed the picture to the Van Gogh Museum, but their curators rejected it. More recently the landscape was brought back for a re-examination.

After an extensive technical examination, the museum eventually confirmed that *Sunset at Montmajour* is indeed the work from that golden evening which the artist had so memorably described.[9] The pigments and canvas correspond to those used by Van Gogh in Arles and the style and

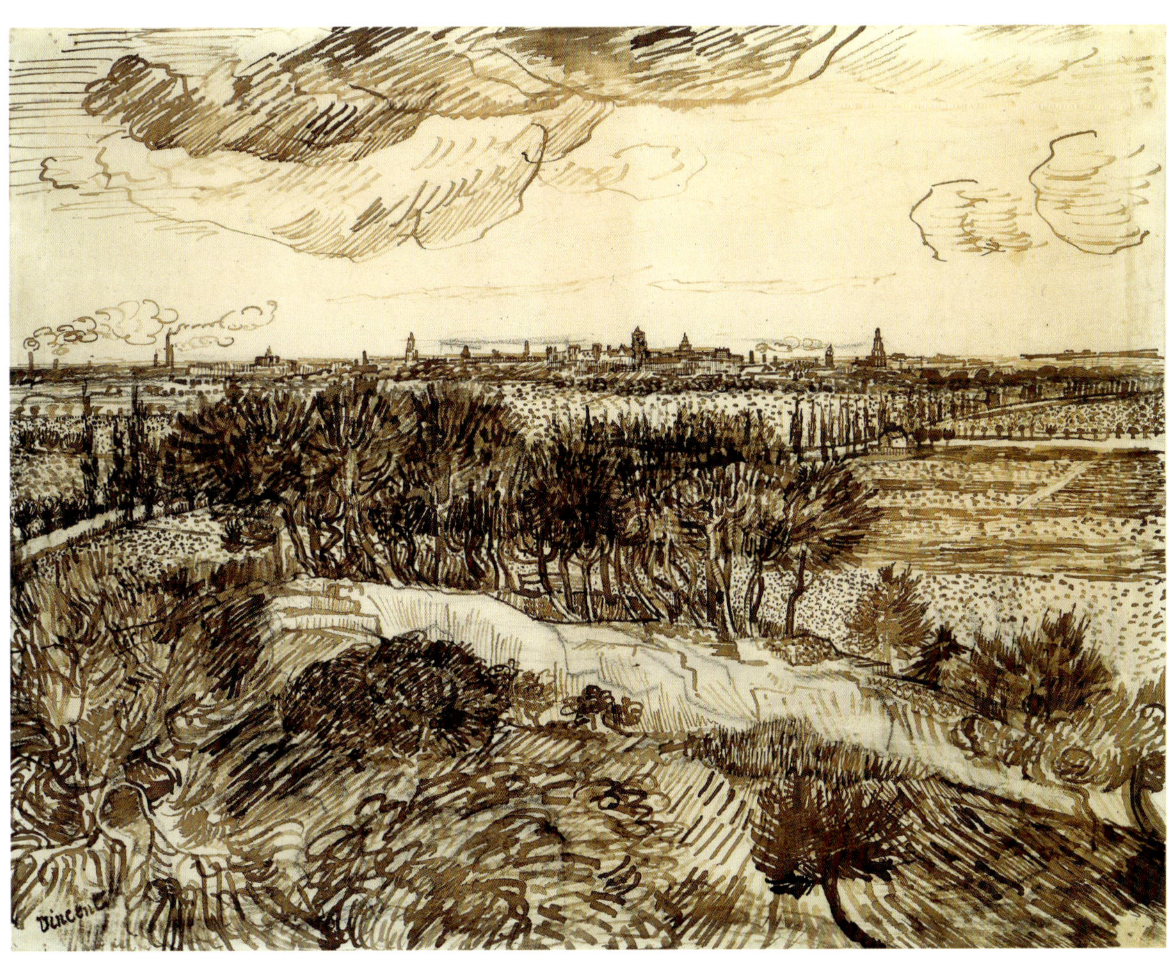

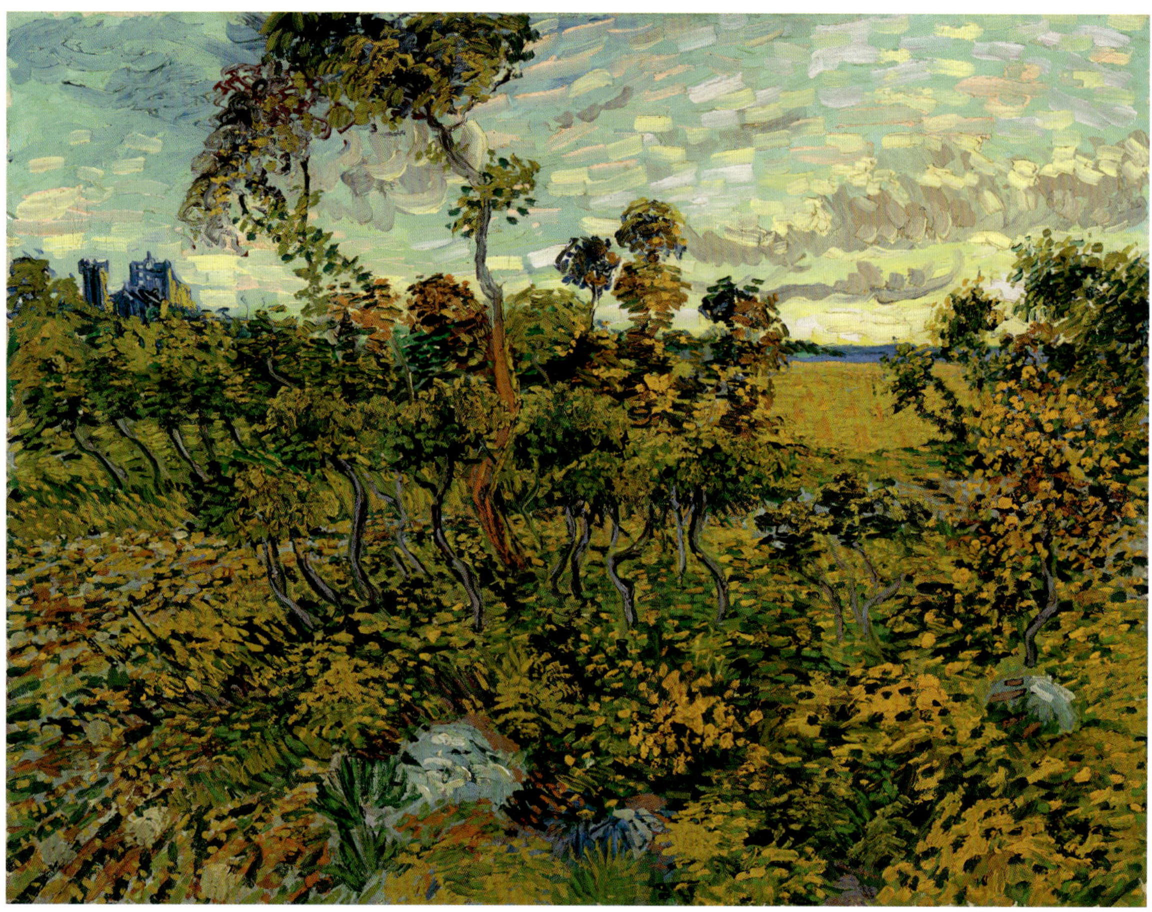

brushwork is typical. On the back of the canvas is a pencilled '180', which links it to a picture with that number entitled 'Soleil couchant à Arles' in an 1890 inventory, compiled just after the artist's death.

The painting of *Sunset at Montmajour* was done from a kilometre east of the abbey, looking back at the distant ruins silhouetted against the sky of a setting sun. Although small, the buildings visible on the far left of the horizon are unmistakably the abbey's tower (with its distinctive defensive parapet) and to its right the Church of Notre Dame de la Major (fig. 25). The large expanse of vegetation covering most of the picture lies in relative darkness, with light from the setting sun reflecting off several small pools as night approaches.

Van Gogh also completed five large and ambitious drawings of Montmajour in early July.[10] On one occasion he was accompanied by his soldier friend Milliet. Walking from Arles, they enjoyed some 'excellent' figs

ABOVE fig. 24 *Sunset at Montmajour*, July 1888, oil on canvas, 73 x 93 cm, private collection (F–)

TOP RIGHT fig. 25 Montmajour, early twentieth-century, postcard[11]

RIGHT fig. 26 Alfred Casile, *The Abbey of Montmajour*, autumn 1888, oil on canvas, 151 x 225 cm, Musée Calvet, Avignon

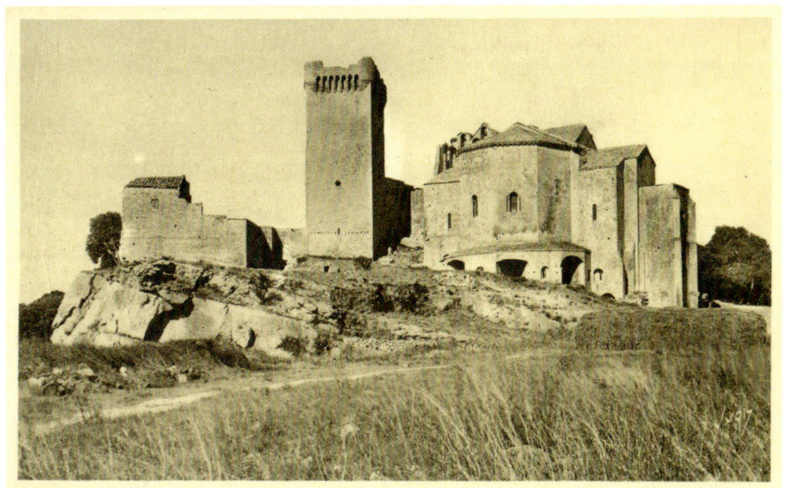

stolen from a garden.[12] Later that day Van Gogh drew *Hill with the Ruins of Montmajour Abbey* (fig. 27) from the southern side. The composition is dominated by a bulky rocky outcrop, looking towards the abbey and its impressive tower. A tiny pair of Arlésiennes carrying parasols pass through the gateway. On the right lies the plain of the Crau, with the Mont de Cordes just visible on the horizon to the right.

In choosing Montmajour as his subject, Van Gogh was far from alone. Many artists were attracted by the evocative abbey with its panoramic views,

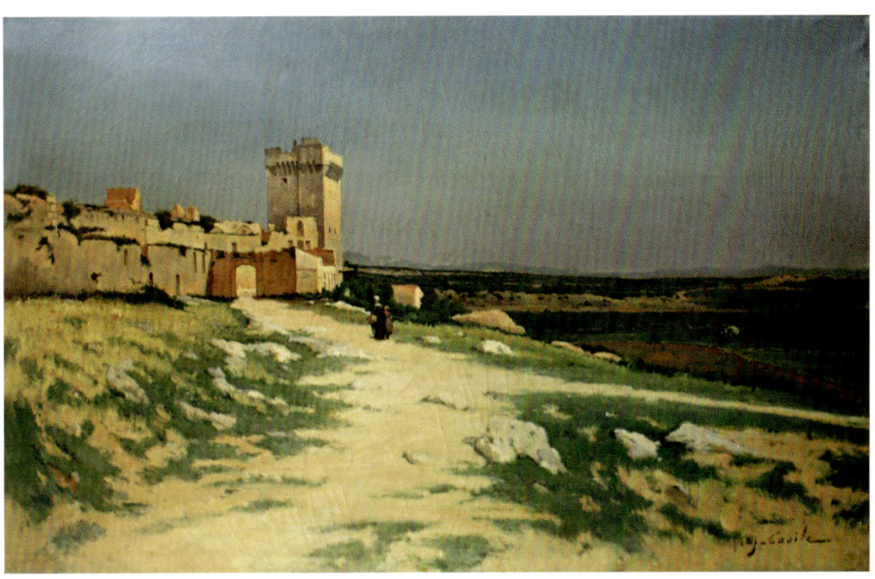

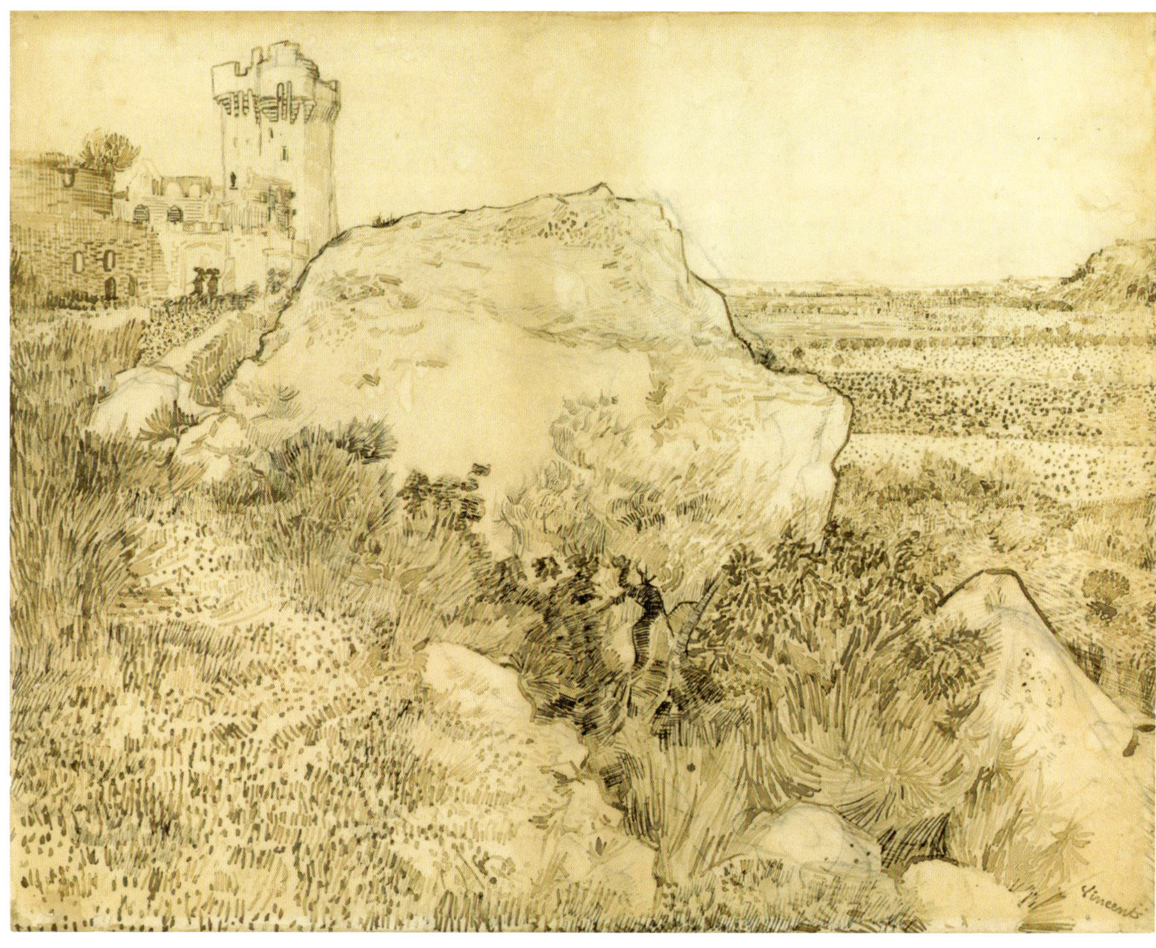

which made it a popular visitor attraction. Another far more established painter worked from almost the same spot only a few weeks later. In September an Arles newspaper reported that several artists were in town, noting that 'Cazil [sic] is installed at Montmajour in order to reproduce the magnificent ruins' (fig. 70). He was Alfred Casile, a Marseille-based painter who had studied in Paris and knew many of the Impressionists, including Monet, Pissarro and Alfred Sisley. The fact that they had friends in common makes it quite possible that Casile and Van Gogh met in Arles or at Montmajour.

Casile's *The Abbey of Montmajour* (fig. 26) must have been the painting which he was working on in September.[13] This picture, which has not been reproduced before, reveals the two artists' widely differing approaches. Casile's large oil painting presents a conventional visitor's view of the

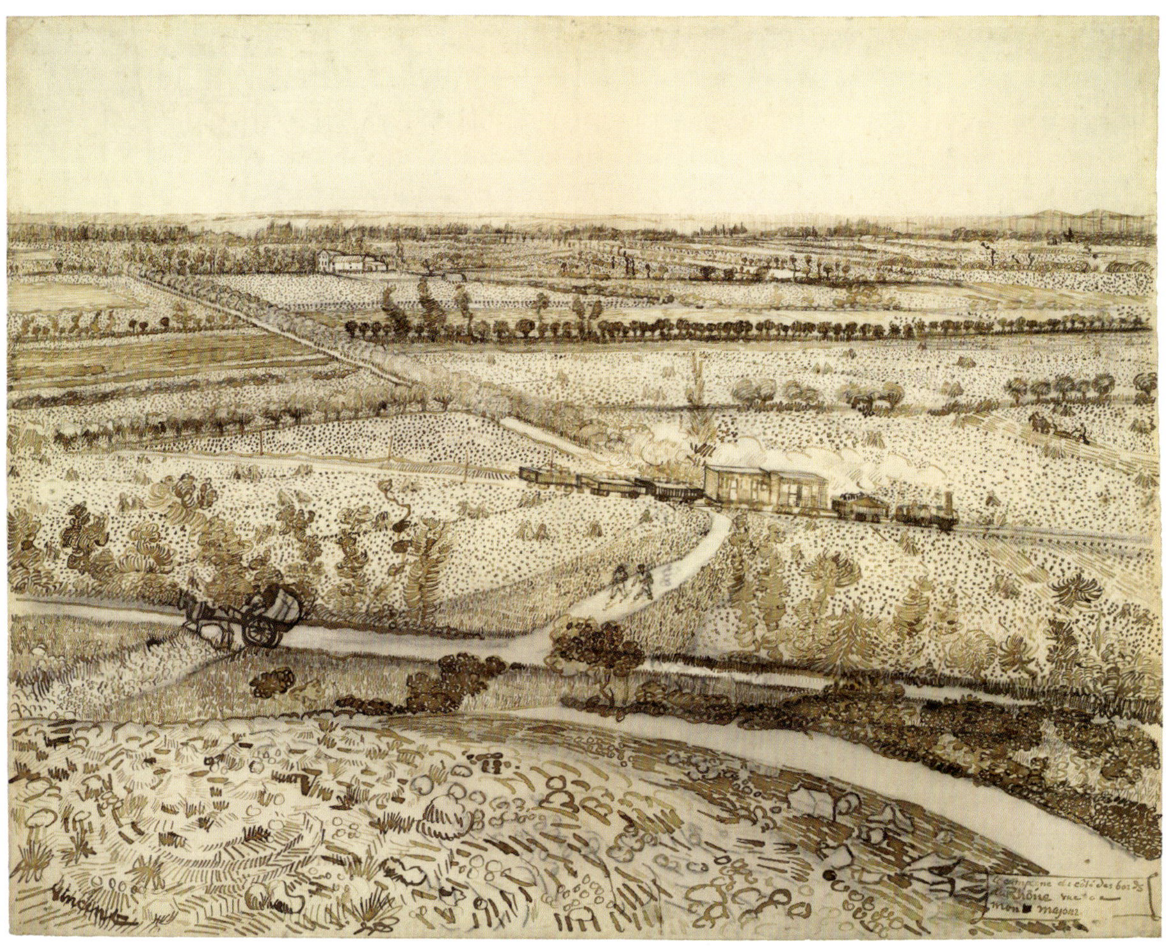

abbey set against the open landscape. Van Gogh takes a more original approach, in which the buildings are almost incidental. Focusing on the rocky outcrop, he is much more interested in the details of the landscape and capturing a mood.

Later that month Van Gogh returned to draw *The Countryside of the Banks of the Rhône seen from Montmajour* (fig. 28), looking from the summit towards the north and north-west. Van Gogh described the panoramic scene to Bernard: 'An immense flat expanse of country – seen in bird's-eye view from the top of a hill – vineyards, harvested fields of wheat, all of it multiplied endlessly, streaming away . . . A microscopic figure of a ploughman, a little train passing through the wheatfields.' He added that the drawing was '*actually* the most Japanese thing that I've done', referring to the high perspective, often seen in their prints.[14]

The straight road with the carriage heading towards Arles is the route from Fontvieille. Further back a train on the Arles-Fontvieille branch line heads in the other direction, with a coal tender, two small passenger carriages and three empty mineral wagons (used for transporting limestone from the Fontvieille quarries). The only visible building, near the horizon towards the left, is the Pavillon de Gaÿ hunting lodge, which still survives among the open fields.

Van Gogh probably added the people back in his studio: the driver and his horse-drawn carriage, the walkers who have just crossed the railway line and the tiny ploughman near the right edge just beyond the track. The lengthy title is inscribed in a cartouche – 'La campagne du côté des bords/ du Rhône vue de/Mon[t]major'. Van Gogh felt that this work, along with another Montmajour view, represented his 'best' Arles drawings. Although he hoped it might be possible to sell them to a Parisian dealer, he failed to do so.[15]

Around this time Van Gogh also made a painting of himself setting off on a morning walk to Montmajour. 'There's a quick [oil] sketch I made of myself laden with boxes, sticks, a canvas, on the sunny Tarascon road,' he told Theo (fig. 29). The artist carries his backpack with his travelling easel and holds another bag and a portfolio. Wearing a straw hat to protect himself from the Provençal sun, his body casts a strong shadow. As Vincent told Wil, he was 'always dusty, always more laden like a porcupine with sticks, easel, canvas, and other merchandise'.[16]

The Painter on the Route de Tarascon was eventually acquired by Magdeburg's Kaiser Friedrich Museum in 1912. During the Second World War the picture was evacuated to a salt mine in Stassfurt, in central Germany, where it was stored deep underground to protect it from Allied bombing. In April 1945, when the Allies liberated Stassfurt, they put their efforts into tracking down a stockpile of uranium which they believed Hitler had been planning to use to develop an atomic bomb. Art was very much of secondary importance. The Van Gogh painting was either looted or destroyed when a fire broke out in the mine. It is more likely to have been burned, but dozens of people had access to the mine during this turbulent period – so the picture could have been stolen. There is a slim chance that one of Van Gogh's most personal Arles paintings may eventually reappear.[17]

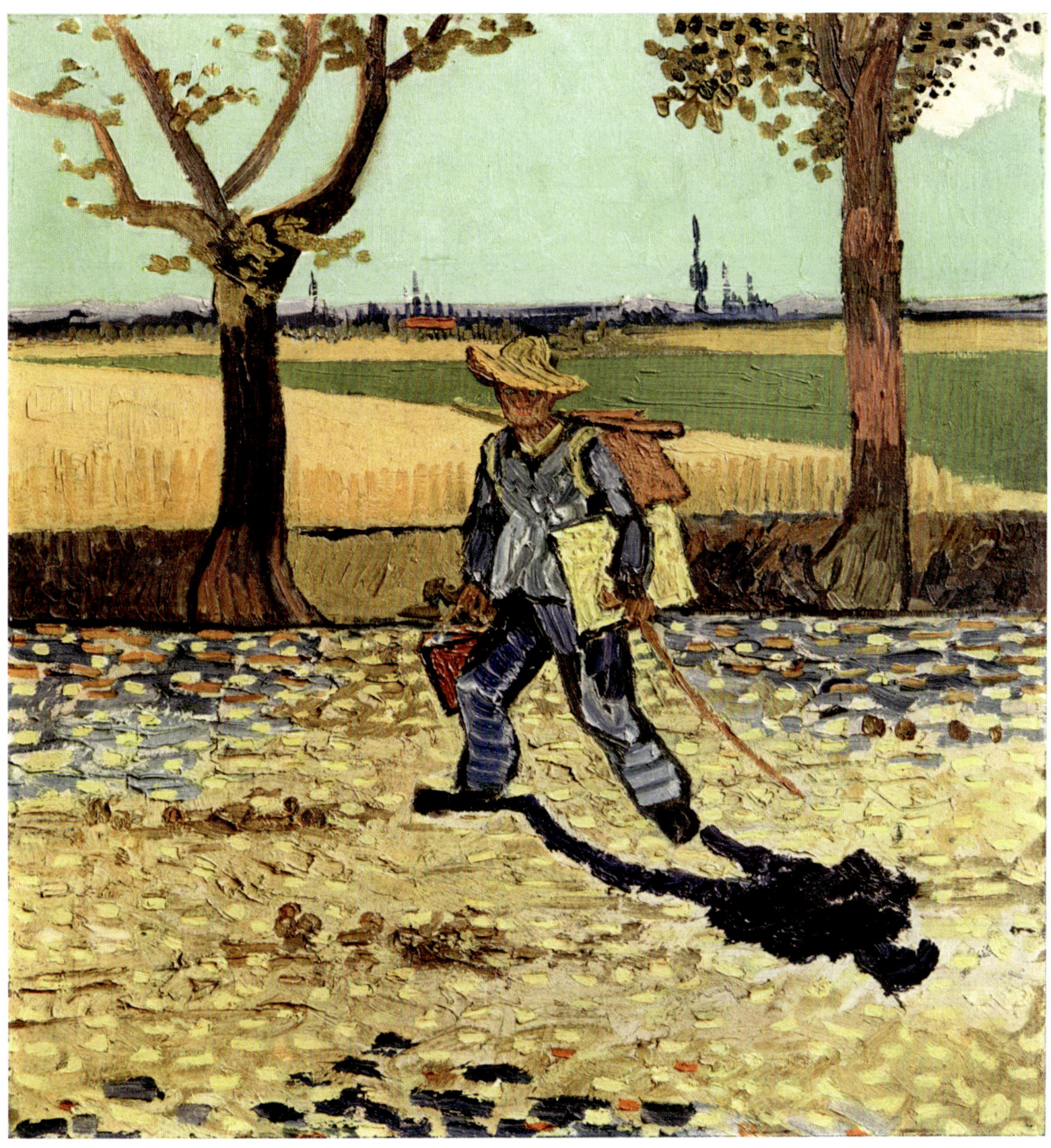

fig. 29 *The Painter on the Route de Tarascon*, July 1888, oil on canvas, 48 x 44 cm, Kaiser Friedrich Museum, Magdeburg (lost in 1945) (F448)

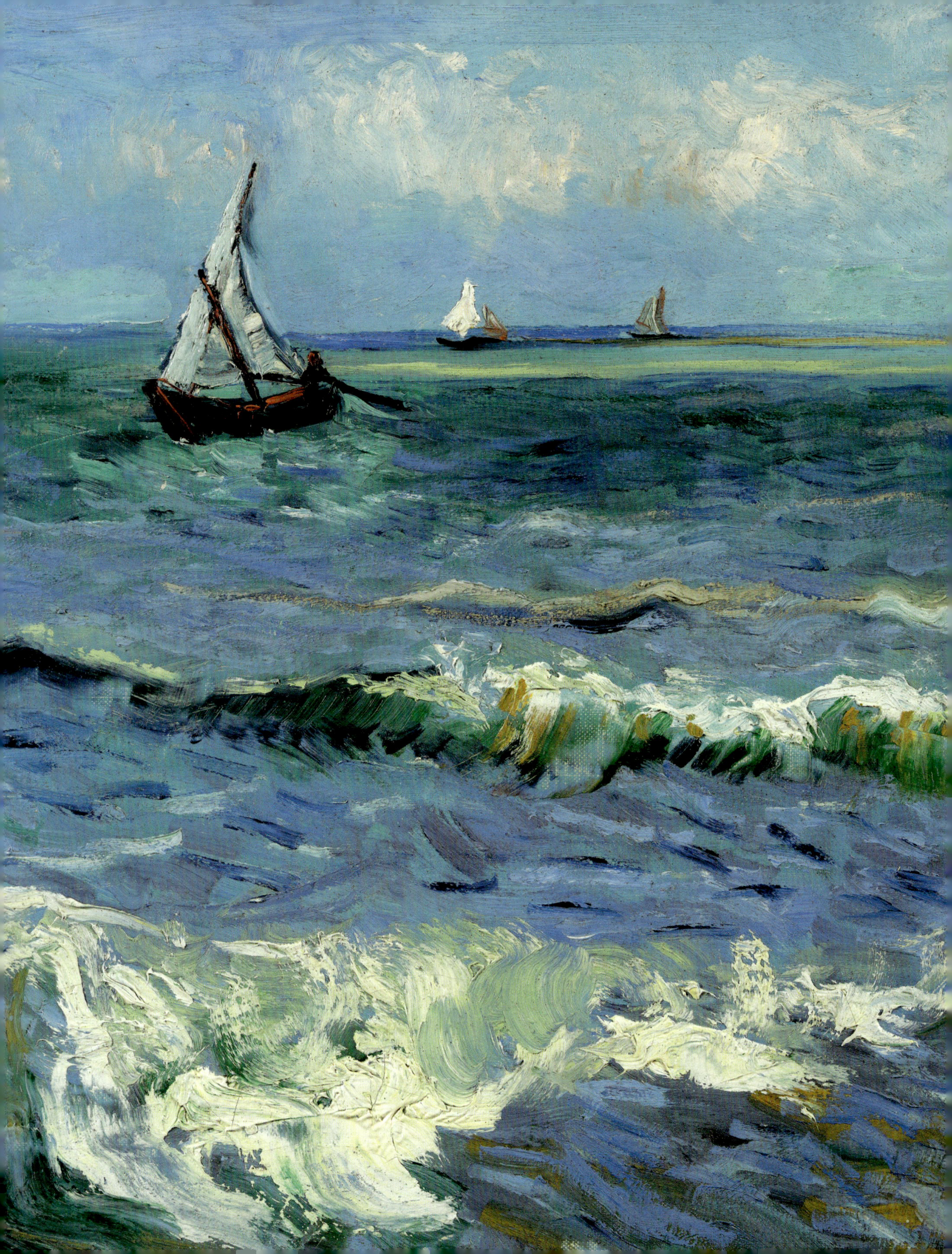

SEASCAPES

'The Mediterranean – has a colour like mackerel'[1]

Van Gogh had long wanted to visit France's southern coast. In late May 1888 he wrote in high spirits to say that he would soon 'see the Mediterranean at last'.[2] He was about to set off for the fishing village of Les Saintes-Maries-de-la-Mer, which lies forty kilometres south of Arles, across the swamps of the Camargue. His week-long stay was to have a much deeper impact on his art than has generally been appreciated.

Saintes-Maries takes its name from two Marys, who according to tradition had sailed from Palestine in 45AD to convert Provence to Christianity. Marie Salomé and Marie Jacobé had both been present at Christ's death. Sara, a servant to the two Marys, is also venerated in Saintes-Maries by the Roma. Every year, on 24–25 May, Roma from all over Europe gather for a festival, ceremonially carrying the statue of Sara from the crypt of the village church to the sea.

Van Gogh heard about this pilgrimage and a few days later, once the fishing village had returned to normal, he decided to go there to paint.[3] Anticipating the journey, he excitedly told Theo that he would see 'herds of bulls and herds of small white horses, half-wild and quite beautiful'. At the very end of the month he took the 6 a.m. *diligence* over the Trinquetaille Bridge and through the remote Camargue (see upper part of fig. 9). After nearly five hours of 'jolting' along muddy tracks, Van Gogh was finally able to pick out the welcoming sight of the bell tower of the church, visible from a considerable distance and rising above the swamps.[4]

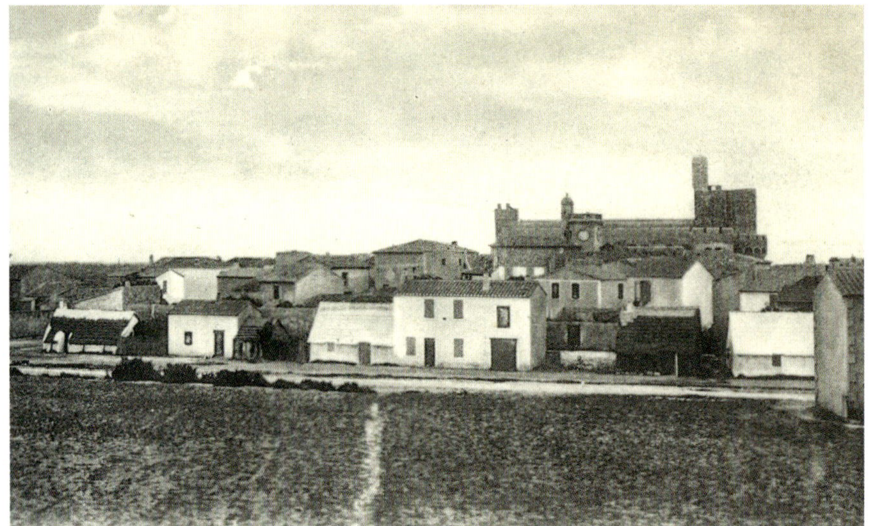

Saintes-Maries was then a village of 800 people. Life was difficult, with its inhabitants struggling to earn a living from fishing, cultivating vines and rice or caring for bulls and horses. Its isolated location meant it attracted few visitors, other than for the annual pilgrimage and for swimming in summer. All was quiet when Van Gogh arrived and he easily found accommodation, probably at the Pension Coulomb. He immediately explored the village, a few short streets surrounding the twelfth-century church. He must have stepped inside the Church of Saintes-Maries to view the relics of the three venerated saints and its collection of *ex-voto* paintings, many given in thanks for miraculous escapes from accidents at sea.

The sandy beach was just a couple of minutes' walk from his lodgings, giving Van Gogh his first view of the Mediterranean. He was instantly struck by its colour which, 'like mackerel', was always in flux: 'You don't always know if it's green or purple – you don't always know if it's blue – because a second later, its changing reflection has taken on a pink or grey hue.' The comparison was apposite, since mackerel was the main fish caught in spring, so he would have watched it being offloaded onto the beach. Van Gogh described the fried fish at Saintes-Maries as 'darned good', although he complained that it was not always available because the fishermen often sold their catch in Marseille.[5]

Van Gogh was immediately inspired to unpack his painting materials. Heading for the sand dunes just to the south of the village, he captured a view of the cottages clustering around its centre (fig. 31). Rows of vines lead towards

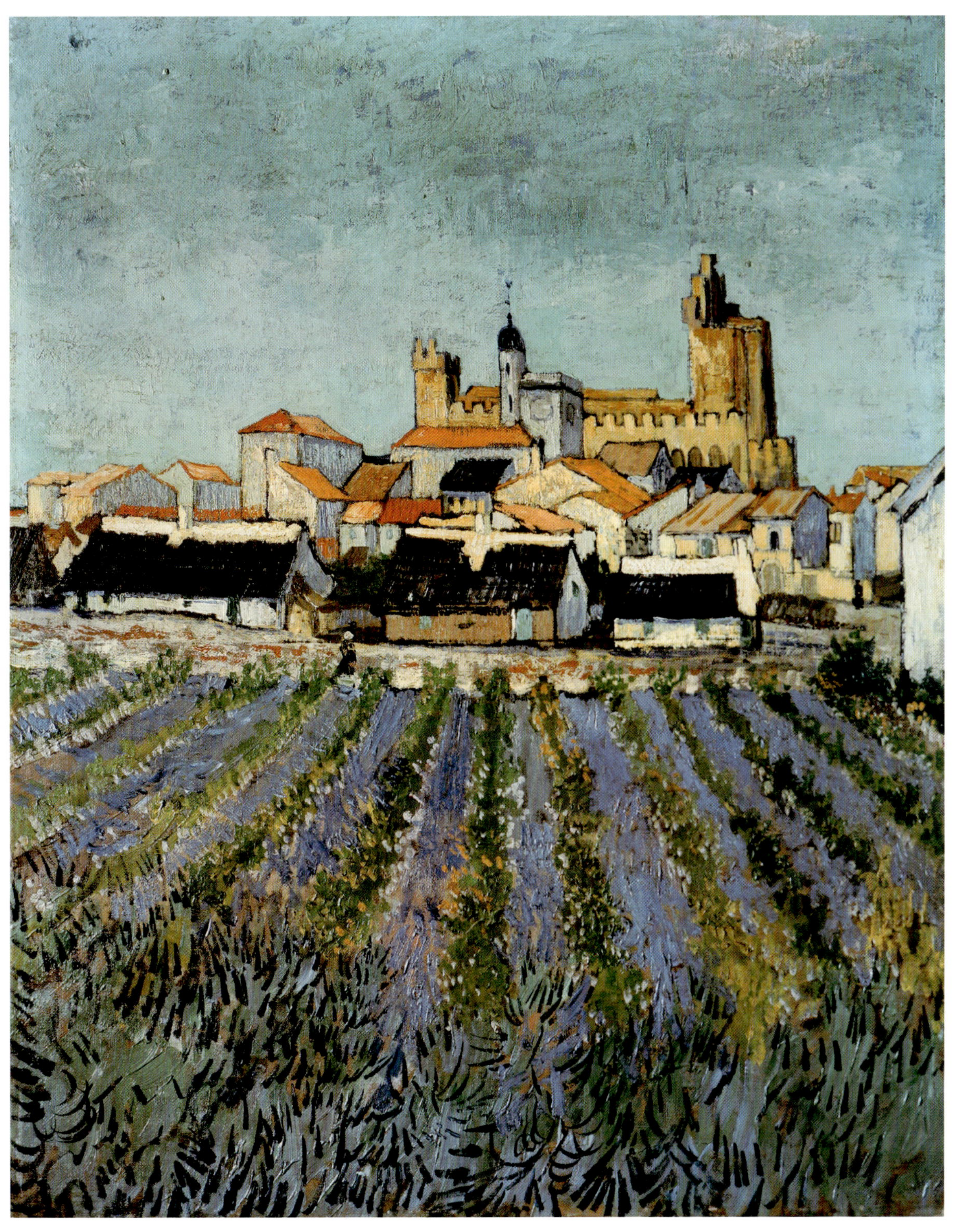

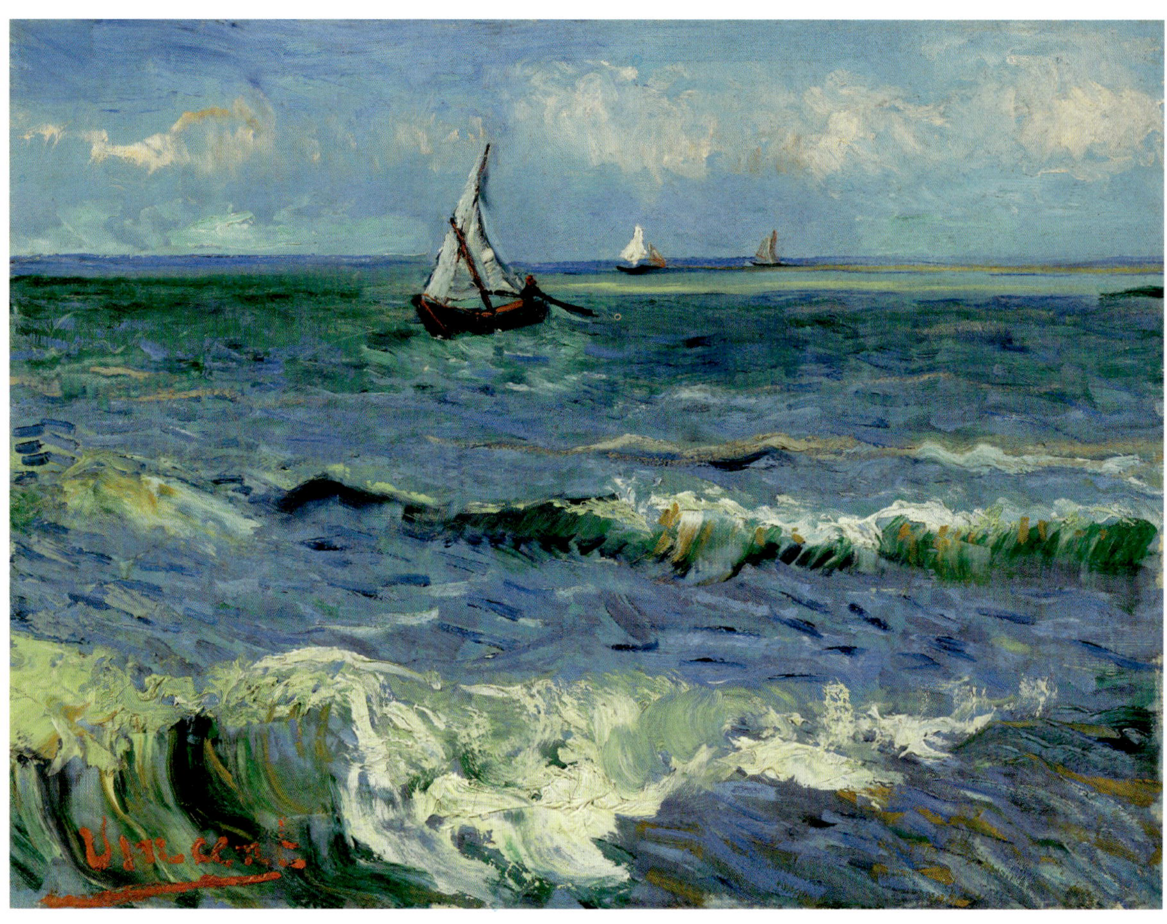

fig. 32 *Fishing Boats at Sea*, June 1888, oil on canvas, 51 x 64 cm, Van Gogh Museum, Amsterdam (Vincent van Gogh Foundation) (F415)

the village, focusing attention on the soaring church with its crenelated roof. An early postcard view suggests that Van Gogh has exaggerated the height of the towers of the church and the closer town hall (fig. 30).

He went on to paint a seascape, *Fishing Boats at Sea*, with three boats bobbing on the water (fig. 32). In the nearest vessel, a fisherman is steering. A tiny spot of red defines his hat and a thin red streak on the side of the boat stands out against the varied blues of the water. The high horizon focuses attention on the sea, with the foreground waves tumbling over each other, depicted in thick impasto. The artist squeezed white paint directly onto the canvas, and then worked the impasto with a palette knife. The curling water in the foreground recalls Hokusai's 1830s print of *The Great Wave*, one of Van Gogh's favourite Japanese works.

Van Gogh signed the seascape with a flourish, his bold red signature standing out against the sea. Grains of sand have been detected embedded in the paint (just visible to the naked eye on the original painting). This confirms that the picture was done on the beach – although he did retouch it a few days later on his return to Arles.[7] Several weeks later Vincent recalled the vulnerability of these boats in a letter to Theo: he and his fellow artists were 'sailing on the high seas in our small and wretched boats, isolated on the great waves of our time'.[8] This is the thought that he must have had while walking alone along the usually deserted Mediterranean beach.

Van Gogh also made eight drawings in Saintes-Maries, mostly of the *cabanes* occupied by fishermen, herdsmen and peasants.[9] These modest cabins, with low thatched roofs, were topped by distinctive triangular windbreaks, positioned to absorb the force of the mistral. Some of these drawings, executed at speed with great spontaneity and verve, would later serve as studies for oil paintings back in Arles.

On his last morning, after a week in Saintes-Maries, Van Gogh walked down to the beach just after dawn. He had previously watched the fishing boats go out, but had not got up early enough to sketch them. This time he drew four sailing boats as they lay moored on the sand (fig. 33). He described the scene to Bernard: 'On the completely flat, sandy beach, little green, red, blue boats, so pretty in shape and colour that one thought of flowers.'[10]

In the drawing Van Gogh used pointillist dots to depict the sand, with deft squiggles to denote the sea. The third boat has the name 'Amitié' (friendship) prominently inscribed towards the stern. Hovering above the beach are several birds, a feature that he often employed to enliven his skies. People are noticeably absent from most of Van Gogh's works from Saintes-Maries, and the fishermen who would have been getting their boats ready do not appear. He captioned the drawing in a cartouche: 'Souvenir de Stes. Maries/Méditerranée'. Van Gogh then painstakingly annotated his sketch with the names of colours inscribed in tiny letters on the sketch in twenty places, to guide him for a similar scene which he planned to paint in Arles.

After finishing his sketch, Van Gogh rushed back into the village to catch the *diligence* back to Arles. Immediately on his return he wrote to Theo, comparing his technique with that of Oriental artists he admired: 'The Japanese draws quickly, very quickly, like a flash of lightning . . . I've been here [in Provence] for only a few months but – tell me, in Paris would I have drawn *in an hour* the drawing of the boats?' Some weeks later he

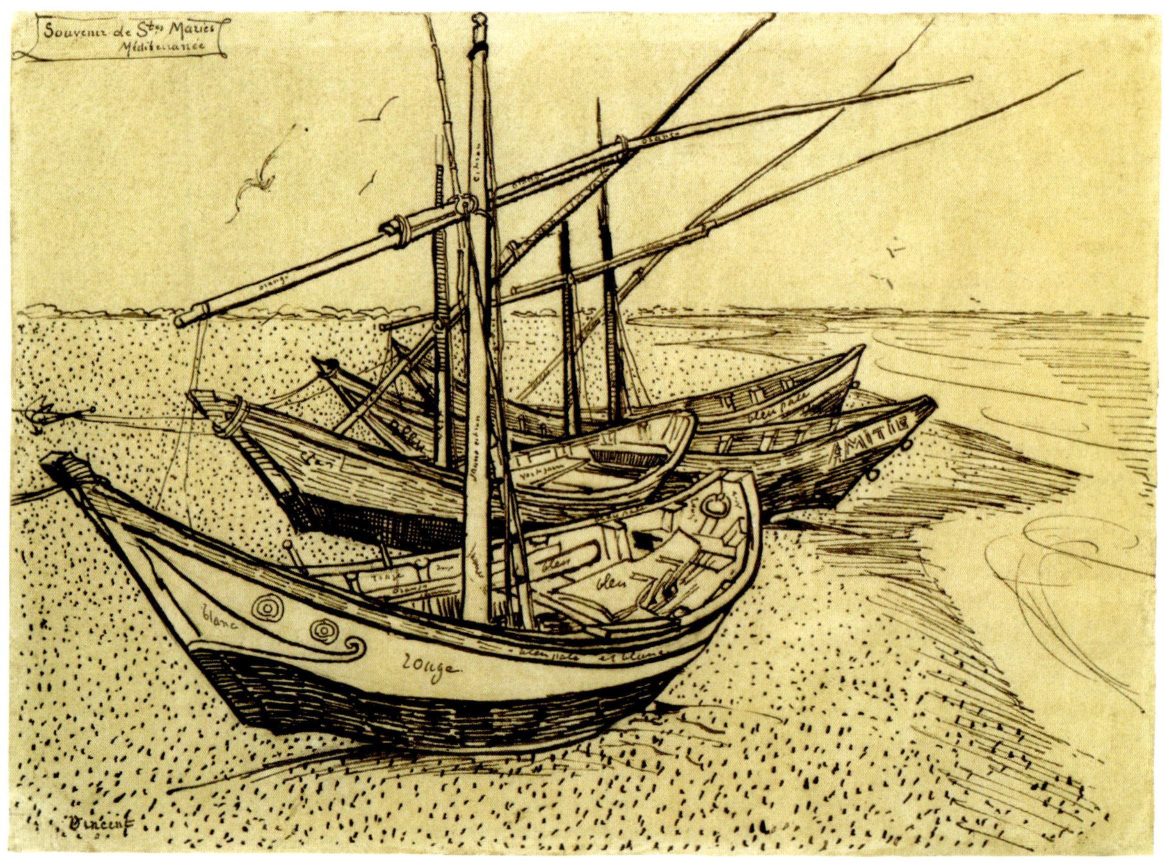

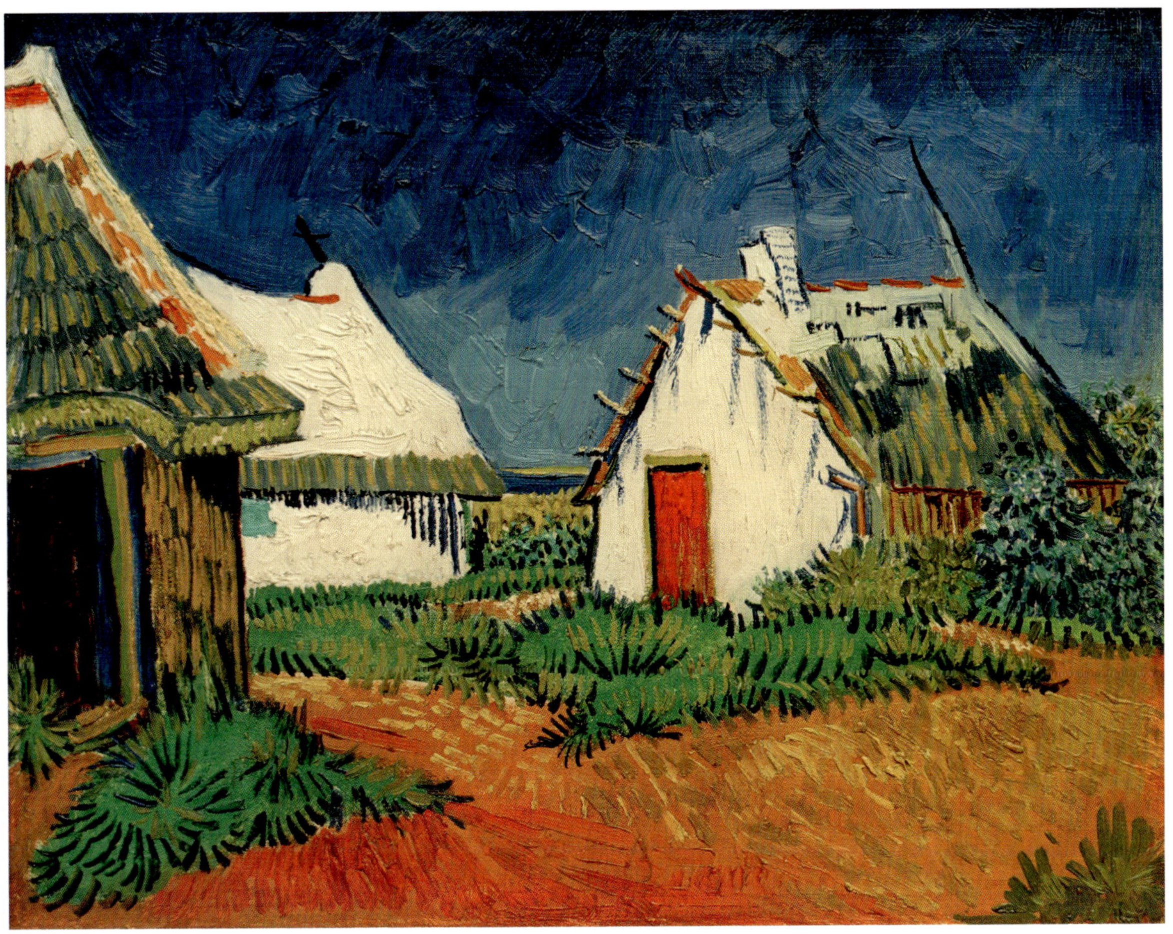

observed that the Japanese draw as easily as breathing, 'they do a figure with a few confident strokes with the same ease as if it was as simple as buttoning your waistcoat.'[11] Within a few days of his return to Arles he had completed an oil painting and a powerfully hued watercolour based on his sketch of the boats on the beach.[12]

Van Gogh also turned two other drawings into paintings, both done with astonishingly bold colouring. One sketch transformed into a painting was *Three Cottages in Saintes-Maries* (fig. 34). This cluster of small *cabanes* was on the outskirts of the village, nestling together for protection against the mistral. Van Gogh used orange for the sandy ground, to emphasise that the brightly-hued earth appears 'more intense' under the blue Mediterranean sky.[13]

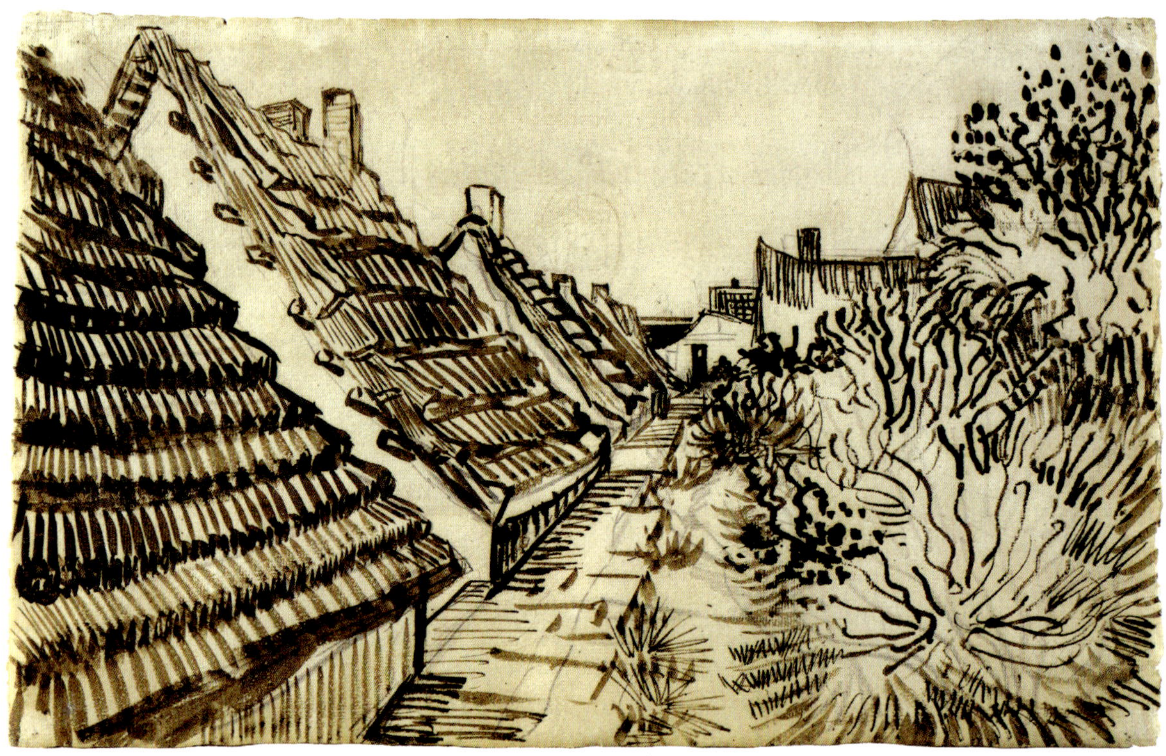

fig. 35 *Street in Saintes-Maries*, June 1888, pencil and ink on paper, 31 x 47 cm, private collection (F1434)

The other drawing that Van Gogh transformed into a painting depicts a row of low-roofed cottages in Rue de la Plage, seen from the village and looking down towards the sea (fig. 35). The composition's strong perspective is heightened by the diagonal lines of the narrow street. The sketch, done with a reed pen, has an immediacy which is partly lost in the painting, but the coloured version has moved into a new realm, almost verging on abstraction – with a play of strong shapes and a riot of colours (fig. 36). The roofs sweep from the village towards the sea, with brilliant red poppies dotted among the foreground greenery.

Van Gogh's week in Sainte-Maries saw a leap forward in his work. A few days before his arrival he had written of his wish to 'exaggerate the essence of things, and to deliberately leave vague what's commonplace'. His few days at the coast saw his confidence grow, spurring him to aim for artistry, rather than settling for realism. 'The effects colours produce through their harmonies or discords should be boldly exaggerated', he wrote. Encountering the ultramarine waters of the Mediterranean under a powerful sun made him even more convinced of the importance of 'staying in the south'.[14]

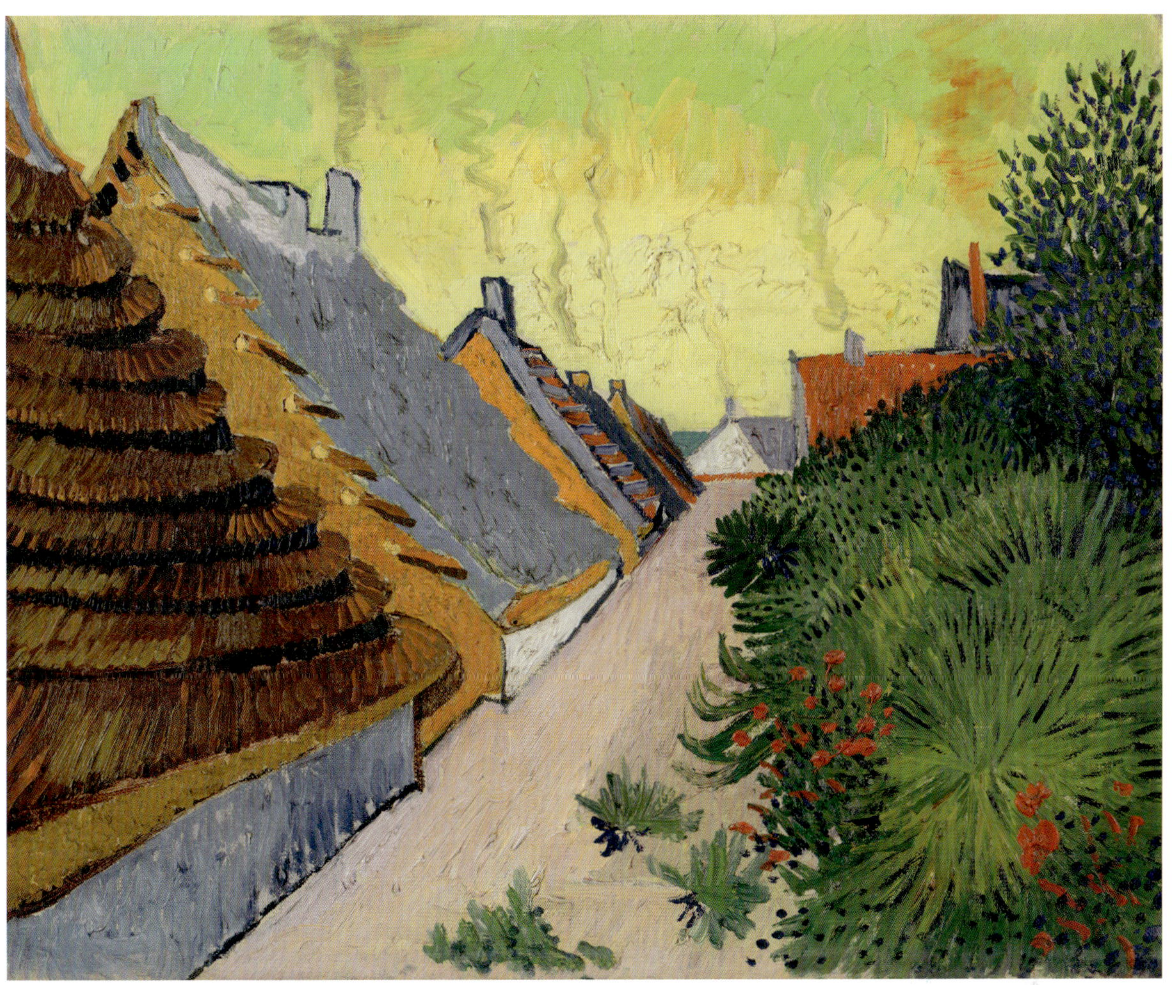

fig. 36 *Street in Saintes-Maries*, June 1888, oil on canvas, 38 x 46 cm, private collection, Fort Worth (F420)

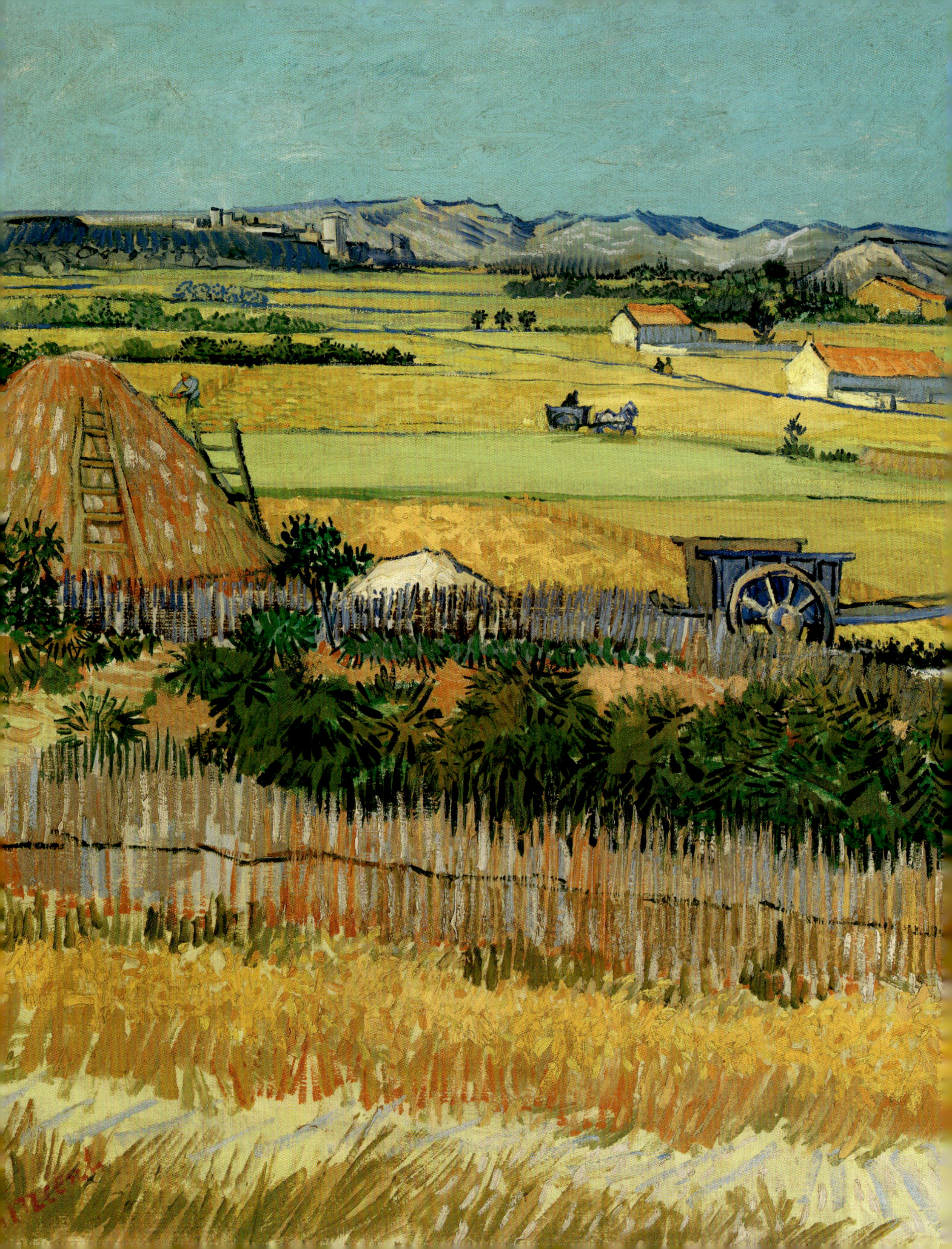

CHAPTER SIX

HARVEST TIME

'I even work in the wheatfields at midday, in the full heat of the sun, without any shade whatever . . . I revel in it like a cicada'[1]

Detail of fig. 37 *Harvest in Provence*, Van Gogh Museum, Amsterdam (Vincent van Gogh Foundation)

When Van Gogh returned from the Mediterranean he was surprised to discover that the wheat harvest had already begun around Arles. As with the orchard blossom, he was instantly captivated. Setting to work around 11 June 1888, one of his first paintings was *Harvest in Provence* (fig. 37), which ranks among his finest Arles pictures. It epitomises the abundance of the south, with the wheat turning a golden brown under the blazing sun. While working on his harvest scenes, Van Gogh acknowledged his debt to the landscapes of Cézanne, who was living in Aix-en-Provence, to the east of Arles.

Van Gogh began with two preparatory watercolours, one of which he entitled *La moisson en Provence* (Harvest in Provence). He then moved on to tackle the carefully planned oil painting. Working in the summer heat was exhausting, as he explained to his brother: 'When I come back from a session like that I can assure you that my brain is so tired . . . I become totally distracted and incapable of a whole lot of ordinary things . . . One's mind is extremely stretched, like an actor on the stage in a difficult role – where you have to think of a thousand things at the same time in a single half hour. Afterwards – the only thing that comforts and distracts . . . is to stun oneself by taking a stiff drink or smoking very heavily.'[2]

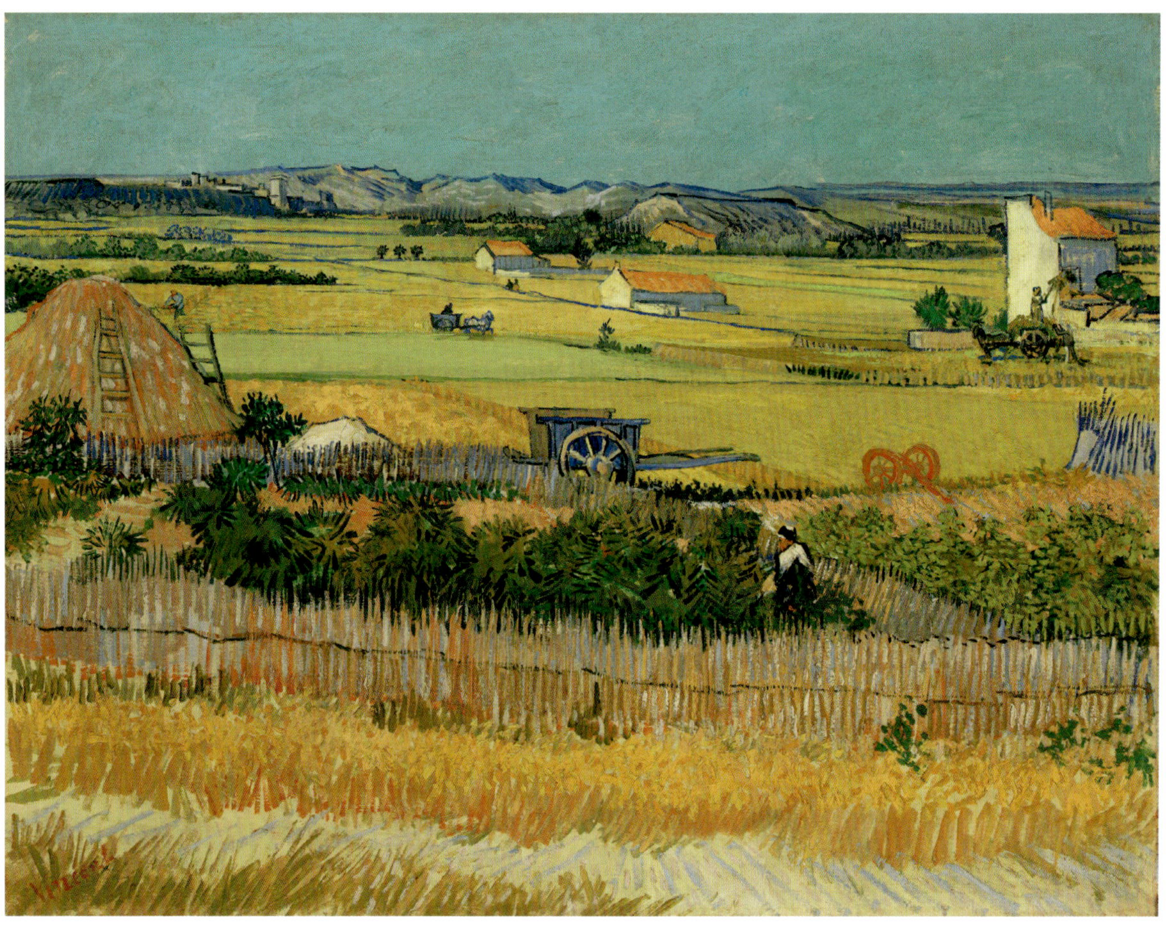

ABOVE fig. 37 *Harvest in Provence*, June 1888, oil on canvas, 73 x 92 cm, Van Gogh Museum, Amsterdam (Vincent van Gogh Foundation) (F412)

RIGHT fig. 38 *Harvest in Provence*, August 1888, ink on paper, 24 x 32 cm, National Gallery of Art, Washington, DC (F1486)

Harvest in Provence shows the panoramic view from the fields just to the east of Arles looking towards the Alpilles, although Van Gogh seems to have altered the topography a little for artistic reasons (the final painting is also slightly different from the pair of preliminary watercolours). The outline of Montmajour is clearly visible on the darker hill on the left and the Mont de Cordes lies beyond the farmhouses, its craggy left flank fringed with a lighter tone. A row of three farm buildings sit along a track among a patchwork of fields, imparting depth and harmony to the scene. The view is angled from slightly above and Van Gogh may have captured the scene from the bank of a canal or a windmill tower.[3]

The rich colours of the golden fields shimmer beneath a deep turquoise sky. A blue cart, in the centre, awaits a load of freshly cut yellow wheat. As the eye is led around, the scene comes to life. An Arlésienne is moving among the greenery in the nearest plot and a small figure of a reaper scythes just beyond a large stack in the middle distance. A horse and cart hurries by, while another stands close to the nearest farmhouse, where a couple are pitchforking wheat. As Van Gogh wrote of this picture: 'I certainly have no less love for nature that is starting to get scorched . . . There's old gold, bronze, copper in everything now . . . and that, with the green blue of the sky heated white-hot, produces a delightful colour.'[4]

Back in his studio Van Gogh set out to 'adjust the workmanship a little, to harmonise the brushstrokes' and then laid the painting on his terracotta floor tiles, enjoying the effect of it being temporarily framed in reddish brown. Pleased with the result, he wrote to Theo: 'On days when I bring back a study [like *Harvest in Provence*] I say to myself, if it was like this every day things could work – but on days when you come home empty-handed and you eat and spend money all the same, you don't feel content with yourself, and you feel like a madman, a scoundrel or an old fool.'[5] Van Gogh lived in hope that in the south he would finally make the breakthrough and begin to sell his work. Another indication that he was pleased with this painting is that he drew copies of it for both Bernard and his Australian artist friend John Russell (fig. 38), to show them what he was doing.[6] This was part of what he described as a set of 'sketches of Provence', based on his best paintings.[7] He now felt success was within his grasp: 'As for landscapes,

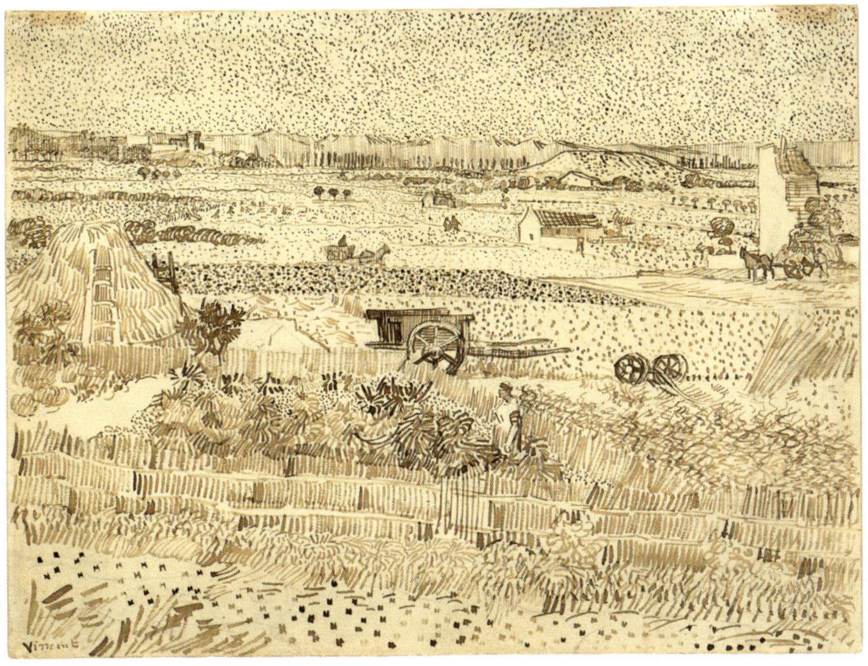

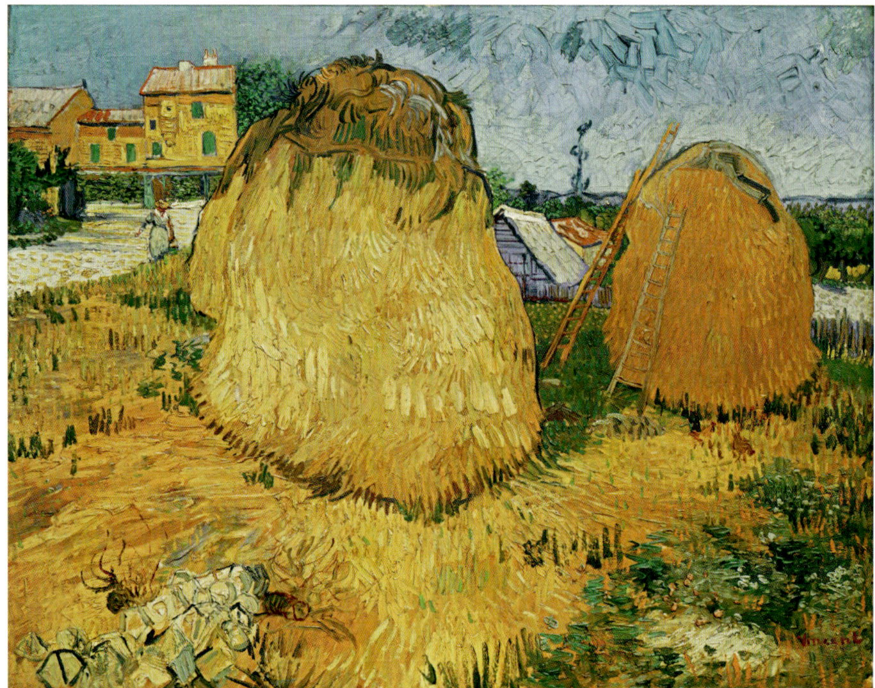

I am beginning to find that some, done more quickly than ever, are among the best things I do.'[8]

Van Gogh initially regarded his subsequent painting, *Haystacks* (fig. 39), as a 'pendant' to *Harvest in Provence* – although he later dropped the idea they should be displayed as a pair. *Haystacks* is centred around three large piles of hay (one is mostly hidden behind the nearest stack). Their bulky shapes dominate the scene, emphasising the fertility of Provence. A woman with a pail adds movement as she walks from the Mas (farmhouse) de Griffeuille.

Two other paintings were done from a similar spot on the north-eastern outskirts, but looking back towards town. In *Arles seen from the Wheatfields* (fig. 40) only a fairly narrow strip of sky is visible, putting the focus on the fields. Old and new jostle on the horizon – four church spires and the tower of the town hall, along with the tall smoking chimneys of the railway workshops to the left. A train on the Paris-Marseille line hurtles by. Below, a reaper and his wife are engaged in the timeless task of harvesting the wheat. Auguste Rodin bought this painting around 1900 and it remains in the Paris museum that was once his studio. The sculptor once described Van Gogh as the 'greatest' painter of modern times, along with Pierre-Auguste Renoir.[9]

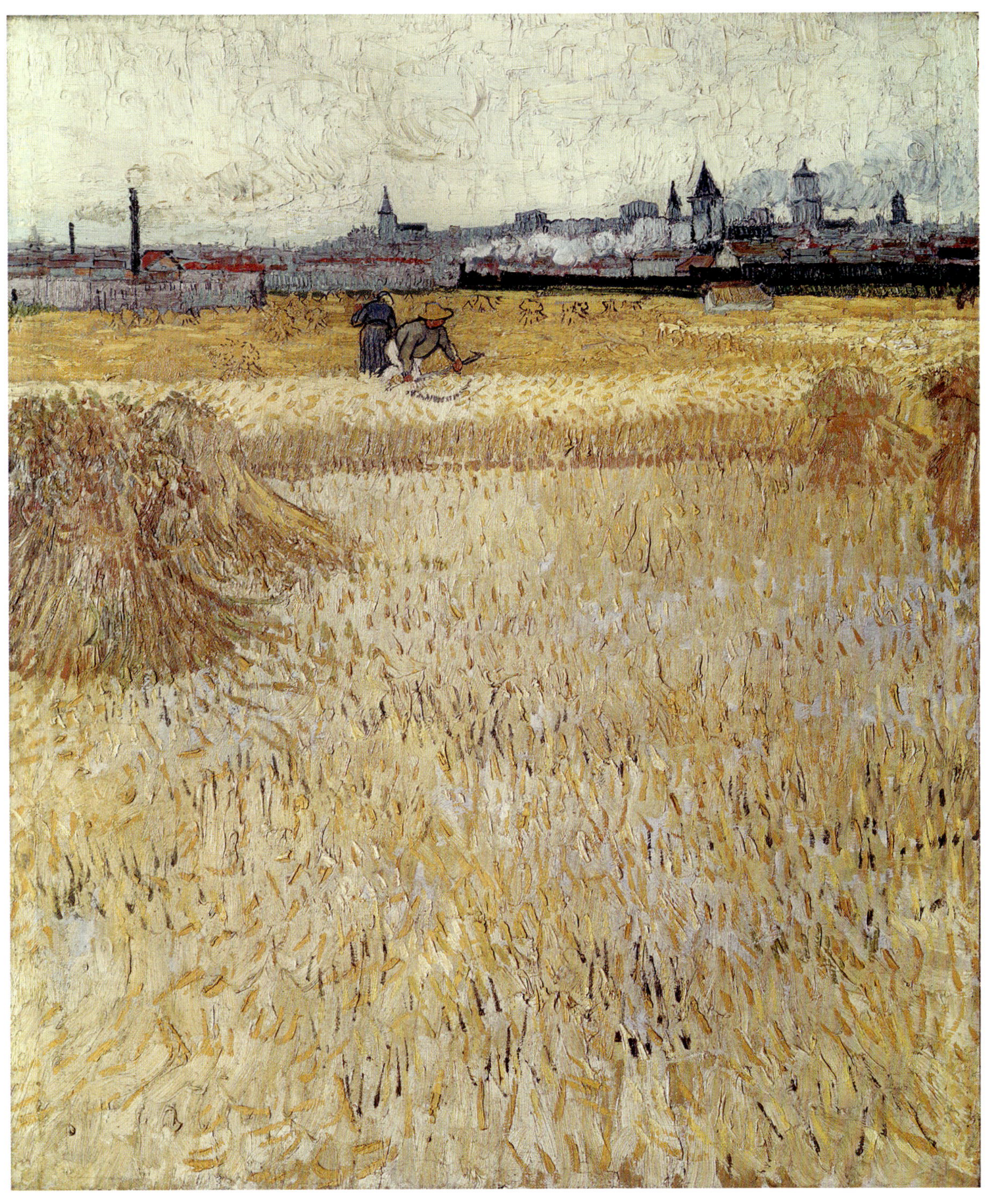

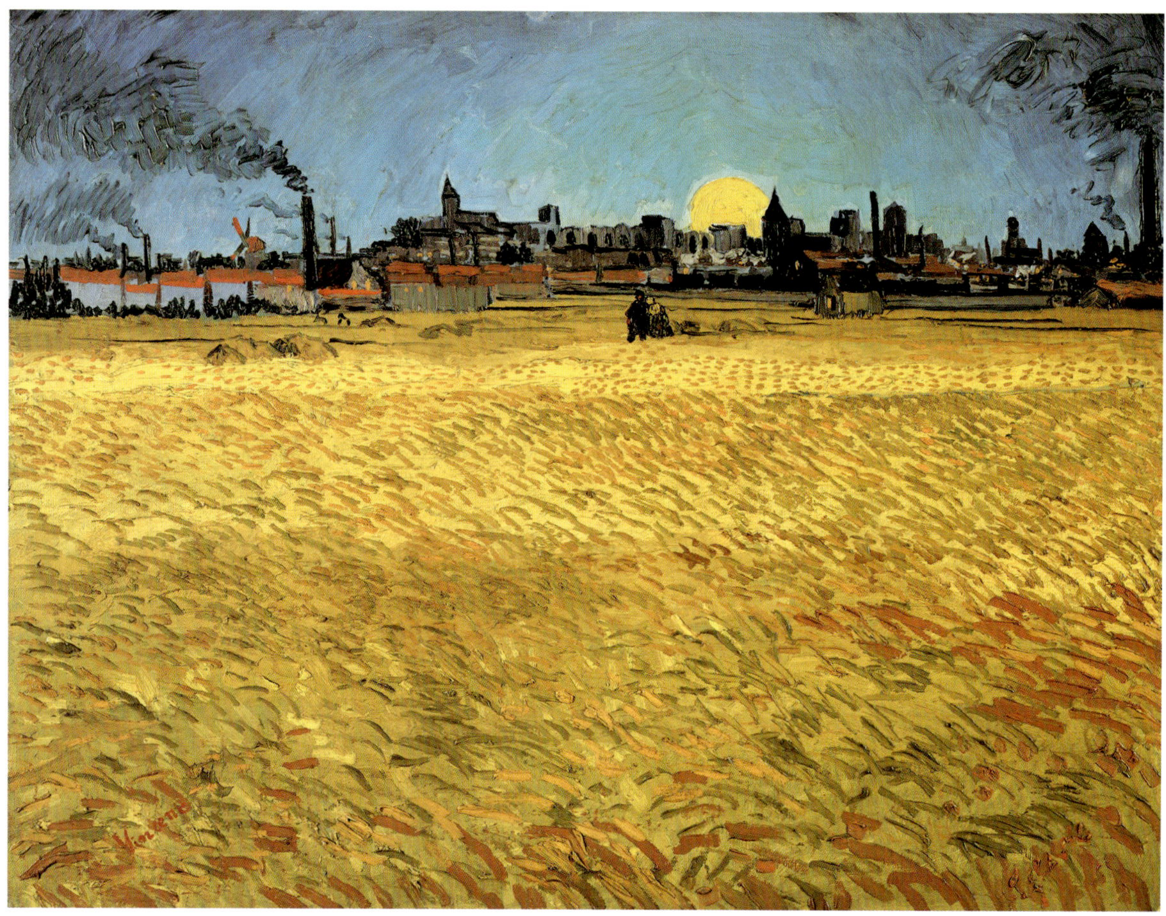

Wheatfield with setting Sun (fig. 41) is a similar view, with the distant figures of a pair of strolling lovers. A huge sun sets behind the Church of Notre Dame de la Major, with the arena just visible to its left. Alongside these ancient buildings are the belching chimneys of the gasworks (on the far right) and the railway workshops (on the left). The setting sun has clearly been placed directly behind the skyline of Arles for dramatic effect, since it would have set more to the north in June.

Van Gogh painted the wheatfield during a mistral, having developed his own personal method for working in gusty weather: 'You shove the feet of the easel in and then you push a 50-centimetre-long iron peg in beside them. You tie everything together with ropes; that way you can work in the wind.'[10] Most artists would have retreated to their studio during mistral conditions, but not Van Gogh. In his painting the smoke from the factory

ABOVE fig. 41 *Wheatfield with setting Sun,* June 1888, oil on canvas, 74 x 91 cm, Kunstmuseum, Winterthur (F465)

RIGHT fig. 42 *Sower with setting Sun,* June 1888, oil on canvas, 64 x 80 cm (including narrow painted border), Kröller-Müller Museum, Otterlo (F422)

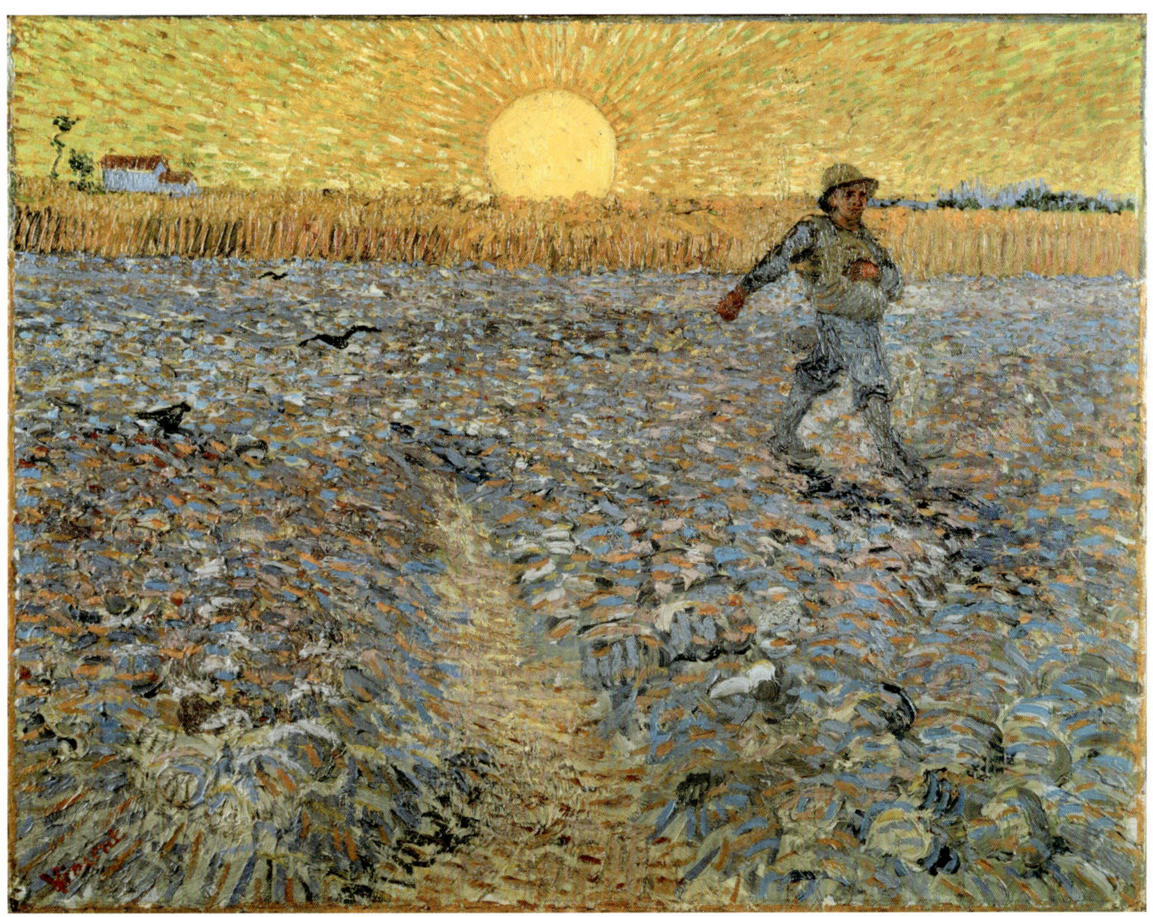

chimneys is being blown southwards, as it would during a mistral, but Van Gogh has (probably mistakenly) got the smoke from the distant train trailing as if there was no wind.

Sower with setting Sun (fig. 42) depicts the subsequent stage in the farming cycle: sowing for next year's crop. For Van Gogh, the act of sowing was highly symbolic. The ripening wheat grows near the horizon, while the farmer strides through the harvested field, scattering the seeds. The furrows are picked out with a mixture of colours, predominantly bluey-violets and ochres. Van Gogh was aiming for impact and effect, particularly when viewed from a distance. 'I could hardly give a damn about the *veracity* of the colour,' he told Bernard.[11] The figure of the sower is directly inspired by the work of Jean-François Millet, an earlier nineteenth-century artist much admired by Van Gogh.[12] A huge setting

I heard Rodin had a beautiful
head at the Salon.
I have been to the seaside for a
week and very likely am going thither
again soon. — Flat shore
sands — fine figures there
like Cimabue — straight stylish
Am working at a Sower. —

the great field all violet. The sky & sun very
yellow. it is a hard subject to treat.
Please remember me very kindly to
Mrs Russell — and in thought I heartily
shake hands.
    Yours very truly
    Vincent

sun (much larger than the farmhouse) symbolically dominates the composition.

Van Gogh began *Sower with setting Sun* out in the fields and his initial composition is sketched in a letter (fig. 43) to Russell (the Dutchman had learned English while working in London as an art dealer in 1873–5). He described his painting as 'the great field *all violet*, the sky and sun very yellow'.[13] A week later he extensively reworked the painting in his studio, heightening the complementary colours. The sower was given a more dynamic striding stance, reinforced by an added shadow, and the farmhouse was moved. Van Gogh finished the picture by painting a very narrow multi-coloured border around it (violet at the top, set against the sky; yellow for the rest, against the bluey-violet earth).

All Van Gogh's efforts were channelled into these harvest scenes. 'I am always in the fields', he wrote to Russell. A few days later he told Theo: 'When I look around me there are many things in nature that hardly leave me time to think about anything else. Because it's harvest time just now.'[14] On 20 June there was torrential rainfall, bringing the season – and Van Gogh's series of paintings   to an end. He had completed eight harvest pictures, nearly one a day.[15]

No doubt Van Gogh's presence in the fields caused considerable surprise, since visitors on the outskirts of Arles would normally only flock to Montmajour. An English guidebook to France commented in 1890: 'The country about Arles is solitary, and suspicious-looking tramps are often seen prowling about. A good thick stick, therefore, is an appropriate companion for a pedestrian.'[16] There is no indication that the writer actually encountered Van Gogh in 1888–9, but the artist was notorious for his shabby clothes and weighed down by his painting equipment he might well have been mistaken for a tramp.

Just after finishing his harvest series, Van Gogh told Bernard that he had needed to paint 'quick quick quick and in a hurry, like the reaper who is silent under the blazing sun, concentrating on getting the job done'. He had spent eight years honing his skills. As Vincent put it to Theo: 'When people say they're done too quickly you'll be able to reply that they looked at them too quickly . . . During the harvest my work has been no easier than that of the farmers themselves who do this harvesting. Far from complaining about it, it's precisely at these moments in artistic life . . . that I feel almost as happy as I could be in the ideal, the real life.' Van Gogh's only regret was not having discovered Provence in his youth. 'My God, if only I'd known this country at 25, instead of coming here at 35,' he wrote to Bernard.[17]

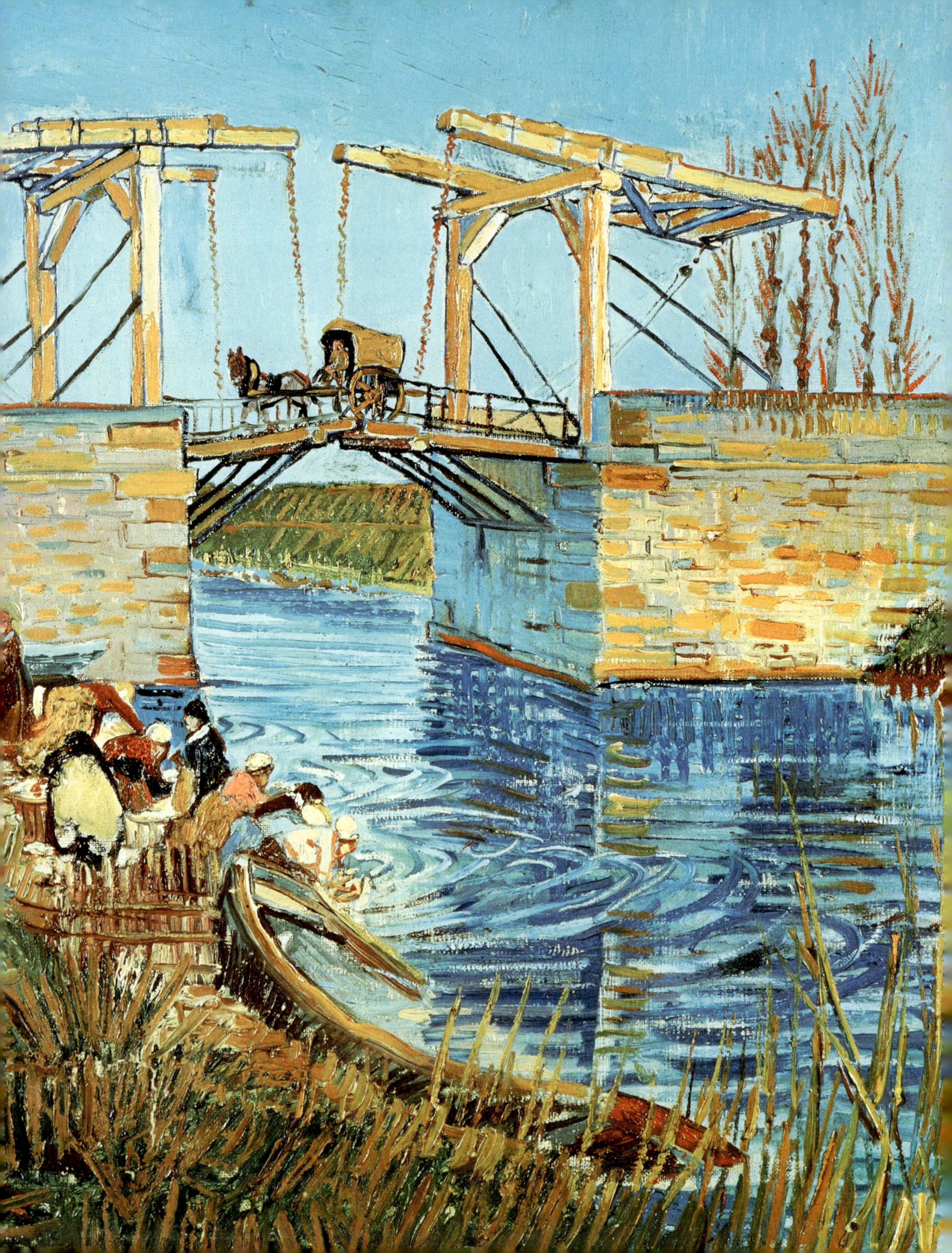

CHAPTER SEVEN

THE RHÔNE AND ITS CANALS

'The stretches of water make patches of a beautiful emerald and a rich blue in the landscapes, as we see it in the Japanese prints'[1]

In Arles Van Gogh was never far from water, which brought back memories of his native Netherlands. With Arles located on the left bank of the Rhône, the river had played a key role in the town's development since Roman days, when it was first bridged. Arles later became a major river port and in the 1830s a canal to Port-de-Bouc provided a more navigable route to the Mediterranean. Smaller canals had also been cut to irrigate the countryside to the east of Arles, an area known as the Crau. Almost any excursion outside town involved crossing waterways.

Van Gogh was captivated by Dutch-style drawbridges on the Port-de-Bouc Canal (fig. 45). He called it the Pont de L'Anglais (Englishman), a name often used at the time, although it was later usually known as the Pont de Langlois.[2] The poet Massebieau recalled encountering Van Gogh while he was painting at this spot, which lay among the wheatfields and orchards just to the south of the town.[3]

Langlois Bridge with Washerwomen was completed in mid-March 1888, just three weeks after Vincent's arrival (fig. 44). Writing to Theo, he described it as 'a drawbridge, with a little carriage going across it, outlined against a blue sky – the river blue as well, the banks orange with greenery, a group of washerwomen wearing blouses and multicoloured bonnets'.[4]

Detail of fig. 44
Langlois Bridge with Washerwomen, Kröller-Müller Museum, Otterlo

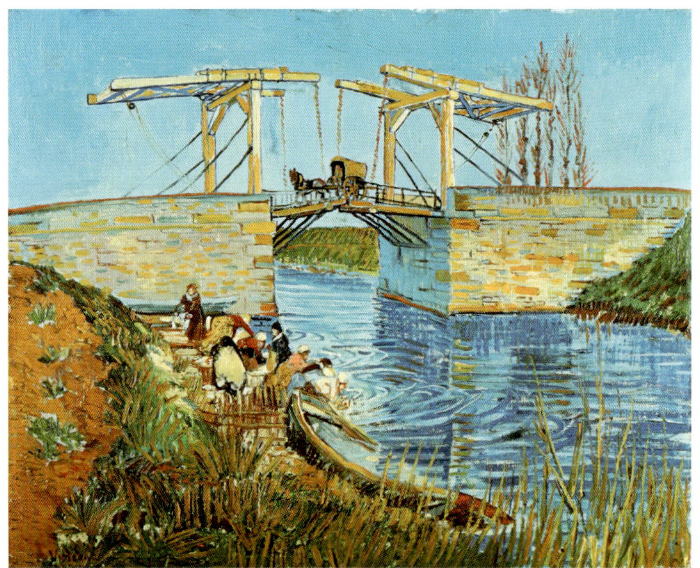

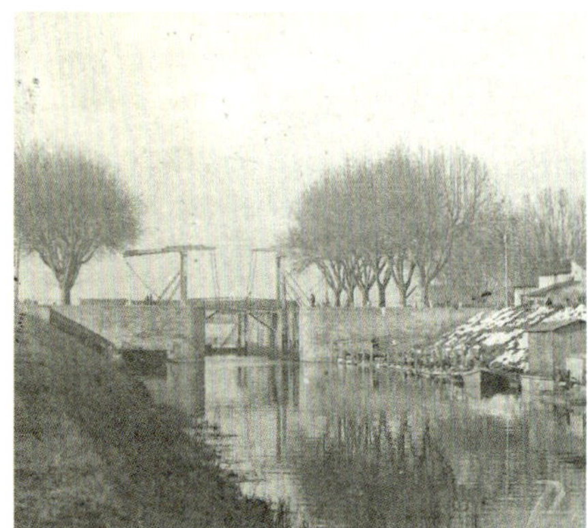

The artist went on to make four further paintings of the Langlois Bridge, although he destroyed the most ambitious of these, saving only a fragment.[5] This picture included a canalside view of 'sailors coming back with their sweethearts', with a setting sun and the distant skyline of Arles. A few days later he explained what had gone wrong: 'As the bad weather prevented me from working on the spot, I completely worked this study to death trying to finish it at home.'[6] Van Gogh liked to paint in front of his subject, finding it difficult to work from his imagination. He ended up discarding most of the canvas, after cutting out a small section showing a pair of lovers, presumably planning to use this as a model for another painting. He never did reuse the lovers, but this abandoned remnant sold for over $7 million in 2013.[7]

The mighty Rhône flowed past the centre of Arles and Van Gogh must have seen the river almost every day. In May, at a spot near the end of Place Lamartine, he drew *Banks of the Rhône* (fig. 46). A moored sailboat and skiff lie by the sandbar, beside a man and two horses. The curving panorama of the town includes the prominent tower of the Church of St Julien, with a setting sun near the horizon.

By coincidence, a similar view would be drawn by the American artist Joseph Pennell just four months later (fig. 47). Pennell, who was making a topographical image to illustrate a travel article on Provence, stood on the embankment, giving a clearer view of the town with its famed arena, its arches emphasised in black. It is uncertain whether the two artists met, but when Pennell visited in September 1888 he would have been sketching only one minute away from the Yellow House.[10]

The Rhône and its river traffic entranced Van Gogh. One evening in late July he described 'a magnificent and very strange effect', with a heavily laden coal boat moored at the quay: 'Seen from above it was all glistening and wet from a shower; the water was a white yellow and clouded pearl-grey, the sky lilac and an orange strip in the west, the town violet. On the boat, small workmen, blue and dirty white, were coming and going, carrying the cargo ashore. It was pure Hokusai.'[11]

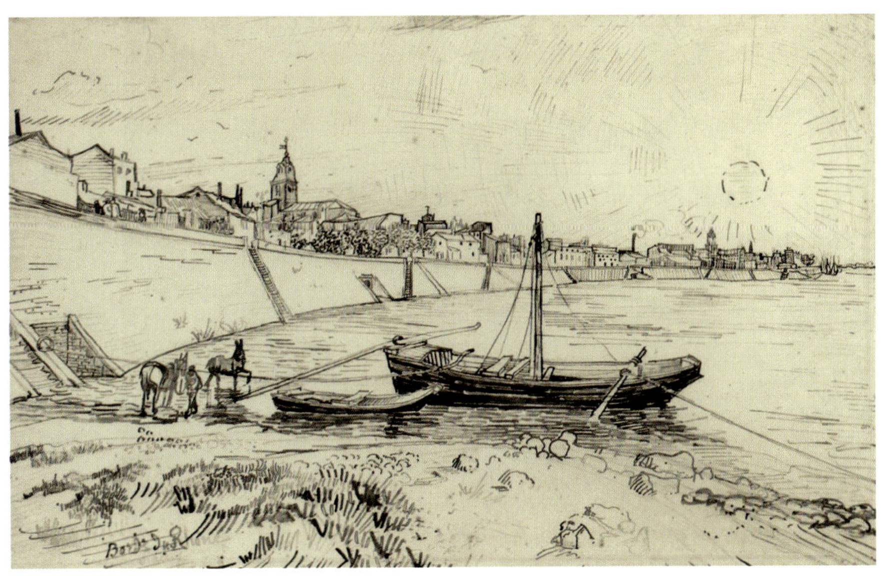

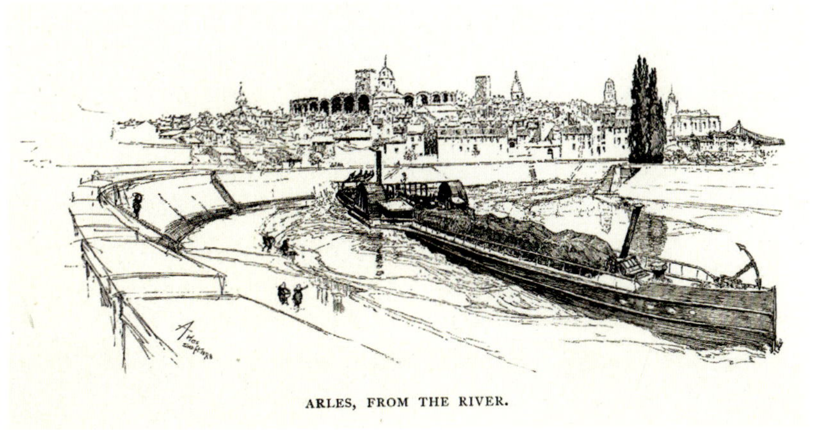

ARLES, FROM THE RIVER.

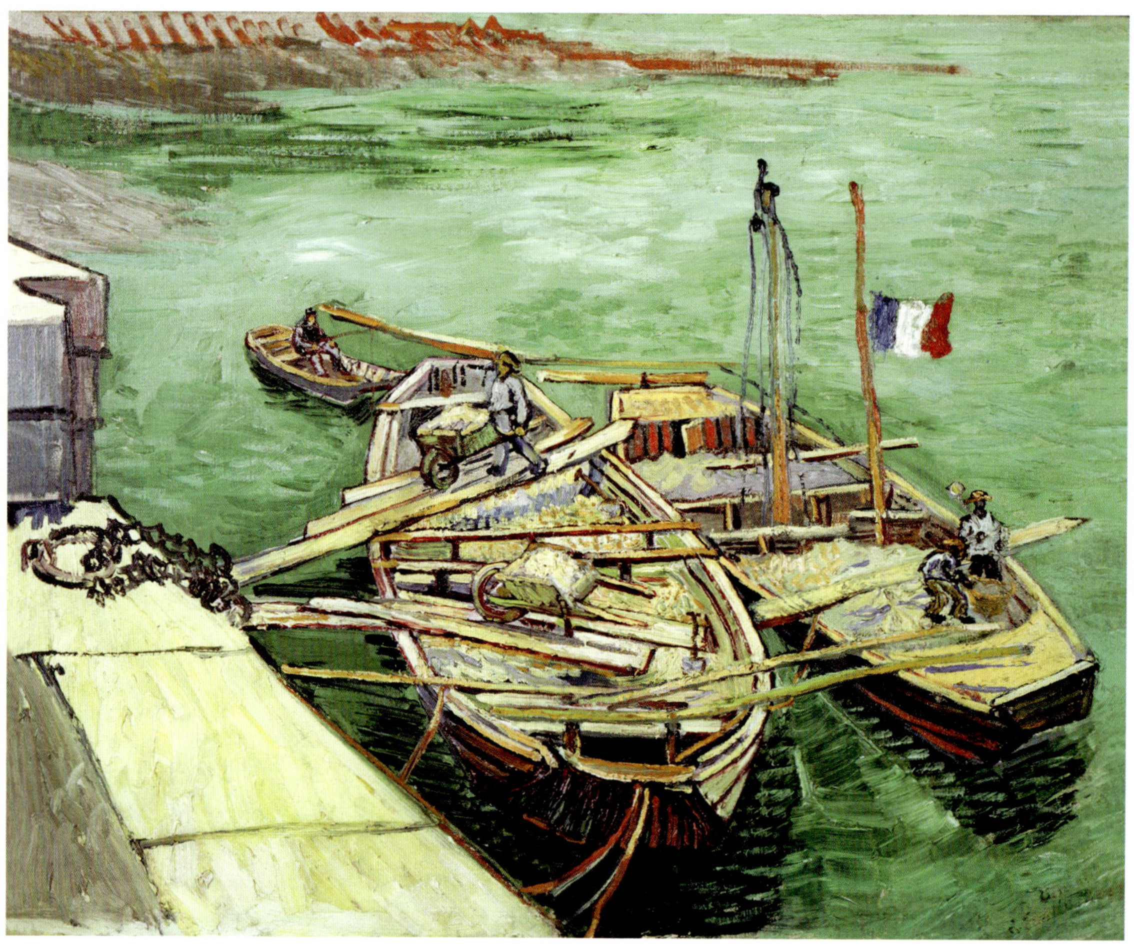

Van Gogh later painted a similar scene, *Quay with Sand Barges* (fig. 48), this time with part of the embankment. His striking perspective omits the sky. He described the scene: 'Boats seen from a quay, from above; the two boats are a purplish pink, the water is very green, no sky, a tricolour flag on the mast. A workman with a wheelbarrow is unloading sand.'[12]

On the other side of the Rhône lay the small town of Trinquetaille, which in 1875 had been linked to Arles by a bridge. Van Gogh painted *Trinquetaille Bridge* (fig. 49) from the Arles side. Selecting a dramatic viewpoint, he looked up the wide steps heading from the street to the embankment and then up to the bridge itself. A sprinkling of pedestrians add scale and movement. The cylindrical object behind the small tree is probably a *pissoire*.

Van Gogh employed considerable artistic licence in capturing this scene. The bridge was later rebuilt and then destroyed during the Second

ABOVE fig. 48 *Quay with Sand Barges*, August 1888, oil on canvas, 55 x 65 cm, Folkwang Museum, Essen (F449)

RIGHT fig. 49 *Trinquetaille Bridge*, October 1888, oil on canvas, 74 x 93 cm, private collection (F481)

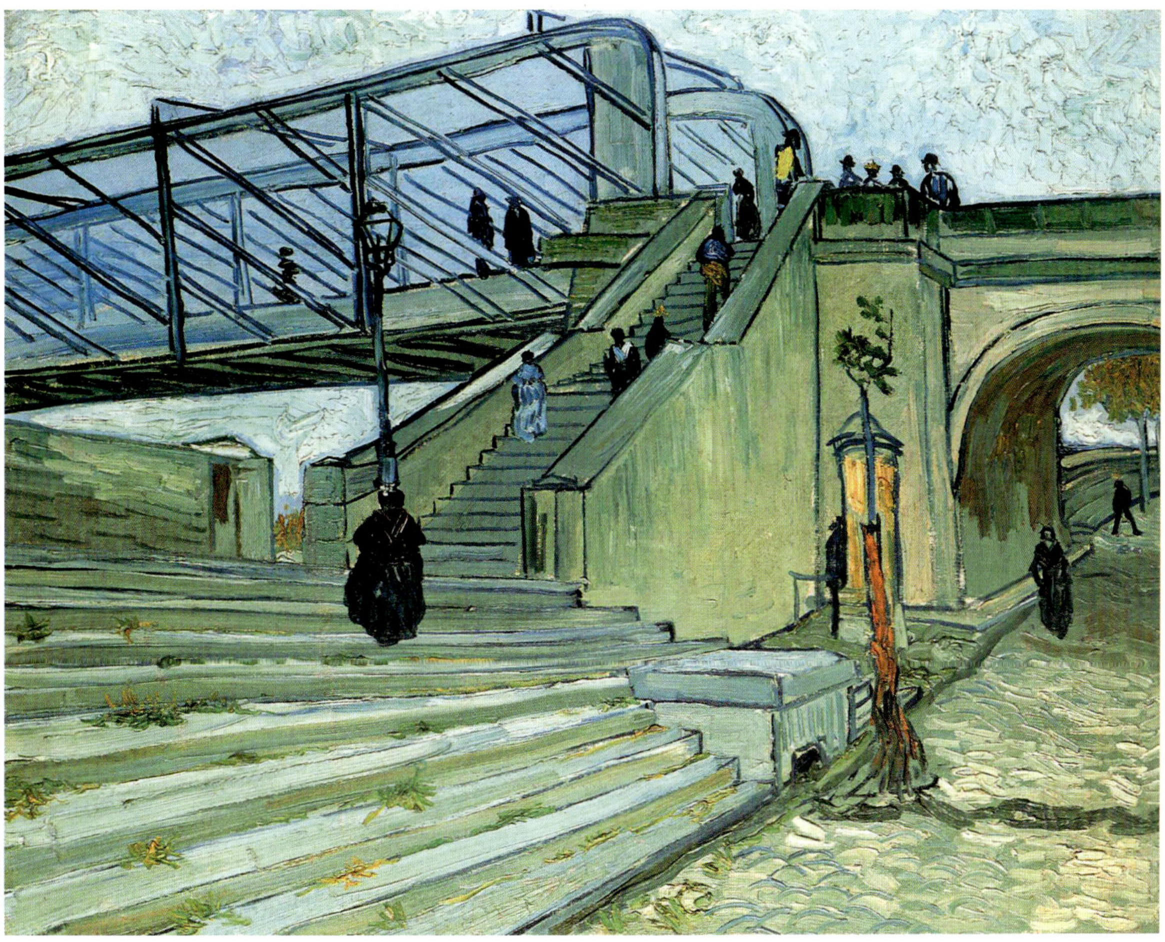

World War, but early photographs show that it had criss-cross struts along its sides, whereas Van Gogh modified them to parallel diagonals. These parallel struts (without others going in the other direction) impart a dynamism to his scene, although from an engineering point of view they would have failed to provide the necessary structural support.

Vincent described his painting to Theo: 'The Trinquetaille bridge with all its steps is a canvas done on a grey morning, the stones, the asphalt, the cobblestones are grey, the sky a pale blue, the small figures colourful, a puny tree with yellow foliage.'[13] By 1935, when the American art historian John Rewald photographed the same scene, what may have been Van Gogh's sapling had grown slightly higher than the bridge. Today the same plane tree is flourishing, some four times taller than the bridge.[14]

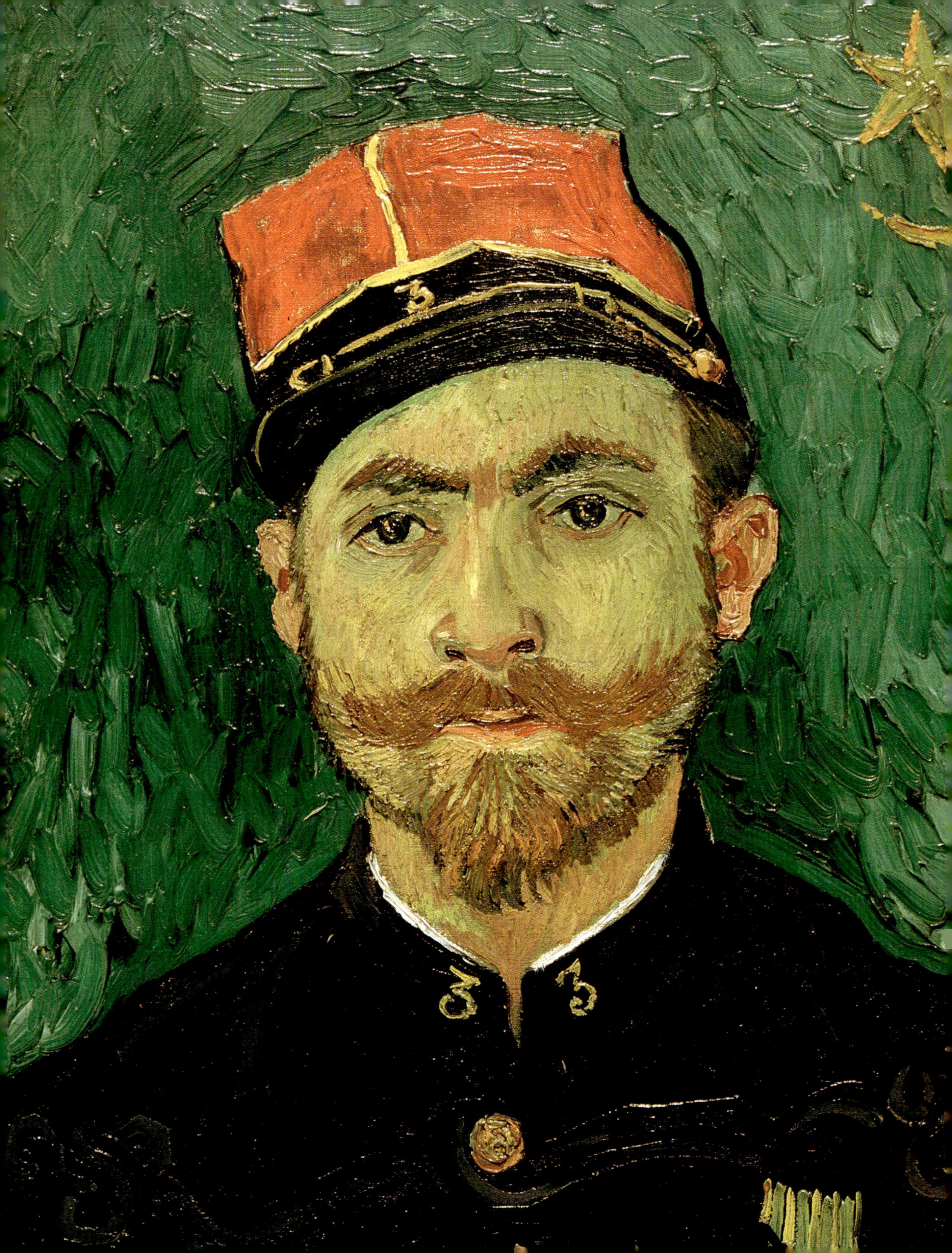

PORTRAITS OF FRIENDS

'A great revolution still awaits us in portraiture'[1]

Van Gogh always found it difficult to get models to pose for portraits. He had little money to pay them and strangers, particularly women, found him awkward. Once he did get sitters, they usually disliked the resulting portraits, expecting something more conventional. Although rarely remarked on, Van Gogh also seems to have found it challenging to paint his family and closest friends, perhaps because this involved too much intimacy.[2]

During the summer of 1888 Van Gogh finally succeeded in persuading several of his Arles friends and acquaintances to sit for him. He did not set out to do straightforward portraits, but expressive depictions of a 'type' – a concept dating back to the seventeenth-century Dutch Golden Age.[3] Thus three of his sitters are portrayed as the peasant, the poet and the postman. Van Gogh may have felt it less inhibiting to aim to depict a type, although he actually proved extremely adept at capturing individual faces and personalities.

The special skill Van Gogh brought to his Arles portraits was his use of colour. Two years earlier he had remarked that most artists produced flesh tones that appear realistic close up, but seem flat from further away. Van Gogh's technique was to use a variety of pigments, 'mostly colours one can't put a name to' – but which were effective 'if one steps back a little'.[4] From nearby, his faces are composed of a wide range of pigments, many looking nothing like flesh – but from a distance they spring to life (unfortunately in some cases Van Gogh's pigments have deteriorated, leaving a slightly blotchy appearance).

One of Van Gogh's early Arles portraits was of a *mousmé* (fig. 50), a term he took from Pierre Loti's Orientalist novel *Madame Chrysanthème*,

Detail of fig. 58 *Paul-Eugène Milliet*, Kröller-Müller Museum, Otterlo

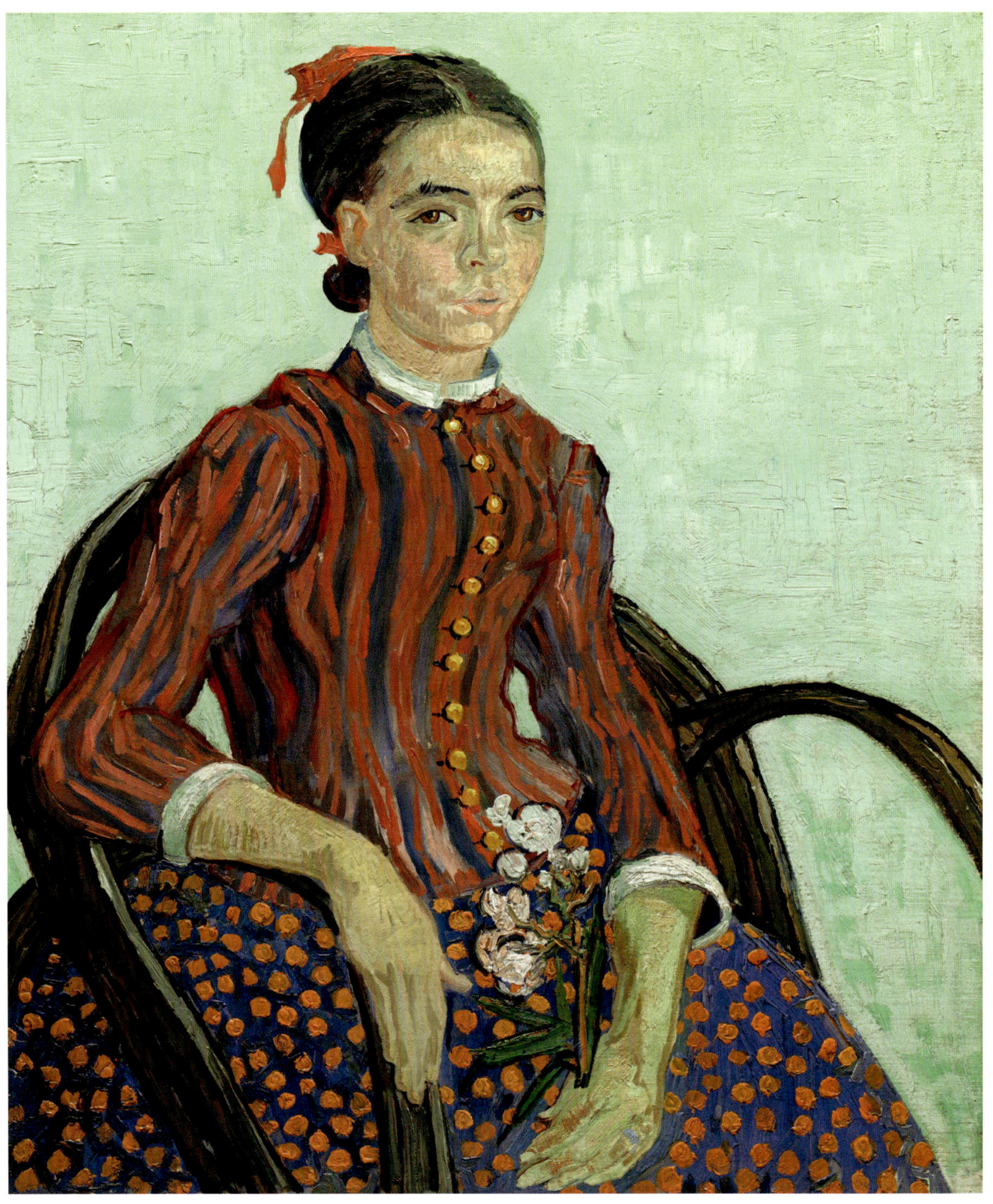

fig. 50 *The Mousmé*, July 1888, oil on canvas, 73 x 60 cm, National Gallery of Art, Washington, DC (F431)

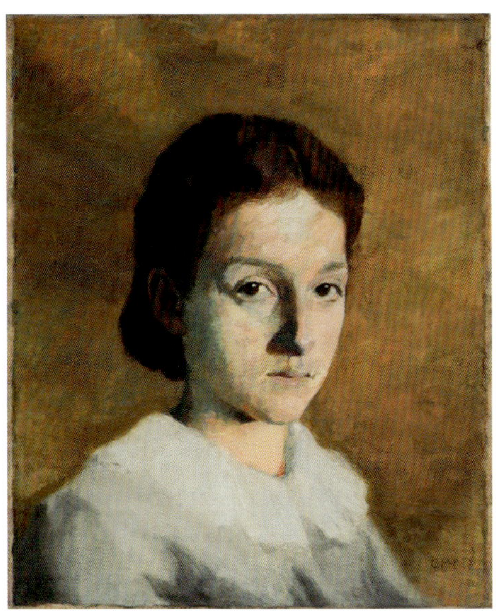

fig. 51 Christian Mourier-Petersen, *Girl from Arles*, early 1888, oil on canvas, 41 x 34 cm, Hirschsprung Collection, Copenhagen

published earlier that year, in which the author explains that a *mousmé* is a young Japanese girl.[5] Van Gogh described his own *mousmé* as aged 12, 'brown eyes, black hair and eyebrows, flesh yellow grey . . . an oleander flower in her sweet little hand'.[6] In fact her hands are quite ungainly (Van Gogh always found hands very difficult to paint). The clumsily placed flowers suggest that she was not holding the sprig while posing, but that it was a later addition. Tradition has it that the *mousmé* was the daughter of a miller at a windmill on the eastern outskirts of the town. The same girl had been painted by Van Gogh's friend Mourier-Petersen a few months earlier (fig. 51).[7] Van Gogh has made her face more rounded and given her eyes a slightly oriental feel, in homage to Loti's novel.

A month later Vincent was tackling a rather different portrait, as he explained to Theo: 'You'll shortly make the acquaintance of Mr Patience Escalier – a sort of man with a hoe, an old Camargue oxherd, who's now a gardener at a farmstead in the Crau.'[8] Van Gogh had painted numerous peasant heads in Nuenen three years earlier, but these were in the dark, sombre colours that characterise his Dutch pictures. His Arles peasant could hardly have been more different, captured in the most exuberant hues. The sturdy figure of Escalier is set against a royal blue background (fig. 52).[9] Escalier sports a yellow straw hat, partly framing his face. What marks him out as a peasant is his weathered complexion, with ruddy cheeks.

The most successful of Van Gogh's summer portraits was of Eugène Boch, a Belgian artist who was staying in Fontvieille. They had met in June through a mutual friend, Dodge Macknight, an American painter who had arrived at the village a few months earlier. Macknight had then summed up his first impressions of Van Gogh in a pithy and revealing comment: 'a stark, staring *crank*, but a good fellow'.[10]

Boch and Van Gogh shared much in common. Boch, whose family owned the Villeroy & Boch porcelain business, came from the Belgian town of La Louvière. This is close to the Borinage, the coal-mining area where

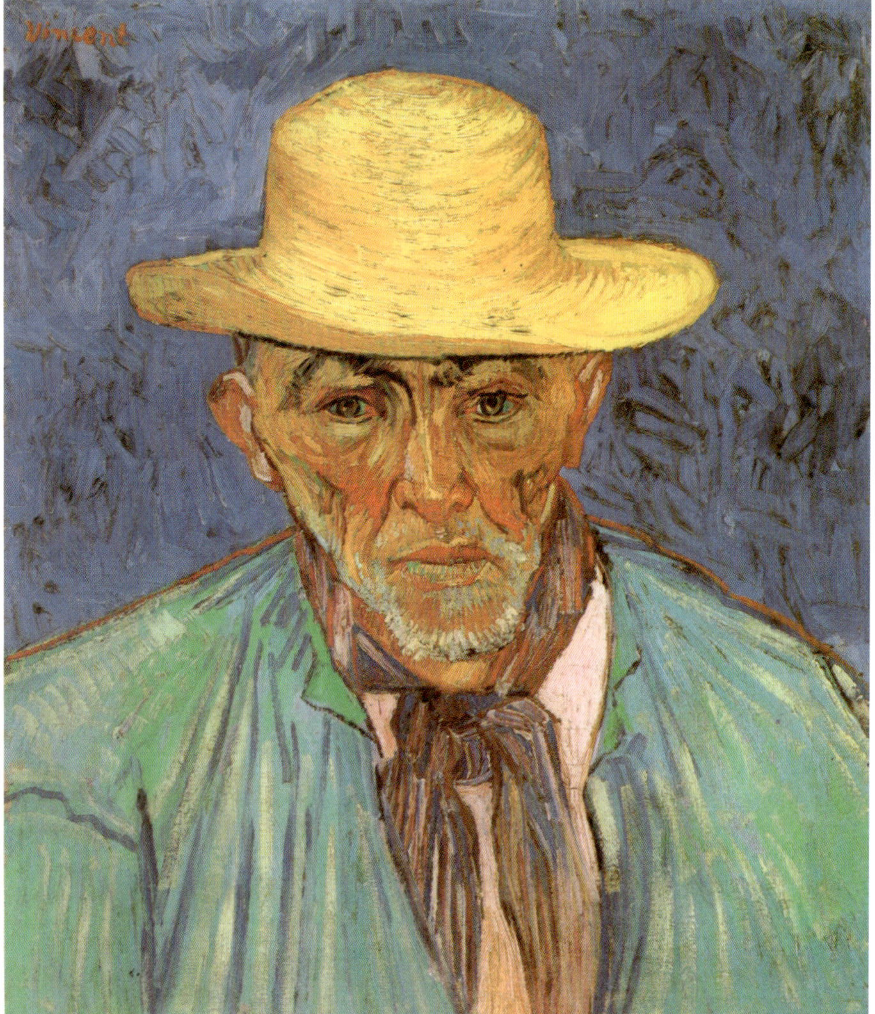

fig. 52 *Patience Escalier*, August 1888, oil on canvas, 64 x 54 cm, Norton Simon Museum, Pasadena (F443)

Van Gogh had served as a missionary a decade earlier. The Belgian had also studied in Paris with Cormon, several years before Van Gogh. In Provence they quickly became friends. Vincent described him to Theo: 'He's a lad whose outward appearance I like very much. Face like the blade of a razor, green eyes, and distinction with all that.'[11]

On 2 September Boch came to Arles for his final visit, en route for Paris. He and Van Gogh walked in the nearby countryside, discussing artistic opportunities in Provence, and then went on to a bullfight at the arena. As Boch was about to head north, Van Gogh seized the opportunity to paint his 33-year-old friend as 'the poet' (fig. 55). Boch does not seem to have written poetry, but he was cultured and Van Gogh saw in his face the features of the medieval Italian poet Dante.[12]

Vincent described the resulting painting to Theo: 'His fine head, with its green gaze, stands out in my portrait against a starry, deep ultramarine sky; his clothing is a little yellow jacket, a collar of unbleached linen, a multicoloured tie.'[13] Boch's face appears strikingly angular, an impression emphasised by the beard. The slumped shoulders give him a slightly melancholic air. A photograph probably taken the same year suggests that Van Gogh successfully captured his appearance (fig. 54).

Boch's head is surrounded by fourteen blobs representing stars in the night sky, along with a larger stylised star in the upper-left corner. Despite its nocturnal backdrop, the portrait was presumably painted in daylight. Van Gogh initially regarded it as a 'first sketch' for a more ambitious work.[14] A month later he tried to paint a larger portrait, but found this very difficult after his model had departed. Dissatisfied with the result, he destroyed the second version. It is interesting to compare Van Gogh's portrait of Boch with a later one done by Bernard, another former Cormon student and also a friend of the Belgian artist. Bernard saw Van Gogh's portrait in Paris in September 1890 and this inspired him to produce his own version (fig. 53). Bernard tackled the task quite differently, exaggerating still further Boch's narrow, triangular head, creating an almost proto-Cubist work.

In July 1891, after the death of Theo, his widow Jo gave the portrait by Van Gogh to Boch. In his letter of thanks, the Belgian artist recalled his memories of Vincent: 'Full of enthusiasm, for art! For pure art! That was the man's only thought.'[15] The portrait remained Boch's most treasured possession. Shortly before his death in 1941 he was confined to bed. Elisa, a sister of Boch, recorded in her diary: 'When Eugène could not move or talk any more, his eyes were fixed on the portrait', which had always hung in his bedroom.[16] Boch bequeathed the picture to the Louvre and it now hangs in the Musée d'Orsay.

The dashing figure of a Zouave soldier was Van Gogh's next subject, portrayed as 'the lover'. Paul-Eugène Milliet was a second lieutenant in the regiment, which was then garrisoned in Arles. He had arrived in Arles in February, the same month as Van Gogh, and they met in June.[17] Van Gogh was impressed by the 24-year-old Milliet's success with the ladies, attributing it to his military prowess: 'Milliet's lucky, he has all the Arlésiennes he wants, but there you are, he can't paint them, and if he was a painter he wouldn't have any.'[18] Van Gogh held the curious notion that it was impossible to be a productive artist and engage in frequent sex, although he felt that such constraints did not apply to virile soldiers.

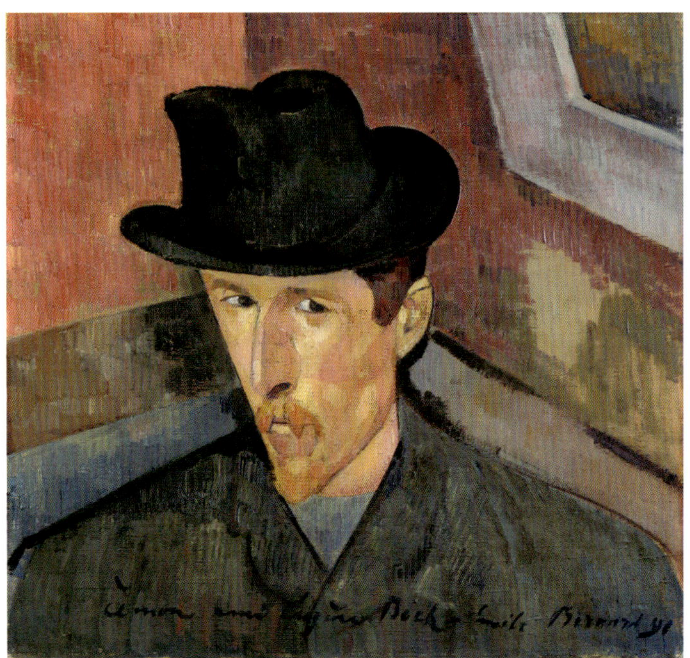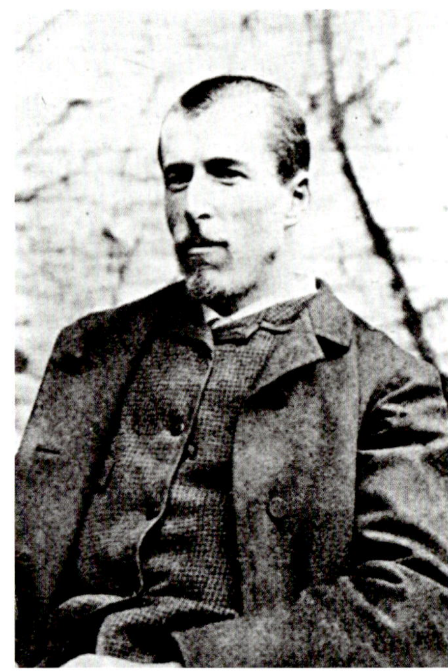

Despite this bizarre belief, Van Gogh nevertheless encouraged Milliet to draw and even gave him lessons.

Vincent told Theo that Milliet 'poses badly', but 'he's good-looking, very jaunty, very easy-going in his appearance, and he'd suit me down to the ground for a painting of lovers.'[19] Van Gogh depicted him wearing the regiment's colourful uniform, which was based on that of the Algerian Zouaves in the 1830s (the Zouaves had originally been recruited from the Zouaoua tribe, but the regiment later also employed Frenchmen). Milliet wears a dark blue jacket with a braided motif and a brilliant red képi – the number three on his collar denotes his regiment. He proudly wears his Tonkin Expedition medal, awarded for his earlier service in French Indochina, now Vietnam. Against the emerald green background, Van Gogh added the emblem of the Zouaves, a crescent moon and five-pointed star. Milliet has a stiff appearance, appropriate for a military man.

Originally Van Gogh planned to do a second version of the portrait to give to Milliet, but time ran out when the soldier was about to be posted to Algeria. Van Gogh commented, in the Zouave's barrack-style humour, that once he received his orders Milliet was far too busy to sit: 'He'll have to say his tender farewells to all the tarts and other pond-life in the Arles stewpond, now that his prick has gone back to the garrison, as he puts it.'[20]

ABOVE LEFT fig. 53 Emile Bernard, *Eugène Boch*, January 1891, oil on canvas, 48 x 50 cm, private collection, Paris

ABOVE fig. 54 Eugène Boch, c.1888, photograph (detail)[21]

RIGHT fig. 55 *Eugène Boch*, September 1888, oil on canvas, 60 x 45 cm, Musée d'Orsay, Paris (F462)

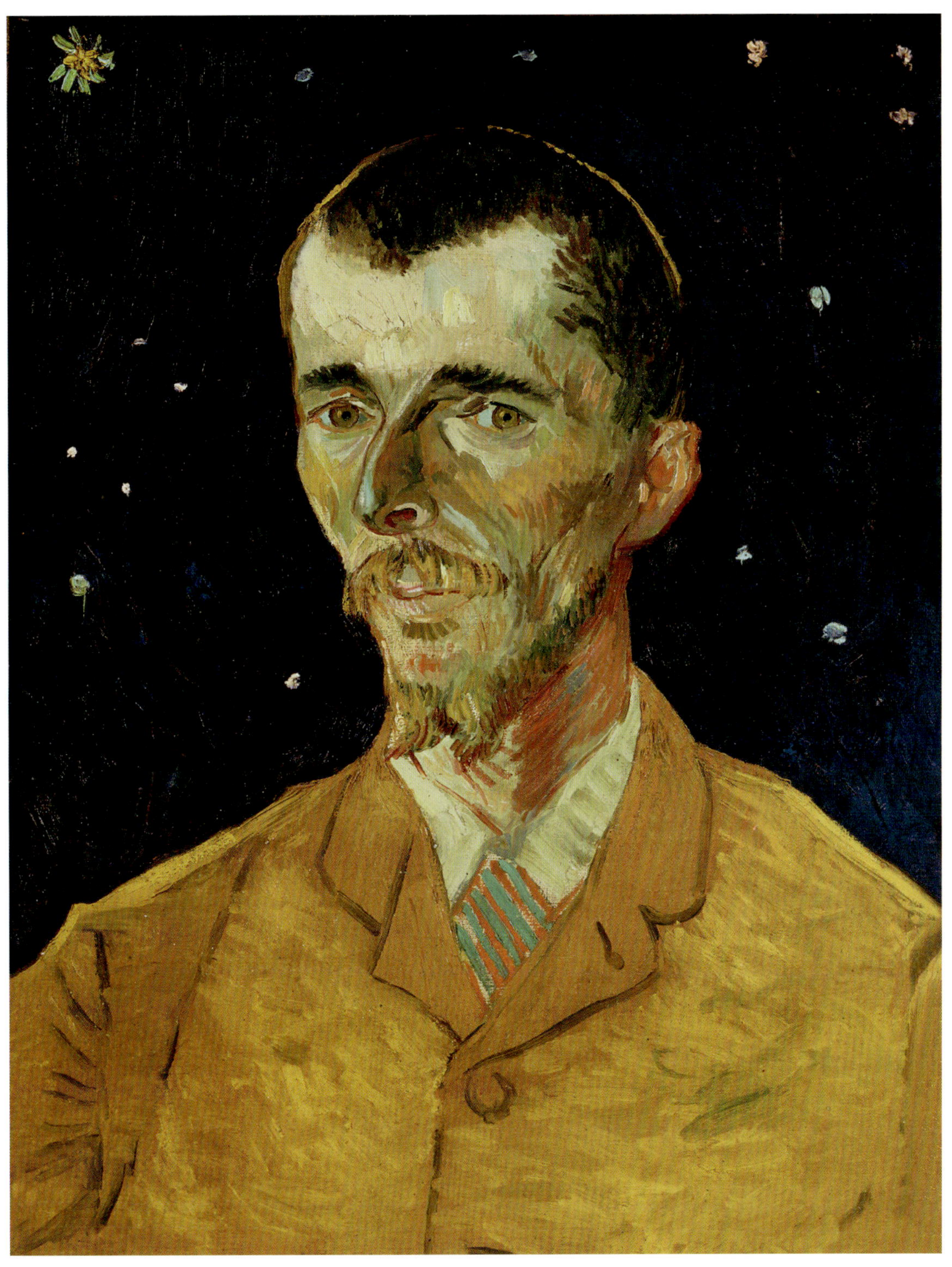

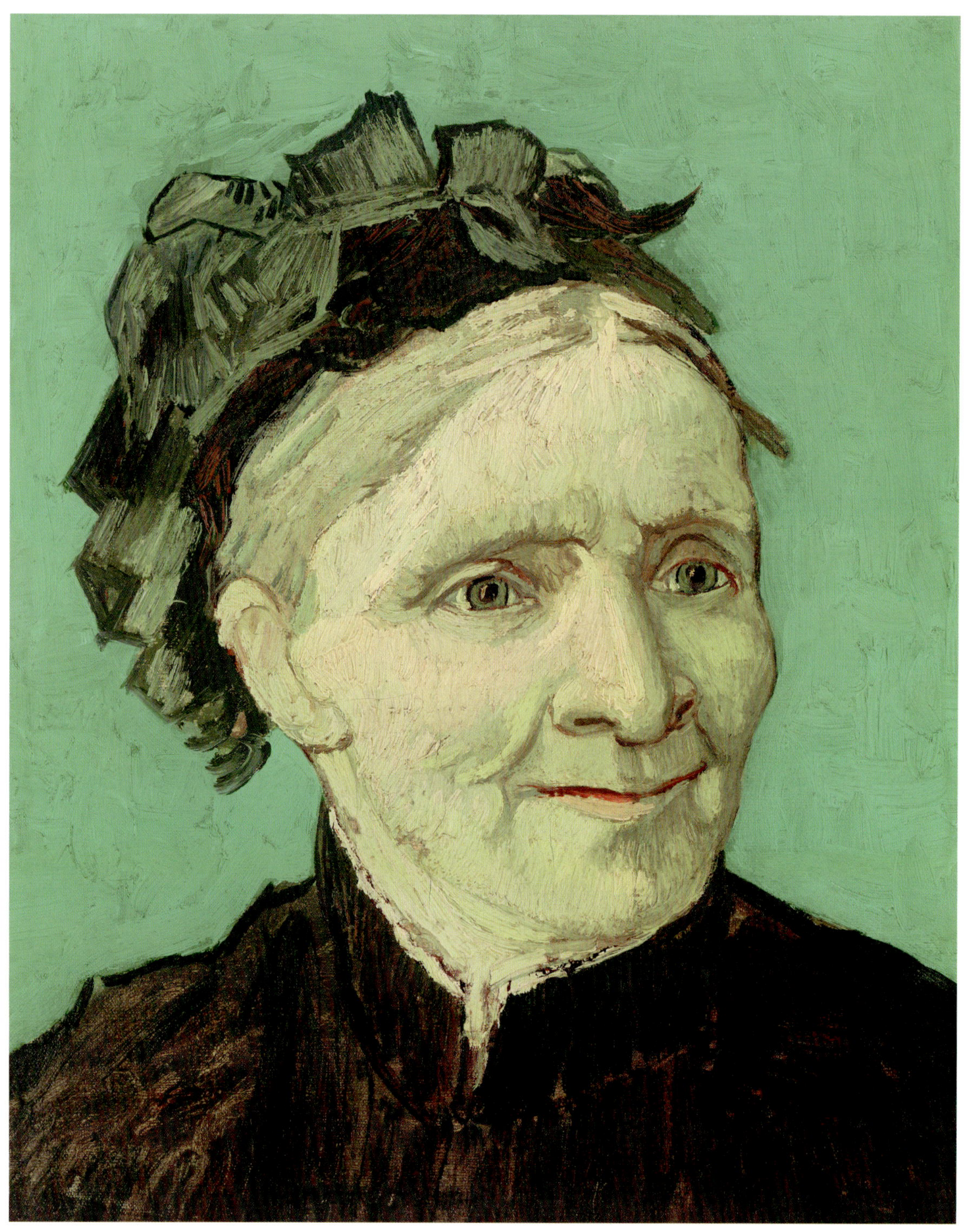

fig. 56 *Anna van Gogh*, October 1888, oil on canvas, 41 x 33 cm, Norton Simon Museum, Pasadena (F477)

After his posting to Algeria, Milliet went on to have a distinguished military career, rising to become a lieutenant colonel during the First World War. In the 1930s, nearly half a century after his friendship with Van Gogh, he vividly recalled his time in Arles. Milliet remembered the Dutchman as 'a charming companion, when he really wanted to be, which didn't happen every day'. The old soldier added: 'He didn't have an easygoing personality, and when he was angry, he seemed crazy . . . He had faith, faith in his talent, faith a bit blind.' As for the portrait, Milliet recalled that although painted quickly, it had represented 'a good likeness'. But the soldier was critical of Van Gogh's style, feeling that artists should paint 'with love', whereas the Dutchman 'raped' his canvases.[22] Milliet died in Paris in 1943.

The most curious portrait Vincent completed in Arles was of his mother Anna, then 69. Their relationship had been fraught since his youth and he had last seen her three years earlier in Nuenen, the family home in the southern Netherlands. From Arles, Vincent wrote to Wil, asking for a photograph of their mother to use as the basis for a painting (fig. 57). In early October Vincent reported to Theo: 'I'm doing a portrait of our mother for myself. I can't look at the colourless photograph, and I'm trying to do one with harmonious colour, as I see her in my memory.'[23] He very loosely based the portrait on her photograph, but gave her the features of a considerably younger woman (fig. 56). In the painting she is middle aged, rather as Vincent would have known her as a child. The result is a curious blend of reality and imagination. This was the only occasion on which Van Gogh painted a portrait based on a photograph.[24]

Van Gogh was rightly pleased with the progress he was making with portraiture. He framed the pictures of Boch and Milliet, giving them pride of place above his bed (fig. 21). As long as he had the sitter in front of him, he could capture a likeness and character in just a few hours – a considerable achievement. Later that year he would use this skill to complete an ambitious series of portraits of postman Roulin and his entire family.

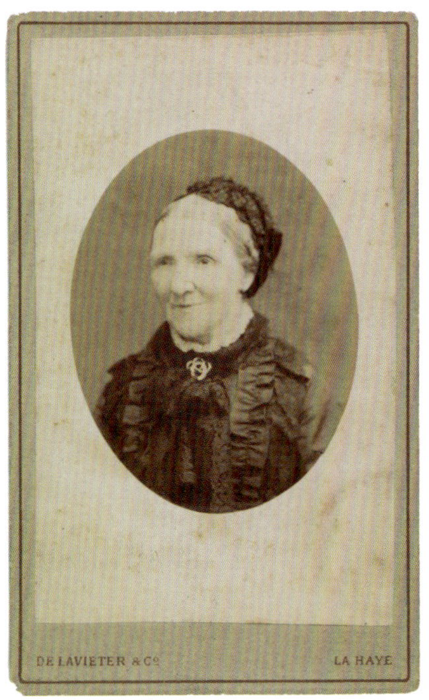

ABOVE fig. 57 Anna van Gogh (Vincent's mother), 1888, photograph by De Lavieter, The Hague, Van Gogh Museum, Amsterdam (Vincent van Gogh Foundation)[25]

BELOW fig. 58 *Paul-Eugène Milliet*, September 1888, oil on canvas, 60 x 50 cm, Kröller-Müller Museum, Otterlo (F473)

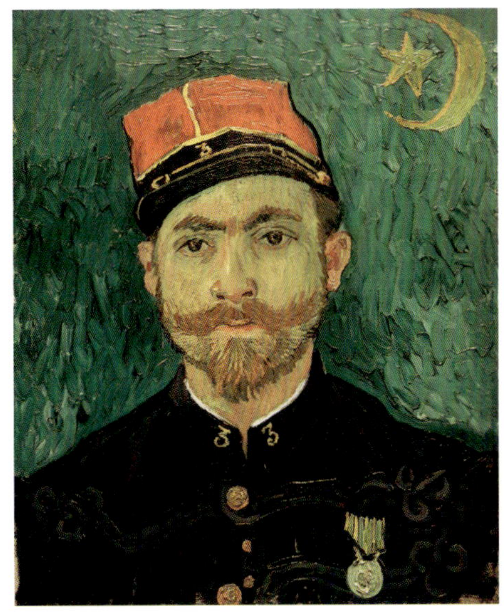

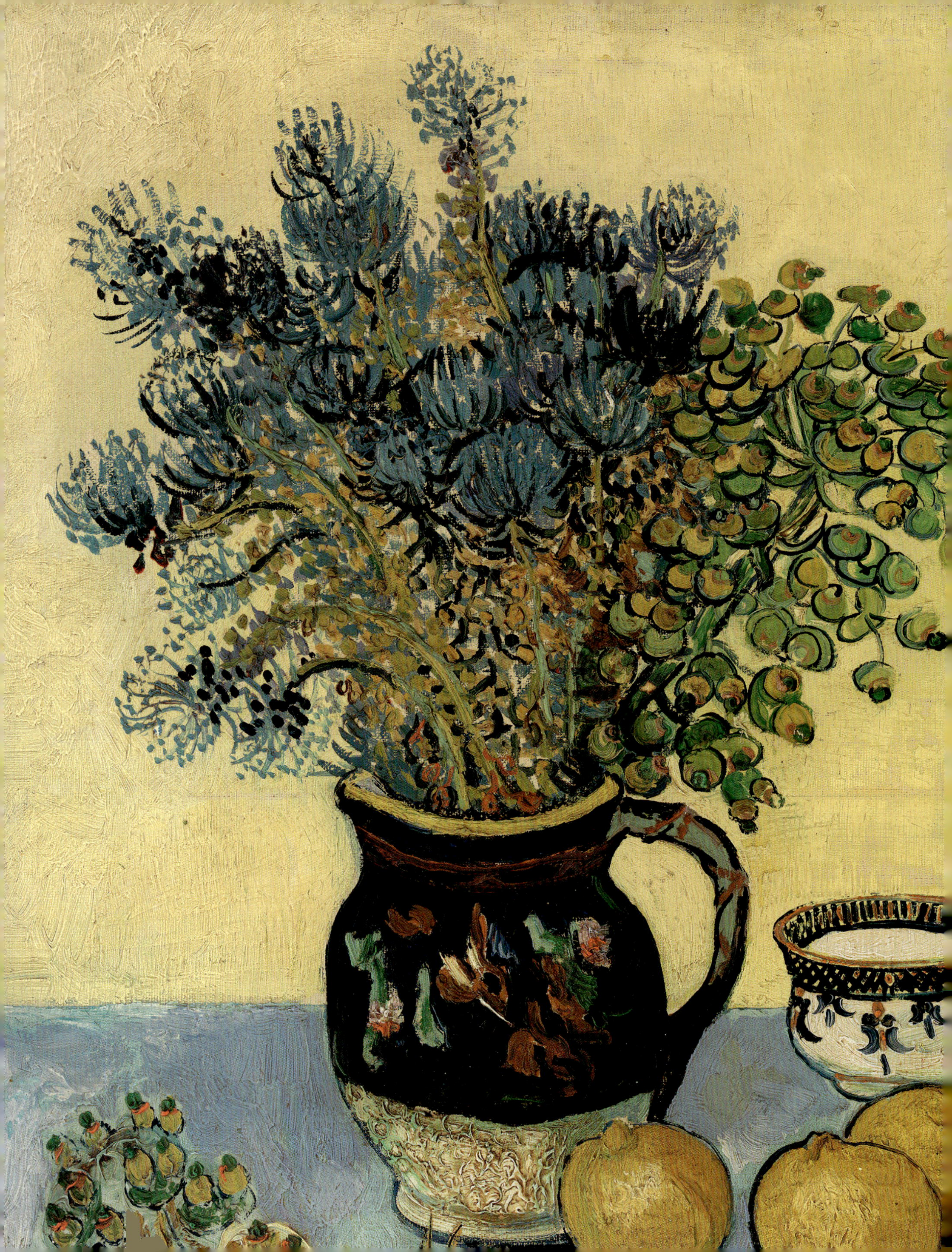

FLOWERS

'I'd like to do a décoration for the studio. Nothing but large sunflowers'[1]

While in Paris Van Gogh had painted dozens of flower still lifes. They were the perfect subject for an artist fascinated by colour, offering an opportunity to explore its effects. In Arles, however, he concentrated on landscapes and as spring turned into summer he had only completed a handful of flower bouquets. By early August 1888 Van Gogh confessed that he was 'annoyed with myself for not painting flowers here'.[2] A fortnight later he rectified this with tremendous power and verve as the sunflowers burst into bloom.

During his early months in Arles Van Gogh had occasionally included flowers as an important element in his landscapes, for example in *View of Arles with Irises in the Foreground* (fig. 59). He described this spring scene to Theo: 'A meadow full of very yellow buttercups, a ditch with iris plants with green leaves, with purple flowers, the town in the background, some grey willow trees – a strip of blue sky . . . a little town surrounded by countryside entirely covered in yellow and purple flowers'.[3] It was painted from just south of the town, which was mainly hidden by a line of trees (the larger tower is St Trophime and the one to the left is the town hall). The irises are particularly sensitively depicted, with swirling lines outlining the flowers.

Garden with Flowers was completed as summer was approaching its height (fig. 60). The scene explodes with colour, from rows of poppies, bluebells, marigolds, geraniums and sunflowers. Van Gogh explained his technique: 'Not a single flower was drawn . . . just little licks of colour, red, yellow, orange, green, blue, violet, but the impression of all those colours against one another is nonetheless there in the painting as it is in nature'.[4] These flowers became a near-abstract composition, symbolising the abundance of Provence.

Detail of fig. 61
Wild Flowers in a Jug,
Barnes Foundation,
Philadelphia

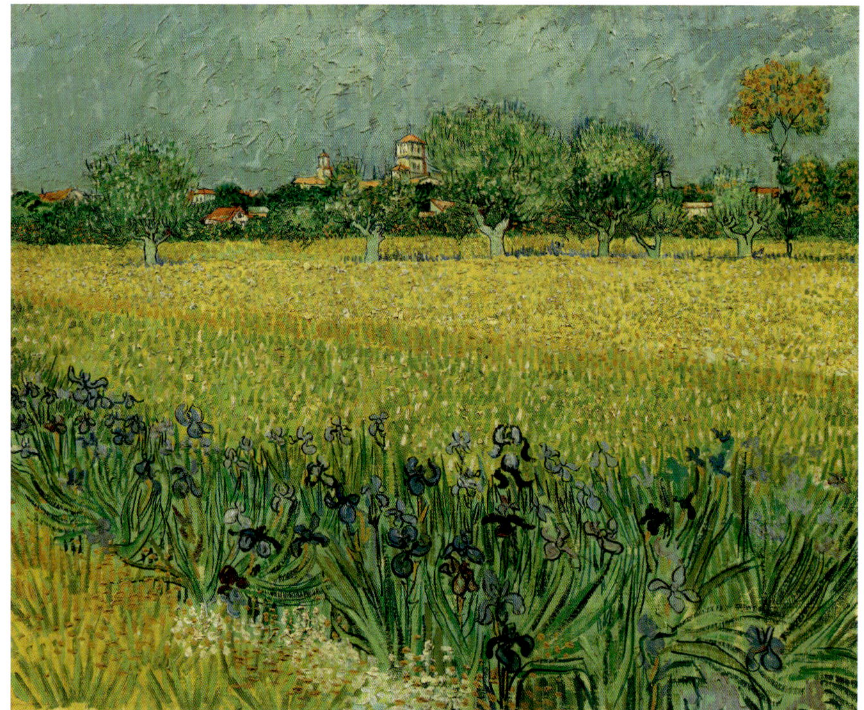

Van Gogh had made his first major flower still life in May.[5] *Wild Flowers in a Jug* (fig. 61) probably depicts euphorbia, picked on a walk in the countryside and brought back to his new studio. The majolica jug appears in three other Arles still lifes and the cup presumably came from his kitchen, since it also features in *Still life with Coffee Pot* (fig. 18).[6] Van Gogh boldly 'framed' the wild-flower composition with a painted red border at the top and sides, but not the bottom. This unconventional device draws the eye towards the objects on the table (our image is the first published reproduction to show this properly).[7]

The wildflower still life prefigured a far grander project, resulting in what has become one of the most iconic images in the history of art.[8] On Monday 20 August Van Gogh began work with a passion on a series of four paintings. Recent research has shown that he completed them in just a week, twice as fast as previously assumed.[9] He worked from dawn to dusk, 'because the flowers wilt quickly and it's a matter of doing the whole thing in one go.' The result was a quartet of sunflower still lifes, created as a key element for the *décoration* for the Yellow House.[10]

Van Gogh began his seminal series with *Three Sunflowers* (fig. 62). He arranged the blooms in a green-glazed earthenware pot, with the yellow-

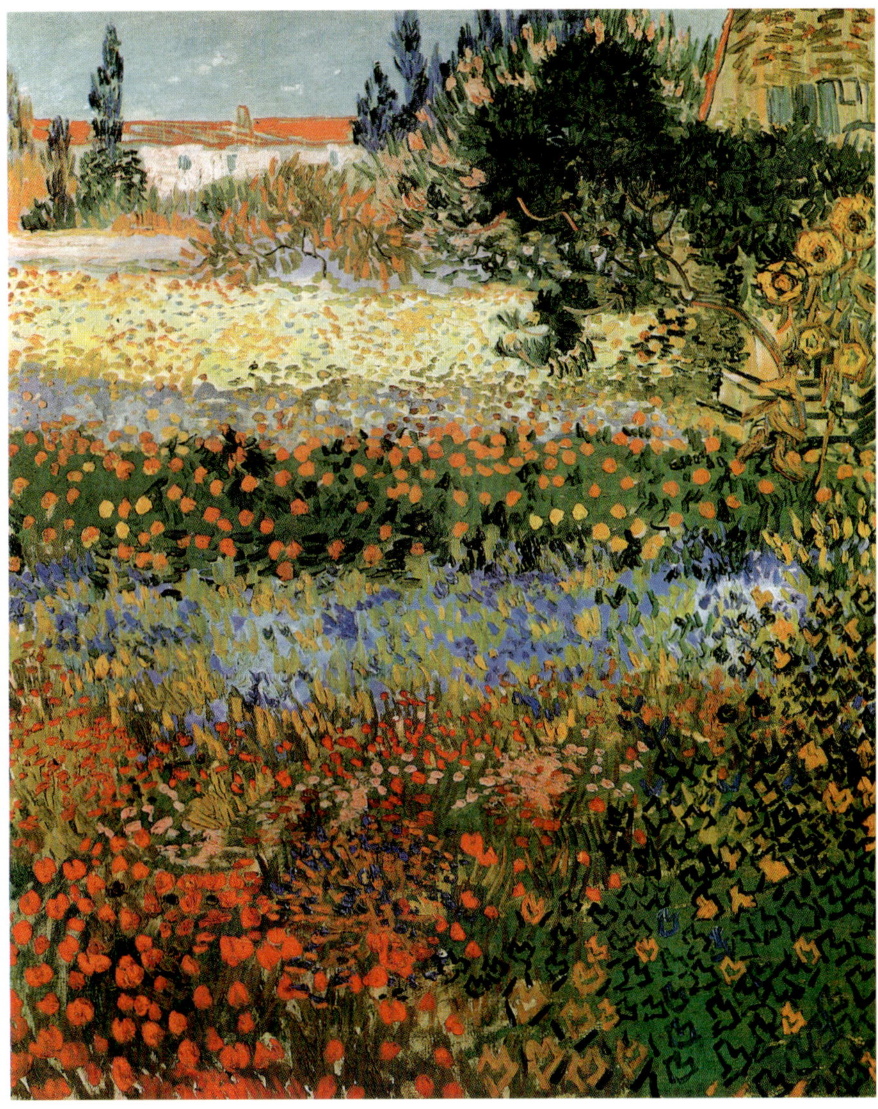

orange flowers radiating out against a vibrant, turquoise background. The flowers are so large that the one on the left seems even wider than its pot. Two are in full bloom, with the one in the centre already turning to seed.

Since leaving his studio, *Three Sunflowers* has led a secluded existence, hidden away in private collections. It was last shown in a one-month exhibition at the Cleveland Museum of Art in 1948. In 1970 the painting was quietly bought by the Greek shipping magnate George Embiricos, who hung it in his villa near Lausanne. Embiricos sold it in 1996 through a leading New

York dealer, and it went to the present anonymous owner, a very discreet collector who owns an extremely important small group of Van Goghs.[11]

Van Gogh's second still life, *Six Sunflowers* (fig. 63), is similar in composition, but with three additional flowers on the table. The turquoise background of the *Three Sunflowers* has been replaced with a rich royal blue. This picture is more stylised than the first, emphasising the spiky petals and sepals. In 1920 *Six Sunflowers* was bought by Koyata Yamamoto, a cotton trader from Ashiya, near Osaka. It was the first Van Gogh to go to a collector in Japan – a highly appropriate purchase given that Van Gogh had been such an admirer of Japanese art. On 6 August 1945, the day that the atomic bomb was dropped on Hiroshima, Ashiya was devastated by Allied bombers in a separate attack. Yamamoto's house was set alight and *Six Sunflowers* was engulfed in the flames.

A very rare colour reproduction of *Six Sunflowers* was recently discovered at the Mushakoji Saneatsu Memorial Museum in Tokyo, set up to honour the writer Saneatsu. This print, dating from 1921, reveals that Van Gogh had created his own frame to surround the picture – made of orange-painted wood, to contrast with the powerful blue background.[12] Although the original painting is lost, we now at least have a good reproduction showing *Six Sunflowers* as the artist intended it to be seen.

While the first two Sunflower paintings have never been displayed in living memory and are generally known only through specialist books, the last two done at the end of that week of feverish activity are now Van Gogh's most popular pictures – made famous from countless reproductions. The third version, *Fourteen Sunflowers*, depicts a huge bunch displayed against a turquoise background (fig. 64). In 1912 this picture was acquired for what became the Neue Pinakothek gallery in Munich. Although nearly sold off by the Nazis in the late 1930s as 'degenerate' art, it was preserved and evacuated during the war to Neuschwanstein Castle, in the foothills of the Alps, to save it from Allied bombing raids on Munich.[13]

The fourth, and greatest masterpiece, *Fifteen Sunflowers* (fig. 65), presents the yellowy-orange blooms against a yellow background – a strikingly bold concept. The composition (like all of Van Gogh's Sunflower still lifes) is deceptively simple: a bouquet, a rustic pot, a table top and a wall. The flowers are at different stages of their life cycle, suggestive of the passing of time. Although each one is carefully depicted, they are stylised. Van Gogh's aim was to capture the essence of the flowers. *Fifteen Sunflowers* remained with Vincent's sister-in-law Jo until 1924, when it was bought for the Tate Gallery in London for £1,304 (and transferred to the National Gallery in 1961). During the Second World War the picture was evacuated to Muncaster

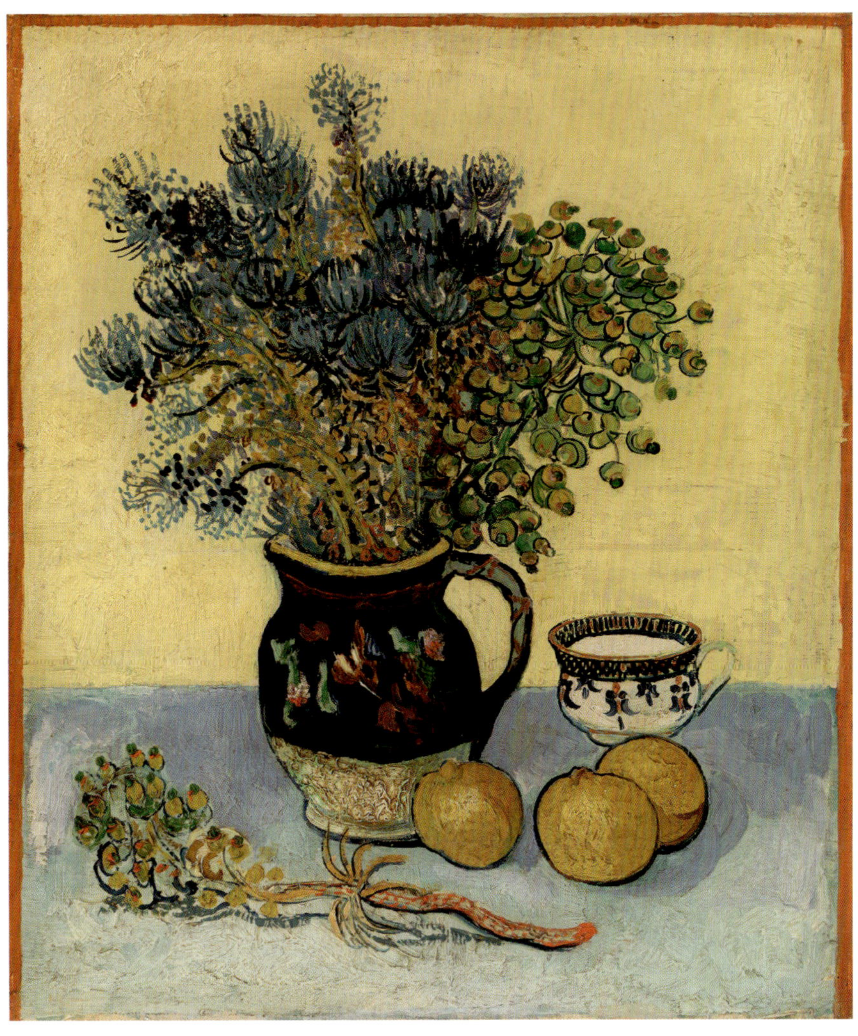

Castle in the Lake District to save it from German bombs. It is now the National Gallery's most popular work.[14]

Van Gogh was rightly proud of his week's endeavours. He framed *Fourteen Sunflowers* and *Fifteen Sunflowers* and hung them in the guest room, anticipating the arrival of his fellow artist Gauguin. In a letter to Theo, Vincent compared his quartet of still lifes with the work of two contemporary French artists who had made particular flowers their motifs: 'The peony is Jeannin's, the hollyhock belongs to Quost, but the sunflower is mine.'[15] Georges Jeannin and Ernest Quost are now virtually forgotten. Although Van Gogh failed to sell any of his Sunflowers in his lifetime, if one came onto the market today it would fetch an astronomical price.

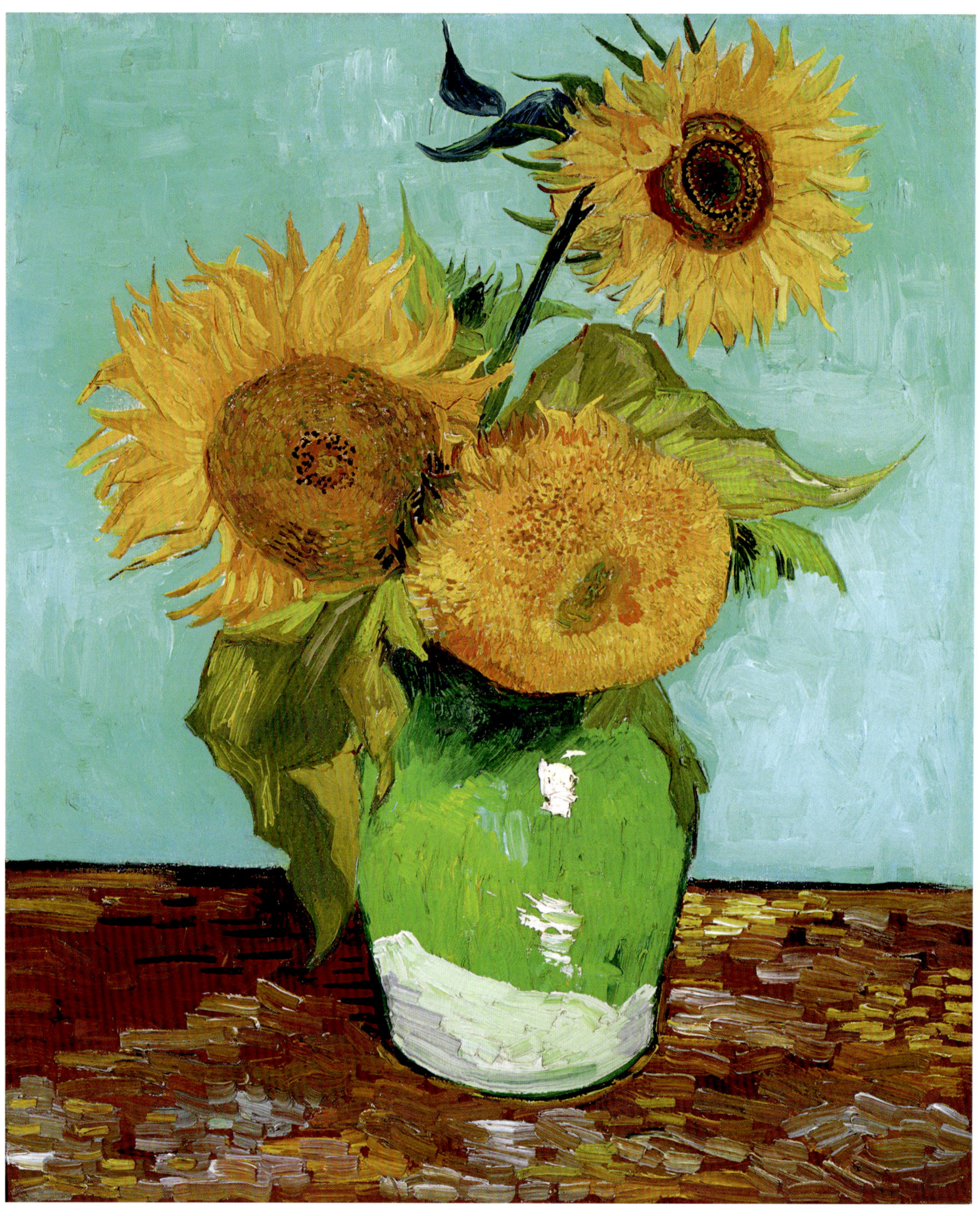

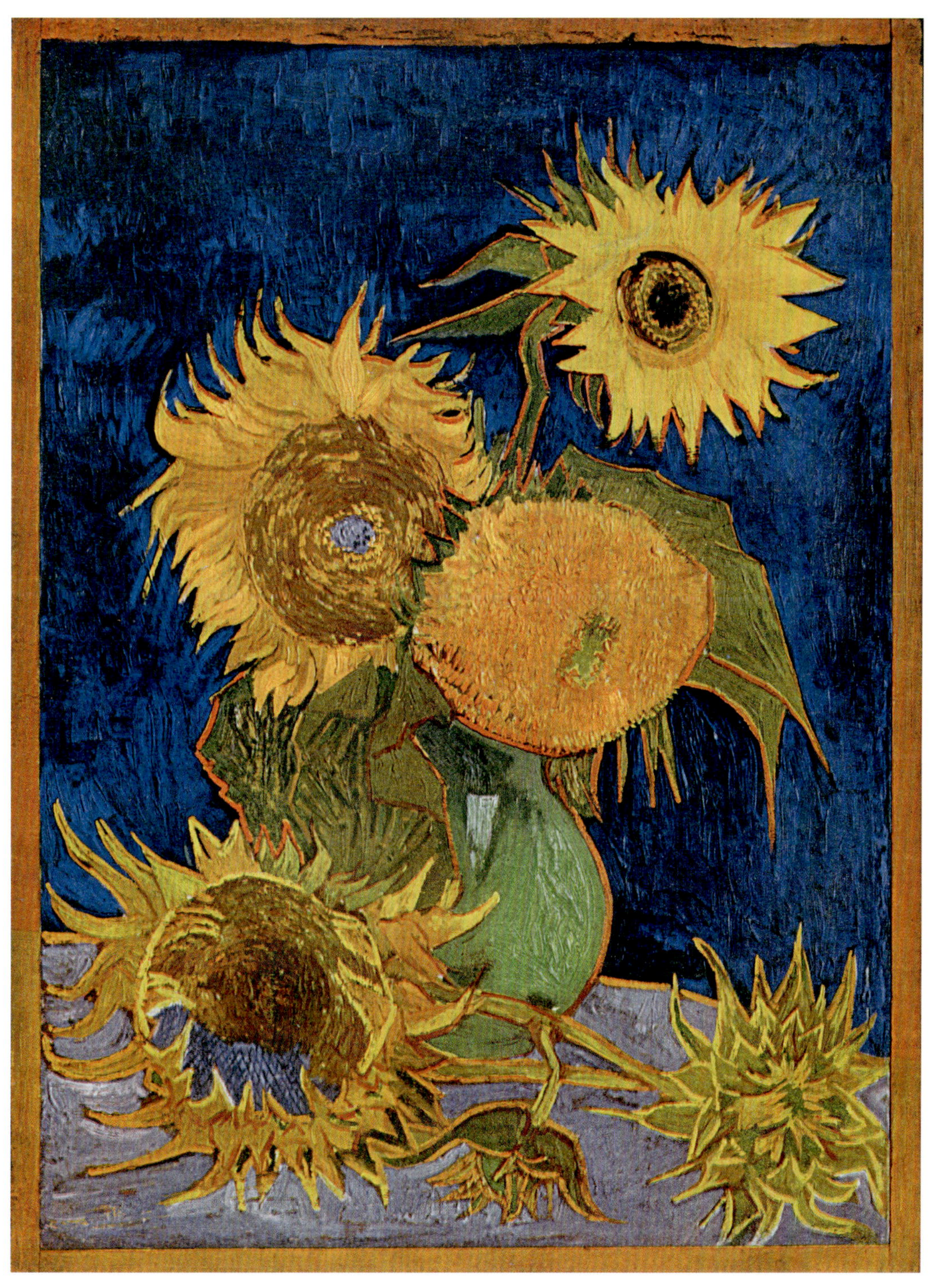

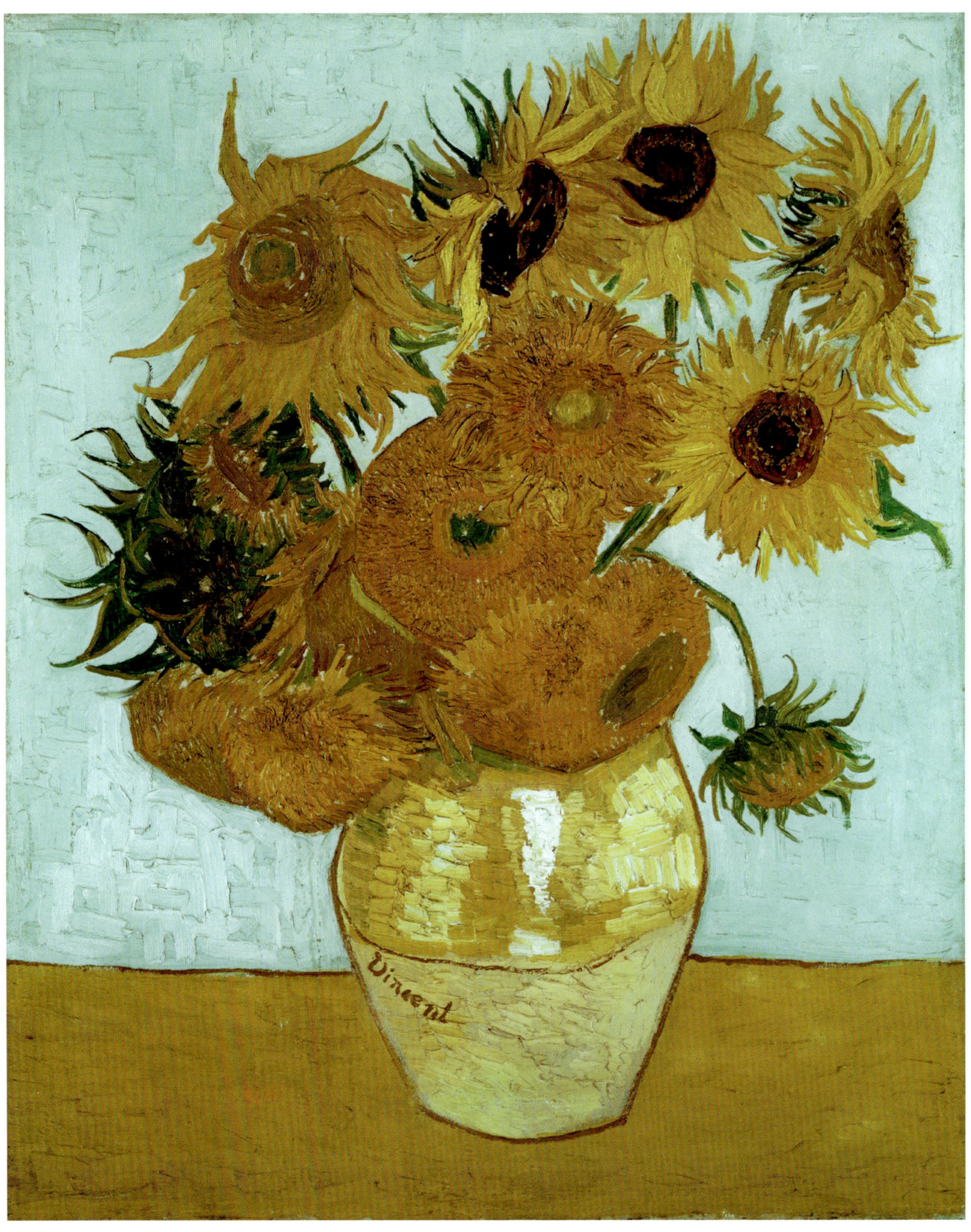

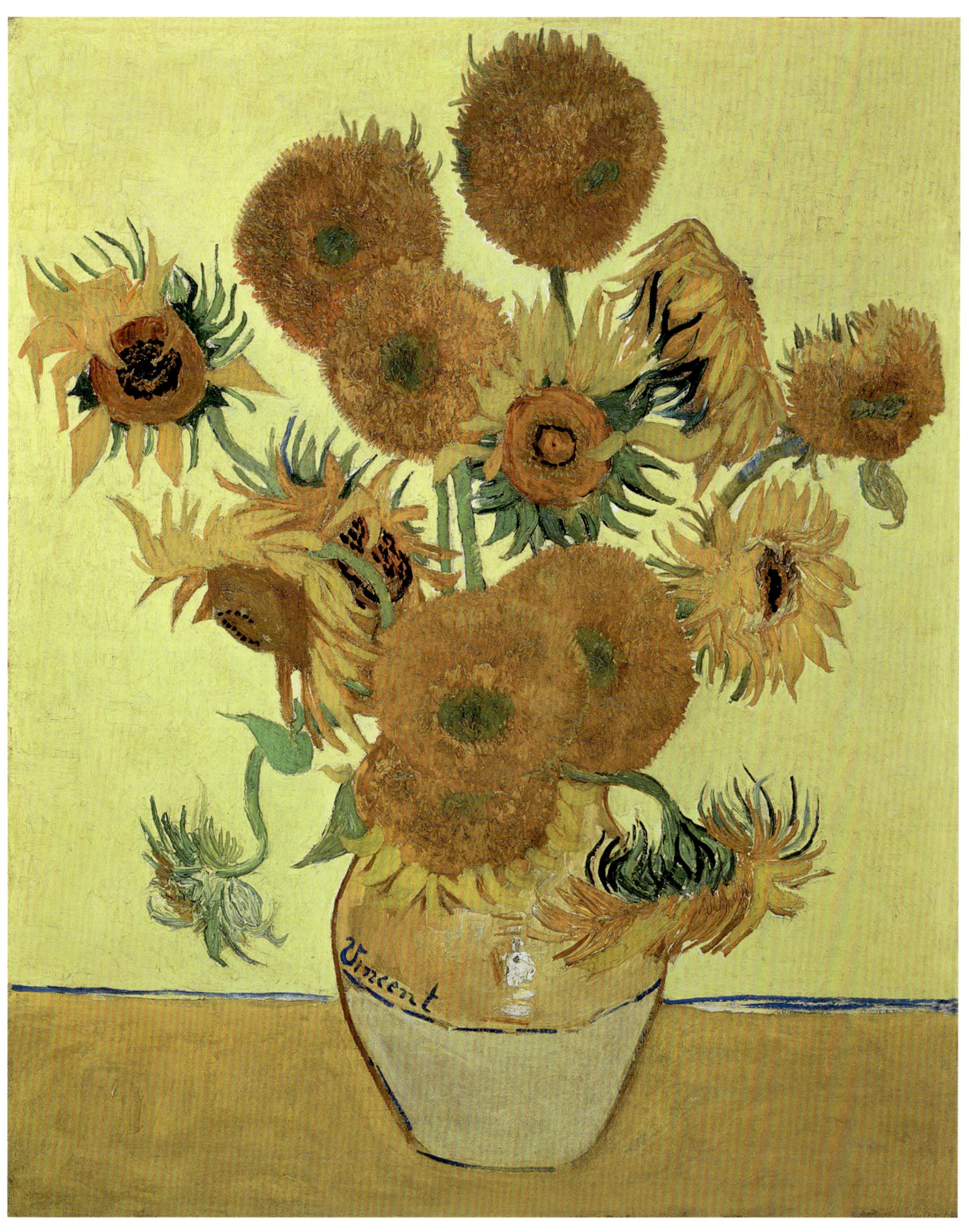

Vincent

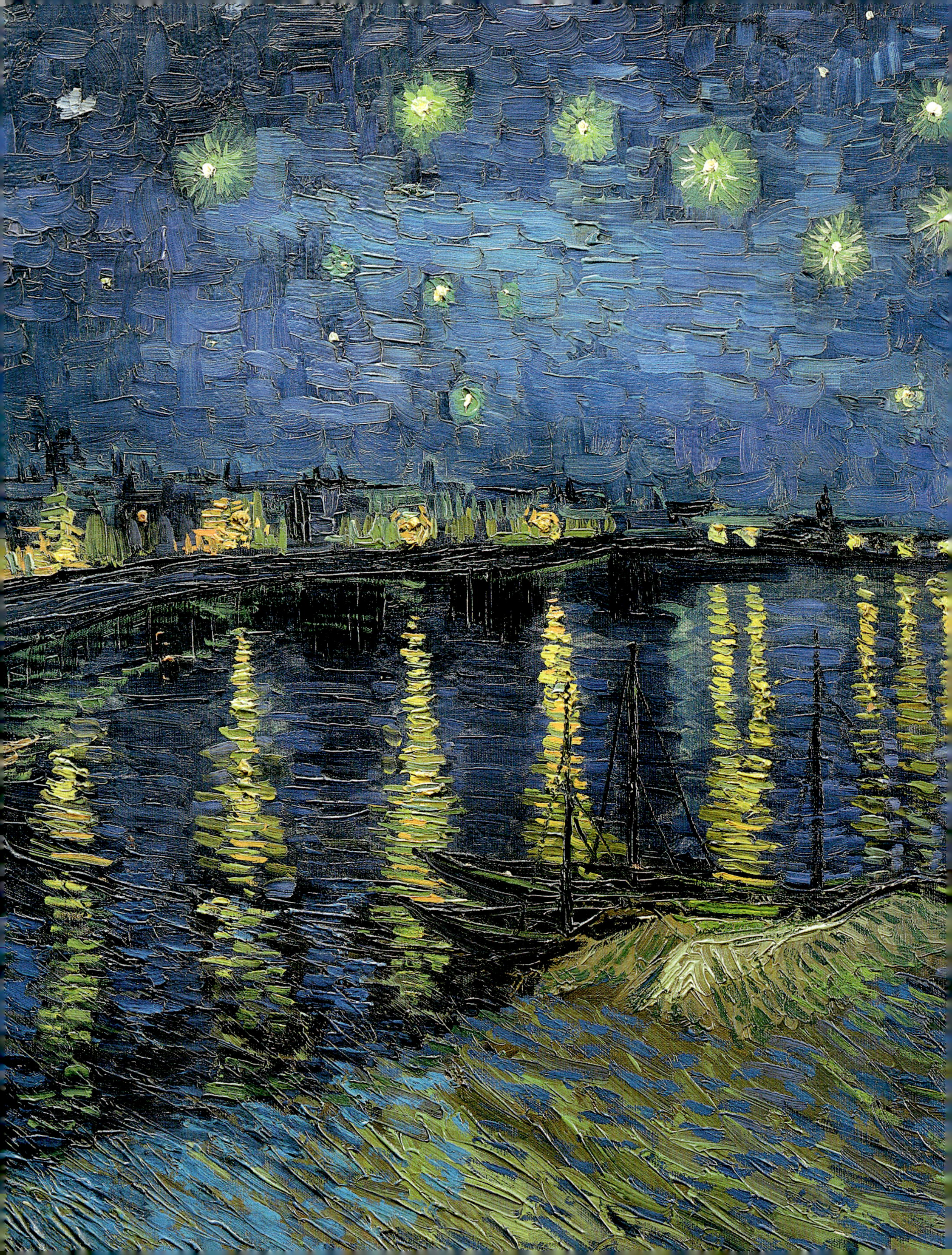

COLOURS OF THE NIGHT

'The night is much more alive and richly coloured than the day'[1]

By the 1880s gas had already been introduced for street lighting and was increasingly being installed indoors. Vincent, with his heightened sense of colour, was fascinated to observe how objects changed their appearance under artificial light. In August 1888 he told Theo about his plan for a night painting: 'I'm probably going to start on the interior of the café where I'm staying, in the evening, by gaslight. It's what they call a "night café" here (they're quite common here), that stay open all night. This way the "night prowlers" can find a refuge when they don't have the price of a lodging, or if they're too drunk to be admitted.'[2]

The following month Van Gogh stayed up for three nights, sleeping during the day. He set up his easel just inside the entrance of the Café de la Gare, no doubt to the amusement of the handful of late and inebriated customers. Using complementary colours, his aim was to convey a mood: 'I've tried to express the terrible human passions with the red and the green. The room is blood-red and dull yellow, a green billiard table in the centre, 4 lemon yellow lamps with an orange and green glow. Everywhere it's a battle and an antithesis of the most different greens and reds.'[3] It is rather unlikely that the café's walls were actually painted bright red (or the ceiling green), so the colouring may well have come from his imagination.

At the centre of *The Night Café* (fig. 66) is the billiard table, presided over by the owner, Joseph Ginoux (the cue and balls forming a rather phallic arrangement). The clock above the well-stocked counter shows it is just after midnight. At the back of the room a couple share a bottle, while three men doze (the one on the right in the straw hat, seen from behind, may represent the artist). As Van Gogh explained, 'it's a house of assignation, and from time to time you see a whore sitting there at a table with her fellow.' If *The Bedroom* (fig. 21) conveys a sense of restfulness, *The Night Café* has quite the opposite effect. 'I've tried to express the idea that the café is a place where you can ruin yourself, go mad, commit crimes', Van Gogh explained.[4]

A week later Van Gogh went on to paint a rather different nocturnal scene, *Café Terrace at Night* (fig. 67). Here the mood is rather more benign. The claustrophobia has gone and half a dozen passers-by stroll along the open, cobbled street. Above it all is the night sky, with hugely exaggerated stars shining over the Place du Forum. A postcard dating from a few years later depicts the setting (fig. 68).[5] Although possibly installed soon after Van Gogh's time, a large *pissoire* stands close to the spot where the artist would have placed his easel.

Known as the Café du Forum, it was one of the two most exclusive coffee houses in Arles[6] – and, astonishingly, the seemingly impoverished Van Gogh seems to have been a regular patron. Mourier-Petersen later recalled the times he and Van Gogh had spent at cafés and the Danish artist regularly drank there (two surviving letters to a friend in Copenhagen were written on the Café du Forum's notepaper).[7] It was also the place where Van Gogh and Boch would regularly drink.[8]

In Van Gogh's painting the illuminated shop on the right is that of a barber, the Salon du Forum. Immediately to the right of the barber's (and just out of sight) would have been the two darkened stone columns and pediment of the original Roman forum. These can be seen in the postcard, embedded in the building just to the left of the hotel entrance. Van Gogh seems to have deliberately excluded these Roman antiquities from his painting, presumably feeling they would distract from his animated café scene. Vincent described his picture to Wil: 'On the terrace, there are little figures of people drinking. A huge yellow lantern lights the terrace, the façade, the pavement, and even projects light over the cobblestones of the

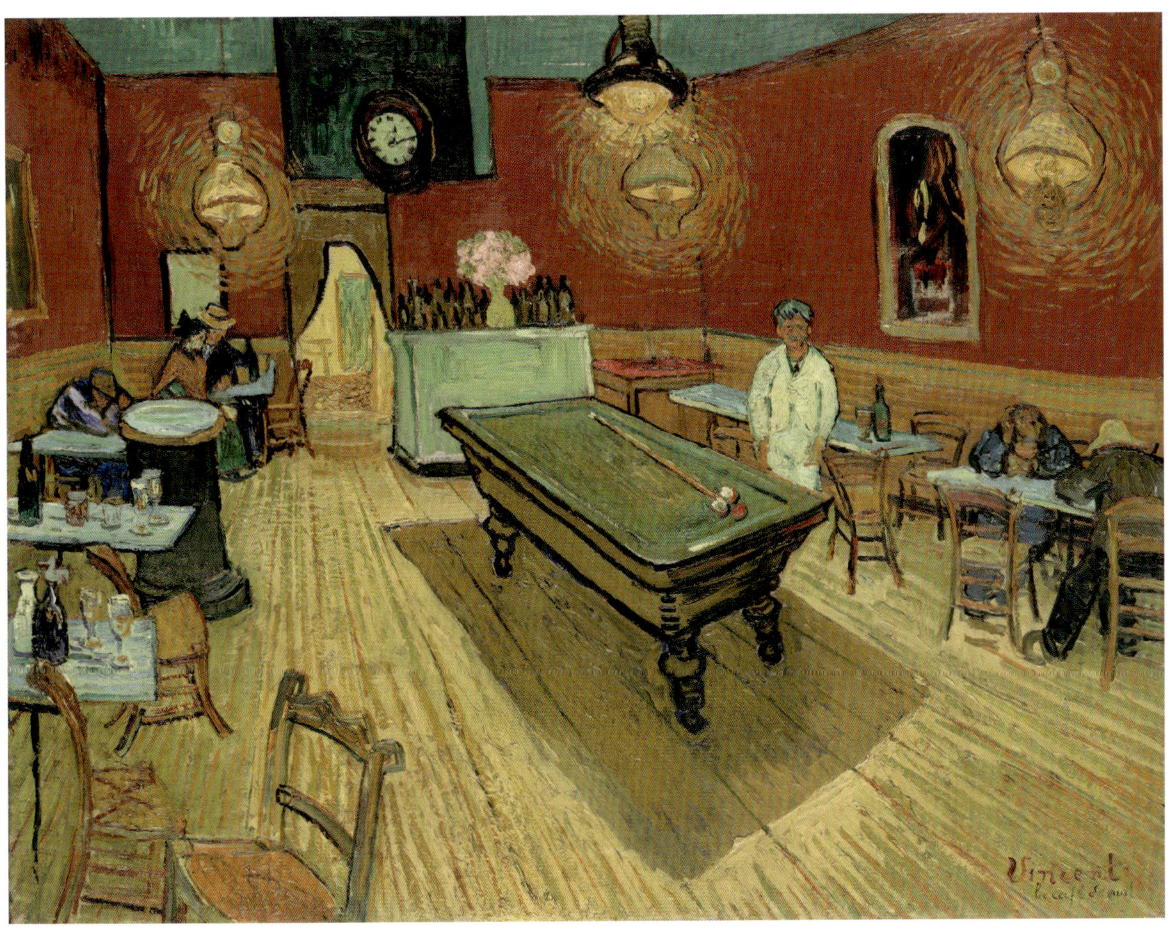

fig. 66 *The Night Café*, September 1888, oil on canvas, 70 x 89 cm, Yale University Art Gallery, New Haven (F463)

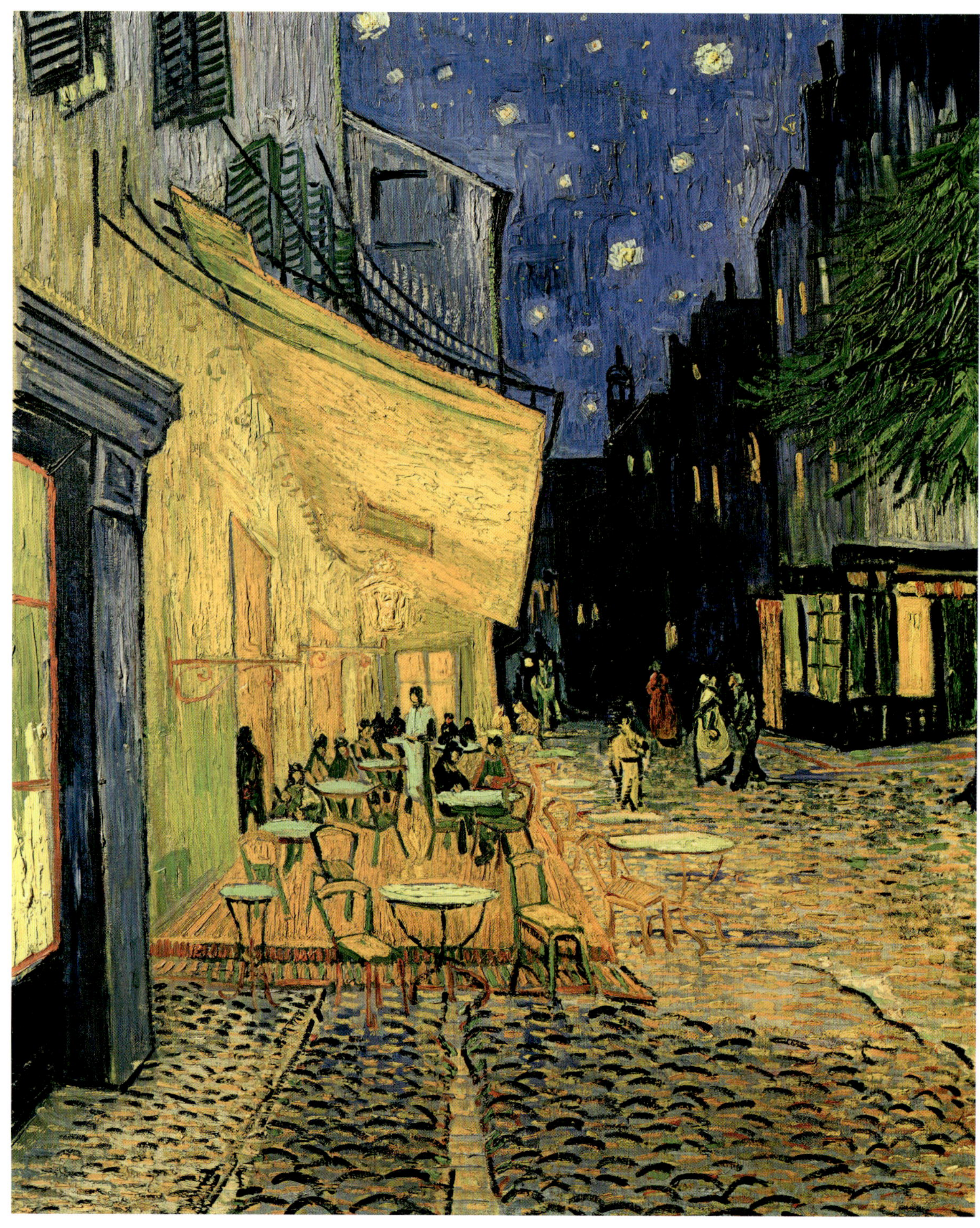

fig. 67 *Café Terrace at Night*, September 1888, oil on canvas, 81 x 65 cm, Kröller-Müller Museum, Otterlo (F467)

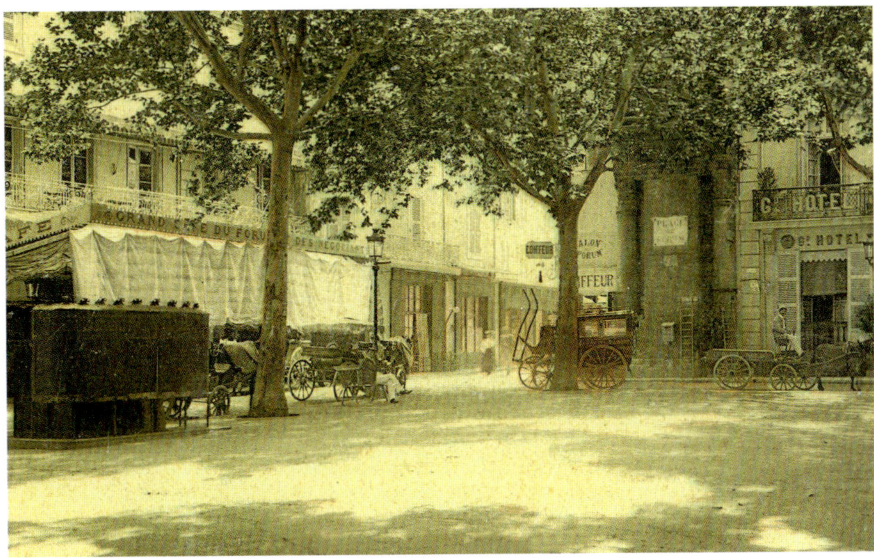

street, which takes on a violet-pink tinge.' It was the colours that excited Van Gogh, 'a painting of night without black'.[9]

'I enormously enjoy painting on the spot at night', he explained. But working in the dark was awkward, since it was only too easy to mistake his pigments and 'take a blue for a green in the dark, a blue lilac for a pink lilac'.[10] Despite these challenges, Van Gogh brilliantly captured the contrast between the warm orange-yellow glow of the gaslight on the welcoming terrace and the deep blue of the infinite heavens.

Van Gogh's third major night-time painting, *Starry Night over the Rhône* (fig. 69), explores the vastness of the river, looking south towards the centre of Arles. The effect of the gaslights reflected in the fast-flowing river is highly exaggerated. An Arlésienne and her lover linger on the sandbar, enjoying their time together. By chance, a newspaper report briefly mentions Van Gogh working on this picture. This article (reproduced here for the first time) names him as one of four artists who were painting in Arles: 'Mr Vincent, an impressionist painter, works, we are told, in the evening, by the light of the gaslamps, in one of our squares' – probably a reference to Place Lamartine (fig. 70).[11] This represents one of the earliest published references to the artist.[12]

His easel was set up on the embankment, a spot he knew intimately. Legend has it that Van Gogh placed candles on his hat in order to paint at night.[13] This bizarre practice had been earlier attributed to Francisco Goya, who depicted himself in a 1790s self-portrait painting in such headgear.[14]

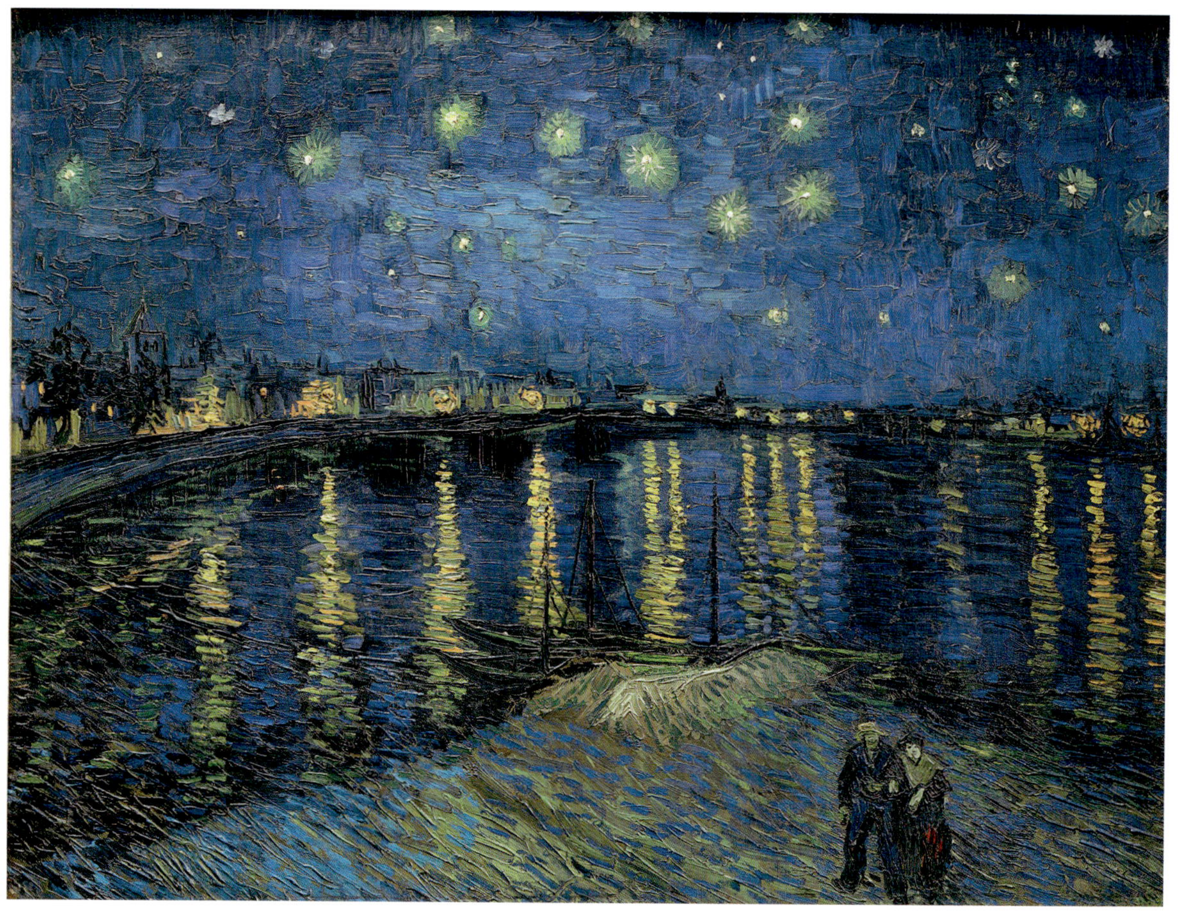

fig. 69 *Starry Night over the Rhône*, September 1888, oil on canvas, 73 x 92 cm, Musée d'Orsay, Paris (F474)

fig. 70 'Chronique Artistique', *L'Homme de Bronze*, 30 September 1888

Wearing a hat with candles would have been quite impractical (and dangerous), so Van Gogh probably had a more mundane method – standing beneath a street gas-lamp, with a candle placed in his paintbox and possibly also on his palette. But however he worked, he no doubt attracted considerable attention painting after dark in Place Lamartine, which was busy at all hours.

Vincent described his picture to Theo: 'The starry sky at last, actually painted at night, under a gas-lamp. The sky is green-blue, the water is royal blue, the ground is mauve. The town is blue and violet. The gaslight is yellow, and its reflections are red gold and go right down to green bronze.'[16] Van Gogh positioned the Plough, the most recognisable stars in the heavens, in the south-west, although it would have been to the north.

Starry Night over the Rhône was the precursor of an even more celebrated painting, *Starry Night*, which he painted the following summer after he had moved to the asylum at Saint-Rémy. In this later picture, the stars and crescent moon illuminate a pair of soaring cypresses. The stars provided great inspiration for Van Gogh, and he relished the warm Provençal nights that offered comfortable viewing conditions. 'The sight of the stars always makes me dream *in as simple a way* as the black spots on the map, representing towns and villages, make me dream', he wrote to his brother.[17]

Van Gogh, with his voracious appetite for work, quickly realised that if he had gaslight inside the Yellow House then it would be feasible to paint after dusk. With the days drawing in, in early October he paid 25 francs to have gas installed in his two ground-floor rooms so that he (and Gauguin after his arrival) could continue working in the evenings. In his painting of *The Yellow House* (fig. 1), the piles of earth in the street probably depict the main gas pipes being laid. Vincent was delighted with the result. Cosily ensconced in the Yellow House, he wrote appreciatively to Theo: 'In the evening especially, with the gaslight, I like the look of the studio very much.'[18]

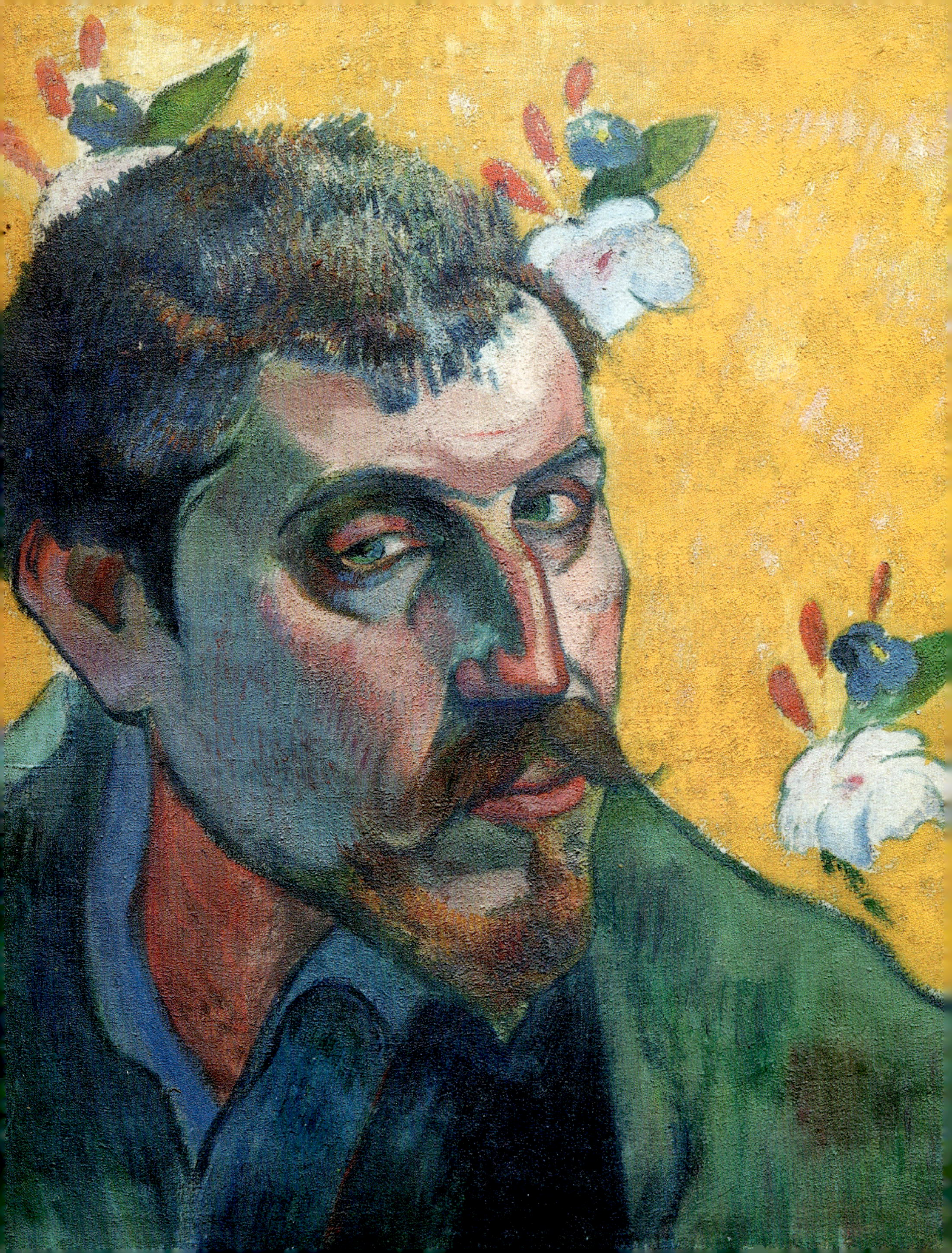

CHAPTER ELEVEN

GAUGUIN'S ARRIVAL

*'He's very, very interesting as a man, and I have every confidence
that with him we'll do a great many things'*[1]

Right from the moment Van Gogh stepped inside the Yellow House he
dreamed of sharing it with a fellow artist – and he quickly fixed on Paul
Gauguin. The two men had met in Paris in December 1887, although they
had hardly got to know each other before going their separate ways. Gauguin
left the following month for the artists' colony in the Breton fishing village
of Pont-Aven. A month later Van Gogh set off for Arles.

On 1 May 1888, only a few hours after renting the Yellow House,
Vincent suggested to Theo that 'perhaps Gauguin will come to the south.'[2]
Gauguin accepted his invitation in July, but then prevaricated, making a
series of excuses. No doubt Gauguin realised that the arrangement would be
financially advantageous, since it would bring him closer to Theo, who was
selling his work at the Boussod & Valadon gallery in Paris. But Gauguin was
also aware that Van Gogh might well prove a difficult companion. As Theo
knew, his brother could be awkward: 'There's something in the way he talks
that makes people either love him very dearly, or unable to tolerate him. He
is always surrounded by people who are attracted to him, but also by lots of
enemies. He cannot be detached in his dealings with people. It is *either* one
thing *or* the other. Even those with whom he is the best of friends find him
difficult to get along with.'[3]

Van Gogh was determined to coax Gauguin to Arles and the next stage
was an exchange of paintings. In August their friend Bernard had joined
Gauguin in Pont-Aven, and a few weeks later Van Gogh suggested that the
two artists in Brittany should paint portraits of each other and send them to
hang in the Yellow House. In exchange, Van Gogh sent them two paintings
in early October – a Rhône riverscape for Bernard (fig. 48) and a self-
portrait for Gauguin, the first he had done in Arles.

Van Gogh's striking *Self-portrait for Gauguin* (fig. 71) shows his stark
face set against a turquoise background. His head is shaven, presumably

Detail of fig. 73 Paul
Gauguin, *Self-portrait
with Portrait of Bernard
(Les Misérables),*
Van Gogh Museum,
Amsterdam (Vincent
van Gogh Foundation)

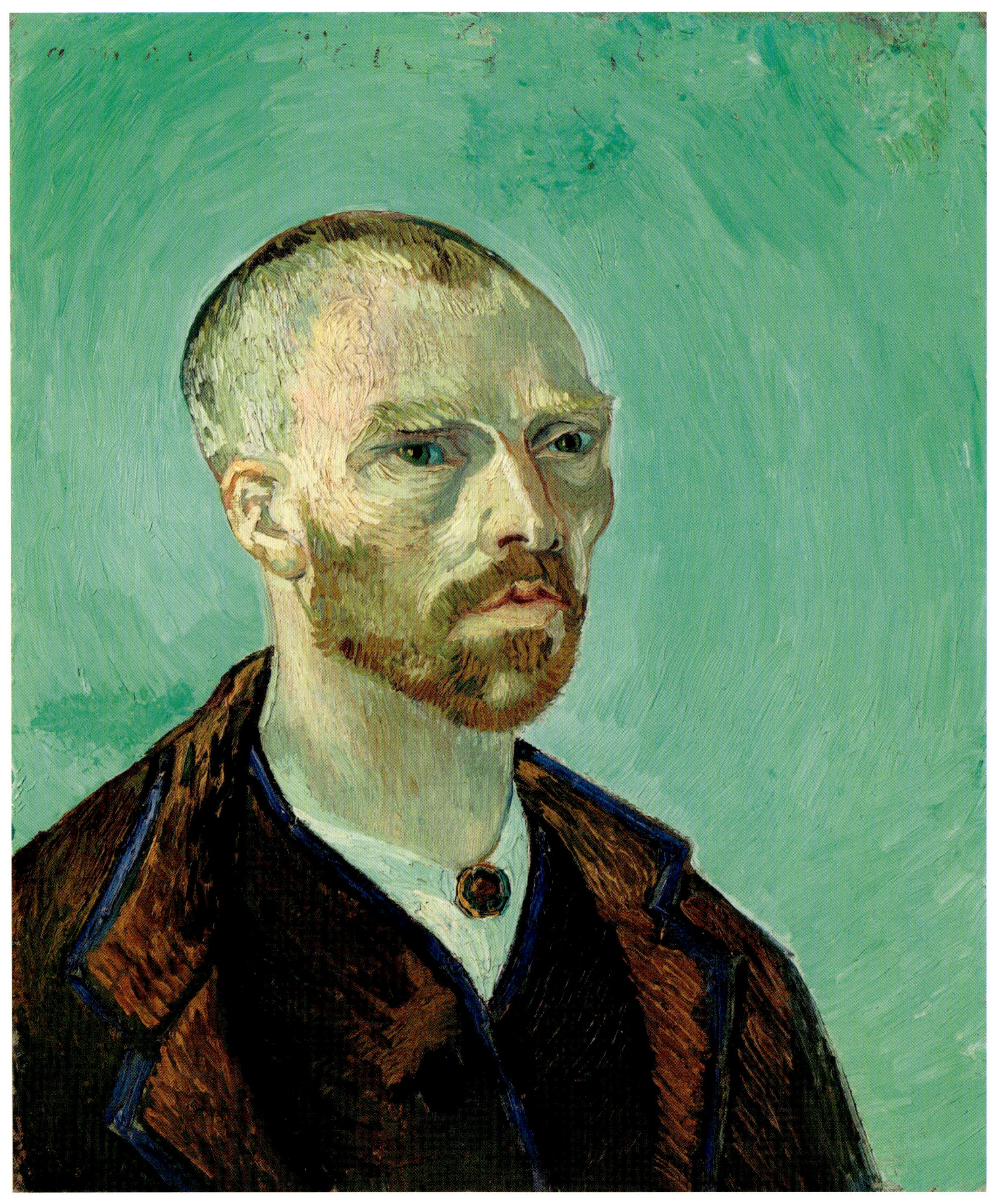

fig. 71 *Self-portrait for Gauguin*, October 1888, oil on canvas, 62 x 50 cm, Harvard Art Museums, Fogg Museum, Cambridge, Massachusetts (F476)

because of the Provençal heat. As he explained, he 'slightly slanted the eyes in the Japanese manner'.[4] Van Gogh set out to depict himself as a bonze, or Japanese Buddhist monk, inspired by his love of the country's art – and his admiration for Loti's latest novel *Madame Chrysanthème* (which also included an illustration of a group of bonzes with shaven heads).[5] Gauguin admired his friend's self-portrait, although Van Gogh's determined look may have given him further pause for thought as to whether he would be an amenable housemate.

Although Van Gogh had asked Gauguin and Bernard to paint portraits of each other, the two Pont-Aven artists had a slightly different idea. They both sent self-portraits, but with small sketches of the other added in the background (fig. 73).[6] Like Van Gogh's self-portrait, Gauguin's had a literary link: he entitled his painting *Les Misérables*, after Victor Hugo's novel. Gauguin saw himself in a similar light to the book's main character, the persecuted outsider Jean Valjean. In the self-portrait, he dramatically emerges from the lower-left corner, with a powerful gaze. Van Gogh praised Gauguin's picture as 'remarkable', giving it pride of place on his studio wall – ready for the arrival of his friend.[7]

As Gauguin dithered, Van Gogh pleaded for him to come, extolling the delights of Arles. Gauguin finally agreed, responding with apparent enthusiasm. 'I like the way you picture your house and its arrangement, and my mouth is watering to see it', he wrote. A few weeks later Van Gogh sent him a small sketch of his painting of the master bedroom, to emphasise the domestic comforts of the Yellow House.[8] As he wrote to Theo, 'in order to do good work you have to eat well, be well housed, have a screw from time to time, smoke your pipe and drink your coffee in peace.'[9]

News of Gauguin's imminent arrival filled Van Gogh with tremendous optimism. 'By staying in the same place I'll see the seasons come and go . . . seeing the same orchards again in spring, the same wheatfields in summer', he told Theo. A fortnight later he elaborated, saying that next year he planned to tackle the blossoms and then the harvest, but 'with a different colour and above all, altered execution'.[10] Van Gogh compared himself to a spider, which 'in its web waits for flies'. He explained: 'As I'm settled now I can take advantage of all the fine days, all the opportunities to catch a real painting from time to time.'[11]

Van Gogh also received formal permission to remain in France. The government had just introduced a system for registering foreign residents and on 15 October he went to the town hall (Hôtel de Ville) to get his certificate. This was the day before he began work on the painting of his bedroom (fig. 21), so registration may well have given him the confidence to feel he was really settled. Van Gogh carefully preserved the vital document until the end of his life. It is reproduced here for the first time (fig. 72).

Gauguin finally arrived on 23 October, after a gruelling journey from Brittany. His train got in very early in the morning, so he first went to the Café de la Gare before waking Van Gogh. The proprietor immediately spotted him, having seen his recent self-portrait. 'You are the friend; I recognise you,' Ginoux told him.[12] Gauguin took a coffee and then knocked on the door of the Yellow House. In great excitement Van Gogh led him upstairs to the guest room, where Gauguin was dazzled by the paintings of the Sunflowers decorating its walls. Van Gogh's dream of a shared studio in the south had finally become reality.

Despite Van Gogh's welcoming efforts, Gauguin was horrified by the domestic chaos. Van Gogh's paintbox epitomised the problem: it was overflowing with tubes that had been squeezed, but not recapped, so the paint had partially dried. 'Everything was in such a mess that I was shocked', Gauguin recalled.[13] Van Gogh's guest insisted that his cleaning lady should be employed for additional hours every week.[14]

Gauguin took over the cooking, after suffering from his host's ineptitude. He complained about Van Gogh's soup, later recalling: 'I don't know how he made the mixture – without doubt like the colours in his paintings . . . we couldn't eat it.'[15] Another of Van Gogh's Arles friends, Dr Rey, later remembered his 'small stove on which he cooked chick-peas which were never cooked'.[16] Gauguin immediately introduced a new routine: 'I did the cooking on a little gas stove, while Vincent got the provisions.'[17] Vincent was rightfully grateful, telling Theo that his new lodger 'knows how to cook *perfectly*'.[18]

Van Gogh was eager to start painting together and had little interest in domestic arrangements. Despite Gauguin's tiring journey, his host insisted that they get down to work right away. Gauguin later pointed out that some artists are keen to pick up their brushes immediately. 'There are those who get off the train,

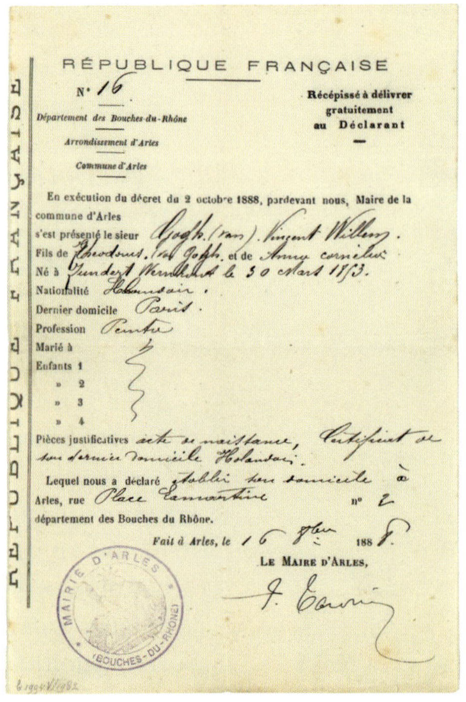

ABOVE fig. 72 Van Gogh's registration certificate, 16 October 1888, Mayor of Arles, 21 x 13 cm, Van Gogh Museum, Amsterdam (Vincent van Gogh Foundation)[19]

RIGHT fig. 73 Paul Gauguin, *Self-portrait with Portrait of Bernard (Les Misérables)*, September 1888, oil on canvas, 45 x 55 cm, Van Gogh Museum, Amsterdam (Vincent van Gogh Foundation) (W309)

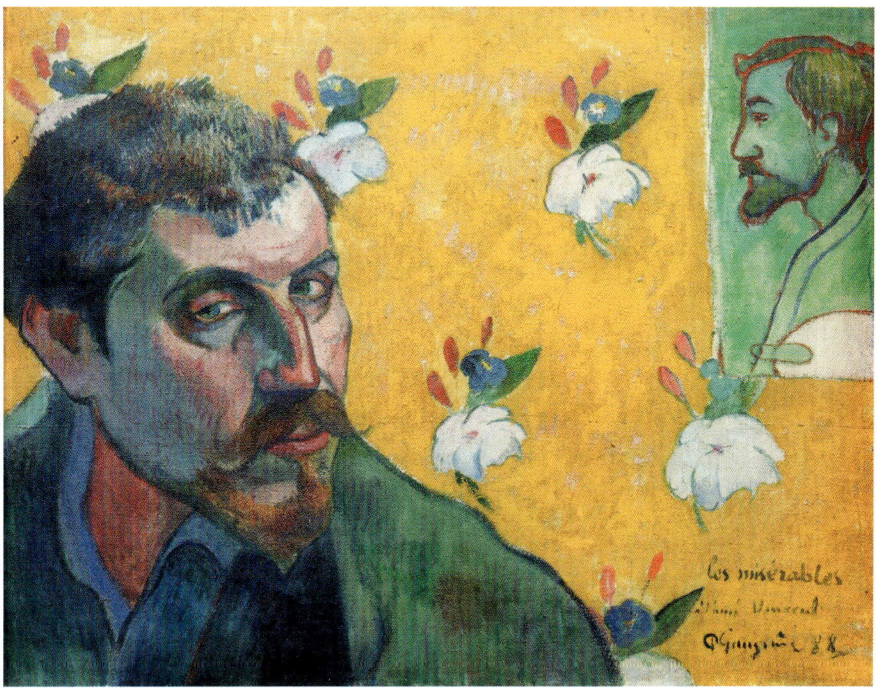

take their palette, and in no time they have done you a sunlight effect', he explained. Gauguin liked to get to know a place: 'I need a period of incubation, to learn each time, the essence of the plants, the trees, in short all nature – which is so varied.'[20]

During their first week together they worked on different subjects. Van Gogh completed two autumnal landscapes of newly-ploughed fields, one with a sower and the other with a dramatic close-up of a tree trunk.[21] Gauguin painted a farmhouse just outside Arles and a negresse (presumably an imaginary work prompted by his sojourn a year earlier on the West Indian island of Martinique).[22]

It was not just working together that was important, but also talking about their work. The two men spent endless hours discussing art, long into the night. They debated the direction of modern painting. They dissected the work of artists they each loved – and despised. They agonised over how they could market their work. All seemed set for a deep and productive collaboration. For Van Gogh, who throughout his life had faced endless challenges, these must have been some of the happiest days in his entire life. He was full of hope. A week after his friend's arrival, Vincent reported back to Theo in triumph: 'The house is going very, very well and is becoming not only comfortable but also an artists' house.'[23]

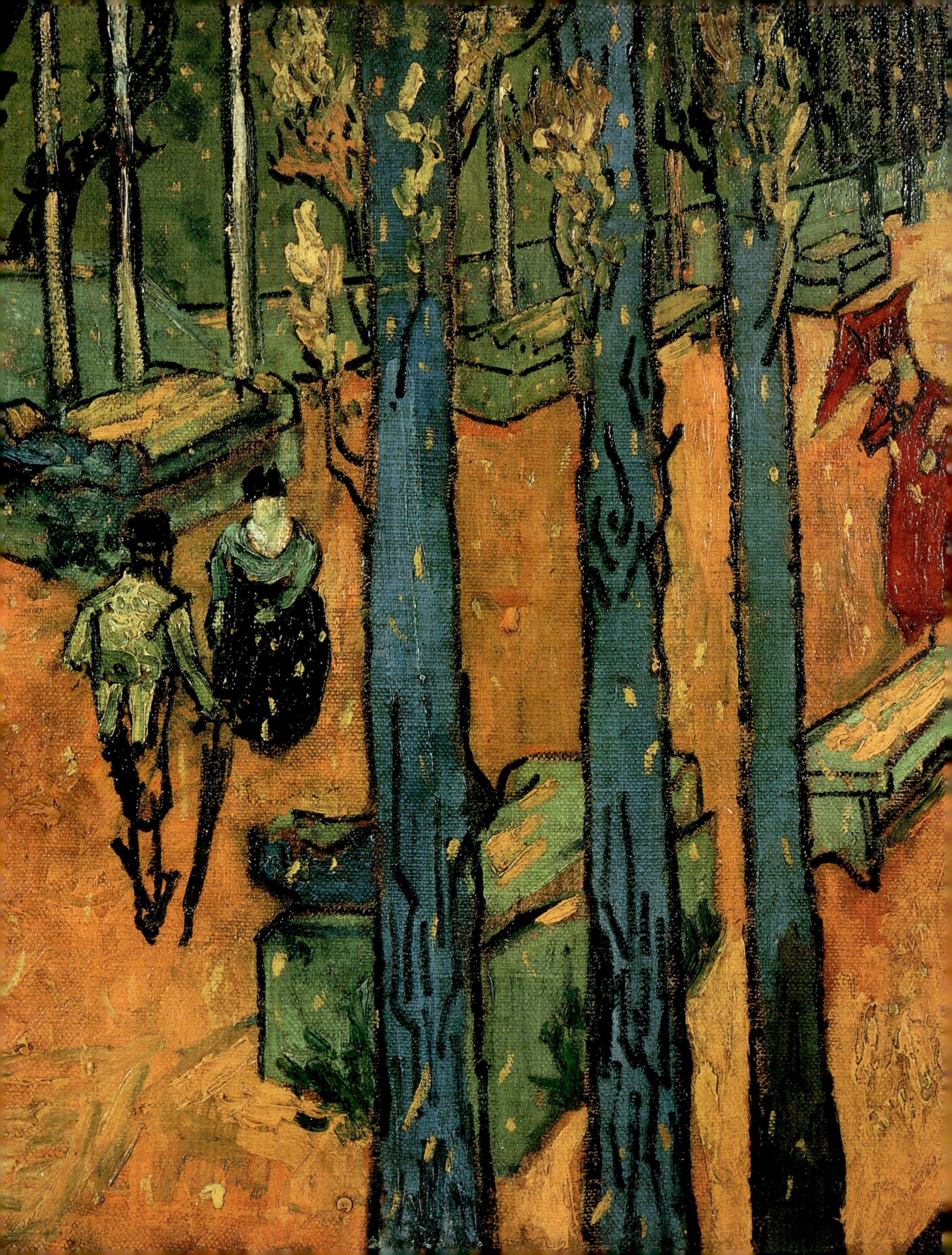

CHAPTER TWELVE

ELYSIAN FIELDS

'Tree-trunks, like pillars, line an avenue where old Roman tombs coloured lilac-blue are lined up . . . the ground is covered as if by a carpet with a thick layer of orange and yellow leaves'[1]

Van Gogh and Gauguin enjoyed walking together in the Alyscamps, the Roman cemetery on the south-east outskirts of the town. Its Provençal name derives from the Latin words Campi Elisii (Elysian Fields) – the mythological paradise where souls of the virtuous rest. It was to become the first place where the two artists set up their easels side by side.

This delightful spot is lined with trees on both sides (fig. 74). Laid out by friars in the seventeenth century, the avenue shelters carved stone sarcophagi recovered from the Roman burial site. It leads to the Chapel of St Accurse, half way along the promenade, and ends at the twelfth-century Church of St Honorat. Although much of the huge Roman necropolis had been destroyed when the railway workshops were built just to the north in the late 1840s, this avenue was preserved. Only a few minutes' walk from the ramparts, this haven became a popular place for an evening stroll – and a rendezvous for lovers.

Artists were also attracted to this famed site. The month before Van Gogh and Gauguin tackled it, two others were working on rather different pictures. An Arles newspaper (fig. 70) recorded that José Belon, a local artist, had painted *Jealous!* (fig. 75). Done in the realist, narrative style popular at the time, it depicts a downcast Arlésienne who has abandoned a dance at the archway of St Accurse. That same month the American artist

Detail of fig. 80 *The Alyscamps (Falling Leaves)*, Kröller-Müller Museum, Otterlo

Pennell was visiting Arles and had portrayed the distant figure of a priest approaching St Honorat, to illustrate a travel article (fig 76).[2]

The Alyscamps was even more dramatic in late October. The day before Gauguin's arrival, Vincent reported to his brother: 'The leaves are starting to fall; the trees are visibly yellowing, the yellow increasing every day. It's at least as beautiful as the orchards in blossom.' He had already asked Theo to urgently send more paint for capturing the autumnal leaves, which 'will surely be amazing and . . . lasts only a week'.[3]

Van Gogh and Gauguin went to stroll and, struck by the changing colour of the leaves, they decided to return the following morning to work. Van Gogh began with two vertical landscapes, emphasising the height of the trees. He had tackled similar motifs from the early days of his artistic career in the Netherlands: an avenue of trees disappearing towards the horizon, giving a sense of depth and drawing the viewer in. This time he put the emphasis on the autumnal colours – poplars rise up like flames above the yellow-orange pathway of leaves.

Both vertical landscapes were painted in the avenue. One scene faces towards St Honorat at the far end (fig. 77). Van Gogh shifted the church tower slightly, so that it appears between the rows of trees (in reality the tower would have been just out of sight on the left and does not have such

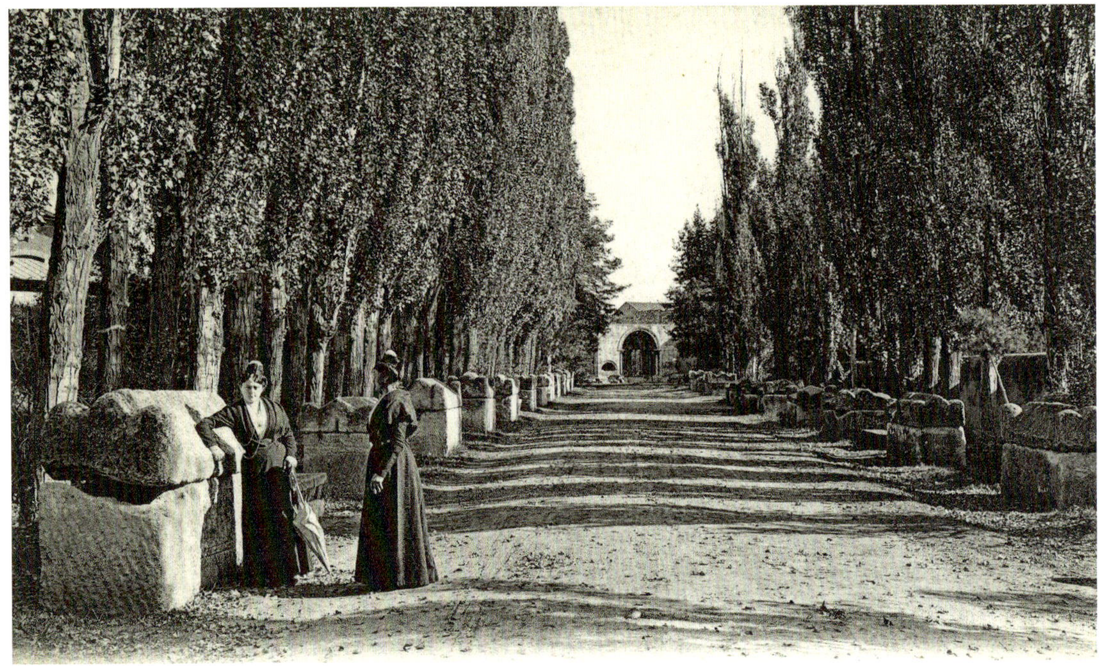

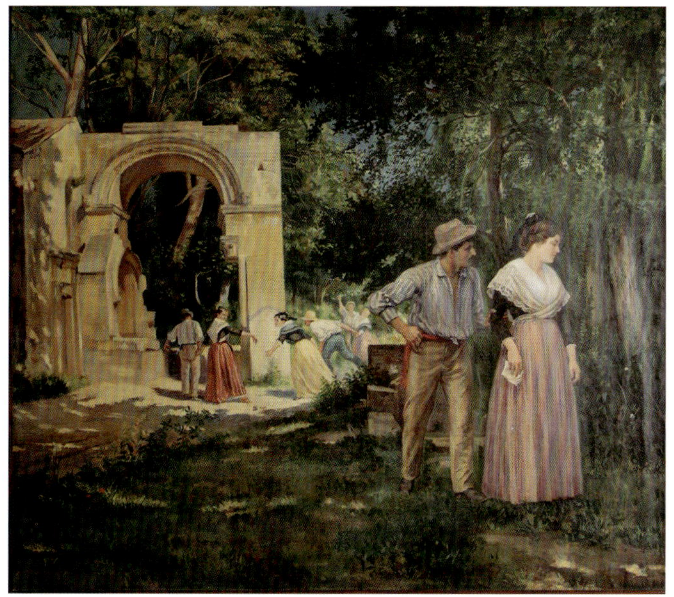

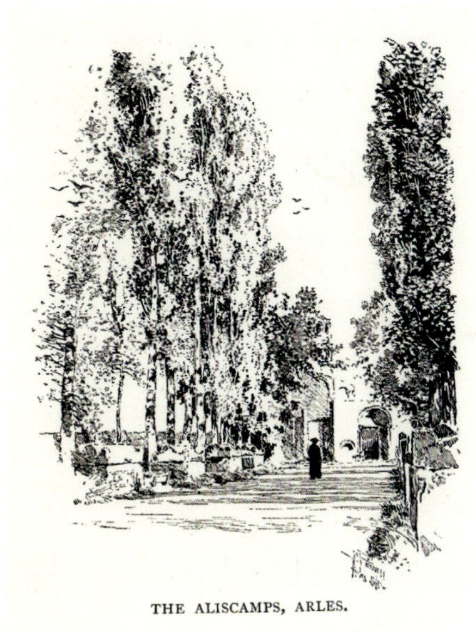

a pointed pinacle). An Arlésienne and her Zouave lover stroll towards the artist. Van Gogh chose to include two smoking chimneys of the adjacent railway workshops, which must have disturbed the peace of this ancient necropolis. The second vertical landscape is angled in the opposite direction, looking from near St Honorat towards the entrance of the Alyscamps (fig. 78). A few sketchy figures amid the sarcophagi are dwarfed by the poplars, which soar up in even richer fiery hues. This painting was bought for $66 million by an Asian collector in 2015.[4]

A day or so later, as the trees became barer, Van Gogh painted two horizontal landscapes, which he called *Falling Leaves*.[5] He positioned his easel on a raised footpath near the northern side of the avenue, on the bank of the Craponne Canal. These twin compositions are notable for their dramatic cropping, in a style reminiscent of Japanese prints. Van Gogh's tree trunks are outlined in black or dark blue, a technique which Gauguin and Bernard were adopting – it is known as cloisonnism (a term derived from *cloisonné* enamels).

Once again, the pair of landscapes face different directions. One looks towards the entrance, through rows of purple trees, as a courting couple approach on the golden, leaf-strewn path (fig. 79). Vincent described the painting to Theo as showing the trees losing their leaves: 'Some are still falling, like snowflakes. And in the avenue dark figurines of lovers.'[6]

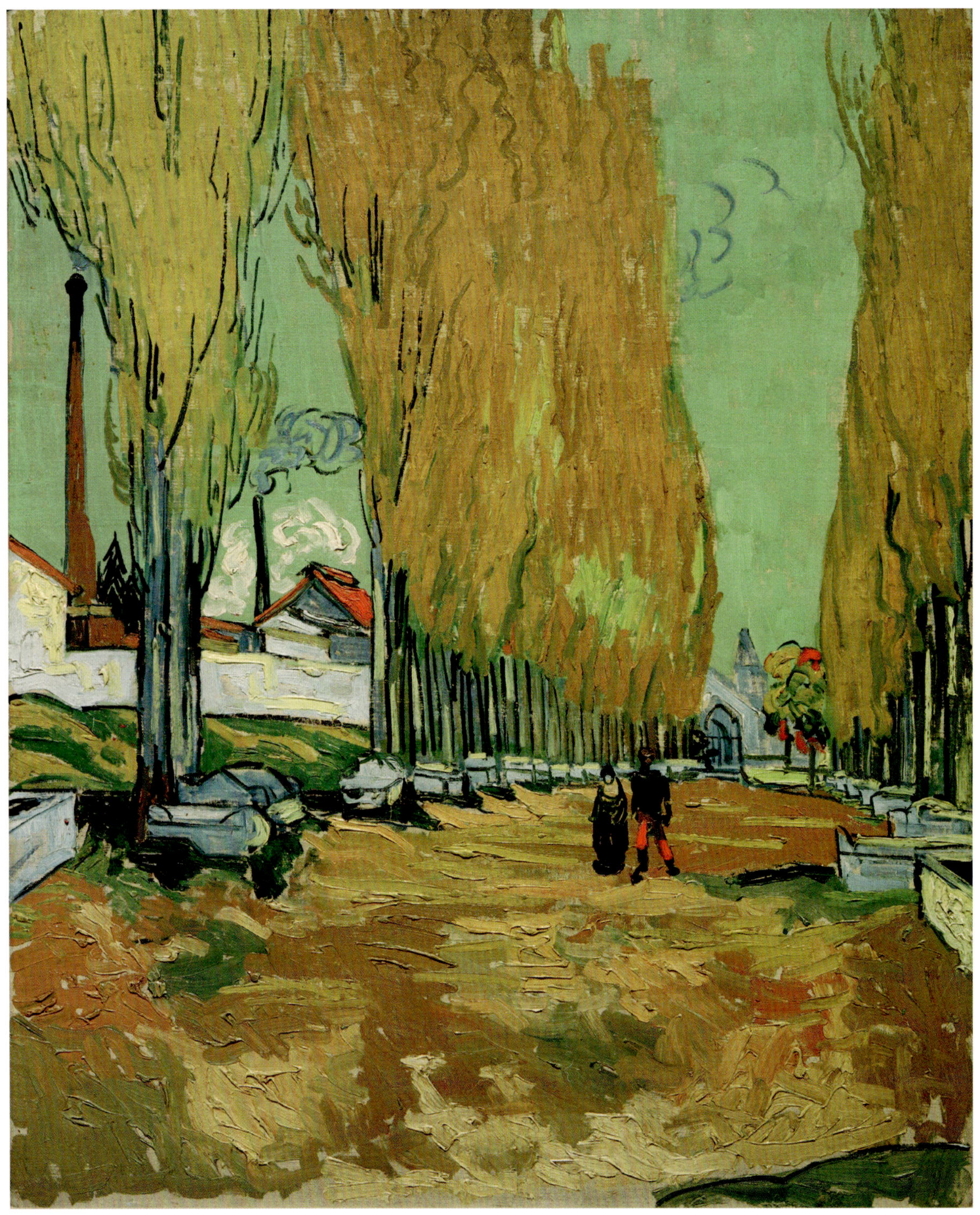

fig. 77 *The Alyscamps*, October 1888, oil on canvas, 89 x 72 cm, Goulandris collection, Lausanne (F568)

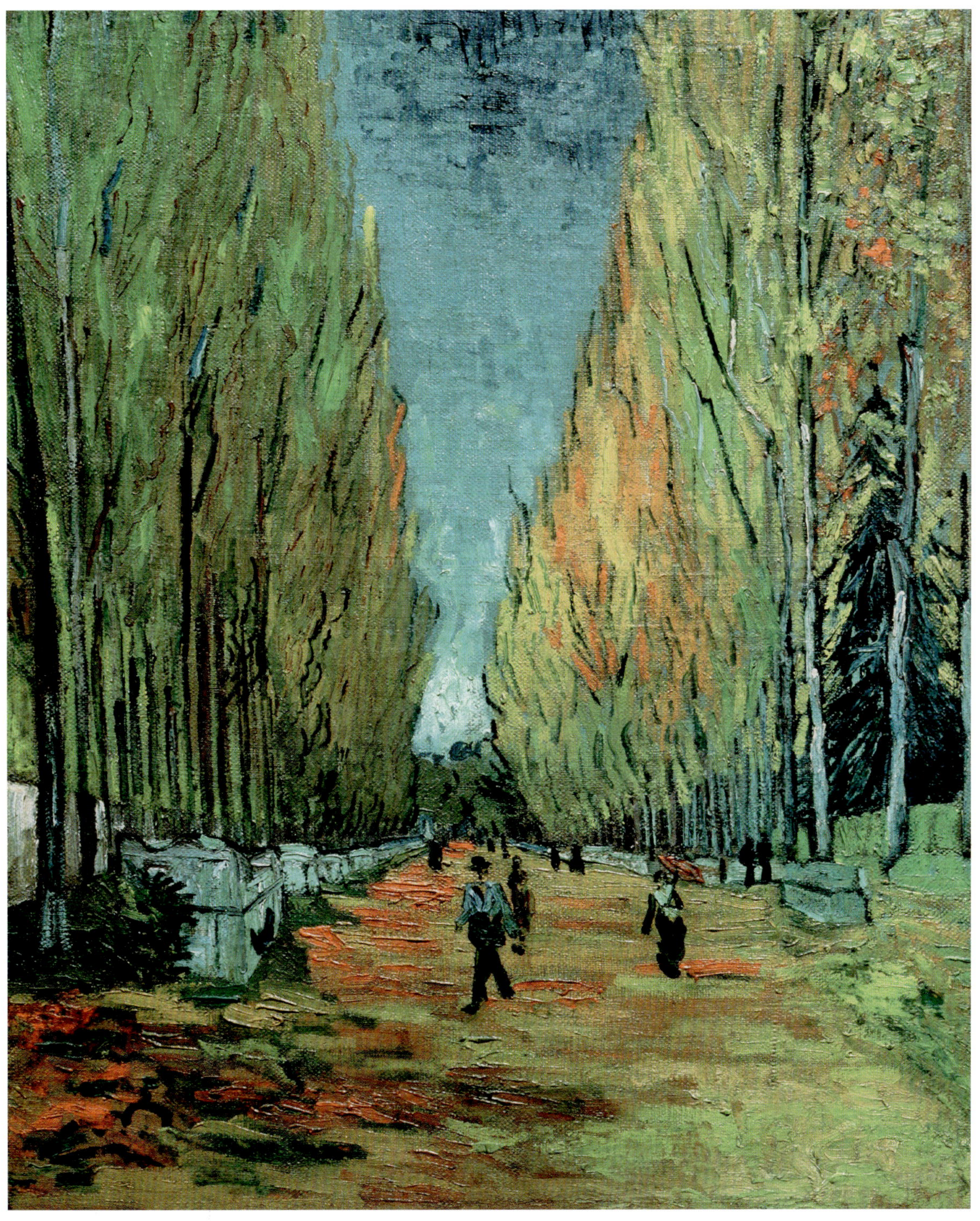

fig. 78 *The Alyscamps*, October 1888, oil on jute, 92 x 74 cm, private collection (F569)

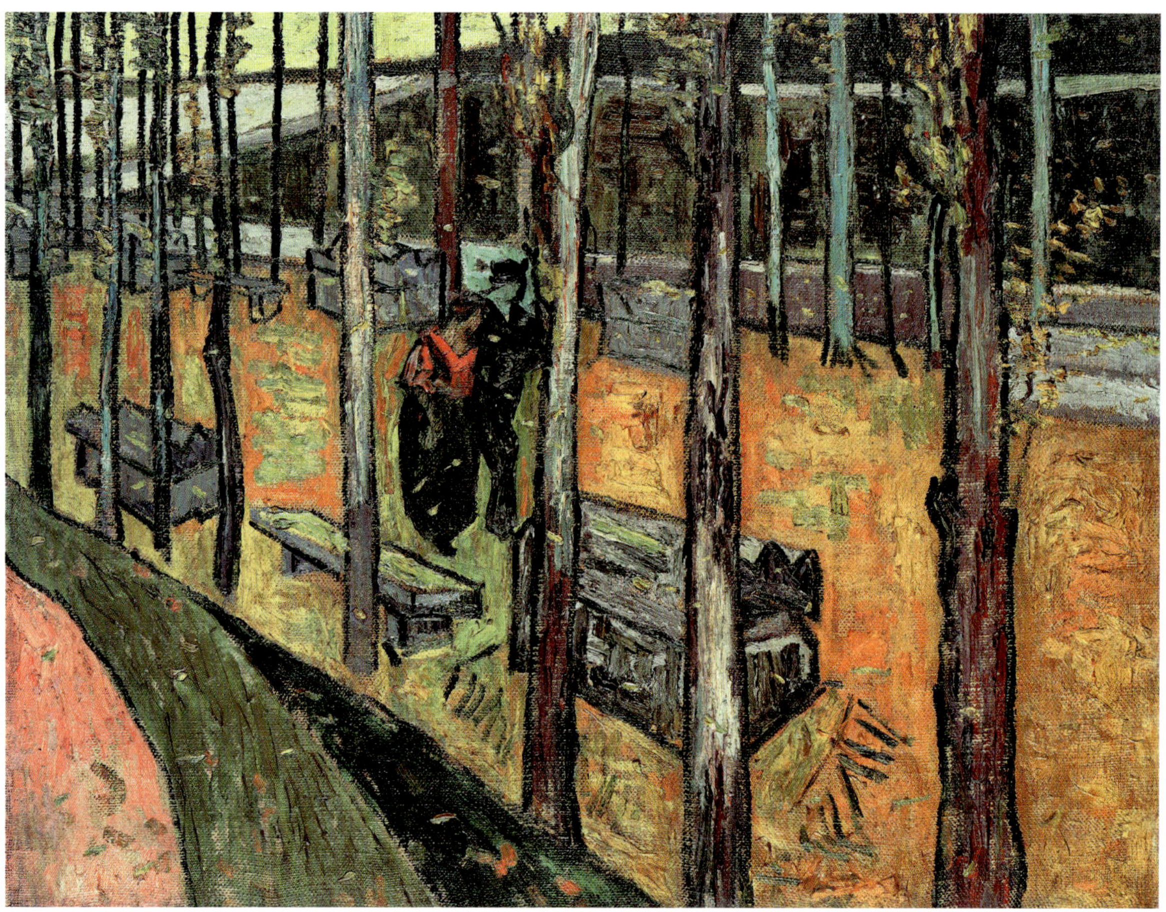

Van Gogh's other horizontal view, with dark turquoise trees (originally more purply, but the red pigment has deteriorated), faces towards St Honorat (fig. 80). Along the avenue an Arlésienne with a red parasol strolls and an elderly man greets a plump woman. Van Gogh probably added the finishing touches back in the Yellow House on 1 November, a day of heavy rain. The two horizontal works were originally conceived as a pair, looking down on the avenue in both directions, and Van Gogh proudly hung them together in the guest bedroom.

Gauguin, who worked close by, chose very different views. For the first, he climbed up the bank of the narrow canal and faced towards the tower of St Honorat (fig. 81). At its centre is a trio of Arlésiennes, whom he described as 'the Three Graces at the temple of Venus'.[9] Conspicuous by their absence are the sarcophagi which lay just below the canal bank on the right. The railway workshops on the left are barely indicated, although a

ABOVE fig. 79 *The Alyscamps (Falling Leaves)*, October–November 1888, oil on jute, 72 x 91 cm, private collection (F487)

RIGHT fig. 80 *The Alyscamps (Falling Leaves)*, October–November 1888, oil on jute, 73 x 92 cm, Kröller-Müller Museum, Otterlo (F486)

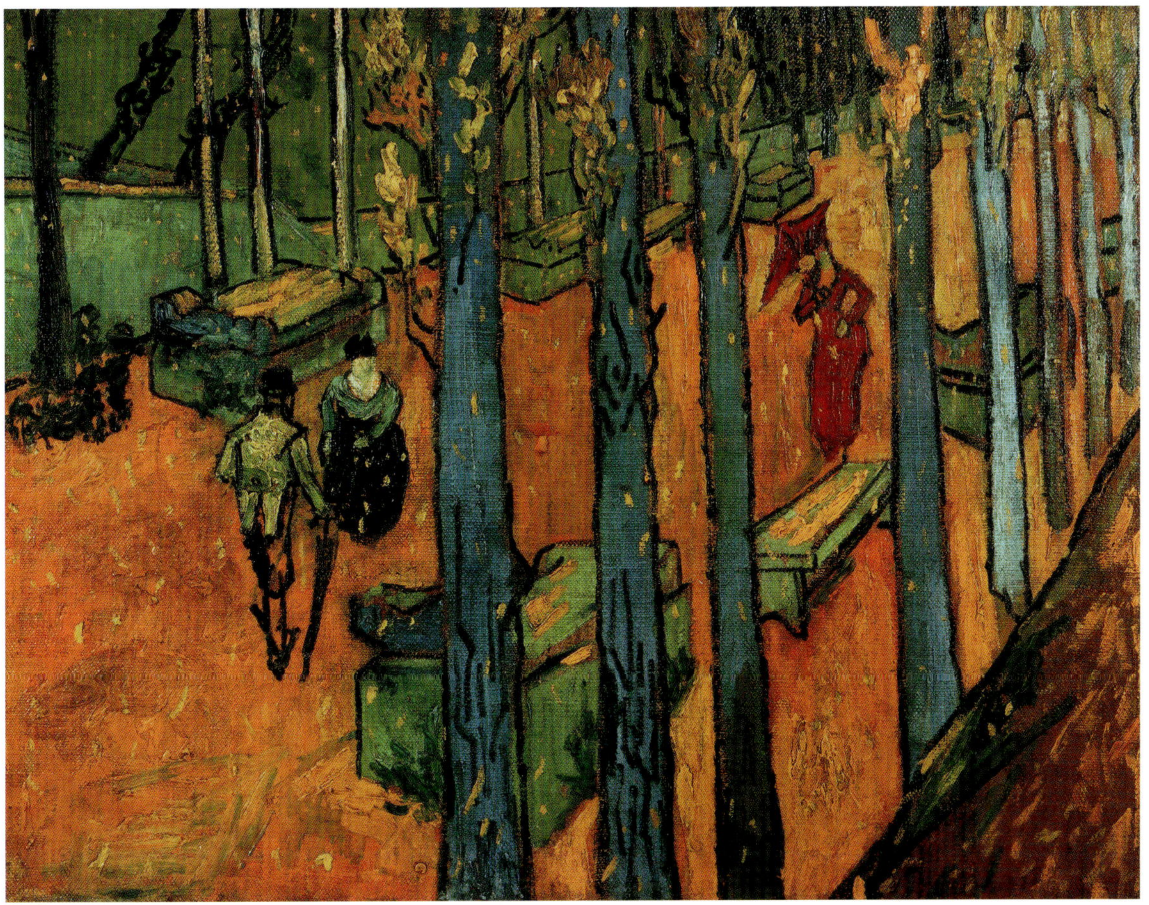

whitish plume of rising smoke is a vague reference to the industrial world just beyond this bucolic scene.

Gauguin's second painting, *The Alyscamps and Portal of St Honorat* (fig. 82), does include several tombs, although the scene is not easily recognisable as the Alyscamps. Gauguin shows the gateway, but excludes the church and its tower (which would be just to the left). Fallen leaves blanket the ground, with others captured in mid-air.

The series of Alyscamps views by the two artists offers an unusual opportunity to compare their contrasting styles. When it came to compositions, Gauguin was the more inventive. He deliberately chose views which were quite unlike the 'tourist' images, as portrayed in postcards of the time. Van Gogh's initial pair of vertical landscapes are more conventional picturesque views, although the two horizontal pictures have become more interesting, using the tree trunks to create a strong grid pattern. Their differing styles are also reflected in the two artists' working methods. Gauguin was quite happy to return to the studio, where he allowed his memory and imagination free rein. Van Gogh felt much more at ease outdoors, in front of his chosen scene.

While working on their Alyscamps scenes, Gauguin introduced an important change to their materials. The two men had used conventional artists' canvas for each of their first works (figs. 77 and 81), but Gauguin preferred a coarser surface. A few days after his arrival he

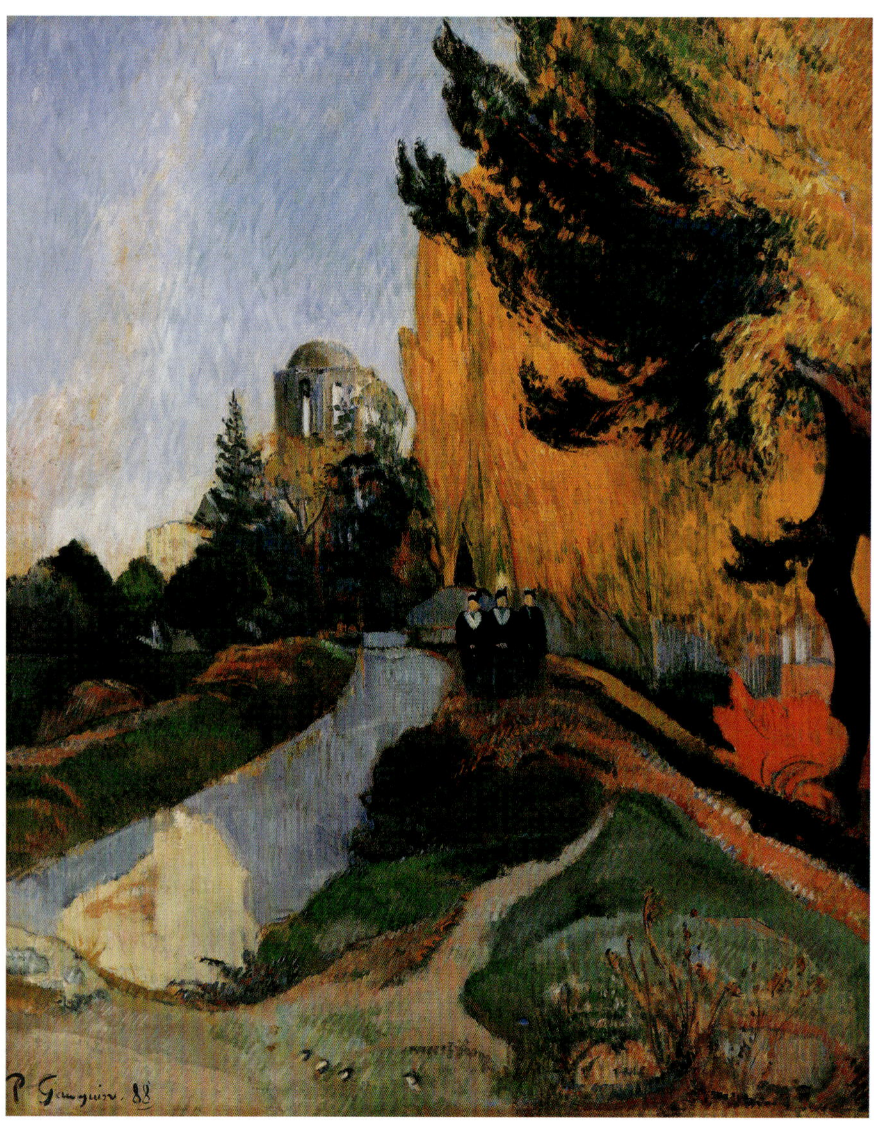

fig. 81 Paul Gauguin, *The Alyscamps*, October 1888, oil on canvas, 92 x 73 cm, Musée d'Orsay, Paris (W314)

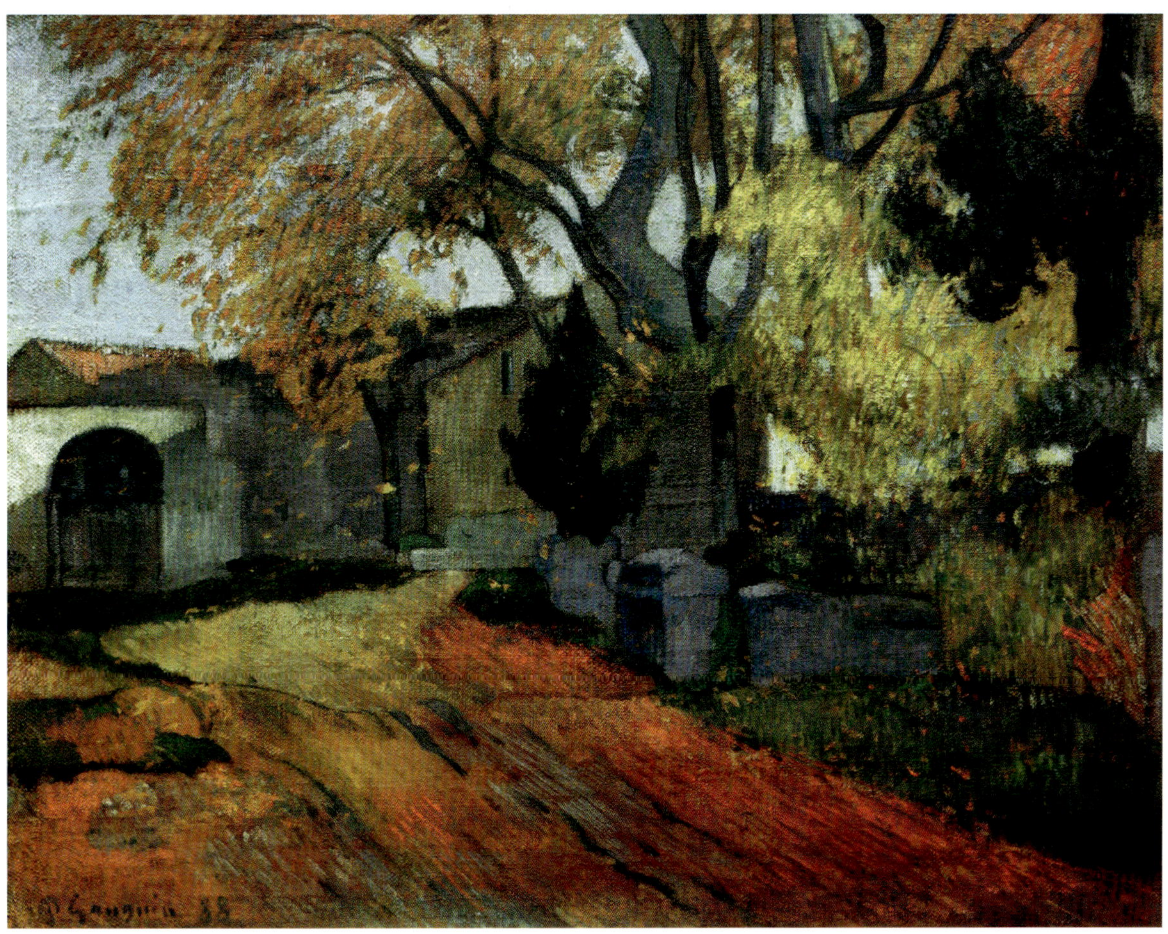

fig. 82 Paul Gauguin, *The Alyscamps and Portal of St Honorat*, October–November 1888, oil on jute, 73 x 92 cm, Seiji Togo Memorial Sompo Japan Nipponkoa Museum of Art, Tokyo (W316)

bought a 20-metre roll of jute, which they then both used, giving their paintings a rougher look.[10] There were several shops in Arles which sold jute, but it is possible that the two artists bought their roll from the Calment shop in Rue Gambetta (and it is just possible that 13-year-old Jeanne Calment would have been working there at that moment). Van Gogh and Gauguin ultimately used the roll of jute for 27 of their autumn pictures.

When it came to technique, Gauguin would paint thinly, whereas Van Gogh preferred thick impasto layers. As for colours, Gauguin particularly loved bold orange tones, making autumnal leaves an ideal subject. Van Gogh went for complementaries, so his orangey leaves were set against purply tree trunks. The two artists both spurred one another on; they were keen to learn from – and ideally surpass – each other.

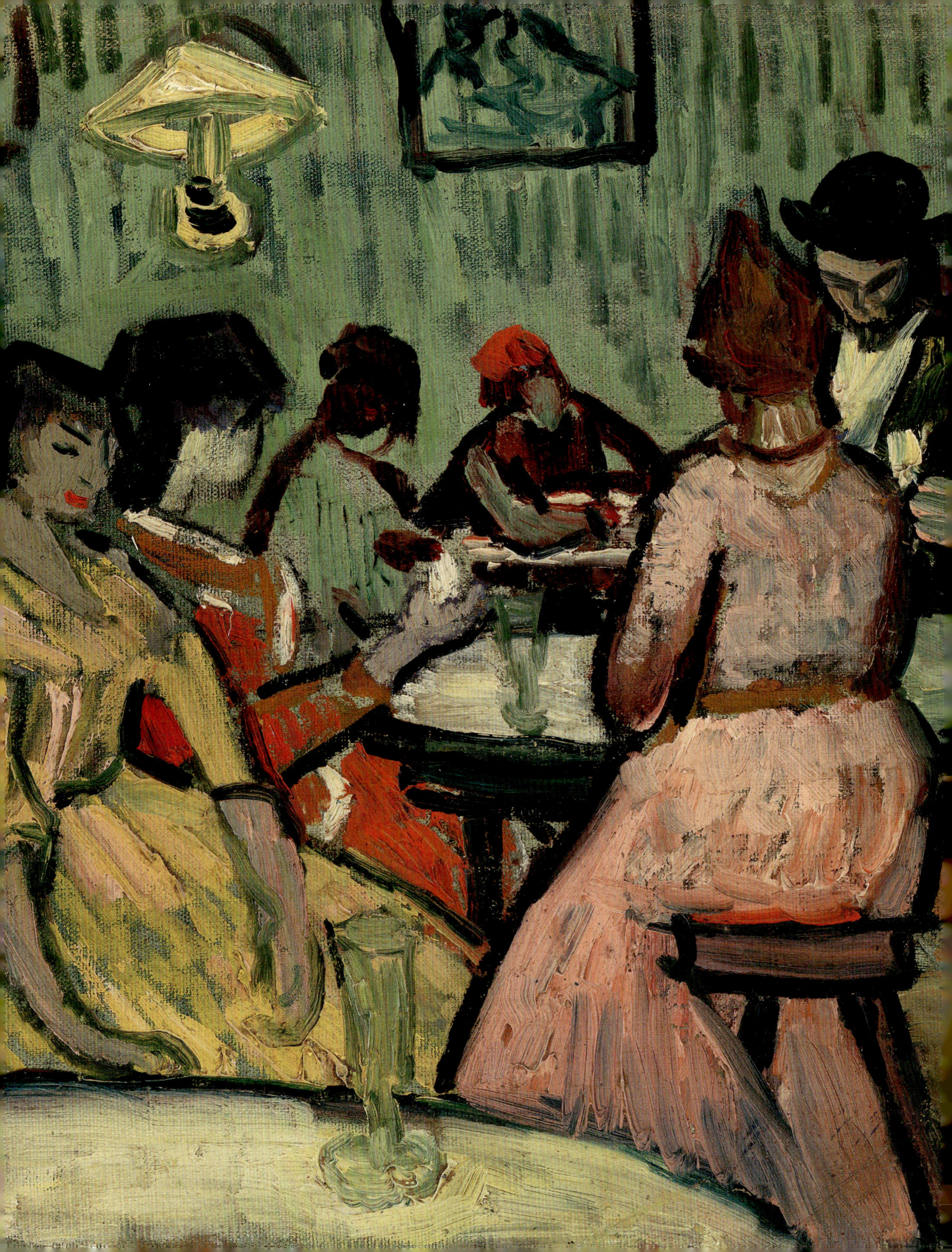

CHAPTER THIRTEEN

STREET OF THE KIND GIRLS

'We've made some excursions in the brothels, and it's likely that we'll eventually go there often to work'[1]

The 'Street of the Kind Girls', as Van Gogh called the brothel quarter, was a place of constant violence.[2] Its actual name was Rue du Bout d'Arles (Street at the end of Arles), because it had been the last street in the north-east corner of the town before the ramparts. The name was also symbolically appropriate, since for the women their trade was usually a last resort. The street is very short, with just seven small buildings on each side in Van Gogh's time. These housed six brothels, as recorded in the 1890 *Annuaire Reirum* (fig. 83). Prostitution was then legal in France. Officially it was confined to *maisons de tolérance* (tolerated or registered houses) with *filles soumises* (submissive girls), although there was also considerable unregulated activity.

The Arles brothels lay almost adjacent to the Convent of the Récollets and the nuns' school in a poverty-stricken area, much to the displeasure of the sisters and local residents. In 1886 they had petitioned the municipality to move the business: 'Since the brothels were transferred to Rue du Bout d'Arles our children, our daughters and our wives are daily witnesses of the most outrageous scenes . . . the nightly noise of the arguments and brawls disturbs the peaceful rest of weary workers after the exhaustion of long, hard days . . . This area is not at all conducive to this kind of trade, given the proximity of an important school and a nunnery.'[3] During Van Gogh's stay, this tiny street witnessed murders and a series of serious assaults. Van Gogh described its habitués as 'ruffians', something of an understatement.[4]

VILLES DE FRANCE

par ordre alphabétique avec la population de chaque ville ¹.

—

Arles (B. du Rhône) S. P. 23,491 habitants :
Virginie Chabaud, rue du Bout d'Arles, 1.
Louis Farce,   id., 5.
Gonouyac,   id., 7.
Legendre,   id., 8.
Léon Bataille,   id., 12.
Driolet, .   id., 14.

fig. 83 Brothels of Arles, from *Annuaire Reirum: Indicateur des Adresses des Maisons de Sociéte (dites de Tolérances)*, 1890[8]

Rue du Bout d'Arles was just three minutes' walk from the Hotel Carrel. Van Gogh's first visit followed a violent incident on the evening of 11 March 1888. Three French Zouave soldiers took supper in a restaurant and went on to what a local newspaper called 'une maison de joie' (house of pleasure) at 1 Rue du Bout d'Arles.[5] This was the brothel which would soon play such an important part in the artist's own story. One of the Zouaves stayed behind at number 1, while the other two went on to number 14. At the entrance of number 14 they encountered three Italians and a dispute ensued over who should enter first. A fight erupted, culminating just around the corner in Rue des Récollets. The Italians stabbed the two Zouaves to death.

Asleep in his hotel, Van Gogh awoke to uproar. The Italians had been caught and Vincent later told Theo that the crowd '*almost* lynched the murderers locked up in the town hall'. Ten thousand people, nearly half the town's population, gathered that morning. Later that day Van Gogh attended the court inquiry and then 'took advantage of the opportunity to go into one of the brothels in the little street called "des Récollets"', commenting that this represented 'the limit of my amorous exploits vis-à-vis the Arlésiennes'.[6]

The short street remained constantly in the news. A month after the Zouave murders a woman faced legal action for encouraging minors to participate in debauchery in an illegal brothel. In November two carpenters got into a brawl, one ending up with concussion and the other with a broken arm. In April 1889 there was a knife fight between a Zouave and the patron of one of the brothels.[7]

Van Gogh soon became a regular in the quarter. He described one of the brothels to Bernard: 'A large room tinged with a bluish limewash – like a village school – a good fifty or so red [uniformed] soldiers and black [clothed] civilians, with faces of magnificent yellow or orange (what tones in the faces down here), the women in sky-blue, in vermilion, everything that's of the purest and gaudiest'.[9] Most men would have focused on the tempting flesh on offer, but even in a brothel Van Gogh remained the artist, acutely aware of colours.

His attitude towards prostitution was ambivalent. Six years earlier in The Hague he had fallen in love with Sien Hoornik, a prostitute, much to the anger of his family. After she agreed to abandon her trade they lived together for nearly two years, so Van Gogh knew only too well the misery faced by these women. But he also needed sex and by now he realised that his awkward character made it difficult to find girlfriends. Prostitution was then widely accepted in France as a necessary evil and Van Gogh's attitude reflected the masculine mores of his time.

Vincent wrote to Bernard saying that he was now living 'like a monk who goes to the brothel once a fortnight'. Surprisingly, he had few qualms about informing his brother about these visits – although Theo was effectively paying for them. In one of his endless begging letters, Vincent even complained that 'for at least 3 weeks I haven't had enough to go and have a screw for 3 francs' (the equivalent of a couple of restaurant meals).[10]

Van Gogh went into more detail with Bernard about these nocturnal visits, arguing that they would provide inspiration for his art. That summer Bernard (who had been influenced by the work of their fellow Cormon student Toulouse-Lautrec) bombarded Van Gogh with sketches of prostitutes. These include a watercolour depicting an outlandishly dressed prostitute in ankle boots who is drinking, with an elderly madame standing behind her (fig. 84). The blue-suited man, with a bottle in front of him, could well be Van Gogh (there are some parallels with Bernard's sketch of him drawn in Paris, fig. 6). In an artistic conceit, hanging on the back wall of the brothel is a picture of Eve reaching up for an apple. Bernard signed his watercolour, 'à mon ami Vincent ce croquis bête' (to my friend Vincent, this silly sketch). Although the watercolour and inscription appear lighthearted, on the reverse Bernard copied out a poem he had written on the evils of prostitution, concluding with the line, 'for your own desire, you force children under pleasure's yoke.'[11] Bernard clearly had an equally ambivalent attitude towards prostitution.

In early October Bernard sent eleven further watercolours in a portfolio entitled 'Au bordel' (At the brothel). It was this set which encouraged Van Gogh to paint his own café scene with a pimp and a prostitute 'making up after a quarrel'.[12] Van Gogh had intended to send this picture to Bernard, but he regarded it as a failure and quickly destroyed it.

Gauguin's arrival in late October would only increase the frequency of visits to Rue du Bout d'Arles. The Frenchman, with his voracious sexual appetite, immediately proposed that they set aside money for 'nocturnal and hygienic promenades'.[13] Needless to say, these sorties were anything but hygienic; Van Gogh's friend Macknight caught what is likely to have been syphilis from a woman Van Gogh had patronised in Arles and Gauguin eventually succumbed to the disease after his move to Tahiti.[14]

Vincent reported back to Theo that he and Gauguin had visited the quarter and planned to return there frequently to work. A week later Van Gogh made 'a rough sketch of a brothel', a small and quickly-painted oil picture.[15] *Brothel Scene* (fig. 86) still remains relatively unknown, since the picture is at the Barnes Foundation in Philadelphia, which does not lend its paintings and until the 1990s did not allow them to be reproduced in colour. Van Gogh depicted the brothel's drinking room. Three women in gaudily coloured dresses sit at the front. On the far side of the table there is a man in a dark hat with a glass of absinthe. At the back are two Zouaves with their partners.

The setting may well have been one of the houses in Rue du Bout d'Arles, quite possibly number 1 (this employed seven women and five appear in this painting). Although Van Gogh observed such a scene, he could hardly have painted there (and no doubt the room was rather dark, despite the hanging lamp). Once again he was forced to work from memory and the result is a rather crude and expressionist work. Van Gogh had hoped to develop this into a larger and more finished painting based on this oil sketch, but he never did so.

Although Van Gogh and Gauguin talked ambitiously of 'working' in the brothels, they never actually depicted naked flesh or produced voyeuristic images of the women. Their plan – largely unachieved – was to explore the social interaction of prostitutes, pimps and punters.[16] But the idea of frequenting the Rue du Bout d'Arles may have been at least partly to legitimise their more worldly indulgences.

Long after his stay in Arles, Gauguin published his reminiscences of a brothel whose owner he named as Father Louis. This must have been the establishment at 5 Rue du Bout d'Arles. The 1886 Arles census and the *Annuaire Reirum* record Louis' surname as Farce (a name which must

fig. 84 Emile Bernard, *Brothel*, June 1888, watercolour and ink on paper, 31 x 20 cm, Van Gogh Museum, Amsterdam (Vincent van Gogh Foundation)

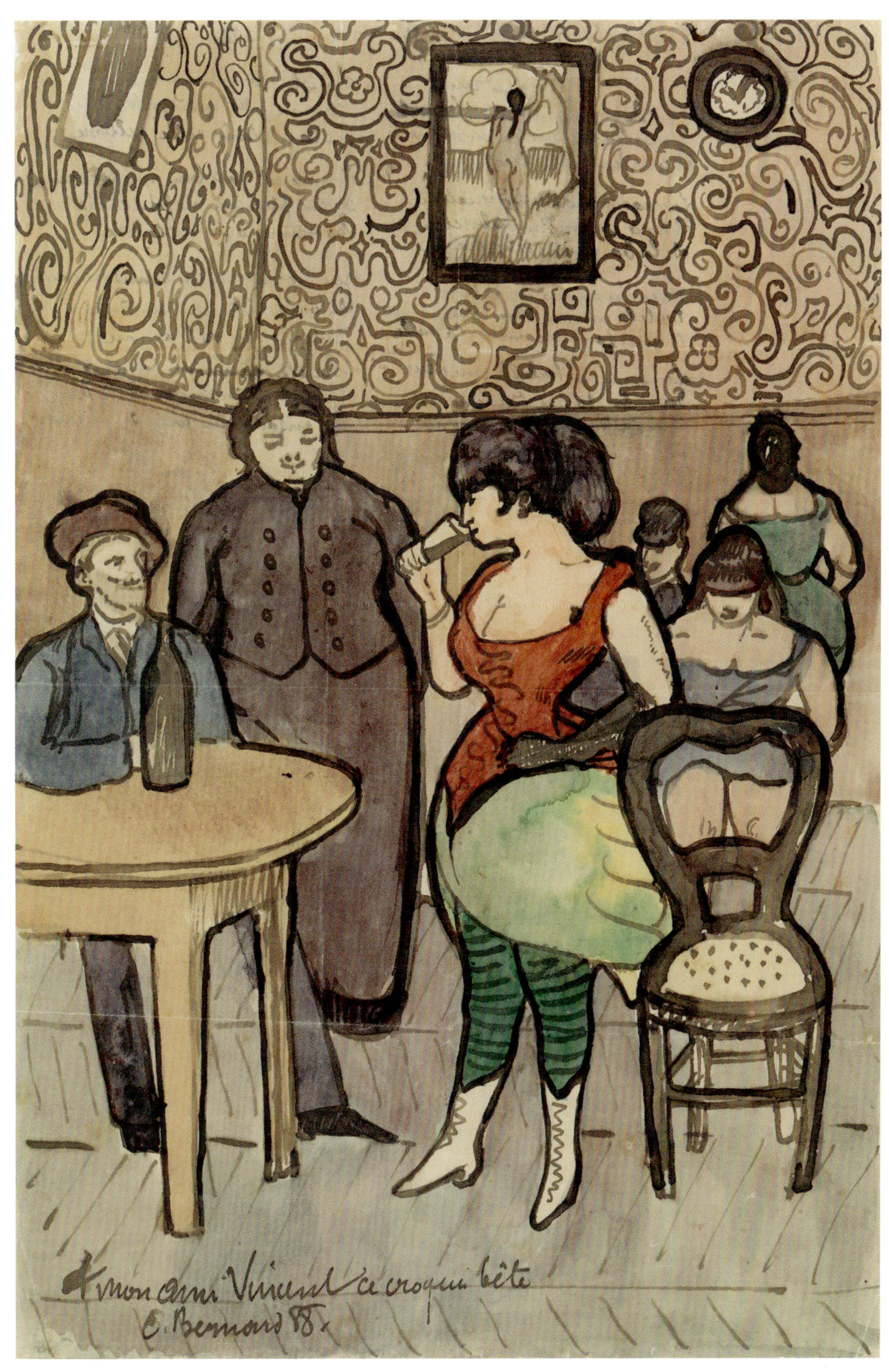
À mon ami Vincent ce croqui bête
E. Bernard 88

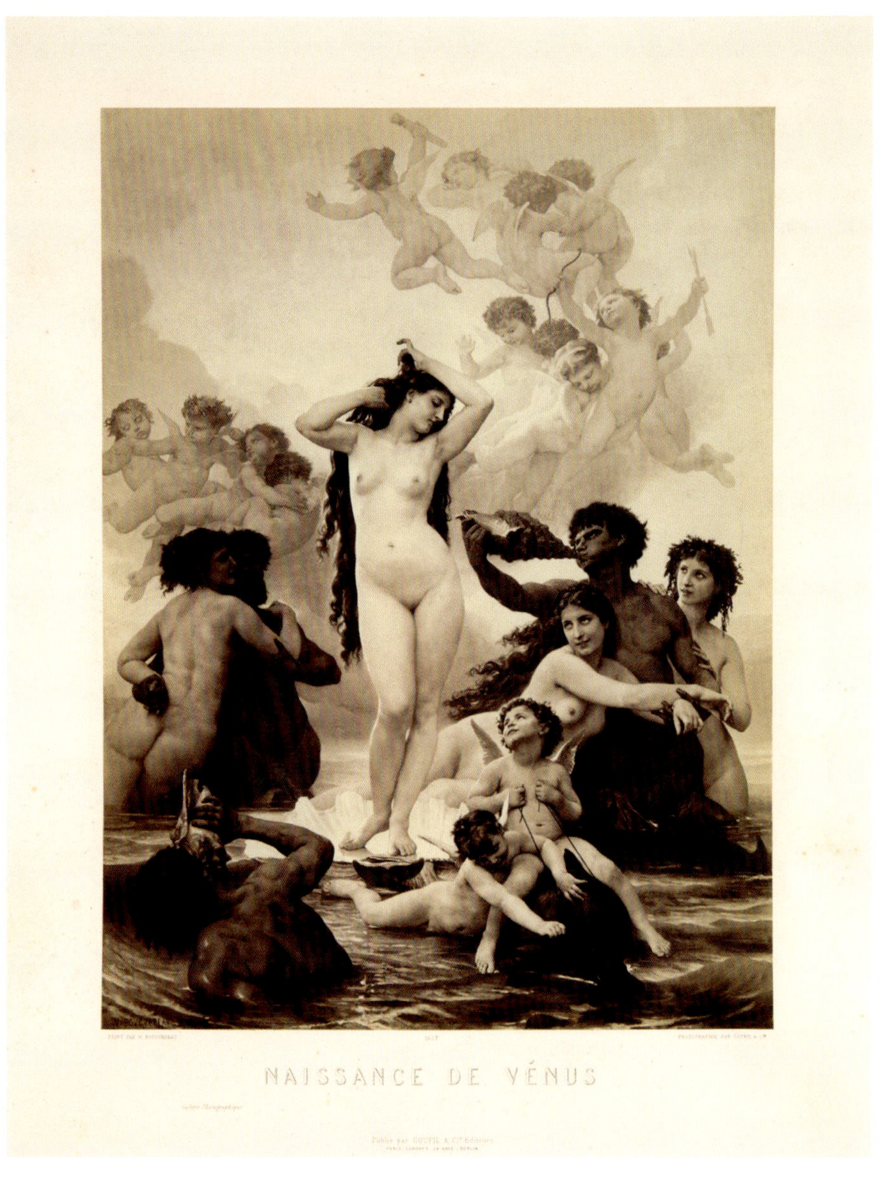

have caused wry amusement with his customers, since it has the same meaning in French as in English). Gauguin recalled: 'At father Louis, he very proudly showed me his special salon. As an artist, I ought to be a good judge, he said. In his salon were two beautiful Goupil prints, a Madonna by Bouguereau and its pendant – by the same artist, a Venus.'[17] Goupil was the Paris gallery where Theo worked, so Gauguin must have been entertained to see his dealer's prints on display in such an establishment. The Venus, representing the goddess of sex, was almost certainly *Naissance de Vénus* (fig. 85). It is unclear whether Farce hung the Venus and Virgin to amuse his customers – or to add a veneer of respectability.

Gauguin and Van Gogh both despised the smoothly painted realism of William-Adolphe Bouguereau. Gauguin commented wittily on Farce's artistic taste: 'Father Louis, on this occasion, showed himself to be a man of genius. The splendid pimp that he was, he had understood the unrevolutionary art of Bouguereau, and where it belonged.'[18]

As for Rue du Bout d'Arles, its risqué character disappeared a few years after Van Gogh's time. The brothels were closed in 1904, following continual complaints that they lay almost next to the Catholic primary school. A year later the street was renamed Rue des Ecoles (Schools), in an attempt to eradicate the memory of its chequered past.

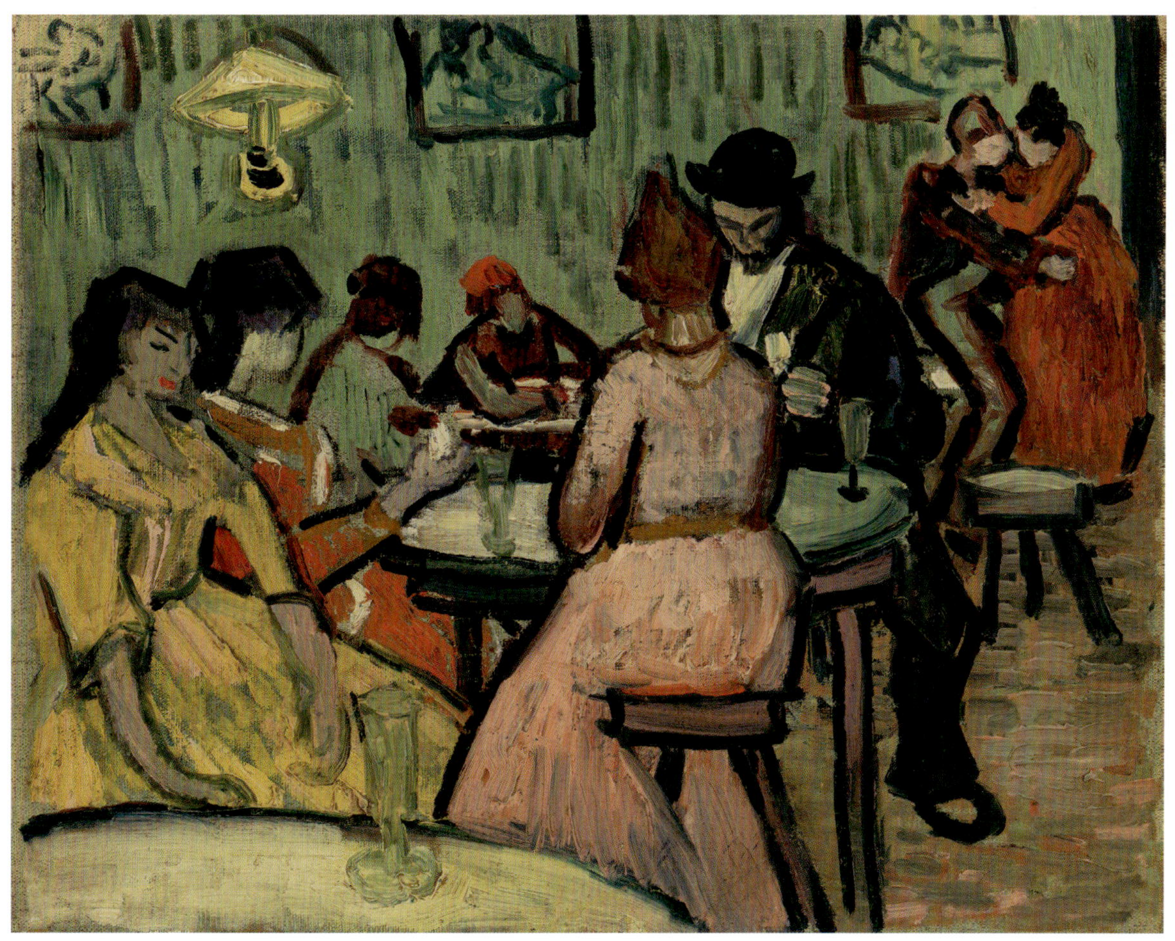

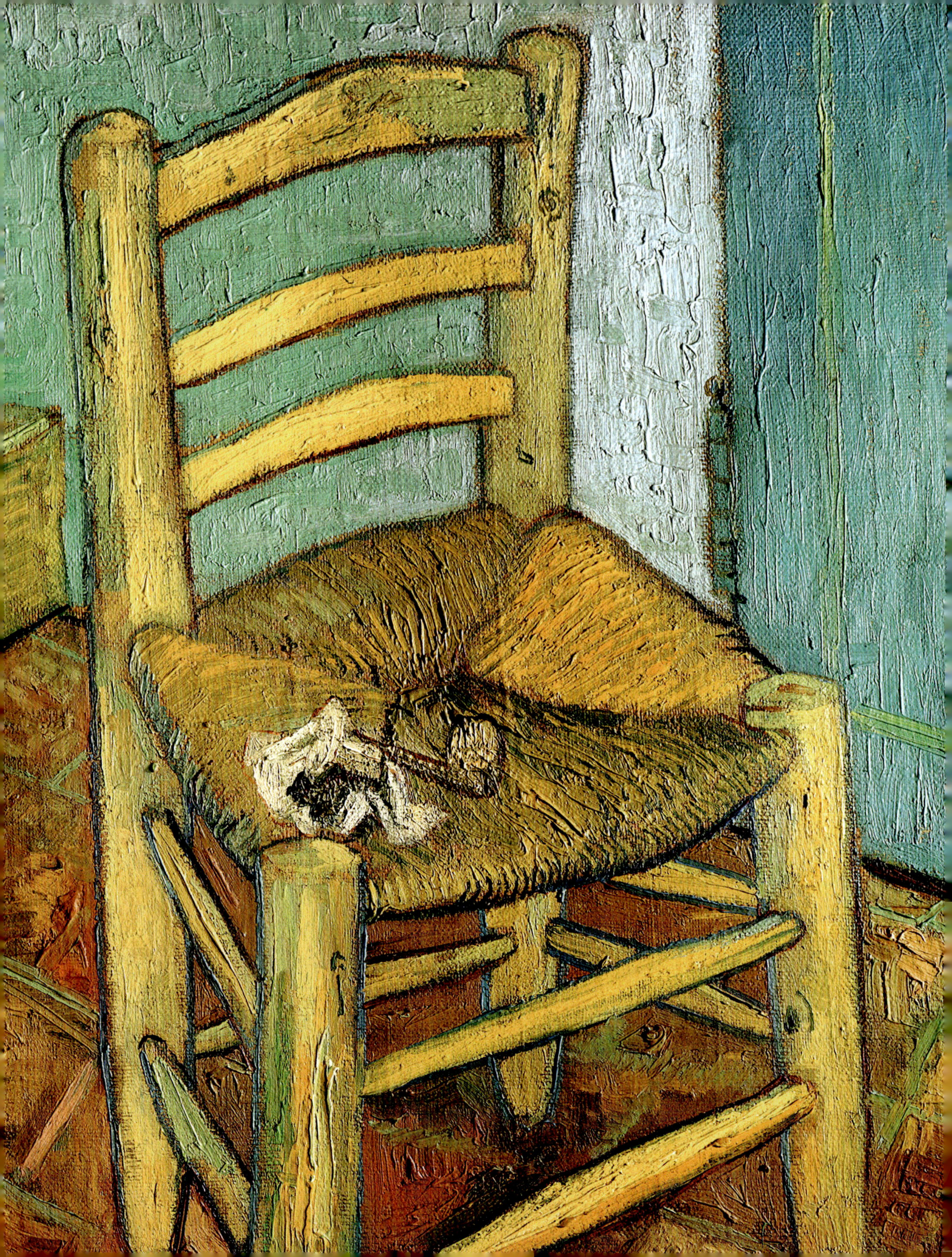

COLLABORATION

'Gauguin gives me courage to imagine, and the things of the imagination do indeed take on a more mysterious character'[1]

'I have an Arlésienne at last . . . knocked off in *one* hour', Vincent wrote excitedly to Theo on 3 November 1888.[2] It was thanks to Gauguin that he secured a model; the Frenchman's guile persuaded the respectable Marie Ginoux to pose. She later recounted how the two artists had tricked her into being painted by inviting her for coffee at the Yellow House. Gauguin then jested with her, saying 'your portrait will be hung in the Musée du Louvre in Paris.'[3] Madame Ginoux recalled this remark in 1922, thirty years before Van Gogh's *Arlésienne* was indeed acquired by the Louvre (the portrait now hangs in the Musée d'Orsay).

Having won Marie's agreement, the two artists swiftly set to work, producing a pair of contrasting works. In Van Gogh's *The Arlésienne* (fig. 87), the 40-year-old café proprietress wears the traditional costume, a dark blue dress and a lace fichu with a flower motif near the lower edge. Her hair is held back by a long ribbon. On the table lie her parasol and gloves, which Van Gogh added a few days later.[4] Ginoux always retained fond memories of 'Monsieur Vincent', describing him as the best man she had ever known.[5]

Detail of fig. 98 *Van Gogh's Chair*, National Gallery, London

Gauguin approached his Arlésienne very differently, making a large drawing while Van Gogh was speedily completing his painting. A few days later Gauguin used this sketch for a painting of the Café de la Gare with its patronne (fig. 88). Although Ginoux is in a similar pose to that in the Van Gogh, the atmosphere is very different. Van Gogh's Arlésienne is portrayed as pensive, her head resting on her hand, a posture traditionally associated with melancholy. Gauguin's Arlésienne appears worldly-wise in the setting of her café, with her elegant parasol and gloves replaced by a glass of absinthe, sugar and soda water.

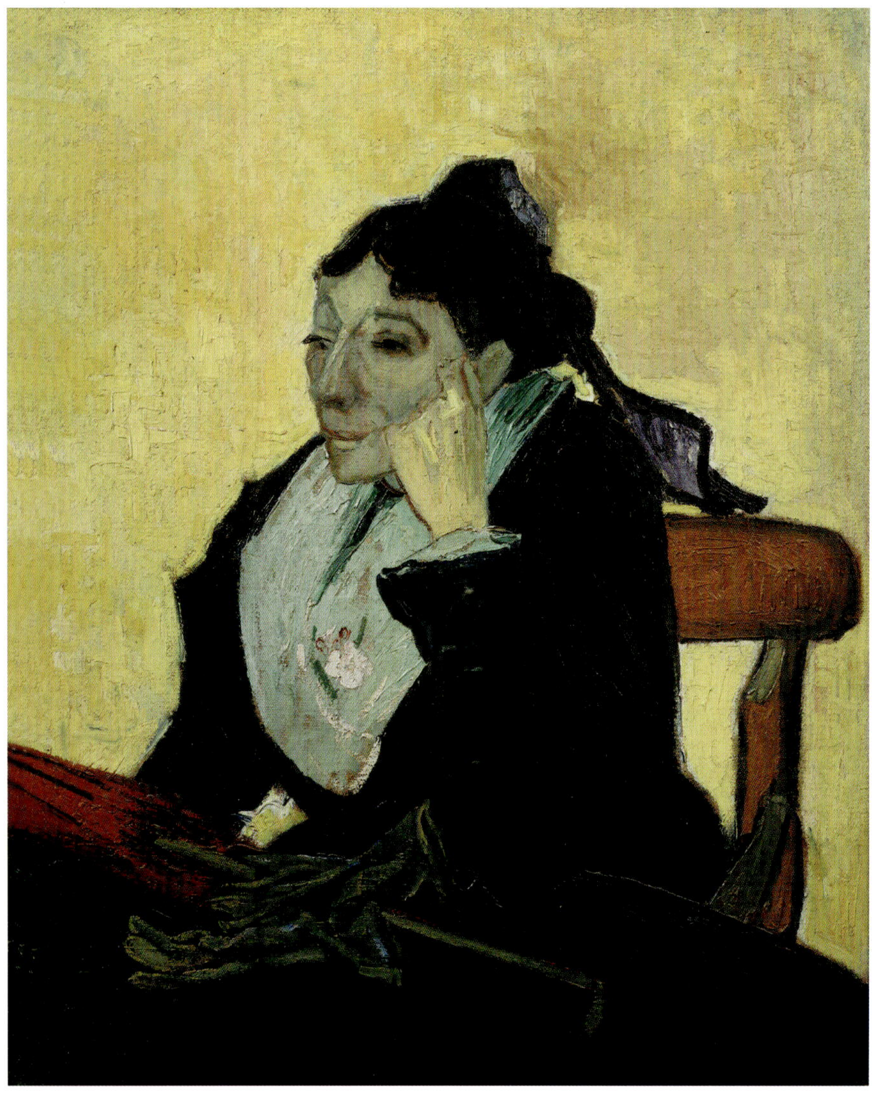

In the Gauguin portrait, painted in the studio of the Yellow House, the billiard table shelters the café's cat. Two groups of customers are at the rear. A man slumps over a table next to a Zouave sporting a képi. The postman Roulin with three exotically dressed and somewhat Japanese-looking women congregate around the other table. These were 'figures seen in the brothels', as Van Gogh commented, a suggestion that would hardly have gone down well with the patronne (or Roulin's wife).[6]

Gauguin's painting represents a direct homage to Van Gogh's *The Night Café* (fig. 66), a title the Frenchman adopted for his own work.[7] The room is similar to that depicted in the earlier Van Gogh, with the bright red walls. But despite the same setting and colours, the effect could hardly have been more different. Whereas Van Gogh focused on the café's harsh atmosphere, Gauguin created a portrait of Madame Ginoux in her environment. Both artists were continuing to spur the other on, while insisting on their individuality.

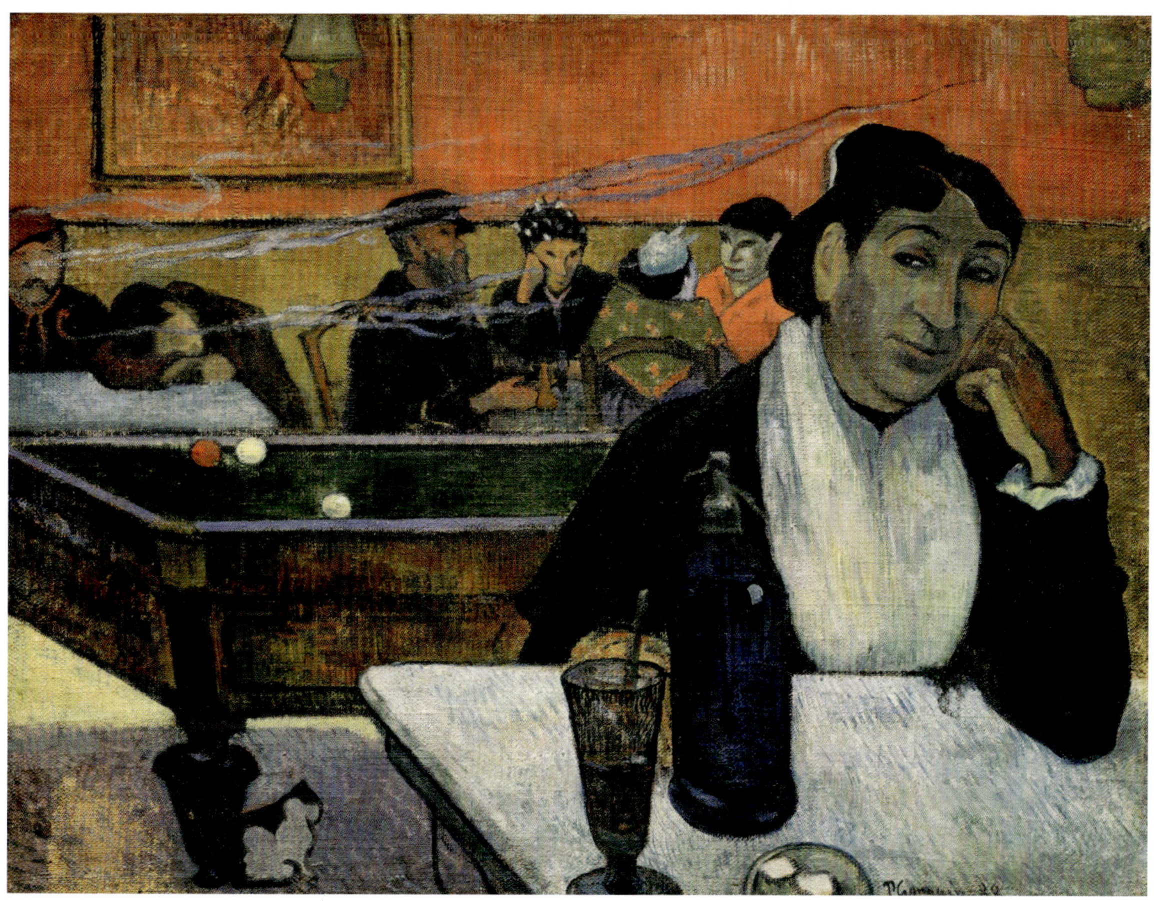

The two painters shared another subject following an inspiring walk through a vineyard on the southern slope of Montmajour. Vincent reported back to Theo: 'We saw a red vineyard, completely red like red wine. In the distance it became yellow, and then a green sky with a sun, fields violet and sparkling yellow here and there after the rain in which the setting sun was reflected.'[8]

Van Gogh painted his interpretation from memory back in the studio. *The Red Vineyard* (fig. 89) captures the view looking towards Arles, with its towers just visible on the far right of the horizon. The harvest had actually been gathered a month earlier, so the group of slightly clumsily painted grape-pickers are from his imagination. The fiery reds and oranges are illuminated by a powerful setting sun. It is often assumed that the red came from the grapes, but it would have been from the leaves quickly changing colour after the fruit had ripened. *The Red Vineyard* ended up being the only

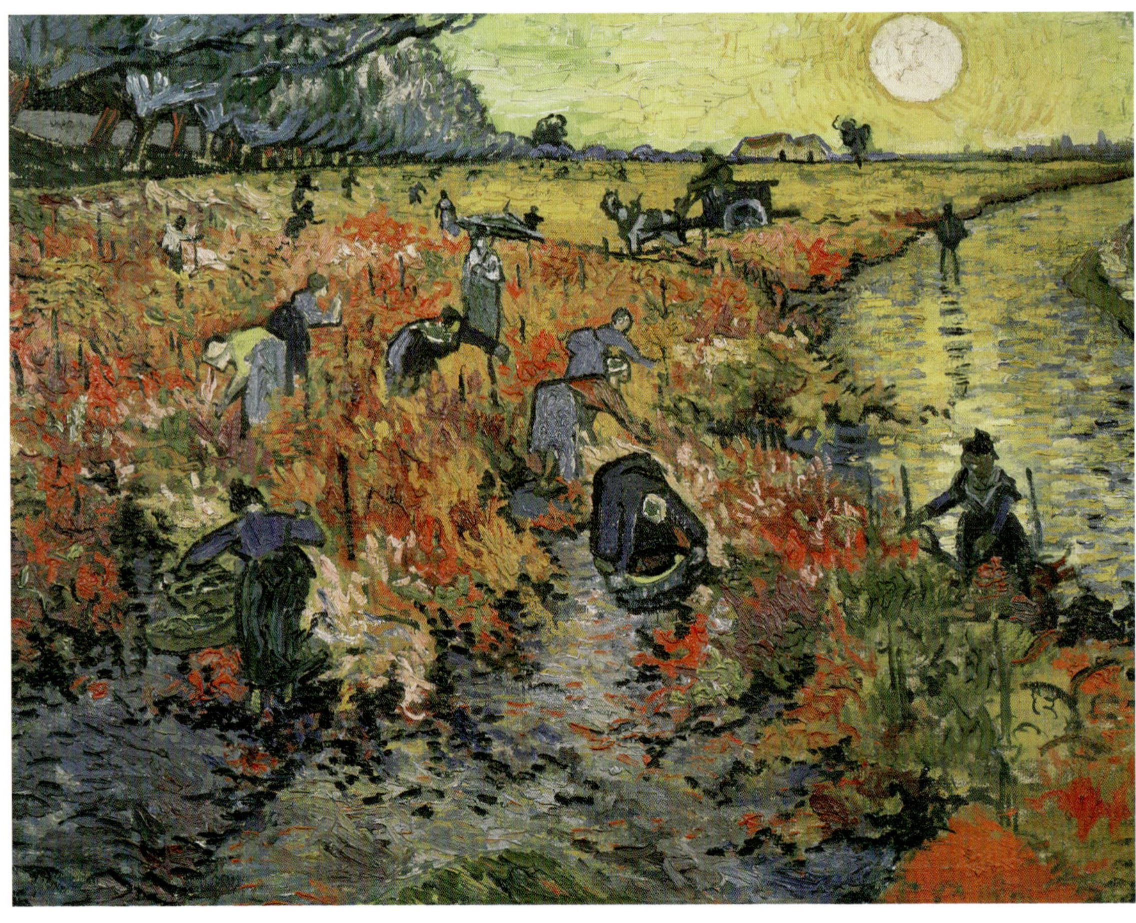

firmly documented painting which Van Gogh ever sold. After being shown in February 1890 at the exhibition of Les Vingt in Brussels, it was bought for 400 francs by the Belgian artist Anna Boch, the sister of his friend Eugène.

Gauguin produced a very different interpretation of the Montmajour vineyard, *Grape Harvest*, which he also entitled 'Human Misery' (fig. 90). In the centre a dejected woman sits with her head resting in her hands. At the side stands an unsettling figure in black, with a container for grapes. Behind them a pair of Breton women stoop over a sea of vines. Gauguin regarded this highly enigmatic work as his 'best canvas of this year'.[9]

Another early evening walk provided further inspiration. After witnessing a 'lemon yellow sunset, mysterious, of extraordinary beauty', Van Gogh used the scene to paint a sower, one of his favourite themes.[10] *Sower with setting Sun* (fig. 91) is dominated by the tree with its sparse autumnal leaves, strongly dividing the composition in the style of Japanese

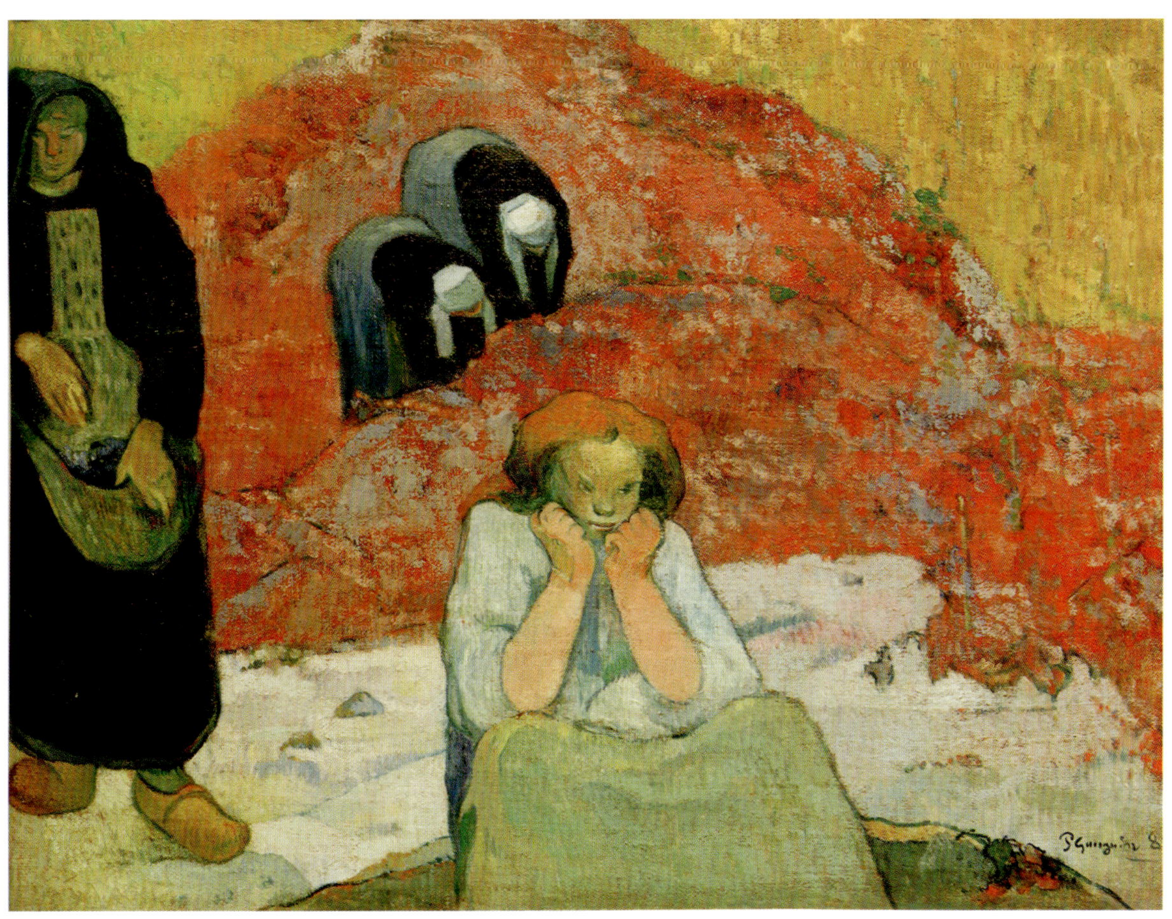

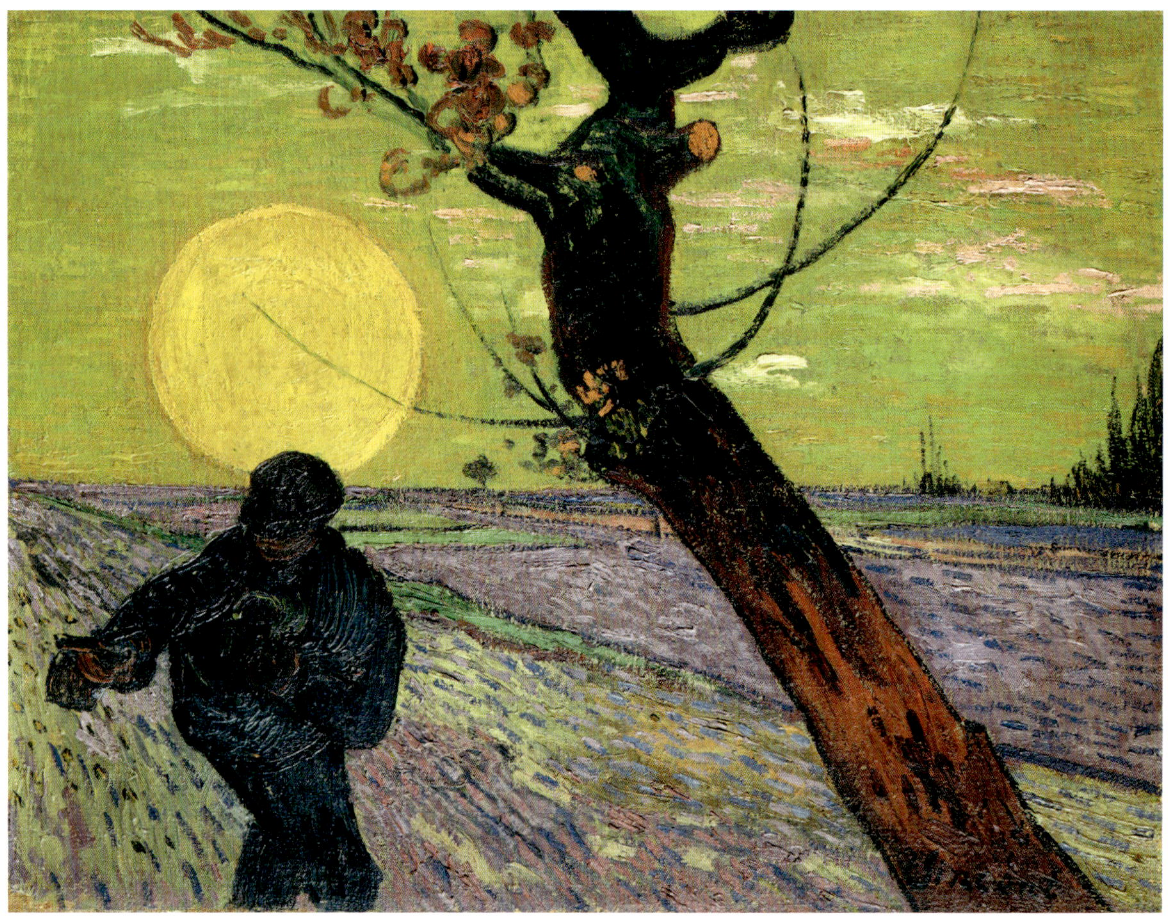

fig. 91 *Sower with setting Sun*, November 1888, oil on jute, 74 x 93 cm, Bührle Collection, Zurich (F450)

prints. Van Gogh may also have been influenced by Gauguin's *The Vision of the Sermon*, painted in Pont-Aven two months earlier, a composition which is also bisected by a tree.[11]

In Van Gogh's autumnal scene the sun becomes a halo for the silhouetted farmer, whose features can barely be discerned as twilight approaches. Van Gogh described his colours: 'Immense lemon yellow disc for the sun. Green-yellow sky with pink clouds. The field is violet, the sower and the tree Prussian Blue.'[12] The setting sun and sower together symbolise the cycle of death and rebirth. Van Gogh signed the painting on the base of the trunk, an indication that he was pleased with the result.

Gauguin encouraged Van Gogh to work from memory, prompting Vincent to create two crowd scenes.[13] The first, *Arena in Arles* (fig. 92), depicts a bullfight in the Roman amphitheatre. As the Dutchman had noted a few months earlier, 'the bullring looks so beautiful when there's sunshine and a crowd.'[14] The fights took place in April and September (when Van Gogh had gone there with Boch), so by the time of Gauguin's arrival there was no chance to paint the scene from life.

In *Arena in Arles* it is the spectators, not the fight nor the imposing Roman architecture, that dominate the scene. Indeed the small, indistinct bull is almost lost on the sand. Most of the crowd is only loosely sketched in, with a black line or two to pick out an individual. It is interesting to compare Van Gogh's close-up view of the crowd with an early postcard, which highlights the arena's vast scale (fig. 93). Pennell, who had been in Arles for the September bullfight, also drew the scene. Positioned slightly higher up, Pennell emphasises the arena's scale, with the audience crammed below (fig. 94).

Applying his imagination to a second crowd scene, Van Gogh then painted *Dance Hall in Arles* (fig. 95). It depicts an evening performance at the Folies Arlésiennes, a café-concert hall for dances and theatrical events.[15] The mass of people has become a mosaic, with individuals delineated by cloisonnist lines. On the right, the woman just below the Zouave in the red képi is Augustine Roulin, the postman's wife, similar to how she appears in Van Gogh's portrait and *La berceuse* (figs. 102 and 104). Vincent proudly told Theo that he was beginning 'to compose from memory'.[16]

Van Gogh then worked on a series of portraits, including one of Gauguin (fig. 97). For sixty years this painting was considered a fake, but it has now been confirmed as authentic.[17] It is not surprising that it was once questioned, since it is an unusually sketchy work for Van Gogh, and perhaps an unfinished study for something more ambitious that was never attempted. Nevertheless, this portrait is important in documenting the collaboration between the two artists in Arles. While Van Gogh was attempting to depict Gauguin, his friend was completing *The Painter of Sunflowers*, showing the Dutchman working on his iconic still life.[18]

In another self-portrait (fig. 96) made around this time Van Gogh adopts a pose similar to the one painted two months earlier for Gauguin (fig. 71). In the earlier work, Van Gogh had a shaven head, although by now his hair has grown back. In this later picture he appears gentler than in the strident image he presented to Gauguin. Van Gogh dedicated his new picture to Charles Laval, an artist friend of Gauguin's (Laval and Gauguin had travelled together to Martinique the year before and Laval had stayed on in Brittany after Gauguin's departure for Arles). Laval had sent his self-portrait from Pont-Aven, so Van Gogh was completing the exchange.[19]

Van Gogh's most unusual 'portraits' done during Gauguin's stay were twin paintings of the chairs they normally occupied, set on the red tiles of the

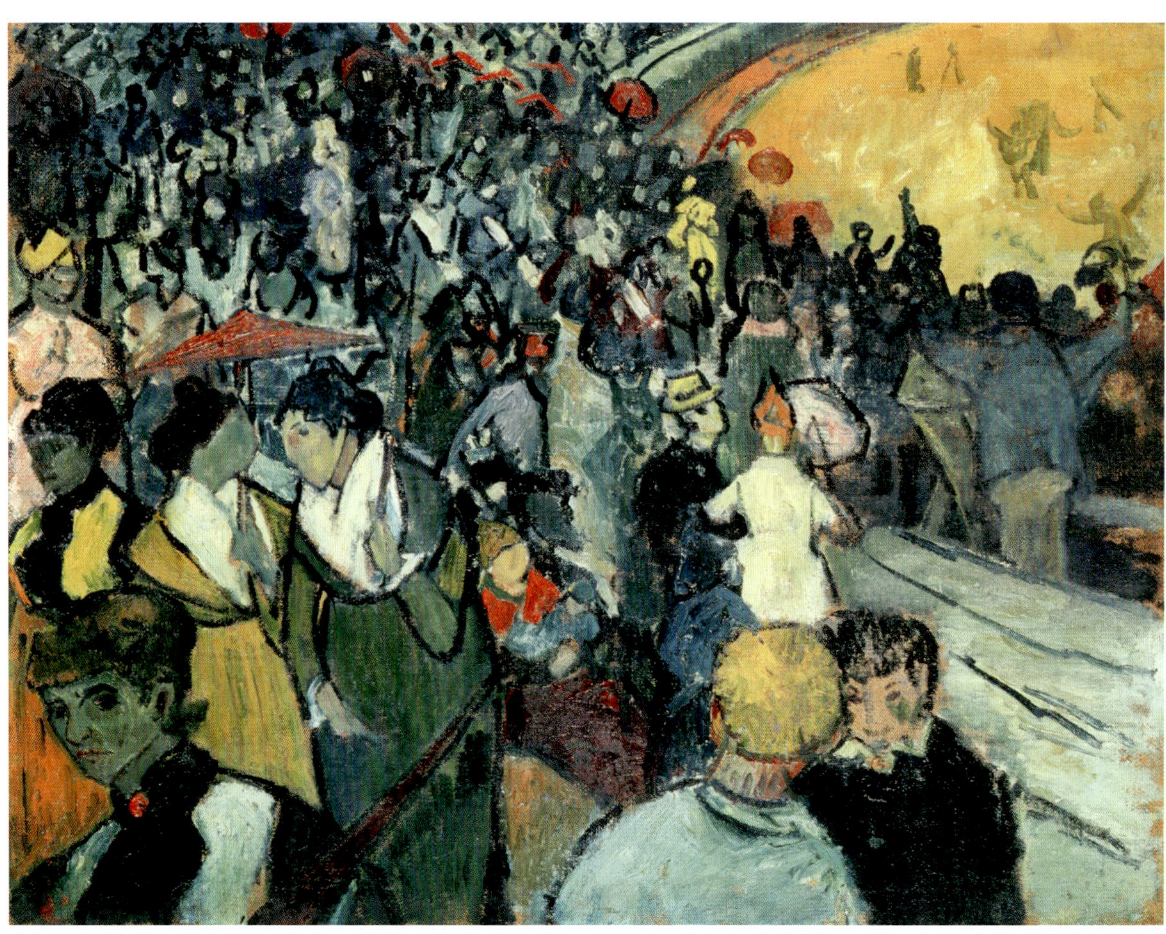

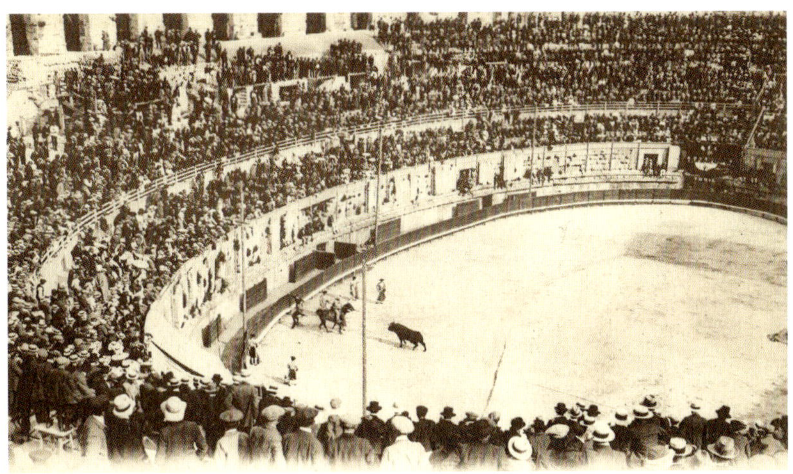

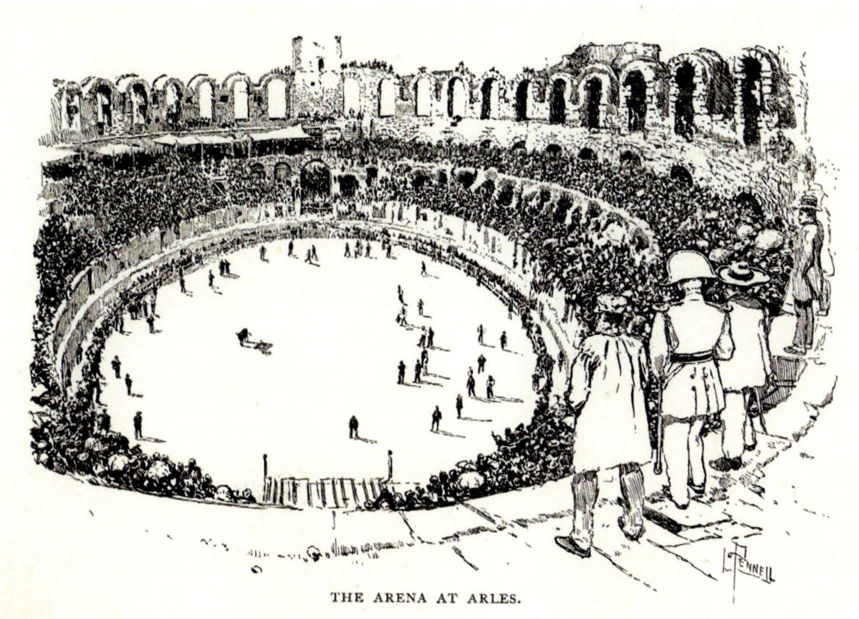

Yellow House. Gauguin was represented by his armchair, illuminated by the newly-installed gaslight.[22] On the seat is a glowing candle and two novels, suggesting that Gauguin would relax in comfort to read in the evenings. The chair appears to be of walnut wood, which would have matched the bed and other furniture in the visitor's room.

Van Gogh then went on to paint what he described as 'my own empty chair, a deal chair with a pipe and tobacco pouch' (fig. 98). His 'rustic'

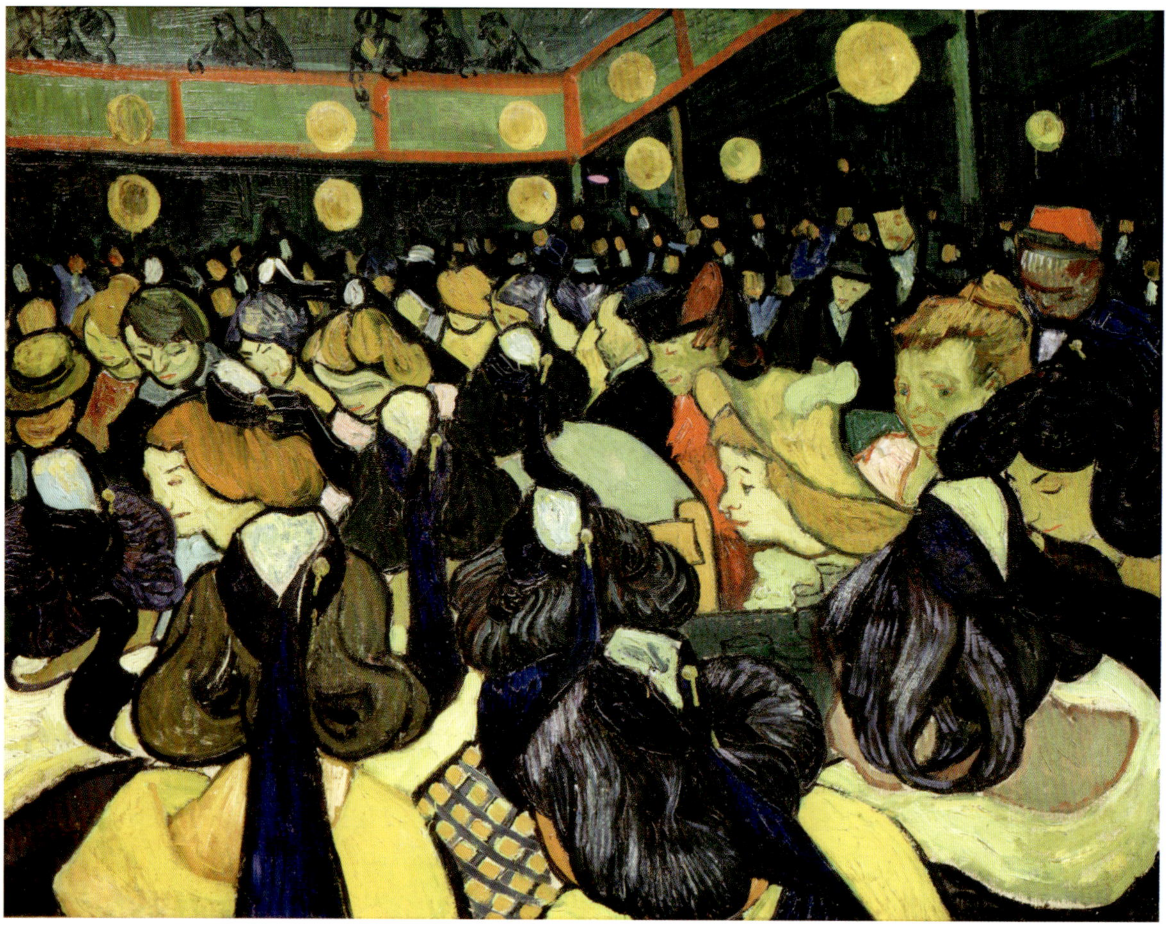

straw-covered chair was probably one of a set of a dozen he had bought in September, while awaiting his friend's arrival.[23] This simple piece of furniture reflects a more modest man, in contrast to the self-assured and ambitious Gauguin. What is striking is the perspective, with the chair almost thrusting into the viewer's space. Although Van Gogh completed most of the painting of his own chair in December, he finished it January, adding his pipe and tobacco.[24] These two intimate objects represent a miniature still life, suggestive of a reflective personality. Smoking was one of Van Gogh's constant pleasures, helping him to relax. The significance of the signed box at the back, filled with what are probably sprouting onions (or garlic), remains a mystery.

It is often assumed that Van Gogh and Gauguin continually rowed, since their collaboration ended badly. The relationship was never entirely easy, and certainly

ABOVE fig. 95 *Dance Hall in Arles*, November–December 1888, oil on canvas, 65 x 86 cm, Musée d'Orsay, Paris (F547)

RIGHT fig. 96 *Self-portrait for Laval*, November–December 1888, oil on canvas, 46 x 38 cm, private collection (F501)

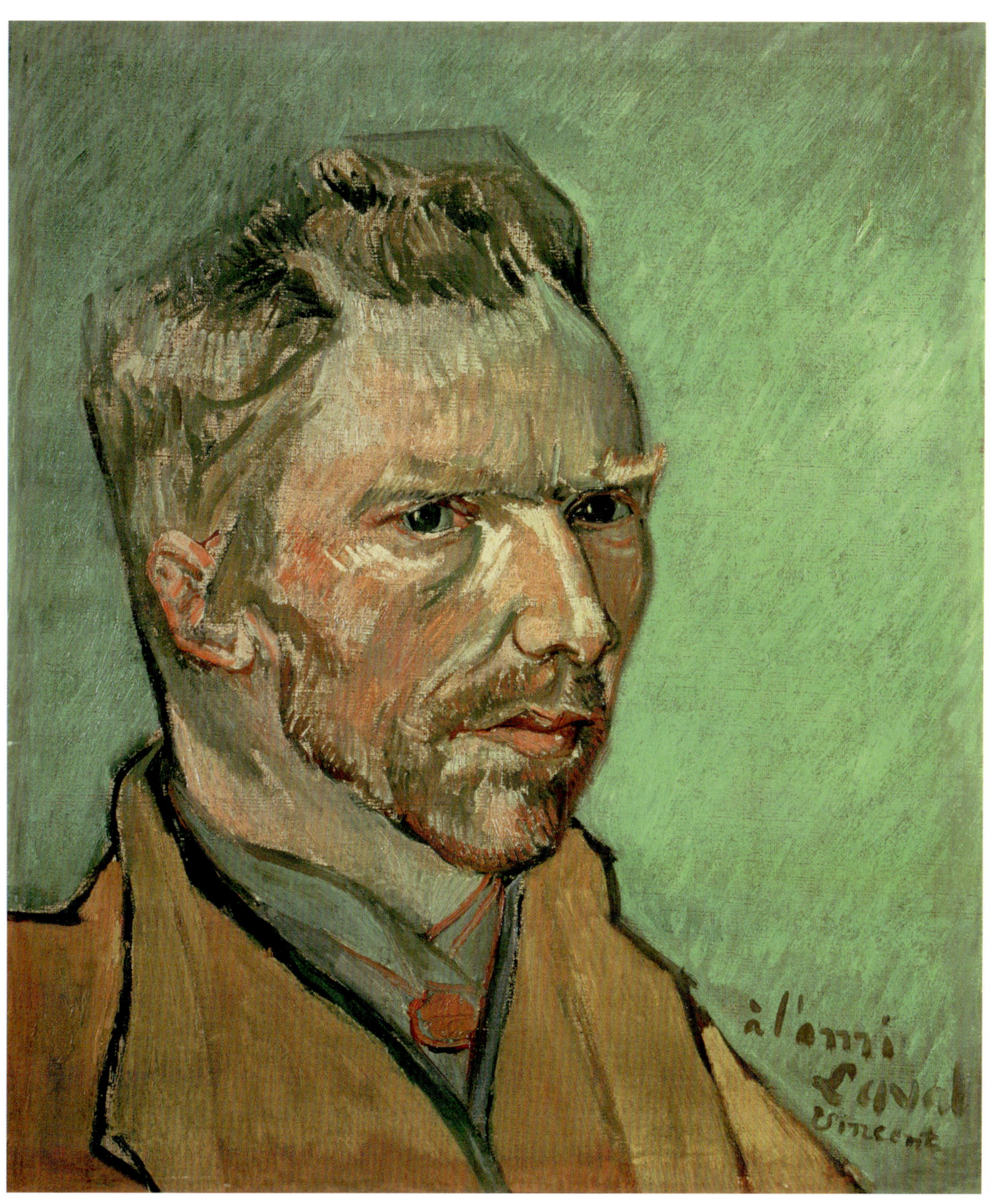
à l'ami
Laval
Vincent

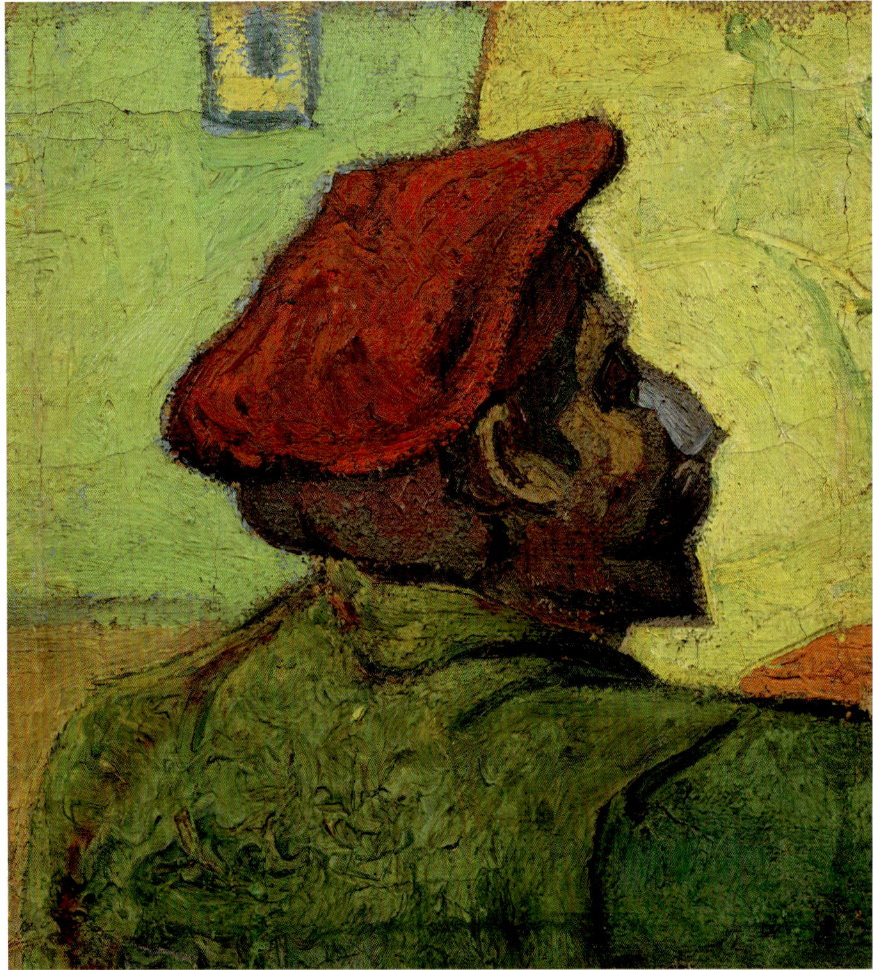

became more fraught. Van Gogh found it difficult to make compromises and was often stubborn. Gauguin, who was five years older and had great self-confidence, was an equally difficult character. While Gauguin had begun to market his paintings, Van Gogh had failed to sell his work – and felt increasingly intimidated by Gauguin's success. But despite their very different personalities, the few weeks they worked together in Arles proved to be highly productive.

Arles and the Yellow House provided what both artists needed. They had companionship, a comfortable home, a regular income from Theo, an abundance of inspiring landscapes to paint and, above all, the stimulation of being able to discuss their work. On 22 November, a month after his friend's arrival, Vincent told Theo that he was 'very pleased to have such good company as Gauguin's'.[25]

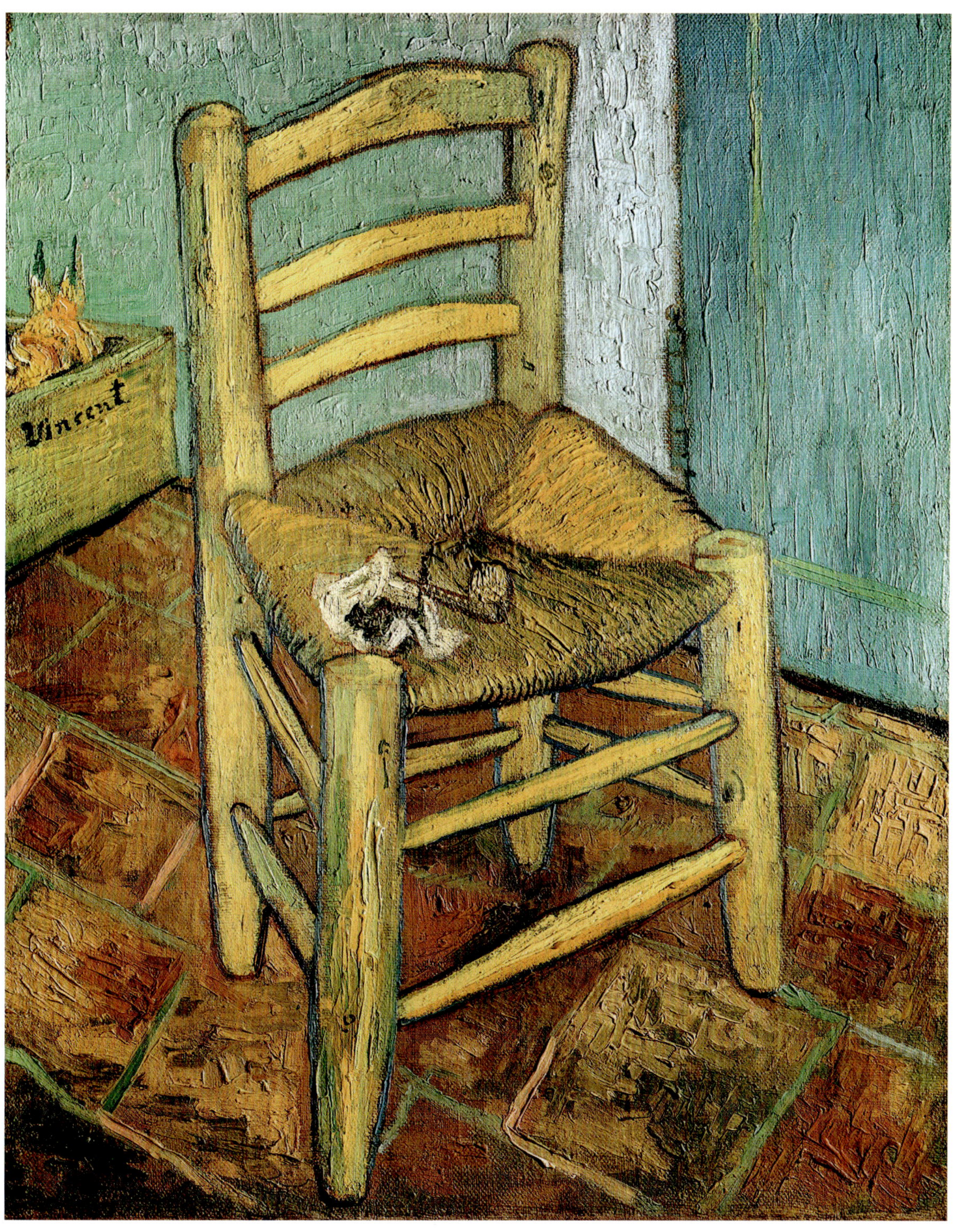

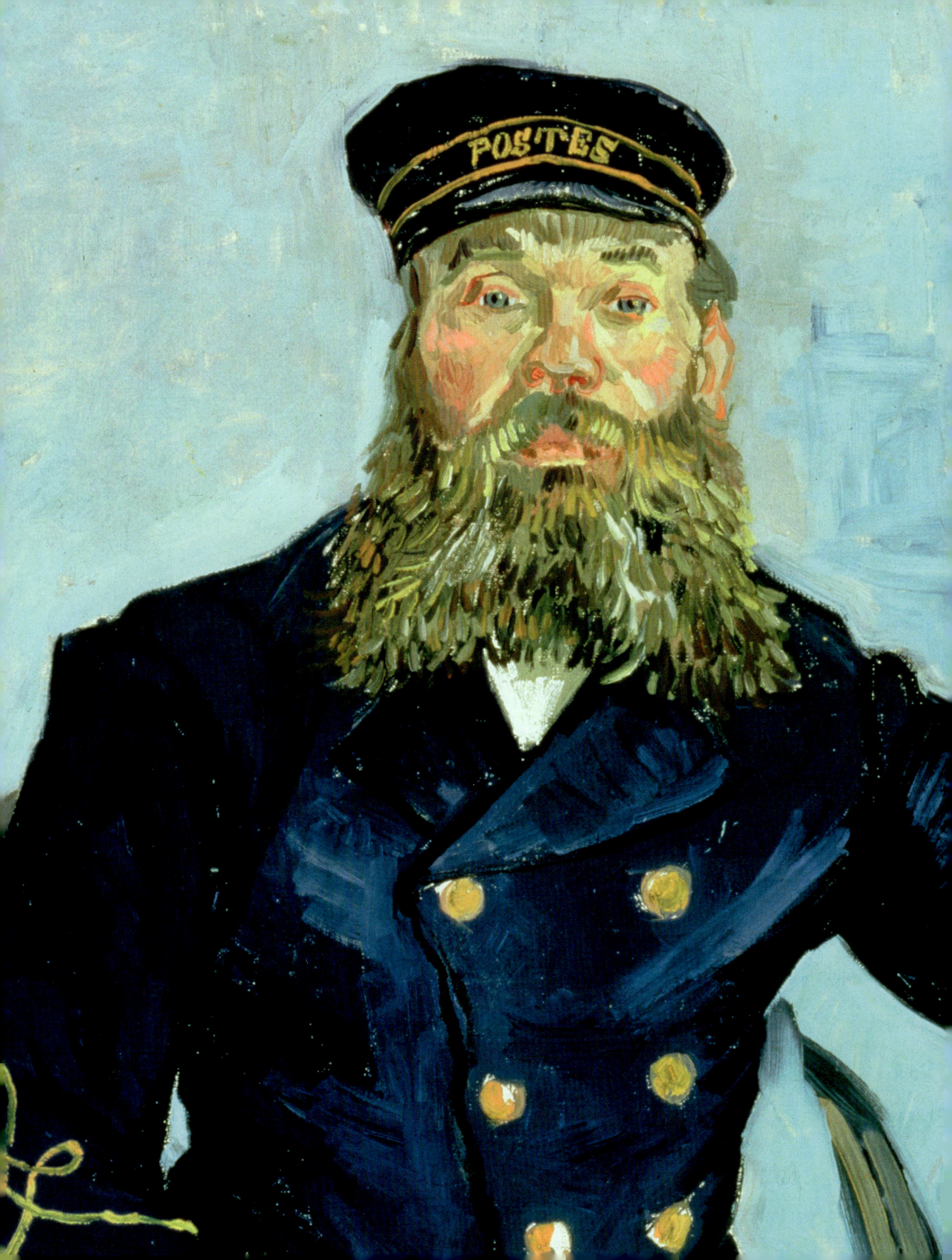

CHAPTER FIFTEEN

POSTMAN ROULIN

'Roulin has been excellent to us, and I dare believe that he'll remain a staunch friend'[1]

Joseph Roulin, the bearded postman, became Van Gogh's closest Arles friend. Aged 47, he was the clerk responsible for loading post at the railway station and lived with his family very close by. The two men became drinking companions, usually meeting at the Café de la Gare. Van Gogh described his new companion as 'a raging republican' and a particularly 'interesting' man.[2]

Roulin and his family soon became Van Gogh's most important subjects for portraits. Vincent first painted Roulin on 31 July 1888 – the day that the postman's wife gave birth to their daughter, Marcelle. Roulin can hardly have been at his most relaxed on this occasion, but perhaps he was looking for an excuse to be out of the house. Van Gogh described his model as 'a *postman* in a blue uniform with gold trimmings, a big, bearded face, very Socratic'.[3] Instead of paying Roulin to sit, the artist took him out to eat and drink, although this ended up costing just as much.

In the three-quarter-length portrait (fig. 99), Roulin sits in a cane armchair, the same one as in *The Mousmé* (fig. 50). His bulky frame fills most of the composition and his beard bushes out below his face, creating a benign demeanour. Roulin's dark blue uniform with golden yellow braid and a cap proudly proclaims his profession. As so often in Van Gogh's work, the arms and hands are clumsily painted. This initial portrait would eventually lead to a much more ambitious scheme four months later. On 1 December Vincent reported to Theo: 'I've done the portraits of *an entire family* . . . the man, his wife, the baby, the young boy and the 16-year-old

Detail of fig. 99 *Joseph Roulin*, Museum of Fine Arts, Boston

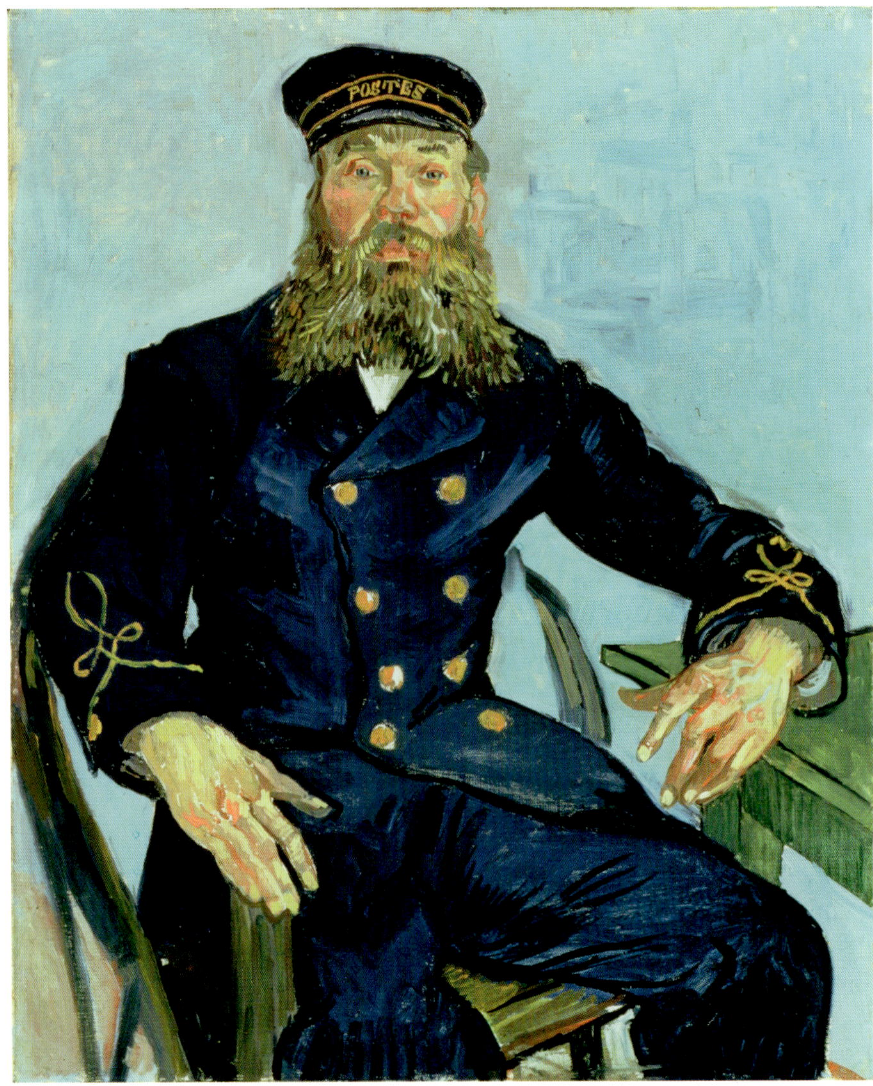

son, all characters and very French, although they have a Russian look.'[4] These paintings were executed very quickly, probably in just over a week. Although in similar sizes, they vary in format, pose, background and style (and quality), and so can only loosely be regarded as a set. The head-and-shoulders portrait of Joseph (fig. 100) is more quickly worked and stylised than the first summer picture.[5] Roulin's dark blue uniform is boldly set against a contrasting deep yellowy background.

Van Gogh's portrait of Roulin's 37-year-old wife Augustine is very different (fig. 102). She sits in another armchair beside a window, outside

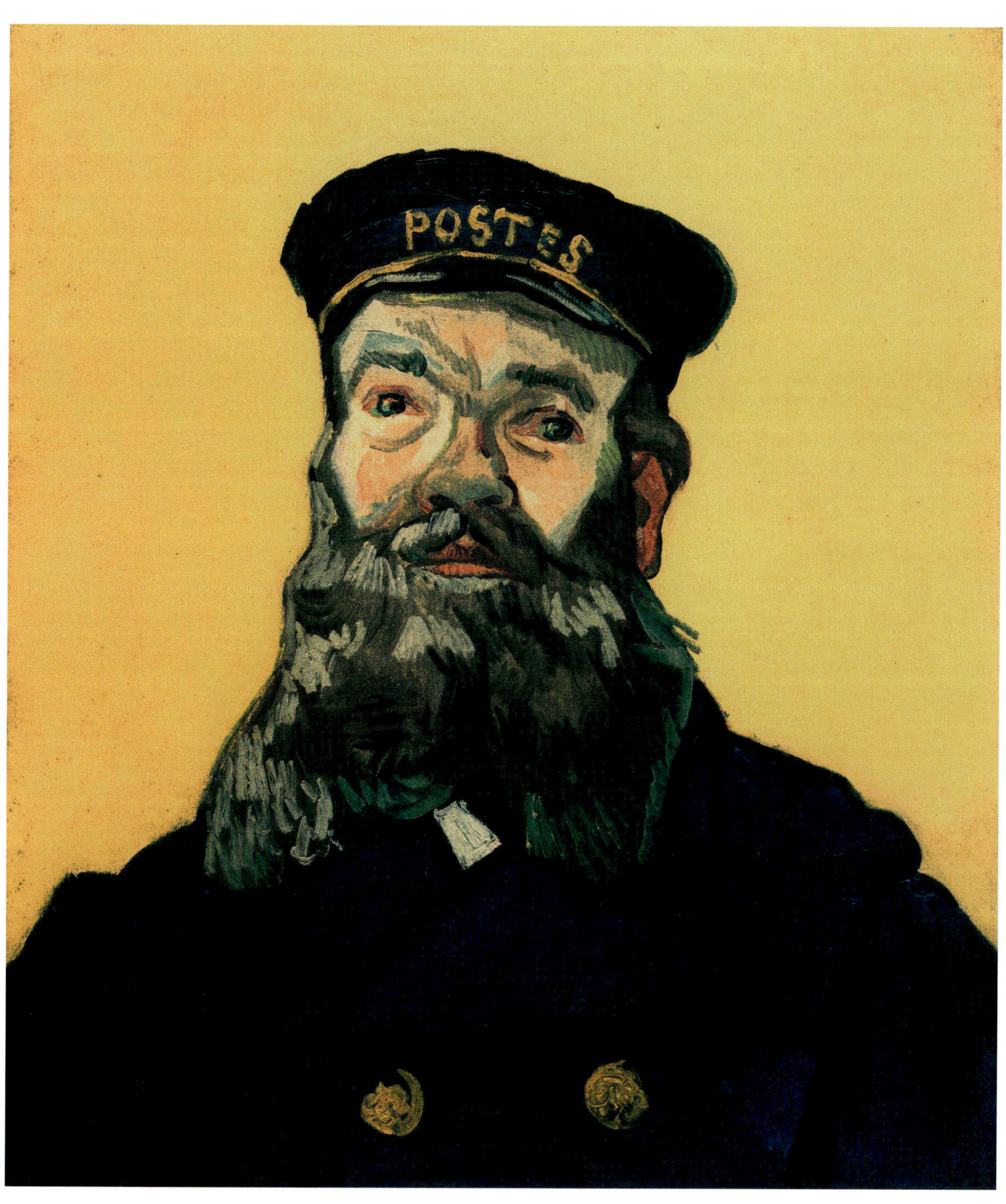
POSTES

of which are six large pots of bulbs and what appears to be a winding path. The bulbs and path must be invented elements, rather than representing what actually lay beyond the studio. Gauguin also did his own painting of Augustine, giving her more rounded facial features (fig. 101). Although the compositions are similar, the window is out of view and part of a door is visible. In the background Gauguin added a depiction of the lower part of one of his own paintings (loosely interpreted), a landscape he had just completed in Arles, *Blue Trees*.[6] The two artists probably painted Madame Roulin on the same occasion, although there are minor differences in the two portraits, such as the shaped top of the chair and Augustine's neckline.

Van Gogh also painted portraits of Augustine holding her four-month infant Marcelle and of the baby by itself. Seeing mother and daughter together reminded Van Gogh of his time in The Hague, six years earlier,

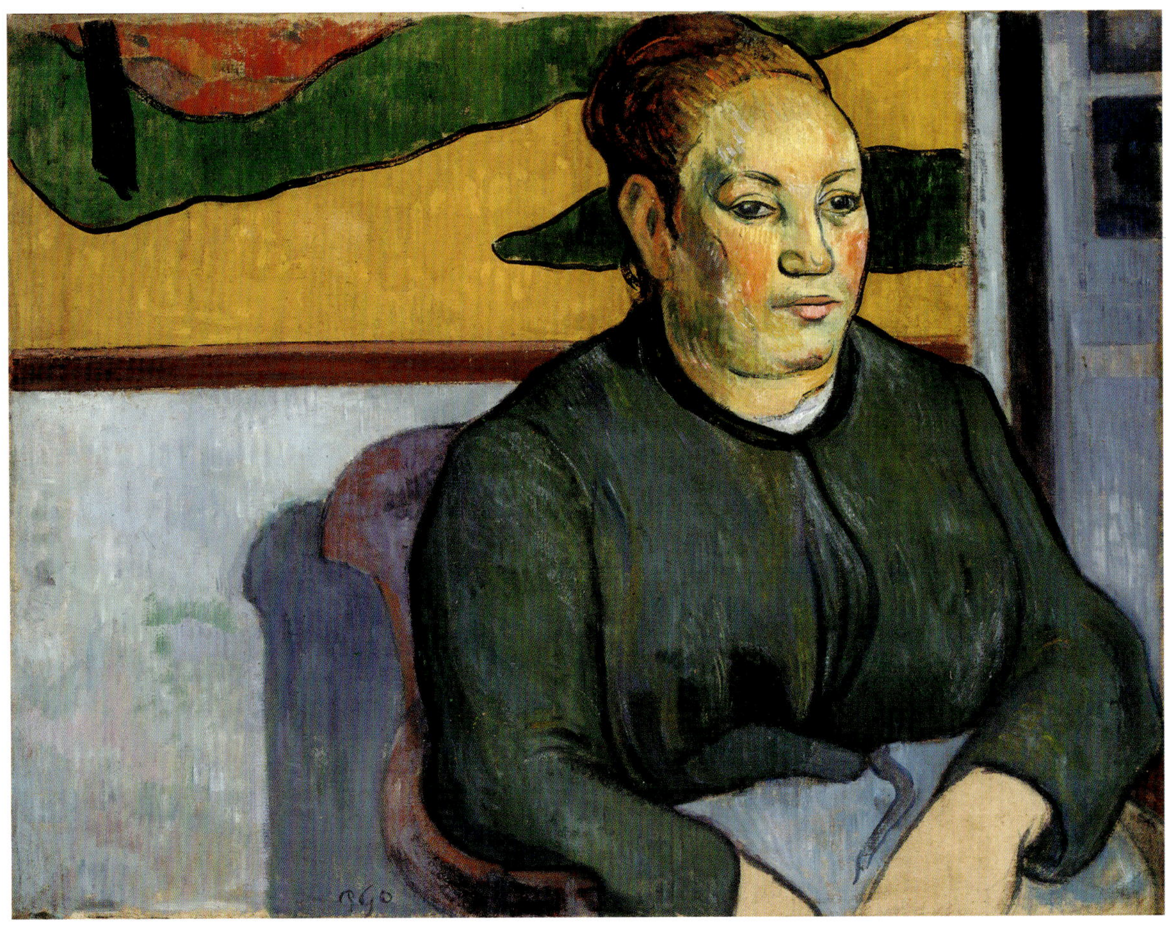

when his companion Sien had given birth to a boy named Willem Hoornik (by another man). On both occasions he was struck by the 'infinite' expression in the eyes of the newborn baby.[7]

Among the most successful of the Roulin portraits was a pair of the elder son, Armand, an apprentice blacksmith. Aged 17, he worked in Lambesc, a village east of Arles where the family had come from.[8] In one of the paintings he is jauntily dressed in a yellow jacket and blue hat, with an unusually pensive expression for a dapper young man (fig. 103). Van Gogh completed the set of portraits with the younger son Camille, a schoolboy of 11.

The Roulins were given the set to thank them for sitting. Over the next couple of months, Van Gogh went on to make further portraits. The most important of these was a stylised portrait of Augustine, which he entitled *La berceuse* (The Cradle Rocker) (fig. 104). The plump mother is holding a rope, which would have been attached to Marcelle's crib.[9] She sits in the

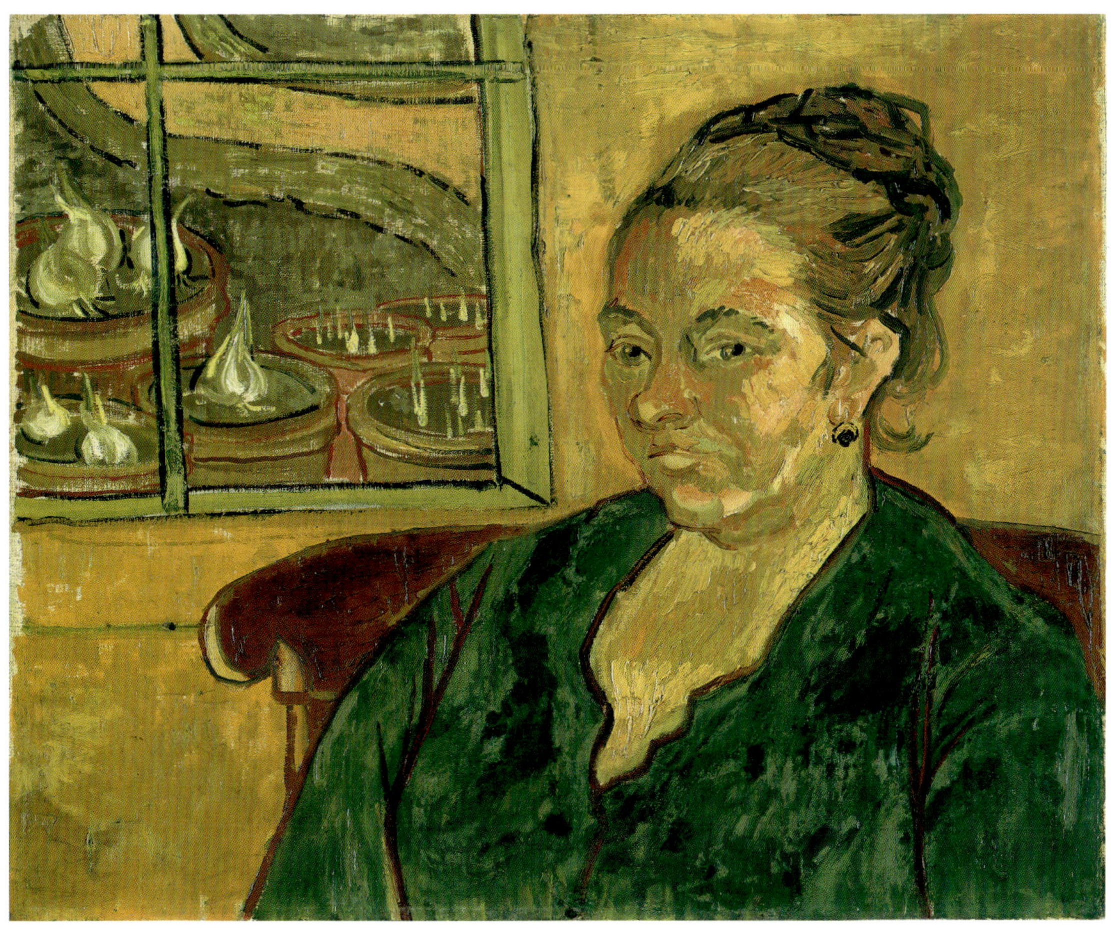

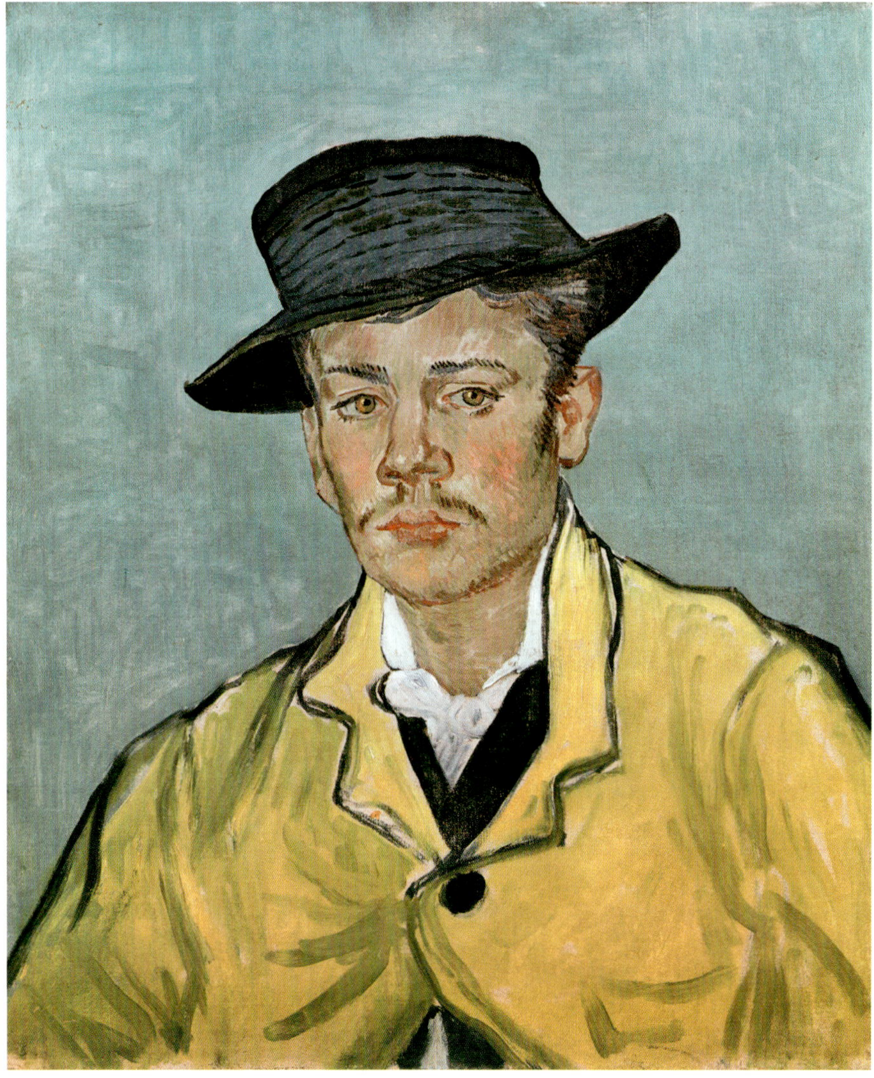

same chair as in the earlier portrait (fig. 102), positioned on the red-tiled studio floor and with a backdrop of gaily patterned wallpaper conjured up from Van Gogh's imagination. However her features are noticeably different from the previous portrait, giving her a more maternal air. He went on to do four other versions of this picture, an indication of its importance.

Van Gogh ultimately painted twenty-three portraits of the Roulin family, accounting for just over half his Arles portraits.[10] The family ended up selling the ones they had been given once the artist's paintings became marketable, with eight going to the Parisian dealer Ambroise Vollard in

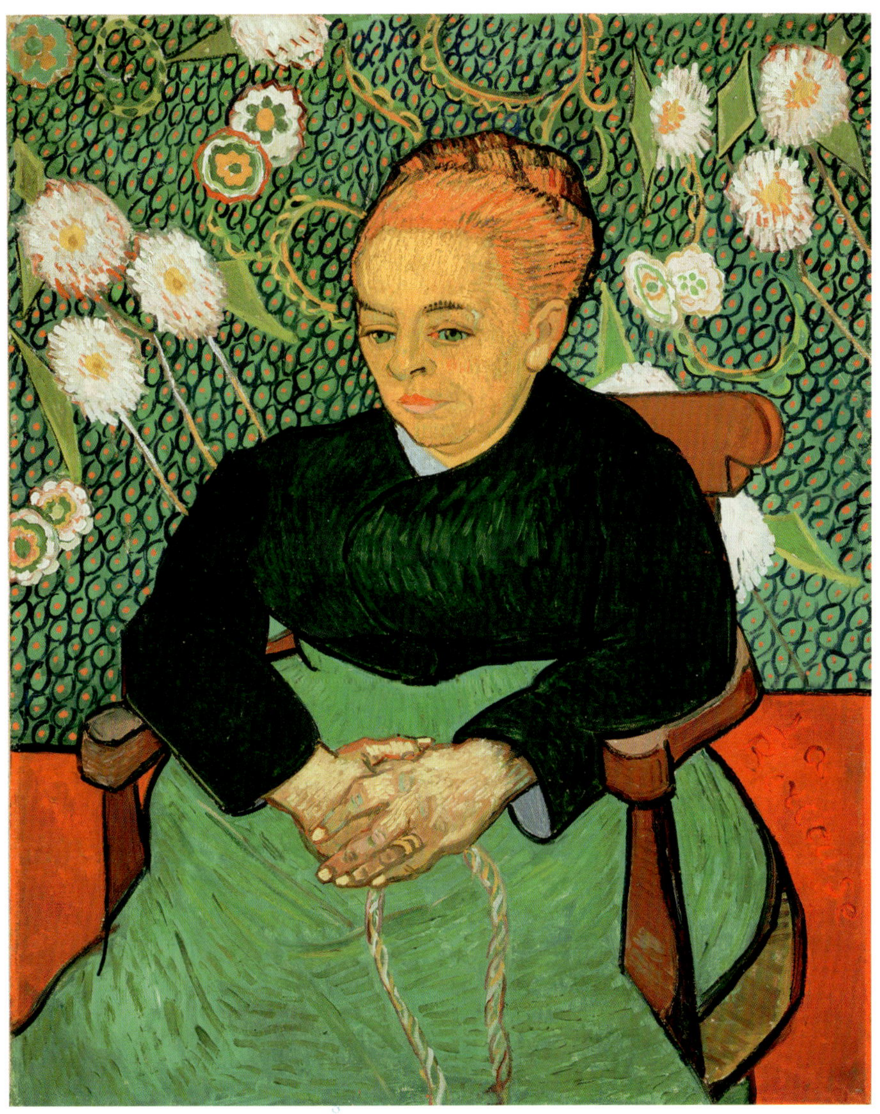

1900.[11] Joseph Roulin died three years later in Marseille and his wife Augustine lived until 1930.

Their daughter Marcelle was to become the last of Van Gogh's surviving sitters. In 1955 she was interviewed about the artist.[12] Obviously she had no direct memories, but the artist had been much discussed within the family. Her father, the postman, would say that Van Gogh often came 'to have soup' at their home. Marcelle, whom Van Gogh saw on the day of her birth, died in 1980, aged 91.

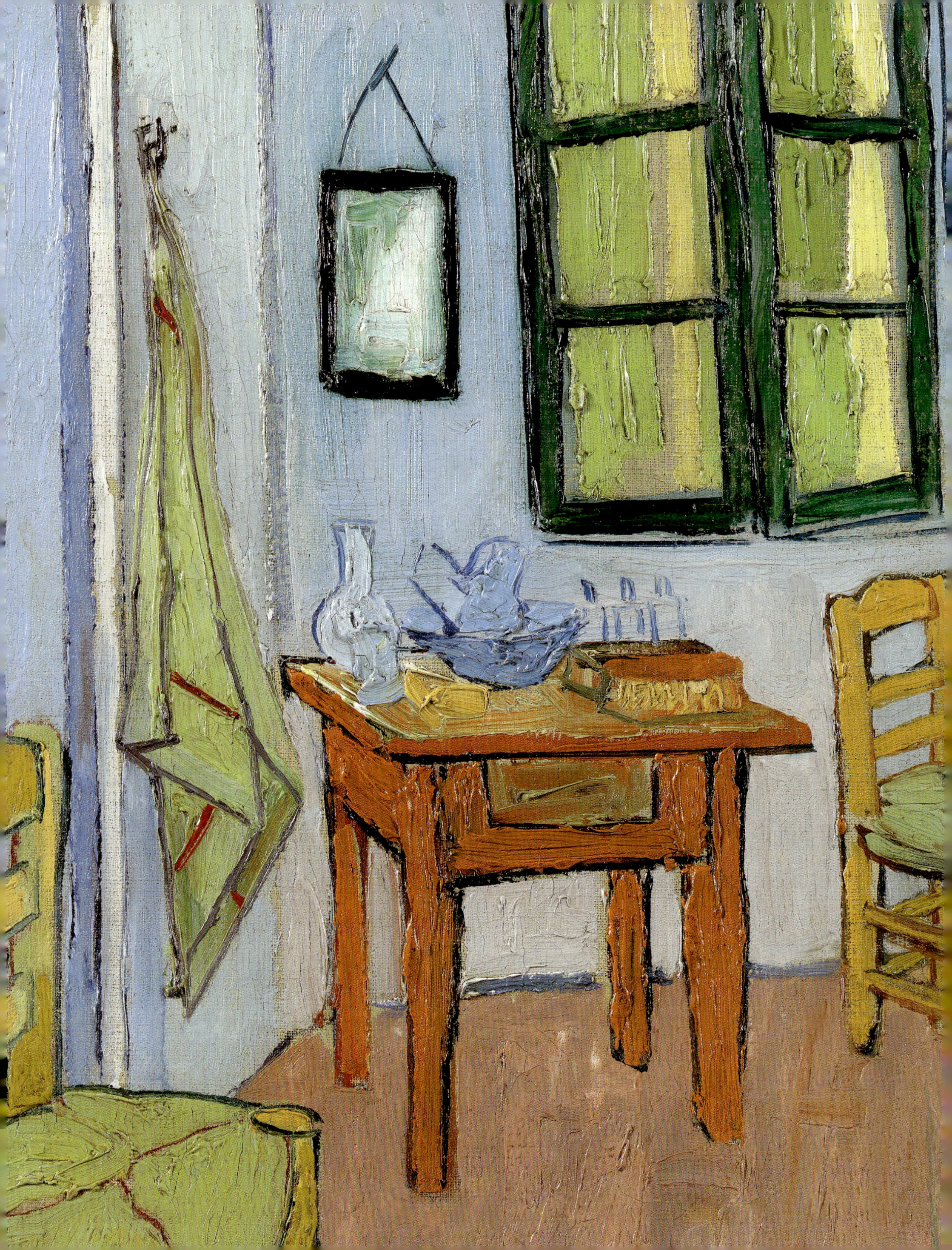

CHAPTER SIXTEEN

OUT OF HIS MIND

'In my mental or nervous fever or madness, I don't quite know what to say or how to name it, my thoughts sailed over many seas'[1]

Van Gogh's hopes for the Yellow House came to a tragic end on the night of 23 December 1888. Trouble had begun looming earlier that month. A fortnight earlier there had been an unfortunate incident in a local bar. As Gauguin later claimed, Van Gogh picked up his absinthe: 'Suddenly he flung his glass and the contents at my head. I avoided the blow and, wrestling him at the chest, I left the café.'[2] The following day Gauguin wrote to Theo to say that he would be returning to Paris. 'Vincent and I can absolutely not live side by side without trouble, as a result of incompatibility of temperament, and both he and I need tranquility for our work', he explained.[3] Gauguin's threat to leave was extremely disturbing for Van Gogh.

The two men made up over the next few days and went on an exhilarating day trip by train to Montpellier, seventy kilometres west of Arles. Their goal was the Musée Fabre, to see its important collection of mid-nineteenth-century paintings donated by the collector Alfred Bruyas. The visit went successfully and the following morning Gauguin told Van Gogh that he felt his 'old self coming back'.[4]

During the evening of Saturday 22 December Gauguin wrote a long letter to his Parisian friend Emile Schuffenecker, saying that he had decided to remain in Arles: 'I am not coming yet. My situation here is difficult; I owe [Theo] Van Gogh and Vincent a great deal and despite some disagreement I cannot hold it against an excellent soul who is ill, who suffers, and asks for me.'[5]

Sunday 23 December was to prove the fateful date. It was the fourth day of continuous rain and the two artists stayed at home, working beside each other in the studio. Sunday for them was like any other day; their work was their life. During the day a letter came from Theo (post normally arrived overnight from Paris and was delivered on Sundays). Vincent opened it with relief; it contained the eagerly awaited 100 francs in cash – the allowance which Theo regularly sent for the two artists.[6]

Although the money was most welcome, the news in the letter was not. A fortnight earlier, on around 10 December, Theo had encountered a Dutch friend, 26-year-old Johanna (Jo) Bonger, who was visiting Paris. The previous year Theo had gone to Amsterdam to propose to her, but Jo had turned him down, partly because she was involved with another man.[7] This time the situation was different and they enjoyed a whirlwind romance. One week after meeting, Jo agreed to marry.

Most writers have assumed that Vincent did not hear about Theo's engagement until after he slashed his ear, but the news almost certainly reached him *on* 23 December. Two days earlier Theo had written to their mother, asking her permission to marry. He would have wanted to share the exciting news with Vincent as soon as possible after that (and had he delayed, Vincent might have heard indirectly from his mother).[8] Jo also appears to have written to her older brother Hendrik on 22 December, since he responded with a congratulatory telegram the following day. There is every reason to think that Theo would have contacted his own older brother at the same time.[9]

Vincent must therefore have learned about the engagement only a few hours *before* he mutilated his ear.[10] It is almost inconceivable that he would have received the letter the following day, when he was extremely ill in hospital, and he appears to have known the news by Christmas Day, when Theo saw him in hospital. After his visit, Theo reported back to Jo that 'when I mentioned you to him he evidently knew who & what I meant.'[11] Presumably Theo's 'mention' was to check that the letter had indeed reached his brother. This timing is backed up by a much later account by the son of Theo and Jo, Vincent Willem, who wrote in the 1950s: 'The trouble with Gauguin in Arles started right after Vincent heard from Theo that he intended to marry . . . It must have passed through his [Vincent's] mind that he would lose his support.'[12]

Theo would soon have a wife and then probably children to support (in fact their child, Vincent Willem, was born in January 1890, nine months and two weeks after their wedding, fig. 105). This would mean that Vincent's financial allowance from Theo might be under threat. Vincent had been receiving these regular payments for nearly eight years and without them he could never have survived as an artist. Equally important, he also feared that he would lose the emotional support of Theo, the only family member he was close to. At a deeper level, there may possibly have been an element of jealousy; Theo had succeeded in finding love, whereas Vincent had failed to sustain long-term relationships (other than that with Sien in The Hague).

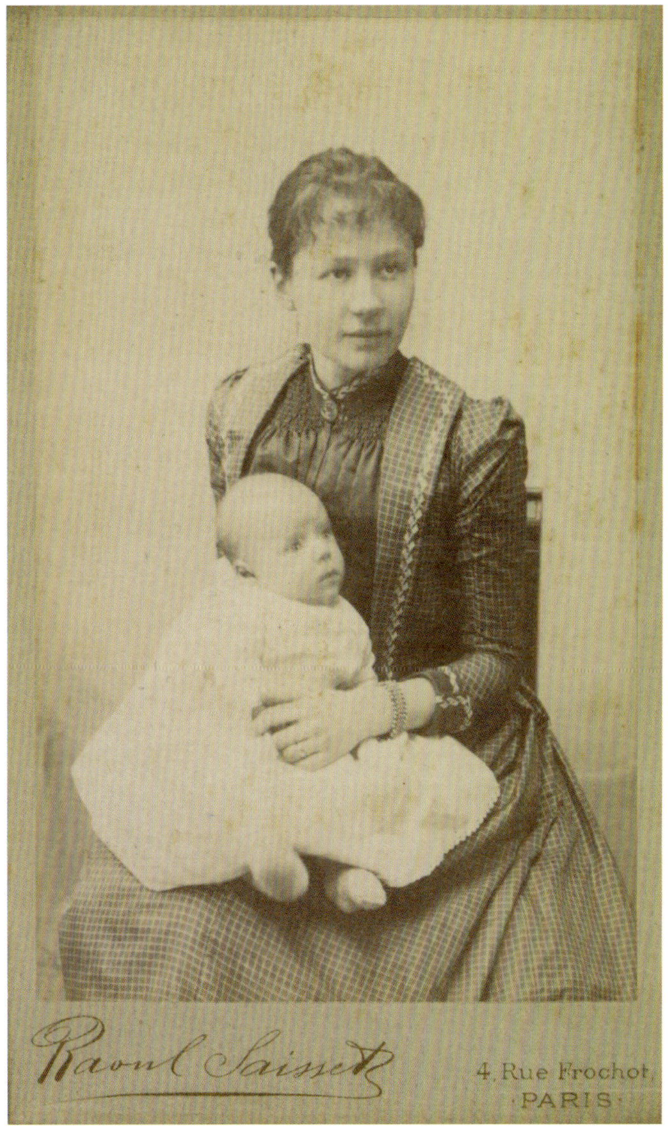

fig. 105 Jo and Vincent Willem van Gogh, April 1890, photograph by Raoul Saisset, Paris, Van Gogh Museum, Amsterdam (Vincent van Gogh Foundation)[13]

On the evening of 23 December Van Gogh and Gauguin had supper and, one suspects, plenty to drink, presumably spending some of the 100 francs enclosed in Theo's letter. The atmosphere in the Yellow House became tense, and Gauguin went out for a walk. Van Gogh chased after him, asking whether he planned to return to Paris. Gauguin said yes, and Van Gogh then showed him a news item he had cut out of that day's *L'Intransigeant* newspaper. Headlined 'Paris coupe-gorge' (cut-throat), it reported that a 19-year-old boy had been stabbed in a violent knife attack. Van Gogh drew Gauguin's attention to the final phrase: 'Le meurtrier a pris la fuite' (the murderer took flight). Gauguin was so struck by these words that he copied them into his Arles sketchbook.[14]

Fifteen years later in Tahiti, in writing his account of that disastrous evening in Arles, Gauguin added a further detail: Van Gogh had threatened him with a cut-throat shaving razor in Place Lamartine. Gauguin recounted: 'I heard a well-known little step behind me, quick and jerky, I turned around just as Vincent rushed at me with an open razor in his hand. The look in my eyes at that moment must have been very powerful, for he stopped, lowered his head and ran back towards the house.'[15] This story, reported long after the event, may have been embellished or even invented to deflect any criticism of Gauguin's behaviour.

Van Gogh returned to the Yellow House and climbed the stairs to his bedroom. His razor probably lay on the dressing-table with the washing bowl. Above it hung the mirror (see detail of fig. 21, p. 152). Van Gogh grabbed his left ear – and turned the razor on himself. Pulling the lobe downwards, he quickly sliced his ear. In the years since his death there has been considerable debate over whether it was the full outer ear or just the lobe.[16] In a sense it did not make that much difference how much flesh he removed, since it was a terrible mutilation, but probably it was the lower half or slightly more of the outer ear.

We will never know for certain what lay behind this unusual act of self-mutilation, but it may well have been a desperate plea for help. Another possibility is suggested by the 1893 letter written by Massebieau, who found that Van Gogh's medical records noted that he was 'prey to aural hallucinations' and heard voices which reproached him. This suggests that he might have cut off his ear in a vain attempt to silence these threatening noises.[17]

Blood gushed from the wound, and Van Gogh grabbed the towel which was hanging on a nearby nail. He carefully wrapped the lump of severed flesh in paper and put on his beret. Despite his weak condition, he walked through Place Lamartine to 1 Rue du Bout d'Arles, arriving there at about 11.30 p.m. He seems to have asked to see his favourite girl.

An Arles newspaper, *Le Forum Républican*, named the woman as Rachel, without recording a surname (fig. 106).[18] Nearly forty years later, the policeman Alphonse Robert, who had been called to the brothel, gave her *nom de guerre* as Gaby, a diminutive for Gabrielle.[19] The 1886 and 1891 censuses record the *filles soumises* at the brothel, but there is no one with either first name (however, prostitution tends to be a transitory trade).[20]

We do know the identity of the madame in charge, which is confirmed in the recently released archival file on the brothels of Arles: Virginie Chabaud, who would have been 40 at Van Gogh's time (her Christian name, too, must have given her customers some wry amusement).[21] She stated her profession as *limonadière* (lemonade seller), although one suspects she sold stronger drinks.

Rachel/Gaby fainted on the spot when she opened the package. Van Gogh immediately fled and chaos ensued at the brothel, with Robert arriving just before midnight. He knew Rue du Bout d'Arles well, having earlier that year arrested one of the Italians who had murdered the two Zouaves.[22] Robert informed his chief, Joseph d'Ornano, and together they went to the Yellow House in the early hours of 24 December.[23]

The incident attracted great attention and it is now known that it was reported in at least four newspapers. The short article in *Le Forum Républican* was noted in the Van Gogh literature in 1955, but the others have only

Uu peintre qui se coupe l'oreille. — Hier soir, un individu se présentant à la porte de la maison de tolérance n° 1, sonnait et remettait à la femme, qui vint lui ouvrir, une oreille pliée dans un morceau de papier, lui disant : « Tenez, cela vous servira. » Il s'en alla ensuite. Je vous laisse à penser l'étonnement et l'effroi que dut avoir cette femme en trouvant une oreille dans ce papier. La police faisant peu après sa ronde, eut connaissance du fait et, avec le signalément donné et grâce aux recherches de M. le secrétaire Barbezier, a été sur les traces de cet étrange personnage. Ce matin M. le commiseaire central et son secrétaire se sont transportés au domicile d'un peintre hollandais nommé Vincent, place Lamartine, et ont appris par la bonne qu'elle avait trouvé ce matin un rasoir ensanglanté sur la table et ont trouvé ensuite l'artiste peintre couché dans son lit avec une oreille coupée et dans un état assez grave. M. le commissaire central l'a fait transporter à l'hôpital.

On ignore quel mobile a poussé cet homme à commettre une pareille amputation et sous quelle influence il a agi.

Le toqué. — Sous ce titre, nous avons, mercredi dernier, relaté l'histoire de ce peintre de nationalité polonaise qui s'était coupé l'oreille avec un rasoir et l'avait offerte à une fille de café.

Nous apprenons aujourd'hui que cet artiste peintre est à l'hôpital où il souffre cruellement du coup qu'il s'est porté, mais que l'on espère le sauver.

Le Petit Journal

DANS LES DÉPARTEMENTS

Télégrammes de nos correspondants spéciaux
(24 DÉCEMBRE)
ARLES

Hier soir un nommé Vincent, artiste peintre hollandais, après s'être coupé une oreille avec un rasoir, est allé sonner à la porte d'une maison mal famée et a remis son oreille pliée dans un morceau de papier à la personne qui est venue ouvrir disant : « Tenez, cela vous servira. »

Il est parti ensuite. La police a recherché cet individu et l'a trouvé couché chez lui. Son état très grave a nécessité son transfert à l'hôpital.

Chronique locale

—

— Dimanche dernier, à 11 heures 1|2 du soir, le nommé Vincent Vaugogh, peintre, originaire de Hollande, s'est présenté à la maison de tolérance n° 1, a demandé la nommée Rachel, et lui a remis. . . . son oreille en lui disant : « Gardez cet objet précieusement. Puis il a disparu. Informée de ce fait qui ne pouvait être que celui d'un pauvre aliéné, la police s'est rendue le lendemain matin chez cet individu qu'elle a trouvé couché dans son lit, ne donnant presque plus signe de vie.

Ce malheureux a été admis d'urgence à l'hospice.

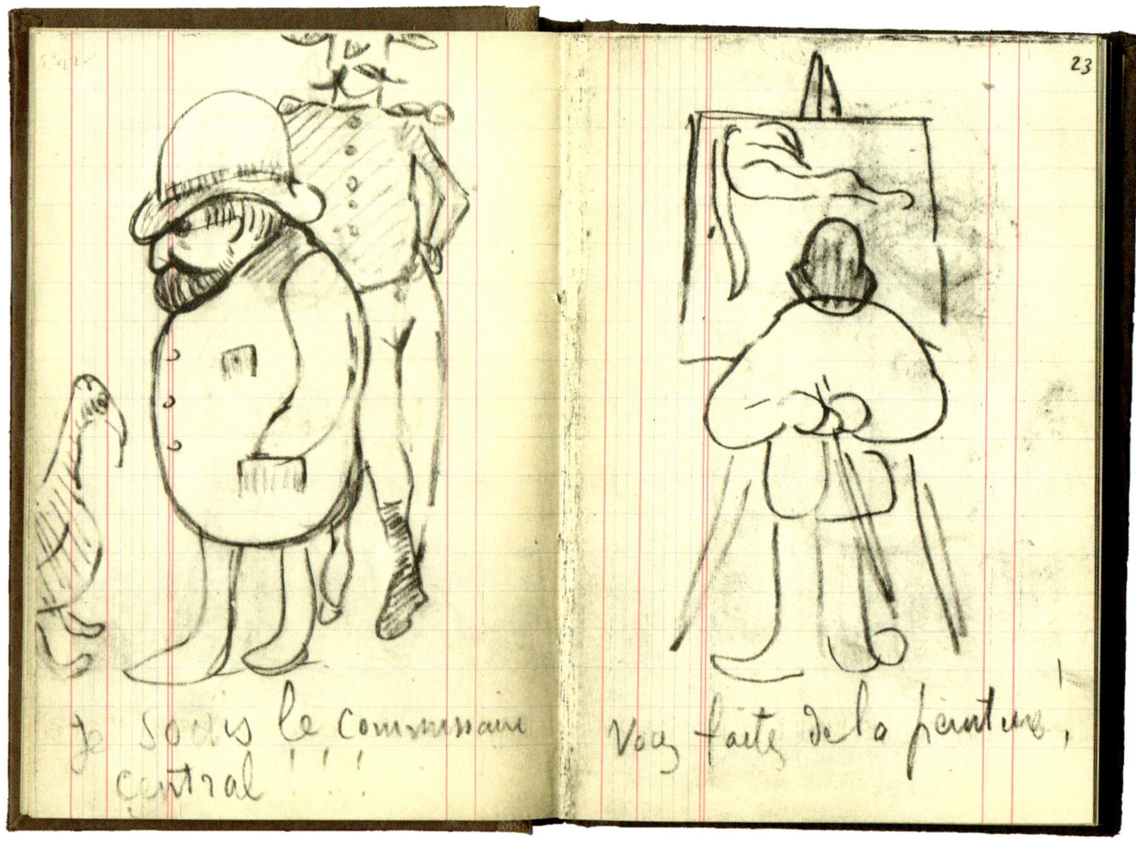

recently emerged (fig. 106).[24] The latest report to surface, in *Le Messager du Midi*, gives some further details, identifying Vincent Barbezier as the police administrator who helped track down Van Gogh after the brothel incident. It also said that Van Gogh's cleaning lady had seen 'a bloody razor' on his table, presumably the dressing-table depicted in the corner of *The Bedroom*. The newspapers found it difficult to spell the artist's surname. *Le Forum Républicain* called him 'Vaugogh', another called him Vincent and a third described him as Polish.

Gauguin, who had fled from Van Gogh in Place Lamartine, did not return to the Yellow House and spent the night at a hotel in town. He came back just before 8 a.m. the next morning to find 'a little man in a bowler hat who was the chief of police'. The police chief asked him: 'What have you done to your comrade?'[25] Gauguin, fearing that Van Gogh might be dead, entered the bedroom – and was relieved to find him alive. Van Gogh asked for his pipe and then agreed to be taken to hospital.

fig. 107 Paul Gauguin, Two sketches of police commissioner Joseph d'Ornano, November–December 1888, charcoal on paper, 16 x 11 cm (each page)[26]

Both artists knew the police chief because the *gendarmerie* was only a few doors away in Place Lamartine. Gauguin despised d'Ornano and drew two caricatures of him in his sketchbook (fig. 107). The first shows a short man in a bowler hat looking at a turkey, inscribed: 'Je souis [sic] le commissaire central!!!' (I am the chief commissioner!!!). The other depicts him with his staff of office, looking up puzzlingly at a painting on an easel, uttering the insulting words: 'Vous faites de la peinture!' (You paint!).[27]

Once Van Gogh had been taken to hospital, Gauguin telegraphed Theo in Paris, where he was preparing to close the gallery for the Christmas break. Theo had been looking forward with great anticipation to spending the holidays with his new fiancée, but instead he had to take the evening train south. Jo, who was staying in Paris with her brother Andries, received a short message from Theo, breaking the news: 'Vincent is gravely ill. I don't know what's wrong, but I shall have to go there.'[28]

Theo arrived in Arles the following morning, Christmas Day, and headed for the hospital, on what was to be his only visit to the town. He was distraught to discover that the injury was self-inflicted and that Vincent's life was 'in danger'.[29] Perhaps surprisingly, he spent only a few hours in Arles, taking the train back to Paris that evening with Gauguin – and not knowing whether he would ever see his brother again. They both arrived back in Paris on 26 December. Jo had left earlier that morning for Amsterdam, to see her family and arrange the engagement announcement.

On his return Theo wrote to Jo in Amsterdam, giving a brief report on Vincent, but sparing her the details: 'For the past few days he had been showing symptoms of that most dreadful illness, of madness, and an attack of fièvre chaude [high fever], when he injured himself with a knife . . . It was terribly sad being there, because from time to time all his grief would well up inside & he would try to weep, but couldn't. Poor fighter, & poor, poor sufferer.'[30]

Few people's medical problems have been so extensively scrutinised over a century after their death than that of Van Gogh. He has been the subject of thousands of papers in medical journals. His own doctors believed it was epilepsy.[31] Other diagnoses in recent decades have included absinthe poisoning, Ménière's disease (of the inner ear), lead poisoning, borderline personality disorder, acute intermittent porphyria (an enzyme deficiency) and bipolar disorder (manic depression). The Van Gogh family are also likely to have had some genetic conditions, since Vincent's younger brother Cor committed suicide in South Africa and Wil spent the last thirty-nine years of her life in a mental asylum.[32] There is still no consensus on Vincent's medical problem.

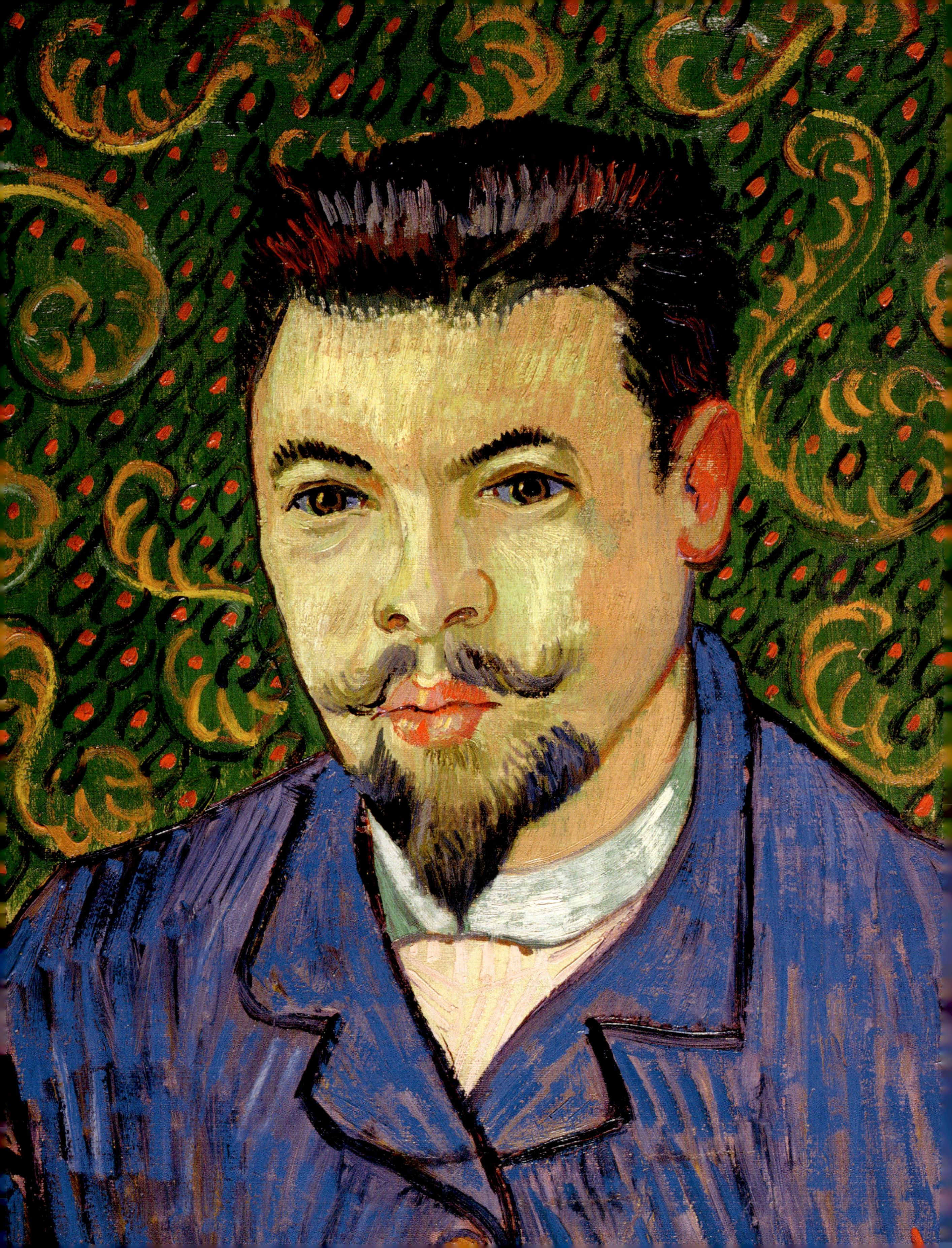

CHAPTER SEVENTEEN

DOCTOR REY

'Rey is a really good fellow, terribly hard-working, always at the daily grind. What people today's doctors are!'[1]

Van Gogh must have endured a terrible night after he had returned from the brothel and made his way up the stairs to his bed. The police then came to interview him. The following morning, on Gauguin's return, Van Gogh agreed to be taken to hospital, which meant suffering a jolting journey by carriage across town through the cobbled streets. In hospital his fresh wound needed to be dressed to reduce the chances of infection and he was then installed in the crowded men's ward. It is difficult to imagine his mental state – and what thoughts were racing through his mind.

The hospital building, converted from a 1573 orphanage, was already antiquated by Van Gogh's time. There was just one men's ward, some 30 metres long with dozens of beds lining the two sides. Although the beds were curtained off, this gave only a modicum of privacy. Nuns served as nurses and at the far end of the ward, beyond the crucifix over the door, lay the chapel (fig. 108).[2] The doctor charged with looking after Van Gogh was Félix Rey, a young intern.

Theo had visited Vincent on Christmas Day. The next day Roulin came, finding the patient in a terrible condition. As Roulin left, Van Gogh told him that they 'would meet again in heaven'. Roulin sent a note to Theo in Paris, saying 'I think he is lost.'[3] One can only imagine how terrible Theo must have felt to receive this letter, with his brother so far away. By 27 December Van Gogh's mental state had deteriorated still further. Rey reported that he had gone 'to lie down in another patient's bed' and 'in his night-shirt he chased the sister on duty'.[4] Van Gogh had to be locked up in the isolation cell, where

Detail of fig. 109 *Félix Rey*, Pushkin Museum, Moscow

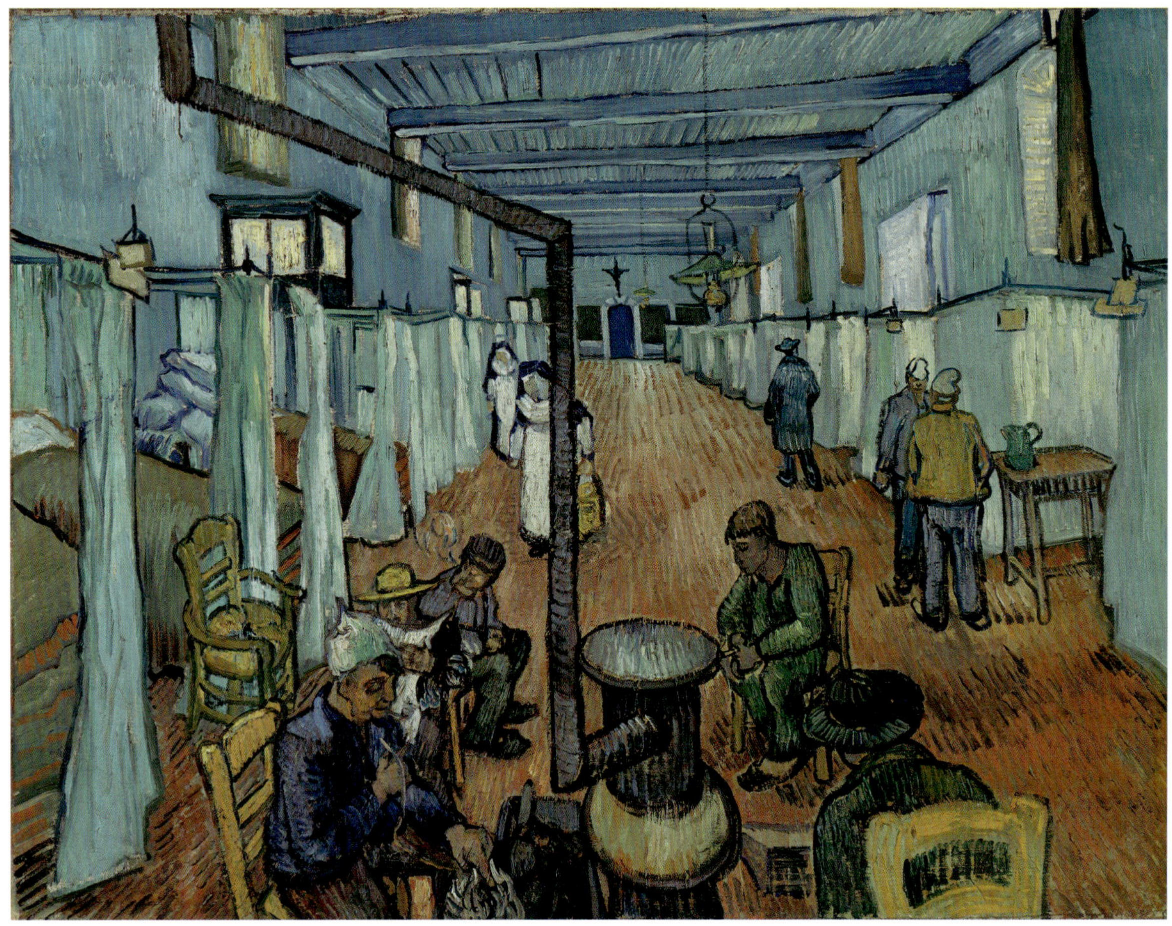

he remained 'without saying a word'.[5] The doctors decided he would need to be committed to an asylum.

Van Gogh then made an astonishing recovery. On 30 December, a week after the ear incident, Rey reported that his patient had 'improved a little' and he was returned to the men's ward.[6] Three days later Van Gogh was well enough to be allowed downstairs to Rey's office, where he wrote a reassuring letter to Theo, saying that he hoped to be discharged shortly. Rey added a friendly note: the 'over-excitement was only fleeting' and he 'will have recovered in a few days' time'.[7] On 5 January 1889 Theo felt that he could leave for the Netherlands for his engagement announcement.

That same day Roulin was allowed to take Van Gogh back to the Yellow House for a few hours. There Vincent wrote to Theo in a mood of astonishing optimism: 'Soon the fine days will come and I'll start on the

fig. 108 *Ward in the Hospital*, April and October 1889, oil on canvas, 72 x 91 cm, Oskar Reinhart Collection, Winterthur (F646)

orchards in blossom again.'[8] On 7 January he was discharged. The hospital register disappeared decades ago, but a transcript of the entry on Van Gogh survives, copied out by Massebieau by 1893. Van Gogh named both parents as deceased, although his mother was still alive; this was probably an attempt to ensure that she would not be contacted with news of the incident. He proudly gave his profession as 'landscape painter'.[9]

On the day of his release an astonishing event occurred – the significance of which has been largely overlooked in the Van Gogh literature. The artist got three senior hospital staff to return with him to the Yellow House to view his paintings. Only a week earlier he had been locked up in the isolation cell. Now he was able to make busy staff feel sufficiently relaxed to join him in his own home. Rey led the trio of guests, although the other two are unnamed in Vincent's letters to Theo.[10] They probably included the hospital bursar, Marius Huard, who was one of the town's leading art connoisseurs. Huard's other job was curator of the Musée Lapidaire, the antiquities museum which had been founded by his father François, an artist.[11] A few months later Van Gogh apparently gave one of his paintings to Huard.[12]

At least three other senior hospital staff were interested in Van Gogh's art, so one of them was presumably the other visitor at the Yellow House.[13] Antoine Rousseau, the hospital secretary, was later given a painting of the hospital ward, which he subsequently handed on to Aimé Nivière, the pharmacist, who liked it more.[14] Van Gogh's letters also mention a doctor from Paris working in Arles who was 'very curious to know about Impressionism'. He was probably Dr Albert Delon, who in 1901 tried to buy Van Gogh's portrait of Rey.[15]

On reaching the Yellow House, the trio of hospital staff saw the finest of Van Gogh's Arles pictures lining its walls, including the Sunflowers. The three visitors must have been astonished, and probably shocked, by what their patient had painted. After their departure, Van Gogh and Roulin went out for a meal to celebrate his discharge. Unfortunately for Van Gogh, the postman was about to be transferred for work to Marseille. Roulin departed from Arles a fortnight later, leaving Van Gogh bereft at a time when he was in desperate need of friendship – Milliet was in Algeria, Mourier-Petersen in Denmark and Boch in Belgium.

Although Van Gogh's wound was healing fast, the mutilated ear was a terrible disfigurement. It represented a constant reminder of what he had done – and it was highly visible to everyone he encountered. Initially he tried to put the incident out of his mind, dismissing it as a fleeting moment of madness. It was, he wrote, 'a simple artist's bout of craziness and then a lot of fever following a *very* considerable loss of blood, as an artery was severed'.[16] On four later occasions he euphemistically referred to it as 'an accident'.[17] Once he used the term 'adventure' and on another occasion he lightheartedly talked of acquiring 'a papier-mâché ear'.[18]

Two days after his discharge Van Gogh returned to hospital to have his wound dressed. He then went out with Rey for a 90-minute walk, a sign of their developing friendship. Vincent told Theo that his doctor had said that he 'likes painting, although he knows little about it, and that he would like to learn'.[19] He asked his brother to send a reproduction of Rembrandt's *Anatomy Lesson* to thank Rey, whom he described as 'the worthiest man one could possibly imagine, the most dedicated, the most valiant, [with] a warm, manly heart'.[20]

While in hospital Van Gogh had planned to paint Rey's portrait and by 17 January he had completed the picture of the 23-year-old doctor (fig. 109). It is a striking work, with the stolid doctor looking straight ahead, impassively. A photograph of the time (fig. 110) shows that Rey's face was rounder and

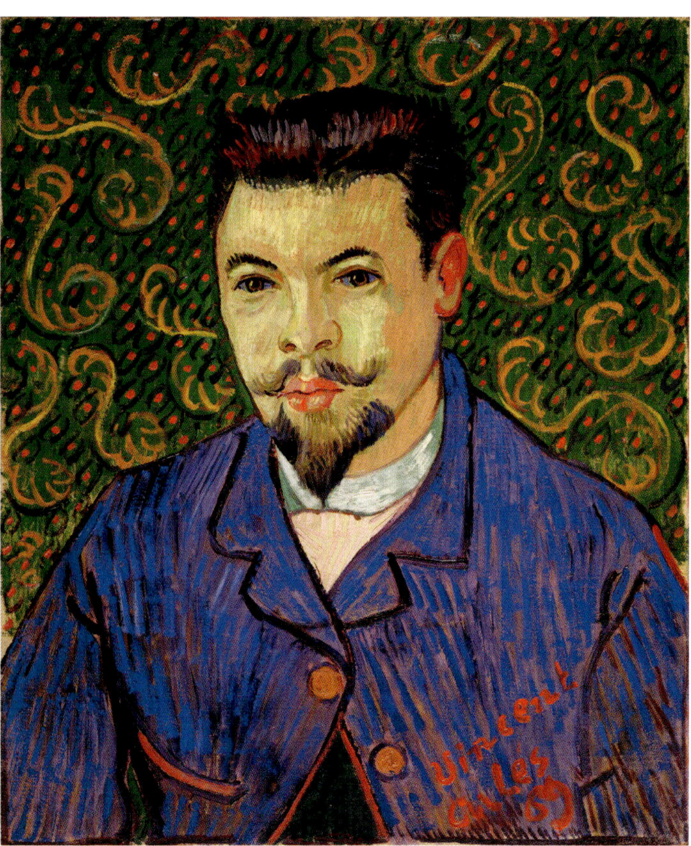

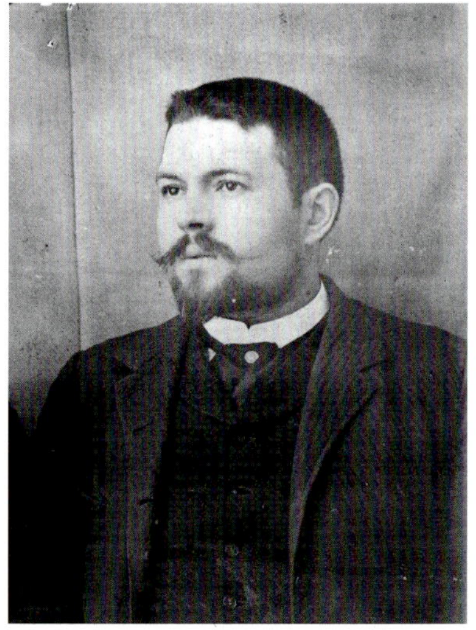

alterations done while doing the painting suggest that Van Gogh slimmed down the face slightly on one side, possibly at his sitter's request. Curiously, Van Gogh has given Rey a red ear. The artist completed the work by painting a partial border around it and then prominently signed his name.

On his return to the Yellow House Van Gogh had been impatient to get back to work. *Still Life with Onions and Letter* (fig. 111), one of his first pictures of the year, provides a fascinating insight into his personal life. He was finding renewed pleasure in his everyday possessions in his own home. His trusty pipe and tobacco sit not far from a matchbox. The lit candle is at the ready – for a smoke, for melting the red sealing wax or for reading. The book is a well-thumbed copy of François Raspail's *Manuel Annuaire de la Santé*, a popular medical guide.[22] There is a bottle and a green water jug (the symbolism of the onions again remains obscure).

But the most intriguing object in Van Gogh's assemblage is the envelope, placed near the front (with the address upside down). A used match lies on top. The envelope, with Theo's handwriting on it, is addressed to 'Monsieur Vincent van Gogh' in Place Lamartine. Clues on the envelope suggest that this is the letter with the cash allowance which Vincent had received on 23 December, along with news of the engagement. The brown 'R' mark for *recommandé* and the blue 15 franc and light ochre 25 franc stamps making up the price of a registered letter suggest that it included cash. Most importantly, the '67' in a circle was a special *jours de l'an* (new year's days) postmark which was used during the holiday period.[23] The number 67 refers to the post office in Place des Abbesses, near Theo's apartment, and the larger black double circle is the normal Abbesses postmark.

Although it is likely that the envelope depicted is that of Theo's letter of 22 December with news of the engagement, its meaning in the painting remains more elusive. Does its inclusion mean that Vincent had come to accept Theo's relationship after nearly a month had passed? Or was he still in anguish over the engagement? Although Vincent later sent most of his paintings to Theo in Paris, it may be significant that this was among the relatively few which he left behind in Arles – and withheld from his brother.[24]

A close examination of the correspondence shows that Vincent remained decidedly cool about his brother's engagement, with the occasional positive comment being far outnumbered by unenthusiastic ones or impolite silences. On 9 January, the day of Theo's engagement party in Amsterdam, Vincent wrote a terse letter, saying that he had already replied to Jo with sincere congratulations – so he simply wanted to 'repeat them here to you'.[25]

A few days later Theo (rather tactlessly) asked Vincent to estimate his expenses for the year to help him budget for married life. Vincent's lengthy

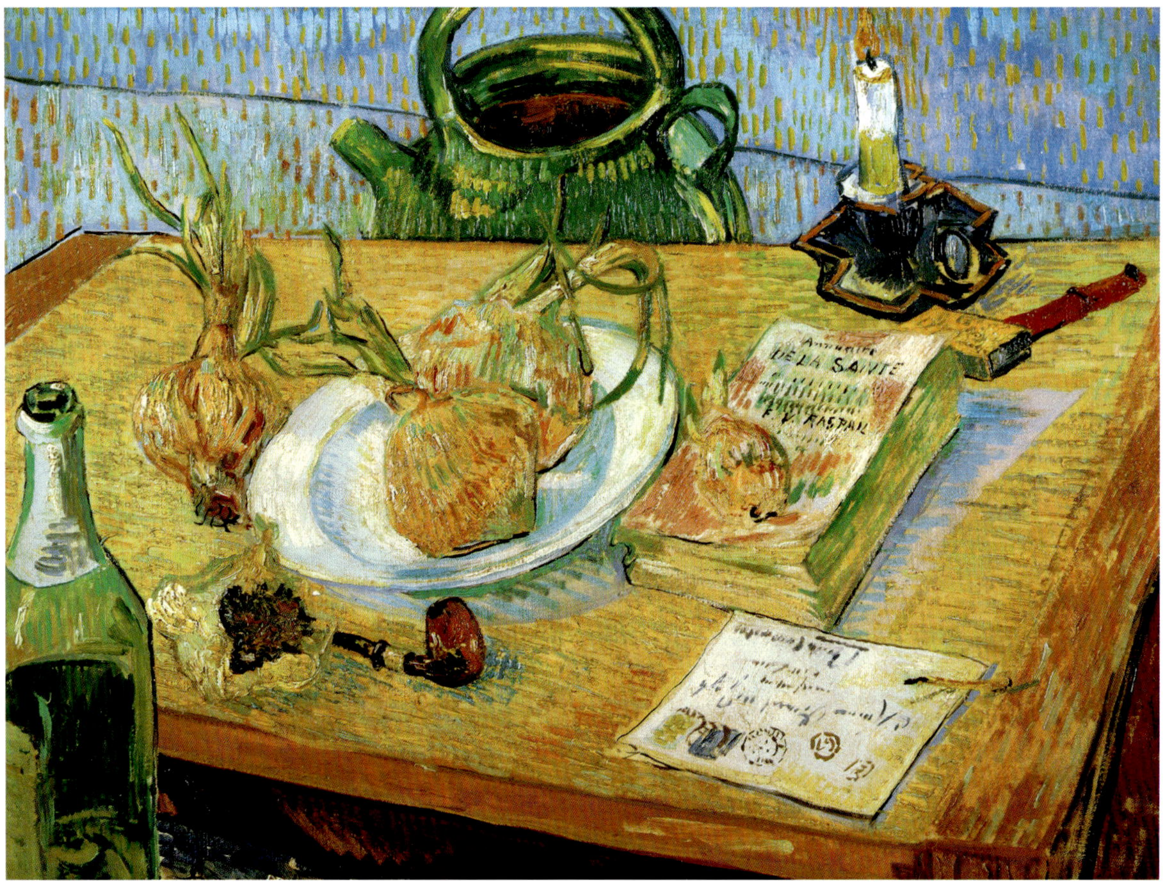

response dealt mainly with his own financial insecurity and did not even ask about the engagement party.[26] In his next letter, he advised Theo to marry because of his social position and to please their mother – but with no mention of love. 'Doing thus what you must do, you'll perhaps have more tranquility than before, even amidst a thousand-and-one difficulties', Vincent commented unenthusiastically.[27]

Within a week or so of Van Gogh's return to the Yellow House he had completed two self-portraits, further evidence that he had lost none of his artistic skills. Both prominently include his bandaged left ear (which appears in the painting on the other side, since he was using a mirror). This was a very deliberate inclusion, since he could easily have depicted his right side with his intact ear.[28] Indeed he did not have to paint self-portraits at all, so they may represent Van Gogh's attempt to come to terms with what had occurred – presenting his injury in a matter-of-fact way. He may not have been able to

fig. 111 *Still Life with Onions and Letter*, January 1889, oil on canvas, 50 x 64 cm, Kröller-Müller Museum, Otterlo (F604) acknowledge what had happened in words, but he could attempt to do so through his art.

Van Gogh's *Self-portrait with bandaged Ear and Japanese Print* (fig. 112) echoes the composition of his last Paris self-portrait (fig. 3). In the early 1889 picture, he is in his Yellow House studio, beside the glass-paned front door opening onto Place Lamartine and the outside world. The print on the wall behind the easel is a modified version of Sato Torakiyo's *Geishas in a Landscape* of the 1870s. The painting was probably done expressly for Theo, to demonstrate that Vincent was back at work.[29]

Self-portrait with bandaged Ear and Pipe (fig. 113) is a simpler composition, with orange and dark red in the background, meeting at the level of the artist's eyes. In both self-portraits, he wears a dark green buttoned-up winter coat. No doubt the house was cold and damp, after having been unoccupied for two weeks during a cold period with extremely heavy rain. The fur hat, which he had bought just a few days earlier, not only kept him warm, but helped hold his bandage in place (and also disguised the worst of his injury).

These two self-portraits were done in the same week as the portrait of Rey. Decades later the doctor vividly recalled Van Gogh's comment while he was painting him, 'there are only two colours, red and green.'[30] Although Rey accepted the portrait (plus a handful of other Van Goghs) as a gift, he privately disliked it, particularly because of its unusual colouring.[31] Rey's mother is said to have used the picture in the 1890s to block up a gap in a chicken coop on their country farm.[32] This story may be apocryphal, and the painting is more likely to have been simply consigned to the attic of their Arles home.

In 1901 Rey met Charles Camoin, a 21-year-old soldier serving in the Arles military infirmary. He was also an artist and a friend of Henri Matisse. Rey mentioned that he had known Van Gogh and then invited his visitor up to his attic.[33] Camoin was instantly struck by the pictures and a few months later he painted a landscape with a canal bridge, in homage to Van Gogh.[34] Rey had no interest in the portrait or his other Van Goghs and decided to sell them, apparently so that his wife Anne could buy a lampshade for their dining room.[35] Camoin contacted Lucien Molinard, a Marseille dealer, who offered to buy the six paintings for 350 francs.[36] Molinard then sold them on to the Parisian dealer Ambroise Vollard. In 1909 the Rey portrait was bought by Sergei Shchukin, a leading Moscow collector of modern art.

Looking back in the 1920s, Rey remembered Van Gogh as having 'a painful, suffering expression'. Van Gogh was nervous, found it difficult to communicate and 'talked fast'.[37] Rey went on to have a successful career, eventually becoming head of the medical services in Arles. He kept

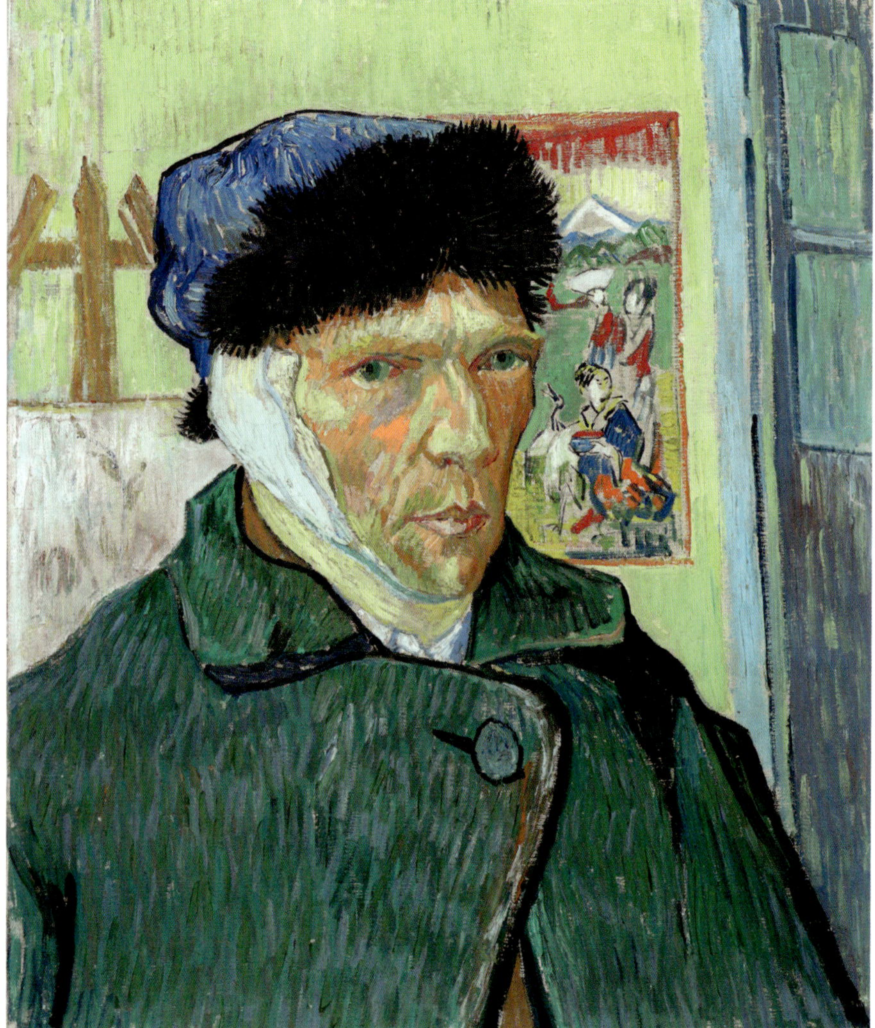

fig. 112 *Self-portrait
with bandaged Ear and
Japanese Print*, January
1889, oil on canvas,
60 x 49 cm, Courtauld
Gallery, London (F527)

Rembrandt's *Anatomy Lesson* from Van Gogh until his death in Arles in 1932, at the age of 67. His daughter, Pauline Mourard, once told me: 'My father understood Van Gogh, but not his paintings.'[38]

As for the severed ear, Rey later claimed that he had been given it a day or so after the incident (presumably from the police, who had been called to the brothel). At this point it would have been impossible to stitch the flesh back on. Although having no medical importance, Rey nevertheless preserved the fragment in a jar of alcohol. Later in 1889, while on a visit to Paris, the jar was cleared from his office and discarded.[39]

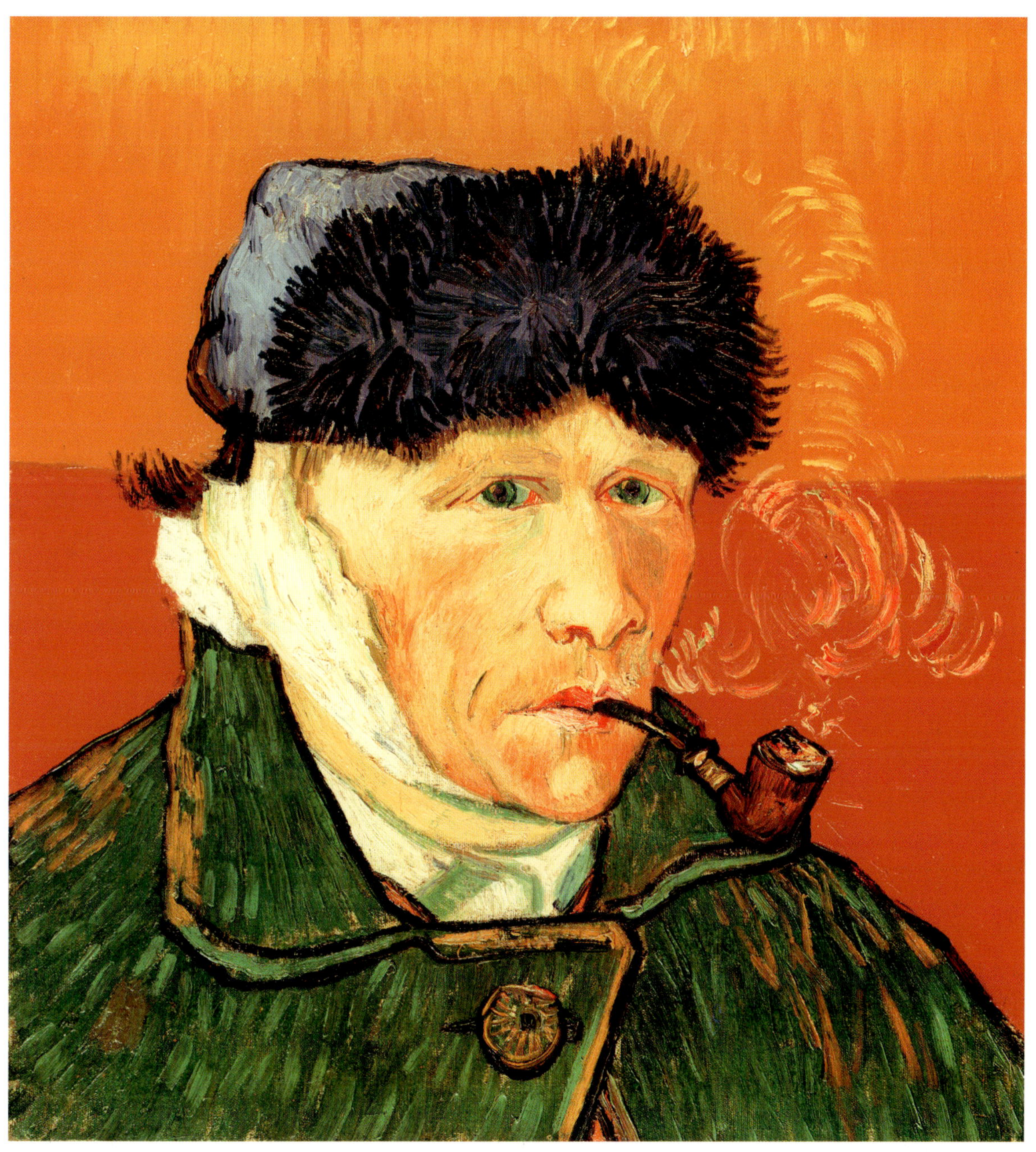

fig. 113 *Self-portrait with bandaged Ear and Pipe*, January 1889, oil on canvas, 51 x 45 cm, private collection (F529)

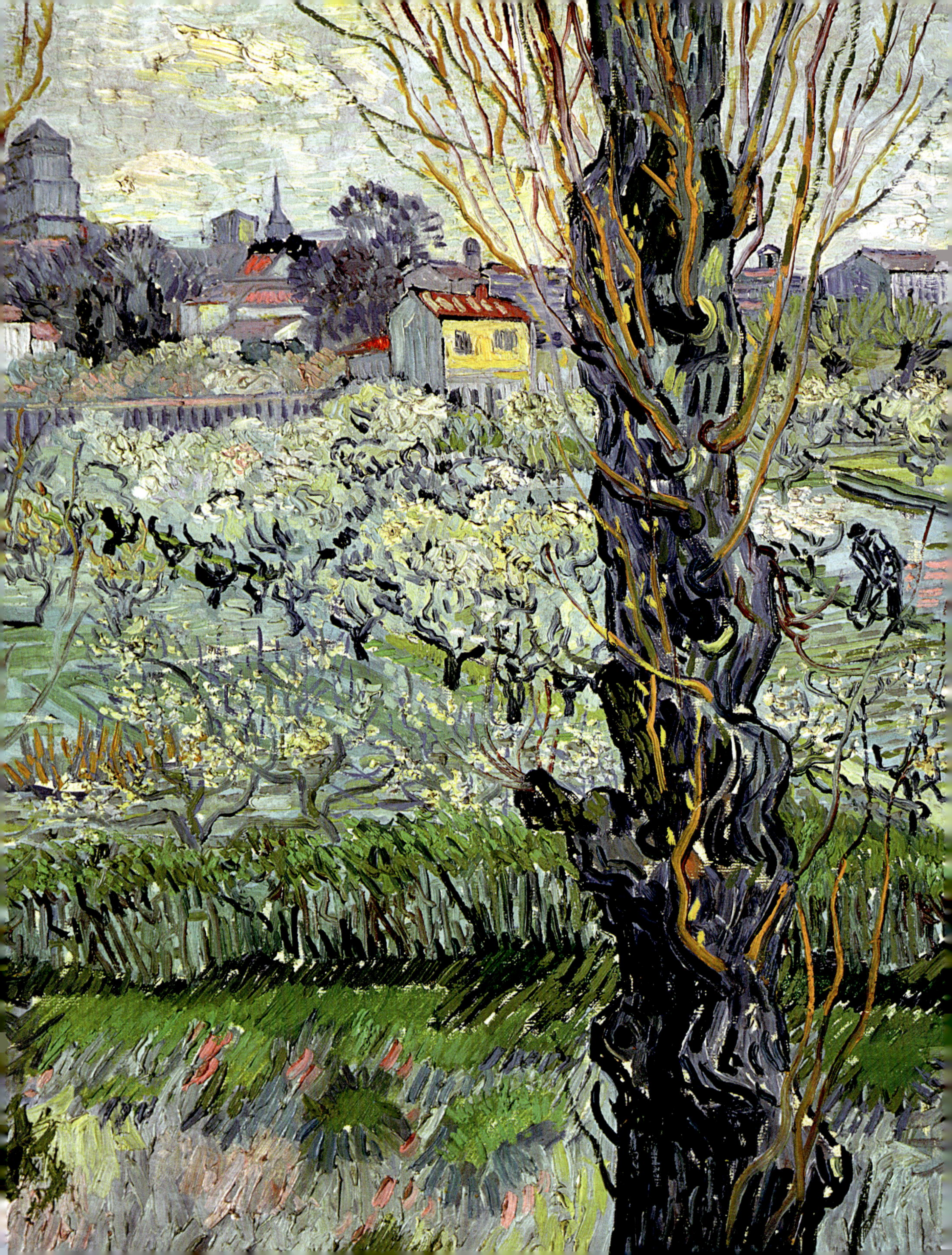

CHAPTER EIGHTEEN

SPRING

'What consoles me a little is that I am beginning to consider madness as an illness like any other'[1]

One can break an arm or leg and it will heal, Vincent wrote to Theo, 'but I didn't know that one could break one's brain and afterwards that got better too.'[2] A month after the ear incident Van Gogh was back at work with a vengeance. In a surge of energy in the second half of January 1889 he had painted Rey's portrait (fig. 109), the still life with the letter (fig. 111), two self-portraits (figs. 112–3), further versions of his finest sunflowers (copies of figs. 64–5) and a handful of other pictures. This represented an astonishing achievement.

On 2 February Vincent returned to 1 Rue du Bout d'Arles (probably the day after receiving 100 francs from Theo). As he explained to his brother: 'I went back to see the girl I went to when I went out of my mind. I was told there that things like that aren't at all surprising around here. She had suffered from it and had fainted but had regained her composure.'[3] It is unclear whether Van Gogh returned to enjoy her services or simply to talk.

Vincent's letter of 3 February was routine, suggesting all was going fine – but the following day he was struck down by another mental attack. Theo received the news from the Reverend Frédéric Salles, the Reformed Church clergyman who was based close to the hospital. Because of Van Gogh's Protestant background, he had been called in to assist. On 7 February Salles wrote to inform Theo about Vincent's condition: 'For three days he has thought he is being poisoned and just sees poisoners and victims of poison everywhere.'[4] That day Van Gogh had been taken back to hospital and locked up again in the isolation cell.

Detail of fig. 116
View of Arles, Neue
Pinakothek, Munich

Dr Delon wrote up a medical report: 'I found this man in a state of extreme excitement, suffering from a true delirium, pronouncing incoherent words, only momentarily recognising the people around him. He is subject in particular to auditory hallucinations (he hears voices uttering reproaches against him).'[5] There was further talk of sending him to an asylum, but within a week Van Gogh began to improve. From 18 February he was allowed to return to the Yellow House during the day, although he continued to sleep in the men's ward.

Van Gogh's daytime return to the Yellow House worried his neighbours, and none more so than the Crevoulins, who shared their staircase with the artist. They had already faced the trauma of Van Gogh wielding a razor to slice his ear only a few metres away from their rooms. Gauguin later recalled the blood on 'the small stairs'.[6] In late February François Crevoulin drew up a petition which he got thirty local residents to sign. This complained that the artist 'is not in full possession of his mental facilities, and that he over-indulges in drink, after which he is in a state of over-excitement such as he no longer knows what he is doing' (inexplicably, the artist was named as 'Vood').[7] Signatories included Soulé (the landlord's agent), Marguerite Vénissac (the restaurant owner) and even Joseph Ginoux. After the petition was submitted to the mayor, the police chief, d'Ornano, was asked to investigate. Since the *gendarmerie* was also on Place Lamartine he was already well aware of the situation.

D'Ornano compiled his report after conducting five interviews with local residents. Madame Crevoulin said in evidence: 'I occupy the same house as Mr Vincent van Gogh, who is truly insane. This individual comes into my shop and makes a nuisance of himself. He insults my customers and is prone to interfering with women from the neighbourhood, who he follows into their residences.' Jeanne Coulomb, a dressmaker at 24 Place Lamartine, reported that she was 'seized around the waist outside Mr Crevoulin's shop by this individual . . . and lifted off my feet'. Soulé said that Van Gogh was 'interfering' with women in the neighbourhood, and 'they actually no longer feel at ease in their homes, because he enters their residences.'[8] The resulting police report recommended that Van Gogh should be sent to an asylum.[9]

These accusations caused Van Gogh great anguish and he was taunted by the locals. He complained to Salles that the police had failed to prevent 'the children and even grown-ups to collect around my home and climb up to my window as they have done (as if I were a strange animal)'.[10] Presumably they peered through the ground-floor windows of the Yellow House.

Van Gogh then suffered another attack, probably on 26 February. Salles broke the news to Theo: 'Your poor brother has again been taken into the hospital.'[11] Once again he was locked up in the isolation cell, but he quickly made a recovery and was taken back to the men's ward. Three days after his first letter, Salles was able to write: 'It has been decided that someone will go with him in order that he may collect his brushes and paints so that he may find some distraction during his stay at the hospital . . . It seems to me, and this view is shared by Mr Rey, that it would constitute an act of cruelty permanently to lock up a man who has done nobody any harm.'[12] For the next month he remained in hospital, not returning to the Yellow House, which had been locked by the police.

On 23 March the Parisian artist Paul Signac stopped in Arles at Theo's request on his way further south and visited Van Gogh in hospital, finding the Dutchman in a reasonable condition.[13] Rey agreed that the two artists could return to the Yellow House for a short visit, although they had to force their way in.

By the following month Van Gogh was considerably better, but he was coming under increasing pressure from his landlord to vacate the Yellow House. He therefore began to look for alternative accommodation for when he would be able to stop sleeping at the hospital. In mid-April Van Gogh was on the verge of renting a small apartment from Rey (probably part of his home in Rampe du Pont), but the artist backed out at the last minute, fearing he would find it difficult to cope with living independently.[14]

Theo had already arrived in the Netherlands for his forthcoming marriage, and once again Vincent was notably unenthusiastic. Vincent's letter mentioning the event came in late March, when he commented to his brother: 'I imagine that you'd prefer to marry without all the ceremonies and congratulations of a wedding, and am quite sure in advance that you'll avoid them as much as possible.'[15] Five days later he wished the couple 'much happiness', but then immediately added: 'It's like a nervous tic with me that on the occasion of a day of celebration I generally experience difficulties in formulating a congratulation, but it shouldn't be concluded from that that I desire your happiness less ardently.' (Van Gogh's reference to a tic was probably meant literally; it is not generally appreciated that he suffered from facial tics.[16])

Just before the wedding Van Gogh wrote that he did not know whether it would be held in Amsterdam (the home of Jo's parents) or Breda (where the mother of Theo and Vincent lived). Immediately after the event, which took place in Amsterdam on 18 April, Vincent thanked Theo for his loyal support, asking him to 'transfer this affection onto your wife as much as possible'.[17] This was a generous thought, but it reveals his deep fear that he would end up being the loser. A few days later Vincent employed emotional blackmail, commenting that without Theo's friendship, 'I would be sent back without remorse to suicide, and however cowardly I am, I would end up going there.'[18] This threatening remark would not have gone down well with Theo and Jo, less than a week before their marriage.

Vincent then focused all his efforts on work, painting a handful of masterful spring landscapes. The fecund springtime beauty of these paintings belies the challenging circumstances in which they were created. He had suffered from three recent mental attacks in as many months. He was sleeping in a crowded hospital ward. He had only limited access to his painting materials and personal possessions at the other end of town. Despite these difficulties, he walked to the orchards on the outskirts of Arles. Witnessing the flowering fruit trees which had so inspired him the previous spring, he set up his easel.

Peach Trees in Blossom (fig. 114) is one of his finest Arles landscapes. Van Gogh gave a staccato description of the picture in a letter to Signac: 'Green countryside with little cottages, blue line of the Alpilles, white and blue sky. The foreground, enclosures with reed hedges where little peach trees are in blossom – everything there is *small*, the gardens, the fields . . . the trees, even those mountains, as in certain Japanese landscapes.'[19]

Orchard in Blossom (fig. 115) is very different in style, although equally successful. In a composition influenced by Japanese prints, the jagged forms of the two closest trees are boldly silhouetted against the town. Van Gogh described the picture as 'almost all green with a little lilac and grey – on a rainy day'.[20] The Church of St Trophime dominates the skyline (on the right), with the tower of the town hall just visible between the branches of the nearest tree.[21]

View of Arles (fig. 116) was done from a similar position, but from an imaginary higher ground, looking down on the scene. The composition is broken up by three tall poplars, framing the fields painted in pastel shades. The orchards create a soothing, harmonious effect. In the background the large tower is that of St Trophime, with the pointed tower of the Church of Notre Dame de la Major slightly to the right.[22]

Van Gogh also occasionally painted inside the hospital, presumably to the amusement of his fellow patients. By this time he had been sleeping there for most of the past four months. One of the pictures was of his ward (fig. 108 represents a version completed in October 1889, after he had left Arles for the asylum).

Courtyard of the Hospital (fig. 117), the garden view, was painted from the upper arcaded gallery in late April, after the flowers had started to

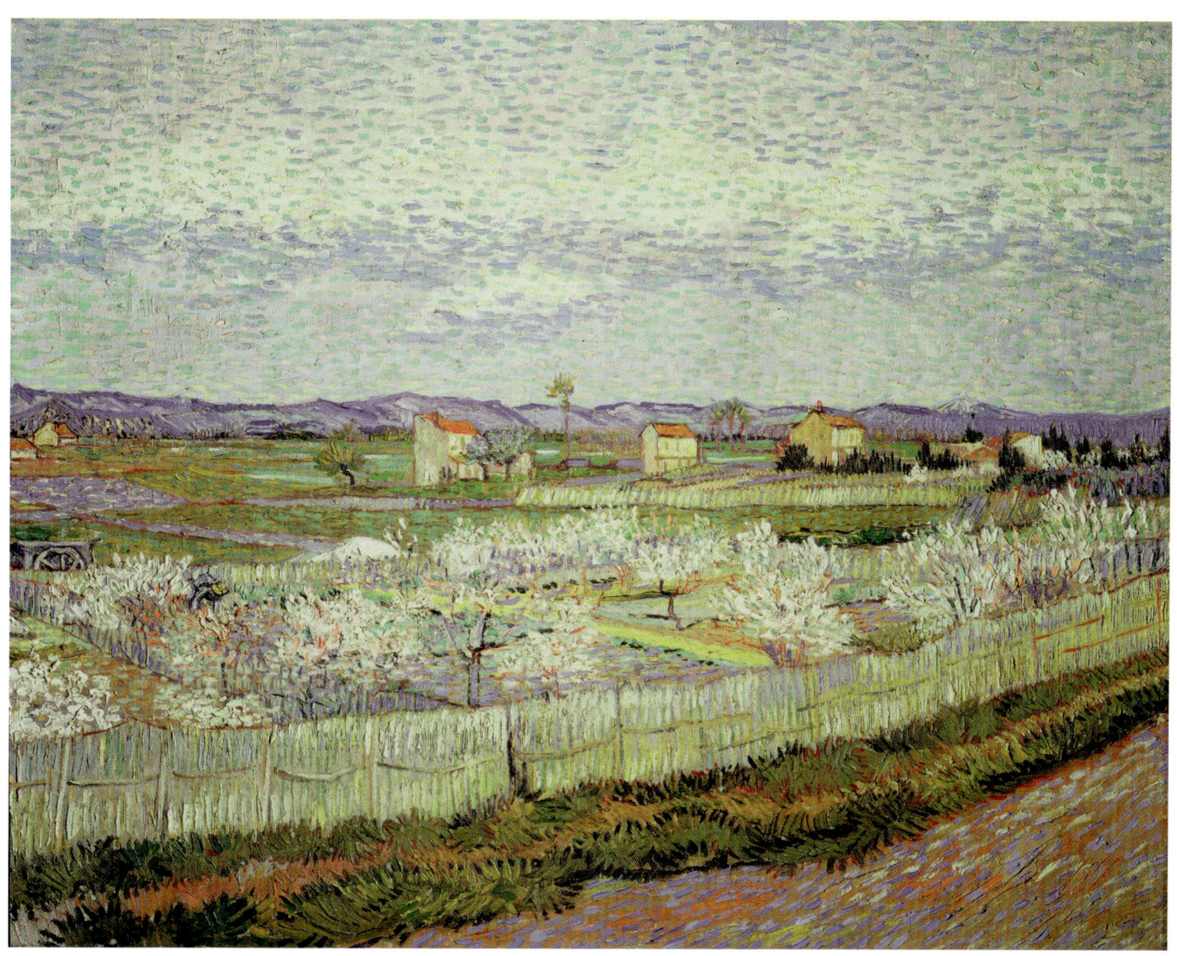

fig. 114 *Peach Trees in Blossom*, April 1889, oil on canvas, 66 x 82 cm, Courtauld Gallery, London (F514)

bloom. Van Gogh must have spent endless hours pacing up and down this walkway or simply contemplating the view from just outside the ward. He lovingly described the picture to his sister Wil: 'An ancient garden with a pond in the middle and 8 beds of flowers, forget-me-nots, Christmas roses, anemones, buttercups, wallflowers, daisies etc. And beneath the gallery, orange trees and oleanders. So it's a painting chock-full of flowers and springtime greenery.'[23] A group of fellow patients relax just outside the men's ward on the upper level, while down below a nun walks along a path at the far end. The goldfish in the pool are a delightful touch, providing an opportunity for the artist to indulge in his love of complementary colours.[24]

Van Gogh's days in Arles were numbered, since he had finally decided to move to the asylum in Saint-Rémy-de-Provence. On around 19 April, the date Theo and Jo moved in together into their new Parisian apartment,

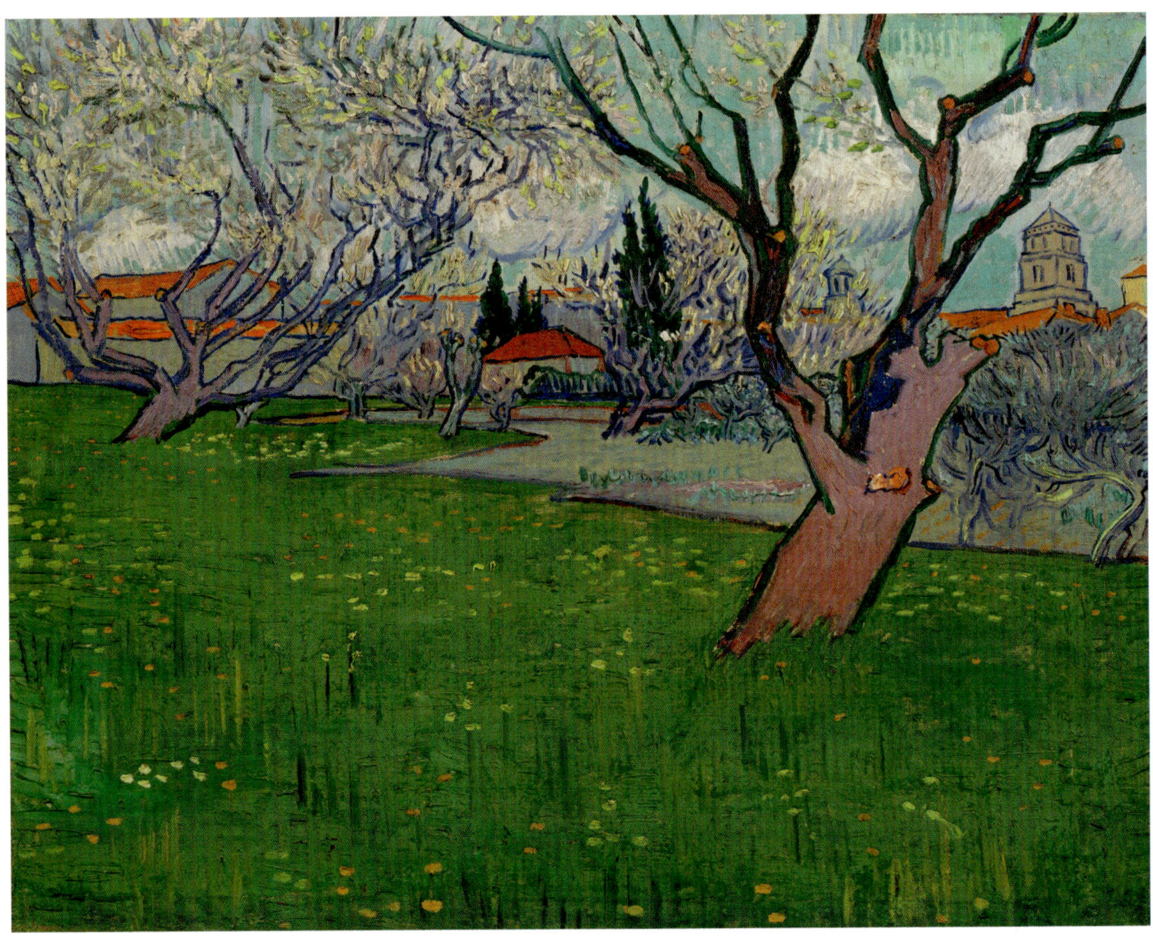

he relinquished the Yellow House and hauled his furniture, painting equipment and personal possessions to the nearby Café de la Gare. Vincent opened up his heart to Theo in rambling words: 'These days have been sad, moving house, transporting all my furniture, packing up the canvases which I'll send you, but above all it seemed sad to me that all that had been given to me by you with so much brotherly affection, and that for so many years, it was however you alone who supported me, and then to be obliged to tell you all this sad story . . .'[25]

Vincent packed most of his pictures into two crates, preparing the first major shipment for Theo since the previous August. The paintings were simply rolled up, to reduce transport costs. On 1 May he took the boxes the very short distance to the station, for dispatch by freight train to Paris. Inside the crates were over thirty pictures, including the Sunflowers, the bedroom, the two chairs, the Café de la Gare at night, the starry sky over the Rhône, portraits of his friends (Boch, Marie Ginoux and the Roulins) and many of the paintings he had done during Gauguin's stay. He could not sell these pictures – and neither could Theo, one of the leading Parisian dealers in modern art. Today the contents of those two wooden crates would be worth billions of dollars.

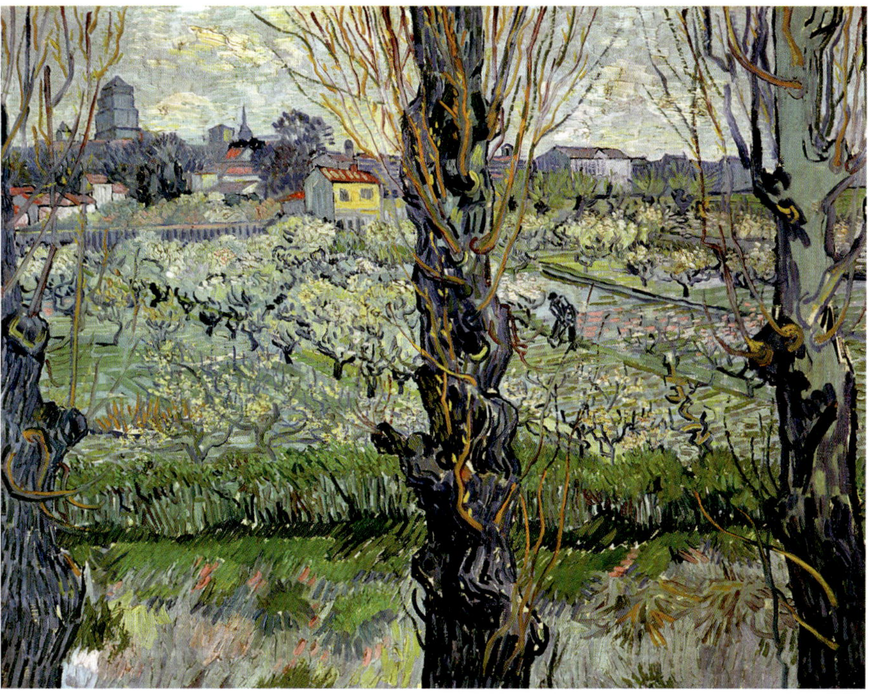

On 8 May 1889 Salles accompanied Van Gogh by train to Saint-Rémy. From the station they took a carriage to the asylum of St Paul de Mausole, a kilometre south of the small town. Salles reported back to Theo: 'When I took leave of him, he thanked me warmly, and seemed somewhat moved at the thought of the entirely new life he was about to lead.'[26]

The following day Van Gogh took his paints into the asylum garden, since he was not allowed outside its walls. He started work on *Irises*, one of the most exuberant pictures of his career.[27] A patch of tall violet-blue bearded irises stand on turquoise stalks, with one dominant white flower. Van Gogh's problems were overwhelming. His mental condition was unstable. He was incarcerated in a remote asylum, far from Theo, his friends and his fellow artists. Many of the other patients were even more seriously disturbed than he was, which must have created a most unpleasant environment. Yet one can hardly imagine a more optimistic picture than *Irises*, so redolent of springtime in the south.

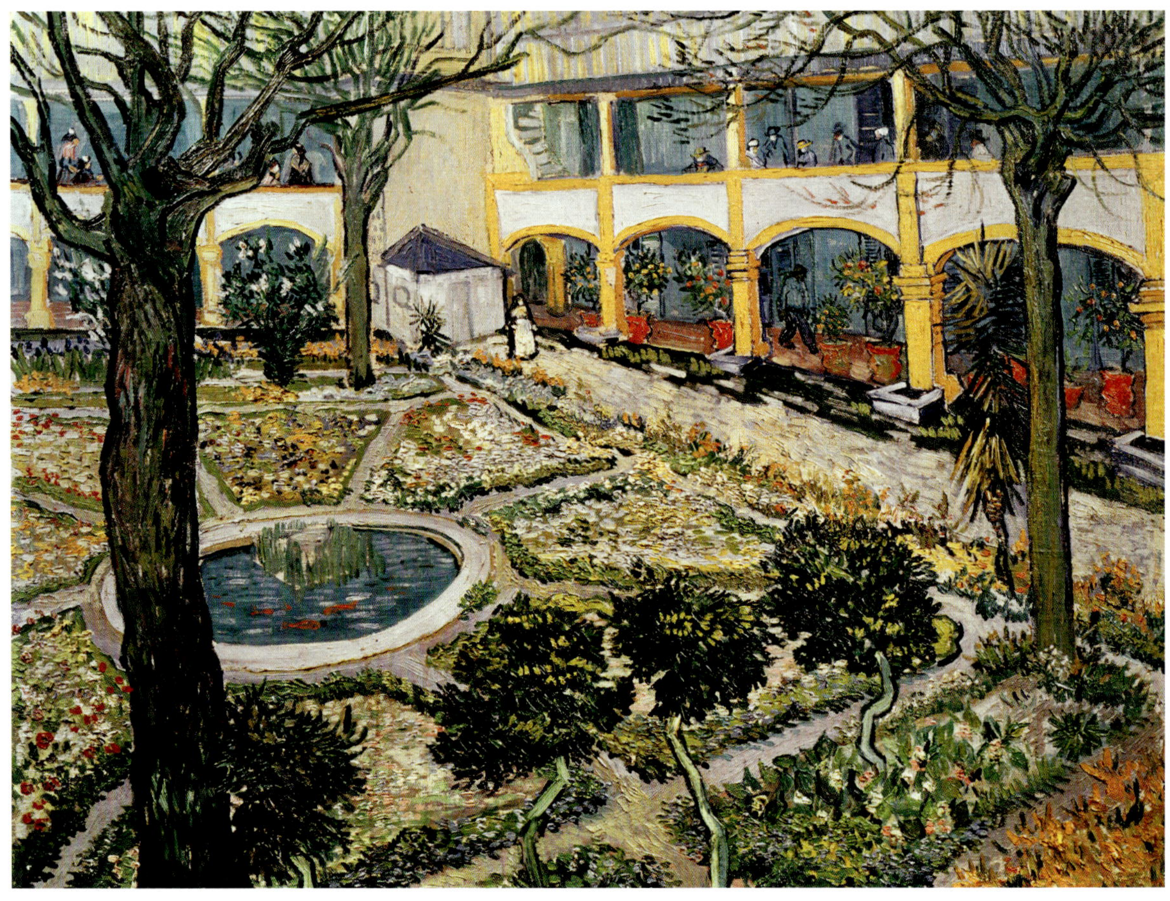

fig. 117 *Courtyard of the Hospital*, April 1889, oil on canvas, 73 x 92 cm, Oskar Reinhart Collection, Winterthur (F519)

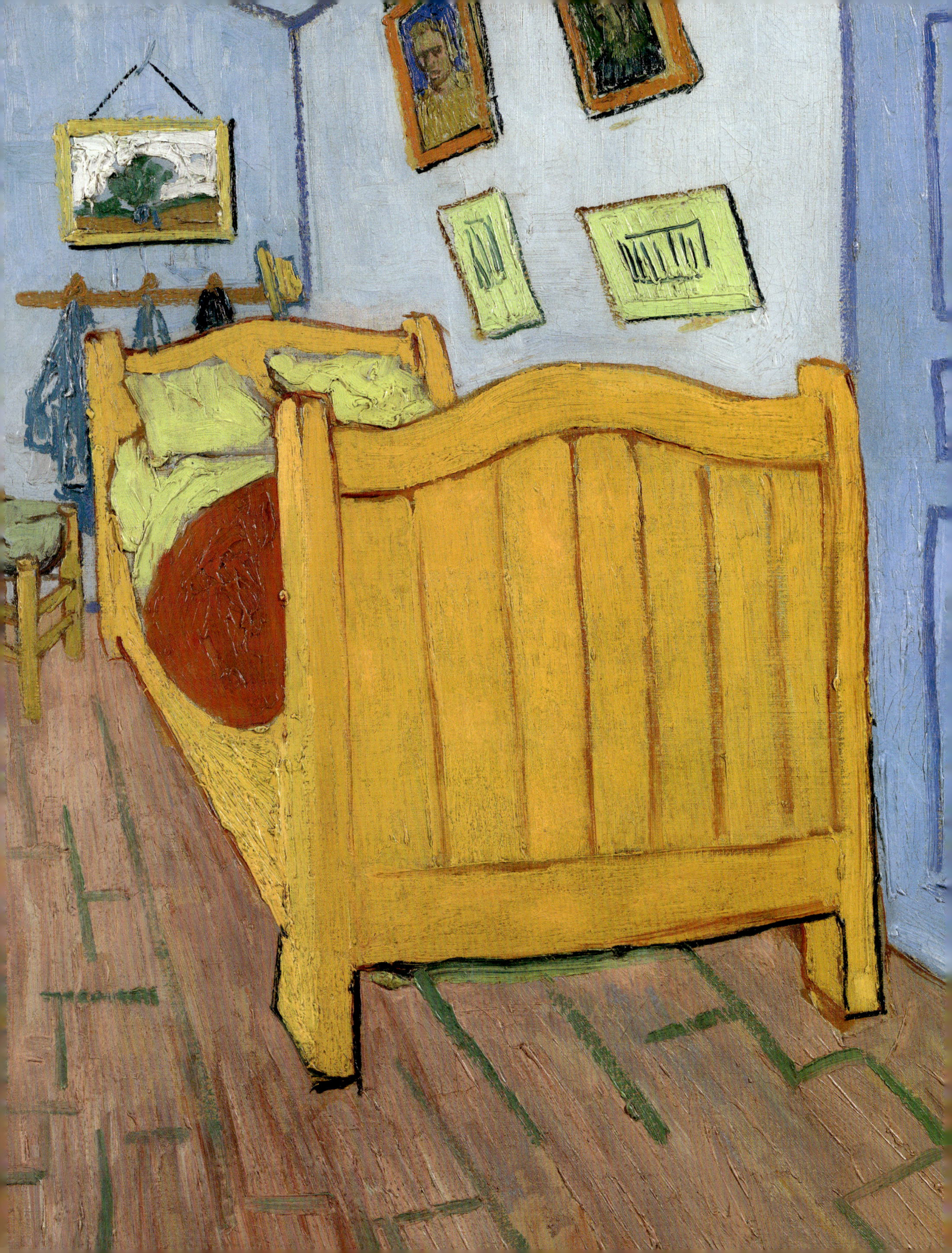

VAN GOGH'S BED

'A portrait is something almost useful and sometimes pleasant, like pieces of furniture one knows, they recall memories for a long time'.[1]

Van Gogh's paintings are now among the world's most treasured art, but what became of the humble objects that furnished the Yellow House? To my astonishment, I discovered that his bed, the very one which features in one of his most important paintings, had survived until after the Second World War. It had ended up over a thousand kilometres from Arles. The vicissitudes of this simple piece of furniture provide a poignant insight into the challenges Van Gogh faced, and shed further light on his legacy.

In May 1888 Van Gogh had rented the Yellow House unfurnished, so one of his first tasks was to acquire a bed. He asked at several furniture shops in Arles if he could rent or buy one on credit, but this was not possible. He even thought of asking Theo to send a bed from his Paris apartment. Without a bed, Van Gogh continued to sleep at the Café de la Gare. Only in August, when he was pressing Gauguin to join him in Arles, did he consider buying more furniture.

'Two beds, if you want something sturdy, will come to 150 francs each', he informed Theo.[2] Three hundred francs was a huge sum, probably more than anything he had bought in his entire life – and equivalent to twenty months' rent for the Yellow House. Yet he was impatient to proceed and went ahead and purchased the beds on around 8 September, a month before Gauguin's arrival. Van Gogh's bed was in deal wood, the colour of 'fresh butter yellow'. The other, for Gauguin, was in walnut (to make the guest room 'as nice as possible, like a woman's boudoir, really artistic'). Locally made, they were both double beds, with 'a look of solidity, durability, calm, and if it takes a bit more bed-linen, that's too bad, but it must have character.'[3]

Detail of fig. 21 *The Bedroom*, Van Gogh Museum, Amsterdam (Vincent van Gogh Foundation)

Van Gogh depicted his newly furnished room – with the bed centre-stage (fig. 21). Writing to Gauguin, he described the colours in his picture: 'The bed chrome yellow, the pillows and the sheet very pale lemon green, the bedspread blood-red'.[4] The twin pillows in the painting suggest that he still had a lingering hope that he might eventually share his bed with a woman. The design of the bed-ends is complicated, since they have curved tops, which would have cost more to make – but this was a typical feature of Provençal furniture of the time. On the day he made the purchase, he told Theo that he intended to paint his own bed. Although he seemed to be saying that he would be painting the actual bed, it is more likely that he meant his bed*room*.[5]

It was here that Gauguin discovered Van Gogh on the morning of 24 December, 'on his bed completely covered by the sheets, curled up'.[6] Soaked in blood, the sheets would have turned the colour of the bedspread. On his return from hospital Van Gogh paid 12.5 francs for laundering the bloodstained bedding.[7]

The early months of 1889 were exceedingly difficult for Van Gogh, and at one point his landlord's agent tried to confiscate his furniture in an attempt to force him to vacate the house. Van Gogh eventually conceded that he was not well enough to live by himself and he decided to move to the asylum in Saint-Rémy, leaving behind his furniture at the Café de la Gare. Altogether he had ended up sleeping barely 140 nights in his Yellow House bed; after the ear incident he had stayed mainly in the hospital ward.

Van Gogh had been very pleased with his picture of *The Bedroom*, although once he was forced to leave the Yellow House, the painting also brought back mixed memories. In April 1889 he wrote to Theo: 'It's one of the best and I think that when you look at it you'll see more clearly what my studio, now foundered, could have been.'[8]

In May 1889 Van Gogh moved to the asylum of St Paul de Mausole in Saint-Rémy. Two months later, feeling more settled, he considered bringing his furniture to the asylum, but instead left it in store at the Café de la Gare. During his year in Saint-Rémy he suffered four further mental attacks, each laying him low for a few days or weeks, although for much of the rest of the time he continued to work. Just before he finally left Provence to return north he considered abandoning his furniture in Arles, describing it as the debris of 'a shipwreck'.[9] He then changed his mind, asking Joseph and Marie Ginoux to dispatch his two beds and a mirror, while leaving the rest of the furniture for them.

In May 1890 Van Gogh made his last move, to Auvers-sur-Oise, a picturesque village north of Paris, where he took a room at the Auberge Ravoux. Joseph Ginoux dismantled and 'flat-packed' the beds and emptied the mattresses of their straw, dispatching the crate by train. When it arrived, Van Gogh had no immediate use for the beds, so they were stored at his inn.

Once settled in Auvers, Van Gogh set to work with gusto. He was astonishingly productive, painting almost a picture a day. Then on 27 July he suffered yet another mental attack. Taking a gun, he climbed up to the wheatfields that spread out above the village. It was there, in the landscape that had inspired so many of his last paintings, that he shot himself in the stomach. Seriously injured, Van Gogh staggered back to the inn, just managing to climb the stairs to his room.

Theo was informed the following morning and rushed to Auvers, remaining at Vincent's bedside until his brother's death in the early hours of 29 July 1890. On hearing the news, Jo wrote immediately to Theo: 'He was still so young and what might he not have done in his life – with his marvellous gifts, his great mind, his wonderful talent – is that all gone, buried for ever?' Theo tried to comfort her by saying that his older brother had finally 'found the rest he hadn't been able to find on earth'.[10]

* * *

While Theo and Jo were in mourning, the Arles beds were brought from Auvers to their Paris apartment, along with Vincent's recent paintings and other possessions. Tragedy would soon strike again. Theo developed syphilis and just two months after Vincent's death he fell seriously ill. He suffered terribly, dying the following January, aged 33. Jo was bereaved less than two years after her wedding and a year after giving birth to their son, Vincent Willem, who had been named after his uncle.

Jo was desperate to escape from Paris and start a new life. She quickly returned to the Netherlands, settling in Bussum, a village outside Amsterdam, where she ran a small guest house to support herself and her infant. Along with nearly a thousand paintings and drawings by Vincent she brought the two Arles beds, which would prove invaluable for her guests. Twelve years later Jo moved to Amsterdam and later to the village of Laren, to the east of the city. There she remained until her death in 1925, when the Laren villa passed to her son Vincent Willem. With every move, Van Gogh's bed came too.

In 1937 Fernand Benoit, the director of the Museon Arlaten in Arles, wrote to Vincent Willem suggesting that a museum dedicated to Van Gogh should be set up in the Yellow House. In the archives of the Van Gogh Museum I discovered Vincent Willem's unpublished reply: 'If you ever have the house in Place Lamartine, I could give you the bed which appears in the painting of the bedroom.'[11] He also generously offered to accompany it with the loan of a few paintings. Although details were never discussed, the obvious ones to be requested would have included *The Bedroom* and *The Yellow House* (fig. 1). Having found the 1937 letter, I was determined to discover what had happened to the bed.

Benoit's dream was never realised.[12] By 1922 'nothing had changed [in the Yellow House], at least inside', Rey reported.[13] That year the French art historian Gustave Coquiot visited Arles, and saw a sign by the door saying 'Furnished rooms to let'. The exterior was then a 'dirty yellow ochre'.[14] A few years later the ground floor of the Yellow House and the adjacent Crevoulin grocery were converted into a café, the Civette Arlésienne. Its owners, who slept in Van Gogh's old bedroom, had no wish for their home to be turned into a museum. One of the two surviving photographs of the room, taken in 1933, shows the wife of the owner standing by the window, beyond which the entrance of the *gendarmerie* is just visible (fig. 119).

The other reason why the museum idea never took off was the lack of interest in Van Gogh in Arles, despite his growing international fame. Widely remembered as the madman, he was sneered at by many residents of Place Lamartine, who probably still included a few elderly signatories of the petition calling for him to be dispatched to an asylum. Although a commemorative plaque had been installed on the facade of the Yellow House in 1922, the dates of his stay were incorrectly incised as 1887–88. This was an indication of how little Arles knew about its former resident.[15]

The artist Signac, who had visited Van Gogh in hospital in March 1889, returned forty-six years later and painted Place Lamartine (fig. 118). It shows

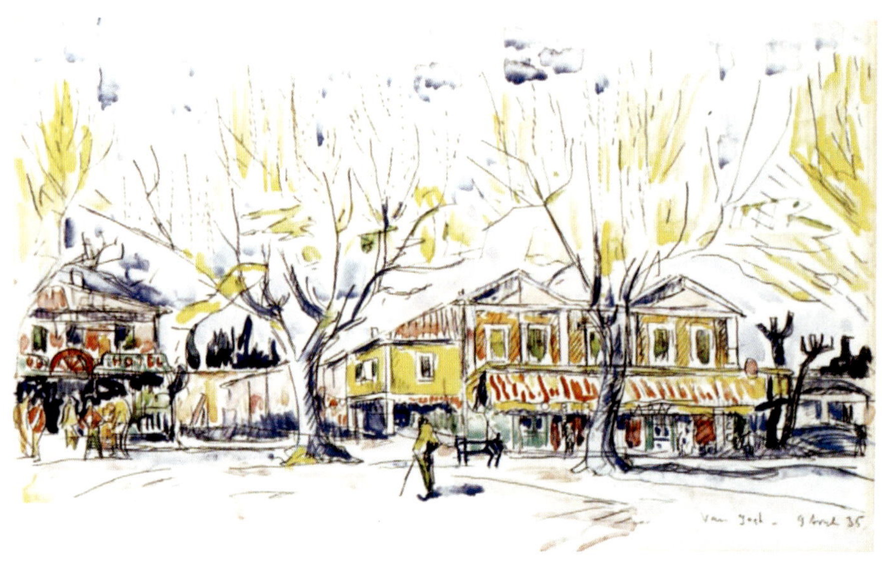

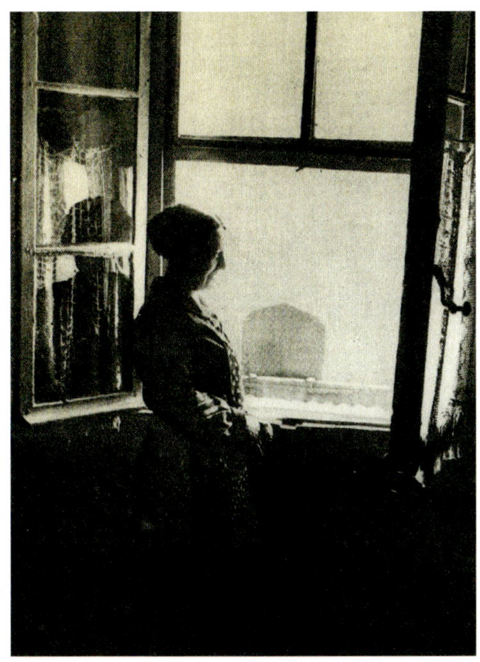

the Yellow House on the right and the Café de la Gare
(then renamed the Hotel Terminus) on the far left.

War finally shattered any hopes of creating a museum.
In June 1944 a wave of American and British bombers
launched their first attack on Arles, then in Vichy France.
Thirty-five people were killed, hundreds were injured
and swathes of the city lay in ruins. Place Lamartine,
located close to the strategically important station and
rail bridge across the Rhône, was devastated (fig. 120
shows another raid a few weeks later, with much of Place
Lamartine already flattened, just above and to the right
of the exploding Rhône bridge).[16]

The former grocery shop was completely destroyed
and the Yellow House was very badly damaged. Van
Gogh's bedroom was gone, although Gauguin's room
partly survived. The walls of the studio and the kitchen
downstairs suffered less damage, but the ceiling
collapsed (fig. 121). The Yellow House could have
been rebuilt, but it was simply demolished. Even the
plaque was lost. Fortunately Vincent Willem had never
lent the bed and paintings to the Yellow House.

* * *

Vincent Willem normally had twenty or so of his
uncle's greatest paintings hanging on the walls of his
Laren villa. Even by the 1930s security was hardly a
concern and his son Johan recalled that they used to
leave the house 'unattended for days on end without
worrying about burglars'.[17] But after war broke out,
with the threat of bombing in the Netherlands, most
of their paintings were evacuated to an underground
bunker in the coastal dunes at Castricum, leaving only
a few behind in Laren. Although not generally known
to Van Gogh specialists, on 30 August 1941 the Laren
villa was struck by lightning. The roof caught alight.
Fortunately the fire was quickly extinguished and
there was only minor damage to the house. Van Gogh's
bed had been stored in the cellar, where it remained
undamaged.

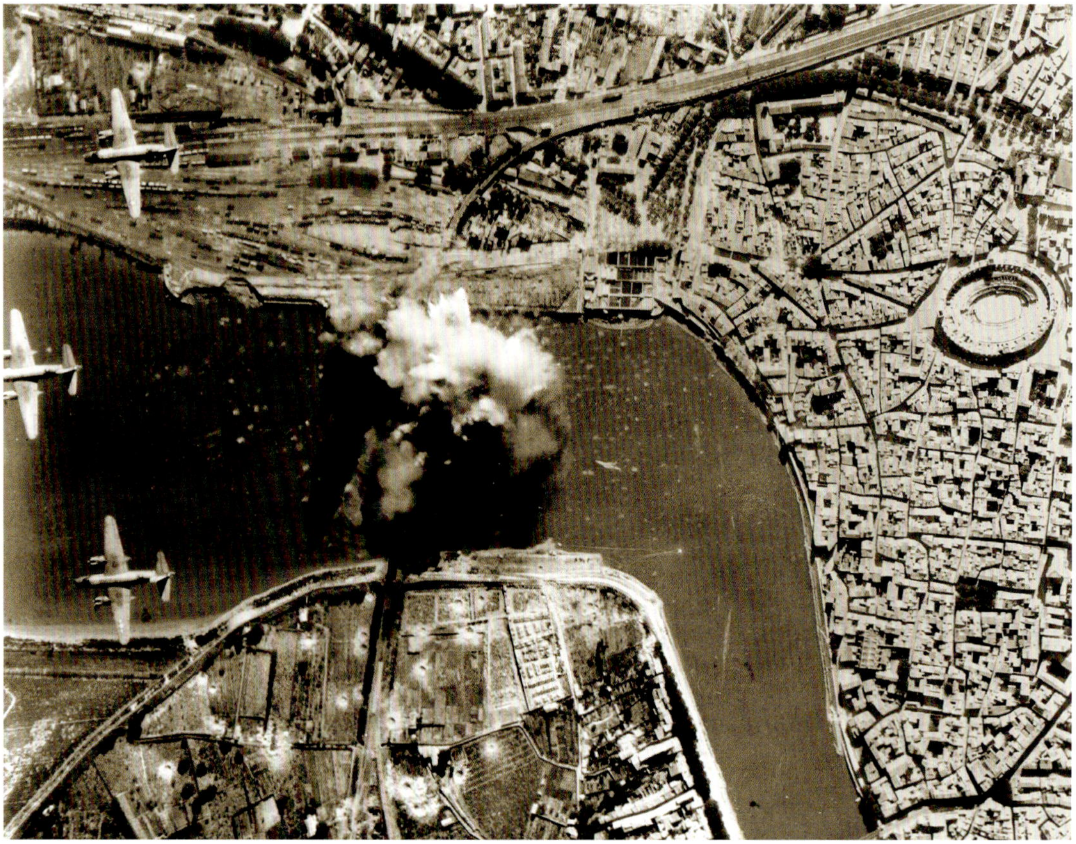

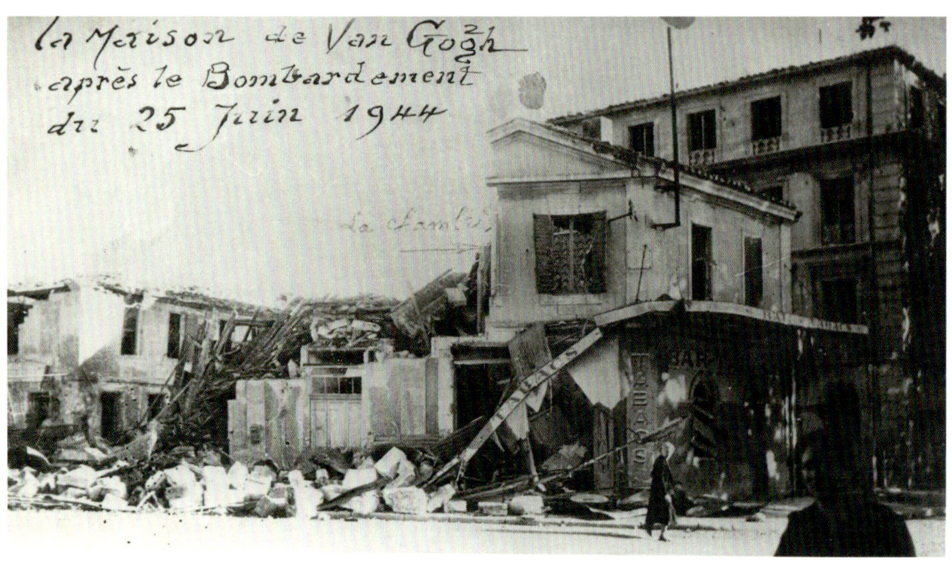

la Maison de Van Gogh
après le Bombardement
du 25 Juin 1944

Johan, the son of Vincent Willem (and grandson of Theo), told me about the fate of the bed during a conversation in 2015, when he was 93. After the Netherlands was liberated from German occupation his father had donated the bed to help those whose homes had been bombed. Some 70 years after the event, he could still recall that after the war the bed had gone 'somewhere in the Arnhem area', in the eastern Netherlands – an area which had suffered terrible losses from Allied bombing.[19] It had been very generous of the Van Goghs to have thought about helping others, since they had suffered terribly: Vincent Willem's oldest son, 24-year-old Theodoor, a resistance member, had been executed by the Gestapo a few months before the end of the occupation.[20]

I managed to track down what had happened to Van Gogh's bed. The village of Laren offered to support Boxmeer, a devastated small town 40 kilometres south of Arnhem, near the German border. Through the Red Cross, the people of Laren provided any furniture that they could spare. A September 1945 photograph survives of a lorry laden with furniture arriving in Boxmeer (fig. 122).[21] The needy Boxmeer recipient of the bed would have had no idea where it had come from – or the identity of its original owner. They would never have known that this was the bed where so many masterpieces had been born. As Van Gogh once wrote from the Yellow House, 'the most beautiful paintings are those one dreams of while smoking a pipe in one's bed.' It was there that the artist often mentally composed his pictures. 'Nature is so lovely these days', Van Gogh had written from Arles, and 'painting comes to me as if in a dream.'[22]

After the war the bed would have been nearly sixty years old and must have suffered from its travels and sojourn in the cellar. The new owner may well have replaced it some years later, when life became easier after the war. But there remains the tantalising possibility that the bed still survives in Boxmeer, a silent witness to the story of Van Gogh in Arles.

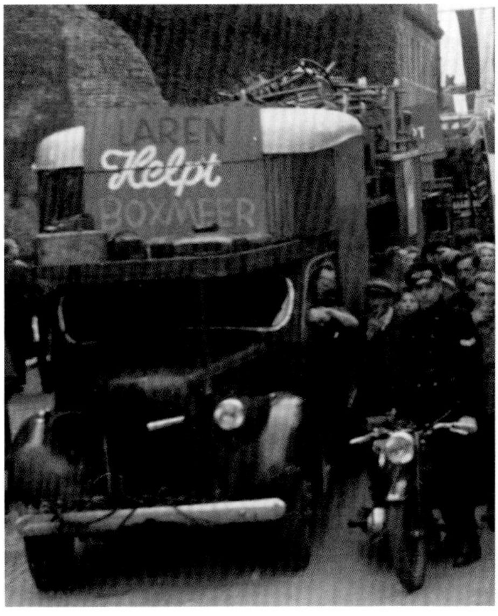

OPPOSITE fig. 120 American bombers over Arles, 6 August 1944[23]

OPPOSITE, BELOW fig. 121 The Yellow House after the bombing of 25 June 1944, postcard, photograph by Emilien Barral[24]

ABOVE fig. 122 Truck with furniture from Laren arriving at Boxmeer, 6 September 1945, photograph by Nico J. de Graaff, Verzetsmuseum, Amsterdam

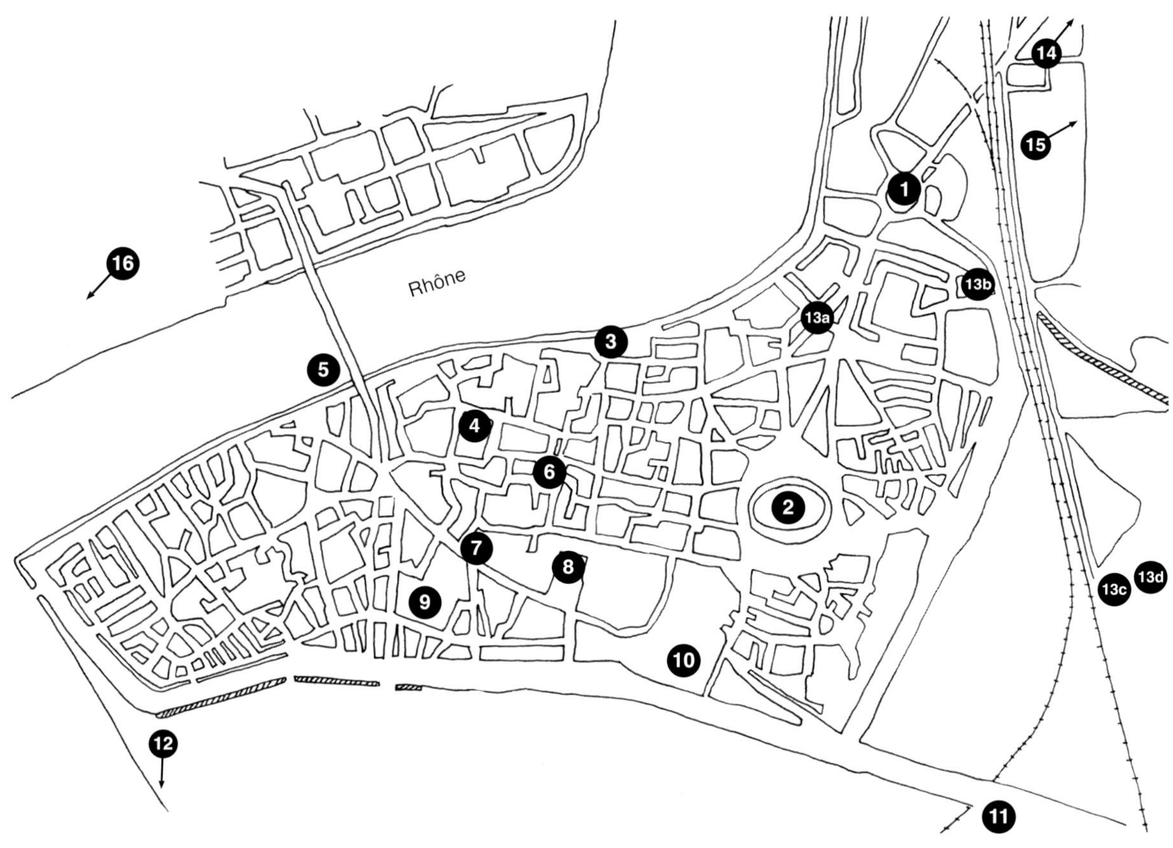

ON THE TRAIL OF VAN GOGH

A stroll around the streets of Arles opens a fascinating window on Van Gogh's life and work. In many of the spots where he worked, panels have been placed with images of the relevant paintings. The full route would take several days to cover, although the highlights can be seen by foot in a few hours or a day – Place Lamartine, the arena, the Fondation Vincent van Gogh Arles exhibition centre, the Place du Forum, the former hospital (Espace Van Gogh) and the Alyscamps. Much of Arles was bombed in 1944, but the historic centre was rebuilt and retains much of the atmosphere of earlier centuries. Low-rise houses with sun-bleached shutters line its narrow streets, where there is little traffic. The sweeping curve of the Rhône embankment is never far away, with remnants of the ancient ramparts remaining on the other three sides. No museum in Arles owns any of Van Gogh's art, but paintings and drawings are sometimes on display at the Fondation Vincent van Gogh, Arles.[1] For a map of Arles in Van Gogh's time, see fig. 10.

1. PLACE LAMARTINE

Start the Van Gogh trail in Place Lamartine, where the Yellow House once stood. Until 1944 the house overlooked what is now a small green area just to the north of the present roundabout (the larger building in Van Gogh's *The Yellow House*, fig. 1, houses a café, as it did when he was there). The road to the right in the painting was Van Gogh's Route de Tarascon or Avenue de Montmajour (now Avenue de Stalingrad), still spanned by the railway viaducts which also appear in two of his other paintings.[2] The Café de la Gare, which was also bombed, would originally have been to the left of the Yellow House, towards the river. For Van Gogh's views of the Rhône, walk over to the embankment (*Quay with Sand Barges*, fig. 48, and *Starry Night over the Rhône*, fig. 69).[3] A very small segment of the former public gardens survives in one corner of Place Lamartine, where the ramparts reach the Rhône.

2. ARENA

Van Gogh painted a view of the crowd from an upper level of the Roman amphitheatre (*Arena in Arles*, fig. 92). There is an excellent view from one of the towers over the rooftops of the town. Looking northwards, one can see Place Lamartine and, in the distance, the ruins of Montmajour and the outline of the Alpilles. To the east and south are the fields which appear in many of Van Gogh's landscapes.

3. MUSÉE RÉATTU

Although Van Gogh described the museum 'dreadful', it is entirely different now, displaying a wide range of art, from Jacques Réattu's original collection to contemporary works. No museum in Arles owns any of Van Gogh's art, but in 1983 the Musée Réattu bought an important letter to Gauguin.[4]

4. FONDATION VINCENT VAN GOGH ARLES

This exhibition centre named after Van Gogh presents excellent changing shows of contemporary art. Loaned works by Van Gogh may well also be on view. In 2014 the Fondation Vincent van Gogh Arles moved to its present location, in a converted fifteenth-century mansion and modern extension, with its entrance at 35 Rue du Dr Fanton.

5. TRINQUETAILLE BRIDGE

Although the bridge was bombed and rebuilt to a modern design in 1951, part of the original stonework approach remains. Van Gogh painted *Trinquetaille Bridge* (fig. 49) from the embankment on the southern side. The tall tree standing there now was probably the sapling in his painting. Rey, Van Gogh's doctor, lived on the upper approach to the bridge at 6 Rue Anatole France (originally Rampe du Pont).

6. PLACE DU FORUM

Van Gogh's *Café Terrace at Night* (fig. 67) depicts what was then the Café du Forum at 11 Place du Forum (it is still a café today). Two columns and part of the pediment of the Roman forum remain, embedded in the building just to the right of Van Gogh's view. The Place du Forum was the social centre of Arles in Van Gogh's time (as it had been since Roman days) – and is still a lively hub of cafés and restaurants, which spill into the square. Although now often packed with tourists, the surrounding buildings give a taste of nineteenth-century Arles and earlier eras.

7. MUSEON ARLATEN

The Museon Arlaten was inaugurated by the poet Frédéric Mistral in 1899 to celebrate Provençal culture and ethnography. Although it opened a decade after Van Gogh's stay, the museum provides a fascinating insight into life in nineteenth-century Arles. Currently closed for major renovations, it is due to reopen in 2018.

8. PLACE DE LA RÉPUBLIQUE

The main square of Arles is home to its town hall and the Church of St Trophime. The Gothic sculptures of the church's magnificent facade include the monstrous figures which Van Gogh described as 'so cruel'. The Church of St Anne, across the square, was the museum of antiquities in Van Gogh's time (the collection has moved to a modern building just south of the city centre). The deconsecrated church now hosts temporary exhibitions.

9. ESPACE VAN GOGH

When the hospital closed in 1986 it was converted into a médiathèque (centred around a library), named the Espace Van Gogh. Its garden, re-planted as it appears in *Courtyard of the Hospital* (fig. 117), remains a delightful spot and riot of colour in the spring and summer. For the view in the painting, walk up the stairs to the upper arcade.

10. PUBLIC GARDEN

The present public garden (formerly known as the summer garden) lies between the Boulevard des Lices and the Roman theatre. Certain sources suggest that Van Gogh painted some of his garden scenes here, but they were probably all done in Place Lamartine. Nevertheless, the present garden gives an idea of what Place Lamartine might have been like. Near the entrance is a 1969 memorial bust to Van Gogh by the American sculptor William Earl Singer.

11. ALYSCAMPS

The Alyscamps, part of the Roman necropolis, is a tranquil tree-lined avenue just outside the centre of the town, to the south east. It shelters two rows of sarcophagi. Van Gogh and Gauguin set up their easels there side-by-side (figs. 77–82).

12. VAN GOGH BRIDGE

The Langlois Bridge, which Van Gogh painted several times (fig. 44), was replaced by the nearby enlarged Réginel Bridge after the war. Only one original canal drawbridge survived the war and in 1962 this structure was moved from further south and re-erected three kilometres south of the former Langlois Bridge. Now known as the Pont Van Gogh, it is much photographed by tourists.

13. OTHER ARLES SITES

The Hotel Carrel (13a), in Rue Amédée Pichot, was destroyed during the war (it stood just to the east of the present junction with Rue Léon Blum, on a site now occupied by a medical laboratory). Rue du Bout d'Arles (13b) was also badly bombed and number 1, at the north-east corner, remains an empty site. Further out from the centre of town, the base of a windmill painted by Van Gogh survives at 27 Rue Mireille (13c).[5] The Mas de Griffeuille (13d, a farmhouse which appears in two of Van Gogh's landscapes, including *Haystacks*, fig. 39) still stands at 3 Rue J. F. Kennedy.[6]

14. MONTMAJOUR

The vast Abbey of Montmajour crowns an imposing hill five kilometres north-east of Arles. Its tower offers magnificent panoramic views and many of the scenes in Van Gogh's drawings can still be identified. Four kilometres beyond lies the village of Fontvieille, where Mourier-Petersen, Boch and Macknight stayed. Van Gogh visited Fontvieille several times, on one occasion drawing the windmill immortalised by Alphonse Daudet.[7]

15. SAINT-RÉMY

The charming market town of Saint-Rémy-de-Provence lies 20 kilometres from Arles, beyond Montmajour and Fontvieille. On the southern outskirts of Saint-Rémy is the asylum of St Paul de Mausole (very close to the Roman site of Glanum). St Paul de Mausole remains a psychiatric hospital, but the twelfth-century cloister and a former patient's room similar to the one occupied by Van Gogh and part of the garden can be visited. The surrounding countryside, just north of the Alpilles, figures in dozens of Van Gogh's pictures. In the town of Saint-Rémy Van Gogh painted two views of the tree-lined Boulevard Mirabeau.[8] The Musée Estrine art gallery, set in an eighteenth-century mansion, shows changing exhibitions of contemporary art and a series of display panels tell the story of Van Gogh's life. The Musée des Alpilles is an excellent local museum.

16. SAINTES-MARIES

The picturesque seaside village of Les Saintes-Maries-de-la-Mer lies 40 kilometres south of Arles, over the Trinquetaille Bridge and across the Camargue. It is renowned for its pilgrimage church dedicated to the two Marys. Van Gogh's *View of Saintes-Maries* (fig. 31) was done from a spot near the sea where a large cross now stands, close to the bullfighting arena. *Row of Cottages in Saintes-Maries* (fig. 35) was drawn in Rue de la Plage (now Rue Frédéric Mistral), which is now packed with restaurants. Van Gogh probably stayed at the Pension Coulomb, now the Hotel Delta in Place Mireille.

CHRONOLOGY

1888

20 February	Vincent van Gogh arrives by train from Paris and stays in Arles at Hotel Carrel (30 Rue Amédée-Pichot)
Early March	Meets Danish artist Christian Mourier-Petersen (who leaves Arles on 22 May, to stay with Theo in Paris 6 June–15 August)
9 March	First visit to Montmajour (five kilometres north-east of Arles)
11 March	Murder of two Zouave soldiers at the end of Rue du Bout d'Arles
24 March–20 April	Paints blossoming orchards
30 March	35th birthday
15 April	Meets American artist Dodge Macknight (who leaves Fontvieille/Arles in late August)
23 April	Probably visits Fontvieille (ten kilometres north-east of Arles)
1 May	Rents the Yellow House at 2 Place Lamartine and uses it as his studio (but initially not for sleeping). Theo's 31st birthday
3 May	Visits Fontvieille
7 May	Moves from Hotel Carrel to sleep at Café de la Gare (30 Place Lamartine)
10 May	Sends 26 paintings to Theo in Paris
Mid–end May	Draws at Montmajour for a first round of work

30 May–4 June
  (or 31 May–5 June)   Visits Les Saintes-Maries-de-la-Mer on the Mediterranean coast (40 kilometres south of Arles)

Early June   Meets Zouave soldier Paul-Eugène Milliet (who leaves Arles on 1 November)

10 June   Visits Tarascon (15 kilometres north of Arles)

11–20 June   Paints harvest scenes

About 15 June   Meets Belgian artist Eugène Boch (who leaves Arles on 4 September)

Early July   Paints and draws at Montmajour for a second round of work

8 or 9 July   Visits Fontvieille

22 July   Gauguin accepts invitation to come to Arles

Late July   Meets postman Joseph Roulin (who leaves Arles on 21 January 1889)

Early August   Meets peasant Patience Escalier

12 August   Sends 36 paintings to Theo in Paris

20–26 August   Paints a series of four Sunflowers

17 September   Starts sleeping in the Yellow House

About 29 September   Paints *The Yellow House* (fig. 1)

16 October   Registers as a foreigner at the town hall

| About 17 October | Paints *The Bedroom* (fig. 21) |

23 October — Paul Gauguin arrives by train from Pont-Aven in Brittany

Late October–early November — Paints with Gauguin in the Alyscamps

Late November–early December — Paints portraits of the Roulin family

About 10 December — Theo meets Johanna (Jo) Bonger in Paris

16 or 17 December — Van Gogh and Gauguin visit Musée Fabre in Montpellier (70 kilometres west of Arles)

About 17 December — Theo and Jo decide to marry

23 December — Receives letter from Theo with news of his engagement to Jo. That evening Vincent mutilates his ear

24 December — Taken to hospital (Hôtel-Dieu St Esprit) in the morning

25 December — Christmas Day. Theo visits Vincent in hospital, leaving that evening with Gauguin (arriving in Paris the following morning)

1889

5 January — Theo travels to Holland for his engagement announcement (Jo had arrived on 26 December)

7 January — Discharged from hospital

9 January — Theo and Jo get formally engaged in Amsterdam (Theo returns to Paris on 13 January)

21 January — Joseph Roulin leaves Arles for Marseille (Augustine Roulin leaves Arles in early February for a stay in Lambesc)

About 4 February — Suffers second mental breakdown

7–18 February	Second stay in hospital
About 26 February	Thirty neighbours around Place Lamartine submit a petition calling for Van Gogh to return to his family or be sent to an asylum
26 February	Suffers third mental breakdown and taken to hospital
27 February	Police commissioner Joseph d'Ornano signs report after receiving the petition recommending that Van Gogh be incarcerated in an asylum
3 March	Committed to hospital by the mayor and the Yellow House is closed
23–24 March	French artist Paul Signac visits Arles and they go from the hospital to visit the Yellow House
27 March	Continues to sleep at hospital, but allowed out during the day (until the end of his stay in Arles)
30 March	36th birthday. Theo and Jo travel to Holland for their wedding
About 4 April	Roulin visits Arles from Marseille and meets Van Gogh
18 April	Wedding of Theo and Jo in Amsterdam (Theo is in the Netherlands from 30 March to 19 April); on their return to Paris they move to 8 Cité Pigalle
About 19 April	Relinquishes lease of Yellow House (from end of April)
1 May	Theo's 32nd birthday
About 2 May	Sends at least 30 paintings to Theo in two crates
8 May	Leaves Arles for the asylum of St Paul de Mausole in Saint-Rémy-de-Provence (20 kilometres north-east of Arles)

ENDNOTES

PREFACE (pp. 6–13)

1   Martin Bailey, 'Van Gogh's Portrait of Gauguin', *Apollo*, July 1996, pp. 51–4 and Druick and Zegers, 2001, pp. 236, 240 and 363–4.

2   Letter 674 (4 September 1888), see also 702 (10–11 October 1888). Van Gogh's expression was 'un atelier dans le midi' (a studio in the south). The Midi, or South, is a common term for southern France. The title of this book uses a slight variant of Van Gogh's phrase. Provence is the eastern part of the Midi, running from Arles towards the Italian border. Arles was the centre of the cultural revival of Provence in the late nineteenth century.

3   Letters 674 (4 September 1888) and 680 (c. 11 September 1888).

4   Letter 678 (9–14 September 1888).

5   Postcard captioned 'Arles – Gendarmerie et Avenue Montmajour', published by J. Poirey.

6   Letter from Pierre Gazanhes to author, 16 November 2015. His grandmother, Victorine Gazanhes, lived there.

7   Letter 626 (16–20 June 1888).

8   He used the term 'landscape painter' in Letter 626 (16–20 June 1888) and in his hospital registration in December 1888 (Massebieau, 1946, p. 232) – and it was also used in the February 1889 petition against him (*Van Gogh à Arles*, 2003, p. 60). Until his arrival in Arles he usually described himself as simply an artist (or painter). Roughly half of Van Gogh's Arles paintings are landscapes, with the remainder being portraits and still lifes.

9   However, in terms of exhibition catalogues I should acknowledge the pioneering work of the British art historian Ronald Pickvance, who curated the only comprehensive show of Van Gogh's Arles works, held in New York (Pickvance, 1984). The short period when Van Gogh and Gauguin worked together in Arles has been excellently covered in both the catalogue of the Chicago-Amsterdam exhibition (Druick and Zegers, 2001) and Martin Gayford's book *The Yellow House* (Gayford, 2006). Roland Dorn's thesis in German represents an important contribution (Dorn, 1990). Bernd Wengler, *Vincent van Gogh in Arles: Eine psychoanalytische Künstler-und Werkinterpretation*, Kassel University, 2013, is a specialist psychological study. There are two slim volumes which provide brief overviews of Van Gogh's time in Arles: Uwe Schneede, *Van Gogh in Arles: Gemälde 1888/1889*, Gutenberg, Frankfurt, 1989 and Alfred Nemeczek, *Van Gogh in Arles*, Prestel, Munich, 1995.

10   The main experts who visited Arles and conducted interviews before 1939 were Julius Meier-Graefe, Gustave Coquiot, Louis Piérard, Edgar Leroy, Victor Doiteau, Max Braumann, Benno Stokvis and John Rewald (see Bibliography, pp. 210–11, for their publications).

11   Interview with author, 19 October 1988. Calment died on 4 August 1997.

12   Interview with author, 19 December 1987. The portrait was shown in the exhibition 'Van Gogh et Arles' in February 1989 (no. 41), when Mourard finally saw the painting.

13   Letter 639 (c.13 July 1888).

14   Email from family member, 2 November 2015.

15   Artists Van Gogh knew in Arles included Christian Mourier-Petersen (Danish), Dodge Macknight (American), Eugène Boch (Belgian) and Jules Armand (from Arles). Paul Signac visited him briefly in Arles. Van Gogh may well have met Alfred Casile (from Marseille) and Joseph Pennell (American).

16   Léon Daudet, *Ecrivains et artistes*, Capitole, Paris, 1927, vol. i, p. 154.

17   See also Bailey, 2013, p. 85.

18   Archives Communales, Arles, file J26 (Maisons de Tolérance, 1871–91). My thanks to archivist Sylvie Rebuttini for her assistance.

19 It was long known from an article in *Le Forum
    Républican* (30 December 1888) that the brothel
    was named 'No. 1' but it had been unclear whether
    this meant it was the first brothel to be officially
    registered or if it was located at 1 Rue du Bout
    d'Arles. Further research confirms that it does refer
    to the street number. Brothels were not allowed to
    advertise their services in the street, so instead of
    signs they simply displayed overly-large numbers
    outside their doors.

20 *Annuaire Reirum: Indicateur des Adresses des Maisons
    de Société (dites de Tolérances) de France, Algérie et
    Tunisie et des Principales Villes de Suisse, Belgique,
    Hollande, Italie et Espagne*, Murier, Paris, 1890. The
    page covering Arles was reprinted in Louis Fiaux,
    Les Maisons de Tolérance: Leur Fermeture, Carré,
    Paris, 1892, p. 353.

21 Alfred Massebieau to Alfred Valette (then editor
    of *Mercure de France*), 10 April 1893 (Massebieau,
    1946, p. 232). Massebieau's letter was in response
    to publication of the first installment of Van Gogh's
    letters to Emile Bernard in *Mercure de France* (April
    1893, pp. 324–30). There is an unsourced mention
    of Massebieau and the medical register in a book on
    Gauguin (Merlhès, 1989, p. 256), but this does not
    cite the 1893 letter.

22 Van Gogh exhibited three paintings at the Salon des
    Indépendants in Paris in March–May 1888 (F316,
    F350 and F359). There is some evidence that Van
    Gogh may have sold a self-portrait in London in
    October 1888 (Martin Bailey, 'Van Gogh's First
    Sale', *Apollo*, March 1996, pp. 20–1).

23 Wil to Theo, 23 December 1888 (Van Gogh
    Museum archive, b2387), see also Letter 719 (11–
    12 November 1888).

PROLOGUE: PARIS (pp. 14–19)

1 Letter 577 (21 February 1888)
2 Letter 626 (16–20 June 1888).
3 Letter 626 (16–20 June 1888).
4 Jo Bonger, 'Memoir of Vincent van Gogh' in *The
   Complete Letters of Vincent van Gogh*, Thames &
   Hudson, London, 1958, vol. i, p. L.
5 Ella Hendriks and Louis van Tilborgh, *Vincent van
   Gogh Paintings: Antwerp & Paris 1885–1888*, Van
   Gogh Museum, Amsterdam, 2011, vol. ii, pp. 440–
   7. The other work, which Van Tilborgh accepts as a
   self-portrait, is F296.
6 Van Gogh Museum archive, b4780a. This photograph was taken to mark Theo's engagement. Theo
   also had other photographs taken by a process
   developed by the British photographer Walter
   Woodbury.
7 Dorothee Hansen, *Emile Bernard: Am Puls der Mod-
   erne*, Kunsthalle, Bremen, 2015, p. 19 and Martin
   Bailey, *The Art Newspaper*, February 2015, p. 8.
8 Marije Vellekoop (ed.), *Van Gogh at Work*, Van
   Gogh Museum, Amsterdam, 2013, p. 147.
9 Letters 870 (11 May 1890), 704 (15 October 1888)
   and 710 (22 October 1888).
10 *Lettres de Vincent van Gogh à Emile Bernard*, Vollard, Paris, 1911, p. 12. See also Letter 692 (1 October 1888).

CHAPTER ONE: DISCOVERING ARLES (pp. 20–7)

1 Letter 612 (c.22 May 1888). The 2009 edition of
   the letters translates Van Gogh's 'coquette' as 'neat'
   (Jansen, Luijten and Bakker, 2009, vol. iv, p. 91).
2 Letter 577 (21 February 1888).
3 *L'Homme de Bronze*, 26 February 1888.
4 Until 1887 it was known as Rue de la Cavalerie.
5 Letters 604 (4 May 1888) and 686 (23–24
   September 1888).
6 The Venus is a first-century BC Roman copy of a
   Greek sculpture. It was excavated in 1651 and was
   in the Louvre in Van Gogh's time. He saw an early
   nineteenth-century copy displayed in the lobby
   of the town hall in Arles. Van Gogh commented
   on the Venus' 'youthfulness' (Letter 683, 18

September 1888, see also 695, 3 October 1888).

7   Reproduced in Tralbaut, 1969, p. 220. The hotel was on the north-west corner of the junction of Rue Amédée Pichot and Rue Métras. Rue Métras was built over after the Second World War and the former location of the demolished hotel is now just to the east of Rue Léon Blum.

8   Letter 578 (c.24 February 1888).

9   Letter 588 (21–22 March 1888), see also 828 (c.13 December 1889).

10 Lithographed by Charles Villemin and coloured, 'Voyage aérien en France', published by Hauser, Paris, c.1850.

11 Letter 578 (c.24 February 1888), see also 583 (9 March 1888).

12 Armand's *Sitting Arlésienne*, 1889, is at the Museon Arlaten, Arles. His Alyscamps scene with an Arlésienne and his evening view at Montmajour are both lost (*L'Homme de Bronze*, 12 February 1888 and 19 August 1888, see also 10 March 1889). Armand's shop was at 30 Rue du Quatre-Septembre.

13 Coquiot, 1923, p. 164, see also Stokvis, 1929, p. 4.

14 Letter 578 (c.24 February 1888). The shop was at 61 Rue Amédée Pichot.

15 Map by L. Thuillier in *Arles et Les Baux, Guides Joanne*, Hachette, Paris, 1896, after p. 2, 16 x 19 cm.

16 Letters 601 (c.25 April 1888), 602 (1 May 1888) and 610 (c.14 May 1888). See Coquiot, 1923, p. 161.

17 Stokvis, 1929, p. 4.

CHAPTER TWO: BLOSSOMING ORCHARDS (pp. 28–33)

1   Letter 592 (c.3 April 1888).

2   Letter 582 (c.2 March 1888). F392 was for Theo and F393 for Wil (who turned 26 on 16 March 1888).

3   In the background of Van Gogh's 1887 portrait of Père Julien Tanguy (F363) he depicted an 1855 print of cherry blossoms by Utagawa Hiroshige. That year Van Gogh also painted his own version of an 1857 plum orchard by Hiroshige (F371). Van Gogh's own copies of both prints survive (Van Gogh Museum, Amsterdam).

4   Letter 594 (9 April 1888).

5   Letter 590 (c.30 March 1888). The same trees appear in F551.

6   Letter 591 (c.1 April 1888). Mauve had died on 5 February 1888, aged 49.

7   Wil to Theo and Jo, 23 December 1888 (Van Gogh Museum archive, b2387), see also Letter 719 (11–12 November 1888). Vincent's mother Anna wrote to congratulate him on the compliment, but her letter arrived in Arles a few days after the self-mutilation, see reference in Anna to Theo, 29 December 1888 (Van Gogh Museum archive, b2425).

8   Mourier-Petersen to Johan Rohde, 16 March 1888 and 4 June 1888 (Rohde papers, Tilg. 392, Royal Library, Copenhagen. Mourier-Peterson initially found Van Gogh's name difficult, calling him 'Van Prut'.). See also Merete Bodelsen, *Gauguin and Van Gogh in Copenhagen in 1893*, Ordrupgaard, Copenhagen, 1984, p. 29 and Håkan Larsson, *Flames from the South: On the Introduction of Vincent van Gogh to Sweden*, privately published, Eslöv, 1996, pp. 9–18.

9   Letters 625 (15–16 June 1888) and 585 (c.16 March 1888). Mourier-Petersen's letters to Rohde (Royal Library, Copenhagen) show that he spent part of 1887 in the village of Fontvieille, where the artists Dodge Macknight and Eugène Boch later lodged.

10 Benni Golf, 'Van Gogh og Denmark', *Politiken*, 6 January 1938, cited in Håkan Larsson, *Flames from the South: The Introduction of Vincent van Gogh to Sweden before 1900*, privately published, Lund, 1993, p. 17.

11 Letter 585 (c.16 March 1888).

12 Letter 591 (c.1 April 1888).

13 Letter 596 (c.12 April 1888). Van Gogh particularly admired the work of the Marseille artist Adolphe Monticelli (1824–86), who also used thick impasto.

14 Letters 593 (5 April 1888) and 594 (9 April 1888).

15 Letters 594 (9 April 1888), 595 (c.11 April 1888) and 615 (28 May 1888).

16 The paintings are: F394, F399, F403, F404, F405, F406, F513, F551, F552, F553, F554, F555, F556, F557 and a destroyed painting of cherry blossom.

17 Letters 598 (19 April 1888) and 608 (10 May 1888).

CHAPTER THREE: AN ARTIST'S HOUSE (pp. 34–41)

1   Letter 626 (16–20 June 1888).

2   Letters 626 (16–20 June 1888) and 602 (1 May 1888). When this drawing arrived in Paris, Theo's flatmate, the Dutch artist Arnold Koning, was oblivious to its significance. He casually used the reverse to scribble a note to Theo: 'If you happen to be awake tomorrow at 5 o'clock, please call me' (Vellekoop and Zwikker, 2007, p. 81).

3   The rent went up to 21.50 francs a month in December, when Van Gogh took over two additional small rooms on the upper floor. His landlord was Aimé Verdier, whose local agent was Bernard Soulé. At the Hotel Carrel he apparently had originally paid 150 francs a month (soon reduced to 120 francs and later to 90 francs), but this probably included meals. After leaving the hotel he paid 30 francs a month for a bedroom at the Café de la Gare.

4   References to the *maison jaune* are in letters 626, 714, 724, 730, 736, 739 and 745 (16 June 1888 to 3 February 1889), see also 678 (9–14 September 1888).

5   Letter 607 (10 May 1888).

6   Three other pictures in this book which have painted borders are figs. 42, 61 and 109. Another has a painted wooden frame (fig. 95).

7   The address of the grocery shop was also 2 Place Lamartine, the restaurant was at 28 and the café at 30. Van Gogh once called *The Yellow House* 'The Street' (Letter 696, 3 October 1888).

8   Letter 685 (21 September 1888).

9   Letter 602 (1 May 1888). The sketch is 4 x 5 cm.

10 Letter 604 (4 May 1888).

11 Letter 703 (13 October 1888). The western section of the gardens, which was the most attractive, was destroyed when a water treatment plant was built near the Rhône in 1907.

12 Letter 704 (15 October 1888).

13 Letter 705 (16 October 1888). In September 1889 Van Gogh painted two other versions of *The Bedroom* (F483 and F484), with different portraits of a man and woman hanging above the bed (probably a self-portrait, F525, in F483 and the other portraits are unidentified).

14 Letter 705 (16 October 1888).

15 Marije Vellekoop (ed.), *Van Gogh at Work*, Van Gogh Museum, Amsterdam, 2013, p. 251. See also Groom, 2016, pp. 89–91, with digital reconstruction, p. 90. Van Gogh originally described the interior of the house as 'whitewashed' (Letter 602, 1 May 1888). He may have redecorated the bedroom in pale violet (or a whitewash with a touch of violet) – or the pale violet may have been an artistic invention for his painting.

16 Letter 705 (16 October 1888).

17 Letter 741 (22 January 1889). He hung the picture in the Yellow House, quite possibly in his bedroom (Letter 706, 17 October 1888).

18 Letter 705 (16 October 1888).

19 Letter 685 (21 September 1888), see also 681 (16 September 1888). Van Gogh probably took the phrase 'maison d'artiste' from Edmond de Goncourt, *La maison d'un artiste*, Charpentier, Paris, 1881, in which the critic described his own home.

20 Enclosed with Letter 705 (16 October 1888).

CHAPTER FOUR: HEIGHTS OF MONTMAJOUR (pp. 42–51)

1   Letter 637 (8–9 July 1888).

2   Letters 613 (26 May 1888) and 639 (c.13 July 1888). Among the motifs that he probably drew on his route was a tile factory (Martin Bailey, *Van Gogh and Britain: Pioneer Collectors*, National Galleries of Scotland, Edinburgh, 2006, pp. 104 and 141, note 28).

3   Letter 583 (9 March 1888). Van Gogh was probably taken there by Mourier-Petersen (see Letters 639, c.13 July 1888 and 641, 15 July 1888).

4   Although the drawing is usually said to show the Route de Tarascon, it may show the side road which turns off it at the Moines (Monks) Bridge and rises to Montmajour.

5   Van Gogh hoped to show some Montmajour drawings at an exhibition in Amsterdam in June organised by the Nederlandsche Etsclub, but the organisers later said they only wanted works from established artists.

6   F1417, F1418, F1419, F1423, F1448, F1452, F1475 and F1493.

7   Letter 618 (29–30 May 1888), see also 617 (29–30 May 1888).

8   Letter 636 (5 July 1888), see also 615 (28 May 1888) for a description of an earlier sunset at Montmajour.

9   Louis van Tilborgh, Teio Meedendorp and Oda van Maanen, '"Sunset at Montmajour": A newly discovered painting by Vincent van Gogh', *The Burlington Magazine*, October 2013, pp. 696–705.

10 F1446, F1447, F1420, F1424 and one drawing not in de la Faille (*Trees, Montmajour*, Musée des Beaux-Arts, Tournai). He also did another painting (F466).

11 Postcard captioned (on reverse) 'Montmajour (Bouches du Rhône), L'Abbaye fondée au VIe s.', published by Yvon, Paris.

12 Letter 638 (9–10 July 1888).

13 This undated painting was exhibited at the Paris Salon in May 1889 (no. 498).

14   Letter 641 (15 July 1888).
15   Letter 639 (c.13 July 1888). The Paris dealer was Georges Thomas.
16   Letters 660 (c.13 August 1888) and 626 (16–20 June 1888).
17   Martin Bailey, 'Could this masterpiece still be found?', *The Art Newspaper,* September 2009, p. 6.

CHAPTER FIVE: SEASCAPES (pp. 52–61)
1   Letter 619 (3–4 June 1888).
2   Letter 615 (28 May 1888). Van Gogh had painted seascapes six years earlier when he was living in The Hague, which was near the fishing village of Scheveningen, but these were done in his Dutch style, with muted colours.
3   There has been considerable discussion among Van Gogh specialists about the dates of his visit, but it was probably from 30 or 31 May to 4 or 5 June 1888 (see Letter 617, 29–30 May 1888, note on dating).
4   Letters 617 (29–30 May 1888) and 619 (3–4 June 1888).
5   Letter 619 (3–4 June 1888). Van Gogh had painted a still life of dead mackerel in Paris in 1886 (F285).
6   Postcard captioned 'Les Saintes-Maries-de-la-Mer: Le Village et l'Eglise', published by Blanchin, Tarascon.
7   Kathrin Pilz, '*En plein air* or in the Studio?', Marije Vellekoop and others (ed), *Van Gogh's Studio Practice,* Van Gogh Museum, Amsterdam, 2013, pp. 100–01. Van Gogh also painted a second seascape (F417).
8   Letter 643 (17–20 July 1888).
9   F1432, F1434, F1436, F1437, F1438, F1439, F1440 and F1479.
10   Letter 622 (c.7 June 1888).
11   Letters 620 (c.5 June 1888) and 686 (23–24 September 1888).
12   F413 (oil) and F1429 (watercolour).
13   Letter 622 (7 June 1888).
14   Letters 613 (26 May 1888) and 620 (c.5 June 1888). In early July he intended to return to the Camargue, but the promised ride with a local vet did not materialise.

CHAPTER SIX: HARVEST TIME (pp. 62–71)
1   Letter 628 (c.19 June 1888).
2   Letter 635 (c.1 July 1888). The watercolours are F1484 and F1483 (inscribed).
3   Possibly the Moulin de Jonquet (or Souchon), which survives at 27 Rue Mireille. It was painted

by Van Gogh (F550). See Schröder, 2008, p. 296 and Teio Meedendorp, 'Van Gogh's Topography' in Standring and Van Tilborgh, 2012, p. 106.
4   Letter 624 (12–13 June 1888). For background on Van Gogh's harvest scenes, see Dorothy Kosinski, *Van Gogh's Sheaves of Wheat,* Dallas Museum of Art, 2006.
5   Letters 635 (1 July 1888) and 625 (15–16 June 1888).
6   The copy for Bernard is F1485. This was part of a wider scheme to make smaller drawn copies of his successful Arles paintings. In July–August 1888 he drew copies of 15 paintings for Bernard, 12 for Russell and 5 for Theo (Ives and others, 2005, pp. 266–77).
7   Letter 643 (17–20 July 1888). The 2009 edition of the letters translates this as 'croquis of Provence'.
8   Letter 635 (c.1 July 1888).
9   Ricciotto Canudo, 'Une visite à Rodin', *La Revue Hebdomadaire,* 5 April 1913.
10   Letter 628 (c.19 June 1888).
11   Letter 628 (c.19 June 1888).
12   Millet, *The Sower,* 1850 (Museum of Fine Arts, Boston). Van Gogh owned a copy of an 1873 print by Paul Lerat after the Millet painting, see Letter 634 (c.28 June 1888).
13   Letter 627 (c.17 June 1888).
14   Letters 627 (c.17 June 1888) and 629 (21 June 1888).
15   F411, F412, F425, F465, F545, F558, F561 and F564.
16   *A Handbook for Travellers in France,* Murray, London, 1890, vol. ii, p.160.
17   Letters 633 (27 June 1888), 635 (c.1 July 1888) and 628 (c.19 June 1888).
18   Letter 627 (c.17 June 1888). The sketch is 10 x 14 cm.

CHAPTER SEVEN: THE RHÔNE AND ITS CANALS (pp. 72–7)
1   Letter 587 (18 March 1888).
2   Letters 595 (c.11April 1888), 597 (c. 13 April 1888), 600 (20 April 1888) and 620 (c. 5 June 1888). It was also called the Pont des Anglais in *Le Forum Républicain* (28 October 1888) and the Pont de L'Anglais in Massebieau, 1946, p. 231 (1893 letter).
3   Massebieau, 1946, p. 231. Massebieau wrote in 1893 that 'during my wanderings on the outskirts of Arles I sometimes encountered him'.
4   Letter 585 (c.16 March 1888). Van Gogh did his painting on the north bank, from west of the bridge facing east (with the carriage going towards town).

5   F400, F570, F571 and F544 (the fragment). Van Gogh's other waterway paintings are of the Gleize Bridge over the Vigueirat Canal (F396) and the Roubine du Roi near Place Lamartine (F427).

6   Letters 587 (18 March 1888) and 589 (c.25 March 1888).

7   Sotheby's, New York, 7 May 2013, lot 59 (F544).

8   Postcard captioned 'Arles – Le Canal', published by B.F., Chalon-sur-Saône.

9   Reproduced in Harriet Preston, 'A Provençal Pilgrimage', *The Century Magazine*, July 1890, p. 333 and Joseph and Elizabeth Pennell, *Play in Provence*, Unwin, London, 1892, p. 15.

10 Pennell remarked nearly 40 years later that 'while I was in Arles, Van Gogh was there', before adding a critical comment about the artist. He did not state whether they had met, although after this length of time he probably would not have remembered. See Joseph Pennell, *The Adventures of an Illustrator*, Little Brown, Boston, 1925, p. 204. Van Gogh's sketch is inscribed 'Bords du Rhône'.

11 Letter 652 (31 July 1888).

12 Letter 660 (c.13 August 1888). Another Rhône view appears in two paintings done in August 1888 (F437 and F438).

13 Letter 703 (13 October 1888).

14 Rewald, 1978, p. 197. The survival of the tree is noted by Teio Meedendorp in Standring and Van Tilborgh, 2013, p. 106. Van Gogh also painted the Trinquetaille Bridge from the quay to the north (F426), this time with the struts vertical.

CHAPTER EIGHT: PORTRAITS OF FRIENDS
(pp. 78–87)

1   Letter 700 (9–10 October 1888).

2   Vincent made one painting of Theo (fig. 5) and none of his other siblings, one of his mother done from a photograph (fig. 56) and none of his father, one unfinished oil sketch of Gauguin (fig. 97) and none of Bernard.

3   The Dutch term is *tronie*.

4   Letter 555 (c.28 January 1886). For background on Van Gogh's portraiture, see Roland Dorn and others, *Van Gogh Face to Face: The Portraits*, Detroit Institute of Arts, 2000.

5   Letter 650 (29 July 1888). Pierre Loti, *Madame Chrysanthème*, Lévy, Paris, 1888, p. 82 (see also illustration by Luigi Rossi on title page).

6   Letter 649 (29 July 1888).

7   The windmill, known as the Moulin de Jonquet (or Souchon), was painted by Van Gogh (F550). For the unconfirmed 1930s story that the *mousmé* was the miller's daughter, see *Van Gogh et Arles*, 1989, pp. 9 and 62. It is possible the girl also appears as the ethereal foreground figure in F426. Two other Mourier-Petersens portraits of the *mousmée* were sold by Rasmussen, Copenhagen, 19 August 1988, lot 328 and 28 November 1989, lot 701.

8   Letter 663 (18 August 1888). The phrase 'man with a hoe' comes from the title of a Jean-François Millet painting of a peasant which Van Gogh admired. Dating from 1860–62, it is now at J. Paul Getty Museum, Los Angeles.

9   A second portrait of Escalier has an orange background (F444).

10 Macknight to Boch, 19 April 1888 (Archives de l'Art Contemporain en Belgique, Brussels, Jean Bouquelle papers). See also Martin Bailey, 'A Friend of Van Gogh: Dodge Macknight and the Post-Impressionists', *Apollo*, July 2007, pp. 28–34. Macknight and Van Gogh had met on 15 April.

11 Letter 637 (8–9 July 1888).

12 Letter 673 (3 September 1888).

13 Letter 673 (3 September 1888).

14 Letters 673 (3 September 1888), see also 676 (8 September 1888).

15 Boch to Jo Bonger, 22 July 1891 (Van Gogh Museum archive, b1184).

16 Extract provided by Ben Solms, a great nephew of Boch.

17 Van Gogh also knew another unidentified Zouave soldier, whose portrait he had twice painted in June (F423 and F424).

18 Letter 686 (23–24 September 1888).

19 Letter 687 (25 September 1888).

20 Letter 687 (25 September 1888).

21 Boch family photograph acquired by John Rewald.

22 Pierre Weiller, 'Nous avons retrouvé le Zouave de Van Gogh', *Les Lettres Françaises*, 24 March 1955 (published twenty years after the interview).

23 Letter 699 (8 October 1888).

24 Inspired by Van Gogh's painting of his mother, Gauguin also painted a portrait of his own deceased mother, Aline, from an early 1840s photograph (she had died in 1867, aged 42). The dating of Gauguin's painting remains uncertain, but it was done

sometime between late 1888 and 1893, after Van Gogh had painted his mother (Georges Wildenstein, *Gauguin*, Beaux-Arts, Paris, 1964, p. 148).

25   Van Gogh Museum archive, b4767.

CHAPTER NINE: FLOWERS (pp. 88–97)

1   Letter 666 (21–22 August 1888).
2   Letter 657 (8 August 1888).
3   Letter 609 (12 May 1888).
4   Letter 653 (31 July 1888). This refers to a similar painting of the same garden, done at the same time (F429).
5   His other flower still lifes are F592, F593 and F594 (lost in the Second World War). Van Gogh may also have done a lost still life of geraniums (Massebieau, 1946, p. 232 and see also Letter 836, 4 January 1890).
6   The same vase appears in F593, F592 and F594, all from August 1888.
7   My thanks to Barbara Buckley, chief conservator at the Barnes Foundation, Philadelphia.
8   For a detailed account of the Sunflowers, see Bailey, 2013.
9   The dating of the letters in the 1993 edition suggested that the Sunflowers were painted between 18–27 August (Han van Crimpen and Monique Berends-Albert, *De Brieven van Vincent van Gogh*, SDU, The Hague, 1990, vol. iii, pp. 1661–8). The revised dating in the 2009 edition of the letters suggests 20–26 August (Letters 665, 21 August 1888 to 670, c.26 August 1888).
10   Letters 666 (21–22 August 1888) and 665 (c.21 August 1888).
11   Bailey, 2013, pp. 52–5, 134–6 and 179–82.
12   Bailey, 2013, pp. 54–6, 139 and 182–5 (see also Letter 665, c.21 August 1888).
13   Bailey, 2013, pp. 56–7, 138–9 and 145–55.
14   Bailey, 2013, pp.17–21, 57, 139–40 and 157–65.
15   *Further Letters of Vincent van Gogh to his Brother 1886–1889*, Constable, London, 1929, p. 283. Van Gogh's response is translated more prosaically in Letter 741 (22 January 1889) as 'but I have the sunflower'. In December 1888–January 1889 Van Gogh made one copy of *Fourteen Sunflowers* (F455) and two copies of *Fifteen Sunflowers* (F457 and F458).

CHAPTER TEN: COLOURS OF THE NIGHT (pp. 98–105)

1   Letter 676 (8 September 1888).

2   Letter 656 (6 August 1888). For background on Van Gogh's night paintings, see Sjraar van Heugten and others, *Van Gogh and the Colours of the Night*, Museum of Modern Art, New York, 2008.
3   Letter 676 (8 September 1888).
4   Letters 684 (19–25 September 1888) and 677 (9 September 1888).
5   The café, located at 11 Place du Forum, was by the early 1900s called the Grand Café du Forum et des Négociants and had a new awning.
6   The Grand Café du Forum (run by G. Lacour) and the Grand Café Brusque are the two top cafés of Arles highlighted in *L'Indicateur Marseillais*, 1888, p. 1744.
7   Mourier-Petersen to Rohde, 23 June 1887 and 10 January 1888 (Rhode papers, Tilg. 392, Royal Library, Copenhagen).
8   Letter 693 (2 October 1888).
9   Letter 678 (9–14 September 1888).
10   Letter 678 (9–14 September 1888).
11   The painting referred to in *L'Homme de Bronze* (30 September 1888) is more likely *Starry Night over the Rhône*, which he finished in Place Lamartine around 28 September (rather than *Café Terrace at Night*, fig. 67, which he painted in the Place du Forum around 8–13 September). See also Dorn, 1990, pp. 85 and 266; Druick and Zegers, 2001, pp. 172 and 385, note 40; and Jirat-Wasiutyński, 2002, pp. 80–1.
12   The only earlier known published reference to Van Gogh, five months before, was a two-sentence comment on his paintings at the Salon des Indépendants exhibition in Paris (Gustave Kahn, *La Revue Indépendante*, April 1888, p. 163).
13   This was claimed by Coquiot, 1923, p. 180.
14   Goya, *Self-portrait before an Easel*, 1792–5, Real Academia de Bellas Artes de San Fernando, Madrid.
15   Postcard captioned 'Arles: Place du Forum', no publisher given.
16   Letter 691 (c.29 September 1888). I have translated *terrains* as 'ground' (not fields, as in the 2009 edition of the letters).
17   Letter 638 (9–10 July 1888). *Starry Night* is F612.
18   Letter 714 (27–28 October 1888).

CHAPTER ELEVEN: GAUGUIN'S ARRIVAL (pp. 106–11)

1   Letter 712 (c.25 October 1888).
2   Letter 602 (1 May 1888).

3   Theo to Jo, 14 February 1889 (Jansen and Robert, 1999, p. 160).

4   Letter 697 (4–5 October 1888).

5   Pierre Loti, *Madame Chrysanthème*, Lévy, Paris, 1888, p. 126 (illustration by Felician Myrbach).

6   The Bernard is *Self-portrait with Portrait of Gauguin*, September 1888, Van Gogh Museum, Amsterdam.

7   Letter 697 (4–5 October 1888).

8   Letters 688 (c.26 September 1888) and 706 (17 October 1888).

9   Letter 690 (27 September–1 October 1888).

10   Letters 680 (c.11 September 1888) and 686 (23–24 September 1888).

11   Letter 686 (23–24 September 1888).

12   Gauguin, 1923, p. 14.

13   Gauguin, 1923, p. 15.

14   The charwoman started in July 1888, working twice a week for 1 franc. She was elderly, with many children, and her husband was employed at the railway station, and therefore knew Roulin. By December 1888 she was working longer hours and was paid 5 francs a week.

15   Gauguin, 1923, p. 17.

16   Rey to Coquiot, 17 March 1922 (Van Gogh Museum archive, b3282), see also Braumann, 1928, p. 453.

17   Gauguin, 1923, p. 17.

18   Letter 718 (10 November 1888).

19   Van Gogh Museum archive, b1994.

20   Gauguin, 1923, pp. 14–15.

21   F494 and F573.

22   The Arles farmhouse is W315 and the negresse is lost.

23   Letter 715 (c.29 October 1888).

CHAPTER TWELVE: ELYSIAN FIELDS (pp.112–21)

1   Letter 717 (c.3 November 1888).

2   For José (or Joseph) Belon's painting, see *Le Forum Républicain*, 9 and 30 September 1888. A watercolour of the Chapel of St Accurse by V. Lamblot was also displayed at the Arles dealer Manson that same month (*L'Homme de Bronze*, 23 September 1888). Armand had earlier made a painting of an Arlésienne at the Alyscamps (*L'Homme de Bronze*, 12 February 1888).

3   Letters 710 (22 October 1888) and 687 (25 September 1888).

4   Sotheby's, New York, 5 May 2015, lot 18.

5   Letter 716 (1–2 November 1888).

6   Letter 717 (c.3 November 1888).

7   Reproduced in Harriet Preston, 'A Provençal Pilgrimage', *The Century Magazine*, July 1890, p. 337 and Joseph and Elizabeth Pennell, *Play in Provence*, Unwin, London, 1892, p. 29.

8   Postcard captioned 'Arles – Arlésiennes aux Alyscamps, Allée des Tombeaux', published by ND.

9   Gauguin to Theo, c.22 November 1888 (Merlhès, 1984, p. 288).

10   Three of Van Gogh's Alyscamps paintings (figs. 78–80) and one of Gauguin's (fig. 82) are on jute. See Druick and Zegers, 2001, pp. 354–69 (on page 174–5 of this pioneering study the caption says F568 is on canvas [it is on jute] and on p. 362 an incorrect Alyscamps view is illustrated for F569.

CHAPTER THIRTEEN: STREET OF THE KIND GIRLS (pp. 122–9)

1   Letter 716 (1–2 November 1888).

2   *The Complete Letters of Vincent van Gogh*, Thames & Hudson, London, 1958, vol. iii, p. 42. The 2009 edition of the letters translates the phrase, more prosaically, as 'the street of the good little ladies' (Letter 683, 18 September 1888; see also 698, 5 October 1888).

3   Archives Communales, Arles, file J26 (Maisons de tolérance, 1871–91). The tower of the convent features in Van Gogh's *Canal with Washerwomen* (F427), in which the sun rises just behind Rue du Bout d'Arles.

4   Letter 683 (18 September 1888).

5   See reports in *L'Homme de Bronze* (18 and 25 March 1888), *Le Forum Républicain* (18 March 1888), *Le Petit Méridional* (13 March 1888) and *L'Intransigeant* (15, 16 and 19 March 1888).

6   Letter 585 (c.16 March 1888).

7   See reports in *Le Forum Républicain*, 22 April 1888, 2 and 9 December 1888 and 21 April 1889, *L'Etoile du Midi*, 2 December 1888 and 21 April 1889, and *L'Homme de Bronze*, 2 December 1888.

8   *Annuaire Reirum: Indicateur des Adresses des Maisons de Société (dites de Tolérances) de France, Algérie et Tunisie et des Principales Villes de Suisse, Belgique, Hollande, Italie et Espagne*, Murier, Paris, 1890, table reprinted in Louis Fiaux, *Les Maisons de Tolérance: Leur Fermeture*, Carré, Paris, 1892, p. 353.

9   Letter 599 (19 April 1888). The presence of 50 men suggests this was a bar where soliciting took place rather than a registered brothel, which would

have been a much smaller establishment.

10   Letters 632 (26 June 1888) and 699 (8 October 1888), see also 659 (c.12 August 1888), where he stated the price as 2 francs.

11   See Letter 630 (23 June 1888).

12   Letter 698 (c.5 October 1888).

13   Gauguin, 1923, p. 16.

14   Letter 637 (8–9 July 1888).

15   Letter 718 (10 November 1888).

16   In Paris, in winter 1886–87, Van Gogh had made a very explicit drawing of a couple copulating, a scene which he may have observed in a brothel. This sketch has never been exhibited and is not recorded in the de la Faille or Hulsker catalogues, but is included in Marije Vellekoop and Sjraar van Heugten, *Vincent van Gogh Drawings: Antwerp & Paris*, Van Gogh Museum, Amsterdam, 2001, vol. iii, pp. 177–8.

17   Gauguin, 1923, p. 220. Gayford identified Farce as Gauguin's brothel keeper (Gayford, 2006, pp. 86–7, 237–8 and 334 and 'Gauguin and a Brothel in Arles', *Apollo*, March 2006, pp. 64–71). In the 1888 voters' register, Farce euphemistically gave his profession as 'loueur en garnie' (renter of furnished accommodation) (Archives Communales, Arles, K38).

18   Gauguin, 1923, p. 220.

CHAPTER FOURTEEN: COLLABORATION
(pp. 130–43)

1   Letter 719 (11–12 November 1888).

2   Letter 717 (c.3 November 1888). He later claimed to have painted it in 45 minutes (Letter 741, 22 January 1889).

3   Coquiot, 1923, pp. 187–8.

4   In December 1888 or early 1889 Van Gogh made another version of *The Arlésienne* for Madame Ginoux, replacing the parasol and gloves with three books (F488).

5   Julius Meier-Graefe, 'Erinnerung an Van Gogh', *Berliner Tagblatt*, 23 June 1914.

6   Letter 716 (1–2 November 1888).

7   Gauguin to Theo, 22 November 1888 (Merlhès, 1984, p. 288). Gauguin later gave his drawing of Marie Ginoux to Van Gogh, who used it as the basis for a series of five paintings in early 1890 (F540, F541, F542, F543 and a lost picture).

8   Letter 717 (c.3 November 1888). Van Gogh had earlier painted *The Green Vineyard* (F475) in the first week of October, during the harvest.

9   Gauguin to Bernard, second week of November 1888 (Merlhès, 1984, p. 275). Another motif that the two artists tackled in November 1888, loosely inspired by the public garden opposite the Yellow House, appeared as Van Gogh's *Reminiscence of the Garden of Etten* (F496) and Gauguin's *Arlésiennes (Mistral)* (W329).

10   Letter 722 (c.21 November 1888).

11   W308. Gauguin had sent Van Gogh a sketch of the painting (Letter 688, c.26 September 1888).

12   Letter 722 (c.21 November 1888).

13   Both were probably painted in November 1888, although possibly in early December.

14   Letter 594 (9 April 1888).

15   René Garagnon, 'Odeon, Van Gogh et Les Folies Arlésiennes', *Bulletin des Amis du Vieil Arles*, September 1995, pp. 14–18. Les Folies Arlésiennes was in Van Gogh's time at 4 Avenue Victor Hugo.

16   Letter 721 (c.19 November 1888).

17   Martin Bailey, 'Van Gogh's Portrait of Gauguin', *Apollo*, July 1996, pp. 51–4 and Druick and Zegers, 2001, pp. 236, 240 and 363–4.

18   W326.

19   Laval's October 1888 self-portrait is now at the Van Gogh Museum. Gauguin also painted a self-portrait (W291) which could well have been done in Arles, although he may have completed it at another point in 1888–89. Although Gauguin originally painted it for Laval, the two men later fell out and the picture was presented to another artist friend, Eugène Carrière.

20   Postcard captioned 'Arles: Les Arènes, Course de Taureaux', published by Selecta.

21   Reproduced in Joseph and Elizabeth Pennell, *Play in Provence*, Unwin, London, 1892, frontispiece.

22   F499.

23   Letters 736 (17 January 1889) and 677 (9 September 1888).

24   My thanks to Ashok Roy, former director of science at the National Gallery, London, for his confirmation that the pipe was probably added a few weeks after Van Gogh had finished the main part of the painting.

25   Letter 722 (c.21 November 1888).

CHAPTER FIFTEEN: POSTMAN ROULIN
(pp. 144–51)

1   Letter 732 (7 January 1889).

2   Letter 652 (31 July 1888). Roulin then lived at 10

Rue Montagne des Cordes.

3   Letter 652 (31 July 1888). For a 1902 photograph of Roulin, see Tralbaut, 1969, p. 229.

4   Letter 723 (c.1 December 1888). The five portraits were probably: Joseph (F434), Augustine (F503), Marcelle and Augustine (F491), Camille (F665) and Armand (F492 or F493).

5   Van Gogh also did four other head-and-shoulders portraits of Joseph: F433 (July–August 1888), F435, F436 and F439 (probably all January–February 1889).

6   W319.

7   Letters 292 (10 December 1882) and 656 (6 August 1888).

8   Although Van Gogh wrote that Armand was 16, he was then 17. Armand later became a police officer in Tunisia.

9   There has been considerable debate on which of the five versions of *La Berceuse* was the first. The 2009 edition of the letters (Letter 739, 21 January 1889) suggests it is F508 (fig. 104), but some specialists believe it may have been F504 (Eliza Rathbone and others, *Van Gogh Repetitions*, Phillips Collection, Washington, DC, 2013, pp. 119–39).

10   These are: Joseph (F432, F433, F434, F435, F436, F439), Augustine (F503, F504, F505, F506, F507, F508), Armand (F492, F493, probably F536), Camille (F537, F538 and F665), Marcelle (F440, F441, F441a) and Augustine with Marcelle (F490, F491).

11   Rebecca Rabinow (ed.), *Cézanne to Picasso: Ambroise Vollard, Patron of the Avant-Garde*, Metropolitan Museum of Art, New York, 2006, pp. 376 and 379. The Vollard records show that some of the pictures passed through an agent, Henri Laget, who had lived in Arles and was later based in Marseille. Marcelle had once said that her father sold six paintings to Vollard in 1895 for 450 francs (Marcelle Roulin to Vincent Willem van Gogh, 23 February 1959, Van Gogh Museum archive, b7015).

12   Articles by Jean-Noël Priou in *Revue des PTT de France*, May–June 1955, pp. 26–32; *Arts Spectacles*, 31 August 1955, p. 6; *Journal de l'Amateur d'Art*, July 1978, p. 9; *Références de la Poste*, autumn 1987, pp. 57–6; and *Relais: Revue des Amis du Musée de la Poste*, March 2006, pp. 32–5 and June 2006, pp. 33–5.

CHAPTER SIXTEEN: OUT OF HIS MIND (pp. 152–9)

1   Letter 739 (21 January 1889).

2   Gauguin, 1923, p. 20. Gauguin's account had been written in 1903, and he appears to have distorted events so that he came out better from them.

3   Gauguin to Theo, c.11 December 1888 (Merlhès, 1984, p. 301).

4   The Montpellier visit was on either 16 or 17 December. See Letter 726 (17–18 December 1888) and Gauguin to Theo, 17–18 December 1888 (Merlhès, 1984, pp. 301–2).

5   Gauguin to Schuffenecker, 22 December 1888 (Merlhès, 1989, p. 238).

6   Theo's letter of c.22 December 1888 does not survive, but the arrival of the money was noted in Letter 736 (17 January 1889).

7   The man was Johann Eduard Stumpff.

8   It is very unlikely that Vincent heard about the engagement *before* 23 December. Theo apparently felt it was important to ask his mother's permission first. If Vincent had received such important news on 22 December, he would probably have sent a response to Theo by the evening of the following day, but no such letter was sent. Gauguin did not refer to the engagement in his lengthy letter to Schuffenecker written in the evening of 22 December (Merlhès, pp. 301–2).

9   Theo to Lies, 24 December 1888 (Van Gogh Museum archive, b918)

10   It is very unlikely that Vincent heard about the engagement *after* 23 December. It would be surprising if a letter from Theo had arrived at the Yellow House on 24 December and was immediately forwarded to the hospital and handed over to him, at a time when he was extremely weak and incoherent. Vincent certainly received *a* letter from Theo on 23 December (as we know from Vincent's letter of 17 January 1889, Letter 736). If this letter had *not* mentioned the romance, Vincent would have been upset to later discover that he had been the last key family member to have been informed (it would have been more sensitive of Theo not to have written at all rather than to have done so and not mentioned his engagement). It is therefore virtually certain that Theo's letter arrived *on* 23 December and *did* indeed contain news of the engagement.

11   Theo to Jo, 1 January 1889 (Jansen and Robert, 1999, p. 76).

12   V.W. van Gogh, 'Some Additional Notes to the Memoir of Vincent van Gogh', *The Complete Letters*

of Vincent van Gogh, Thames & Hudson, London, 1958, vol. i, p. lviii.

13 Van Gogh Museum archive, b4822.

14 *L'Intransigeant*, 23 December 1888. See René Huyghe, *Le Carnet de Paul Gauguin*, Quatre Chemins, Paris, 1952, facsimile volume, p. 220.

15 Gauguin, 1923, p. 20 (this account had earlier been published in Charles Morice, 'Paul Gauguin', *Mercure de France*, October 1903, p. 130).

16 Some sources suggest that Van Gogh cut off his entire ear: Massebieau, 1946, p. 232; Gauguin, 1923, p. 21; Bernard, based on Gauguin's comments, in letter from Bernard to Albert Aurier, 1 January 1889 (Neil McWilliam, *Emile Bernard: Les Lettres d'un Artiste*, Réel, Dijon, 2012, p. 87, where the letter should be dated to 1 January 1889); Rey (Doiteau and Leroy, 1936, pp. 9 and 15) and the policeman Robert (letter from Robert to Doiteau/Leroy, 11 September 1929, Doiteau and Leroy, 1936, p. 6). Other knowledgeable sources state it was only the part of the ear: Signac (Coquiot, 1923, p. 194) and, most importantly, Bonger (Jo Bonger, 'Memoir of Vincent van Gogh' in *The Complete Letters of Vincent van Gogh*, Thames & Hudson, London, 1958, vol. i, p. xlvi). However, many of those involved would not have had a reason to distinguish between the whole or part of the ear. Physically, it would have been difficult to cut the ear off without pulling it with the other hand, and a single cut would have resulted in the loss of only part of the outer ear.

17 Massebieau, 1946, p. 232. However, if the cut was only to the outer ear, this might well have only resulted in a relatively minor loss of hearing. There is no evidence in Van Gogh's later letters of any hearing problems.

18 *Le Forum Républicain*, 30 December 1888. Pablo Picasso apparently always kept a copy of *Le Forum Républicain* article, sent to him in 1957, on his bedside table (*Les Picasso d'Arles*, Musée Réattu, Arles, 2013, p. 72). His copy is now preserved in the archive of the Musée Picasso in Paris (RMN 149952).

19 Alphonse Robert to Victor Doiteau/Edgar Leroy, 11 September 1929 (Doiteau and Leroy, 1936, p. 6). A later writer, Pierre Leprohon, claimed that Rachel/Gaby died in 1952, aged 80, which meant she would have been 16 in 1888, rather young for a registered prostitute (see Leprohon, *Tel fut Van Gogh*, Sud, Paris, 1964, pp. 307 and 311 and Leprohon, *Vincent van Gogh*, Bonne, Paris, 1972, pp. 235 and 355).

Leprohon gives no surname or source.

20 The six *filles soumises* recorded in the 1886 census were aged between 26 and 30 (one was Spanish, the remainder French). The 1891 census recorded eleven women aged between 22 and 43 (one was Belgian, the remainder French). The 1886 census listed Margueritte Aubert, Madeleine Montchamps, Prudencia Allonzo and Marie Laroche. The 1891 census listed Marie Leon, Marie Denande, Henriette Chauvet, Antoinette Mesognan, Agathe Fouchon, Marie Colliard, Marie Thérèse Estèves, Marie Albertine Azaïs and Marie Anne Ballandy. Marie Magnier (or Magnis) and Louise Bourdenove (or Bourdeneuve) were the only women listed in both censuses. Records at the Archives Communales, Arles.

21 Her Christian name was given by Robert and her full name is in the Archives Communales, Arles (file 26, Maisons de tolérance, 1871–91), in the 1886 and 1891 censuses and the *Annuaire Reirum*, Murier, Paris, 1890.

22 *Le Petit Marseillais*, 20 September 1929 (cited in Doiteau and Leroy, 1936, p. 7). Robert lived in Rue des Récollets, very close to Rue du Bout d'Arles (Voters register 1888, Archives Communales, Arles, K38).

23 Alphonse Robert to Victor Doiteau/Edgar Leroy, 11 September 1929 (Doiteau and Leroy, 1936, p. 6). For another account of Robert's memories, see Benno Stokvis, *De Groene Amsterdammer*, 30 December 1933.

24 *Le Forum Républicain* (cited in Henri Perruchot, *La Vie de Van Gogh*, Hachette, Paris, 1955, p. 284), *Le Petit Méridional* (Bailey, 2005, pp. 34–6), *Le Petit Journal* (Bailey, 2013, pp. 12–13 and 210) and *Le Messager du Midi* (reproduced here). The article in *Le Petit Méridional* is not in most editions of the newspaper, but is in a copy inspected at the Bibliothèque Inguimbertine in Carpentras.

25 Gauguin, 1923, p. 22.

26 Reproduced in René Huyghe, *Le Carnet de Paul Gauguin*, Quatre Chemins, Paris, 1952, facsimile volume, pp. 22–3 and see text volume, pp. 95–8.

27 René Huyghe, *Le Carnet de Paul Gauguin*, Quatre Chemins, Paris, 1952, facsimile volume, pp. 22–3 and text volume, pp. 95–8.

28 Theo to Jo, 24 December 1888 (Jansen and Robert, 1999, p. 67).

29 Theo to Jo, 28 and 30 December 1888 (Jansen and Robert, 1999, pp. 70 and 74).

30 Theo to Jo, 28 December 1888 (Jansen and Robert, 1999, p. 70).

31 Admission record at St Paul de Mausole asylum, 8 May 1889; report by Dr Théophile Peyron, 9 May 1889; and Letters 767 (2 May 1889) and 776 (c.23 May 1889).

32 Cor died in 1901 and Wil in 1941. On Cor, see Chris Schoeman, *The Unknown Van Gogh: The Life of Cornelis van Gogh*, Zebra, Cape Town, 2015.

CHAPTER SEVENTEEN: DOCTOR REY (pp. 160–9)

1 Letter 760 (21 April 1889).

2 The architect Auguste Véran drew a plan of the hospital, known as the Hôtel-Dieu St Esprit, on 8 January 1889, while Van Gogh was there (Archives Communales, Arles, 1Fi 124).

3 Roulin to Theo, 26 December 1888 (Van Gogh Museum archive, b1065).

4 Rey to Theo, 29 December 1888 (Van Gogh Museum archive, b1055).

5 Massebieau, 1946, p. 232.

6 Rey to Theo, 30 December 1888 (Van Gogh Museum archive, b1056).

7 Letter 728 (2 January 1889).

8 Letter 729 (4 January 1889).

9 The entry reads: 'Vincent Van Gogh, peintre paysagiste, 35 ans, célibataire, fils de feu Théodore et de feue Anna Carbentus, Jundert [Zundert] (Hollande), mutilation volontaire d'une oreille. Entré le 24 décembre 1888, sorti le 7 janvier 1889.' It is also recorded that Theo left 100 francs for Vincent to cover his expenses and help him on his discharge. See Massebieau, 1946, p. 232. Massebieau may have got access to the register from Aimé Nivière, the hospital pharmacist, who was a friend (Massebieau hand-dedicated a book of his poems to Nivière in 1893 [Massebieau, *L'Or des Songes*, Vanier, Paris, 1893, copy in private collection]).

10 Letter 732 (7 January 1889). Van Gogh referred to "doctor friends", but he may well have used the term loosely for senior hospital staff.

11 On François Huard, see Pascale Picard-Cajan, *Le Voyage immobile de Monsieur Huard: Peintre et Archéologue Arlésien, 1792–1856*, Museon Arlaten, Arles, 1995.

12 Van Gogh ordered a 'fine' walnut frame for Huard, presumably for one of the artist's paintings (Letter 778, 31 May 1888). See also Stokvis, 1929, p. 6.

13 Many of the senior hospital staff were active supporters of Provençal culture. Rey, Huard, Nivière and Delon were key Arles members of the Félibrige movement, set up by the poet Frédéric Mistral (Claude Férigoule, 'Vincent van Gogh et les Félibres', *Bulletin des Amis du Vieil Arles*, March 1990, p. 8).

14 See Stokvis, 1929, p. 6 (Stokvis misspells Nivière as Nevière) and Doiteau and Leroy, 1936, p. 22 (who misspell the name as Neuvière).

15 Letter 732 (7 January 1889). Delon wrote to Dr Rey in 1901 to ask if he could buy Van Gogh's portrait of Rey (René Garagnon, 'Histoire du Tableau de Van Gogh', *Bulletin des Amis du Vieil Arles*, December 2007, pp. 6 and 10). Other doctors in Arles included: Th. Arnaud, Béraud, Castellanet, Duffaut, Denis Amédée Gay, C. Martin-Raget, Antoine Talon and Marie Jules Joseph Urpar. Rey also knew Dr Aussoleil from Montpellier, a specialist on epilepsy.

16 Letter 732 (7 January 1889).

17 Letters 739 (21 January 1889), 764 (28 April–2 May 1889), 767 (2 May 1889) and 779 (9 June 1889).

18 Letters 736 (17 January 1889) and 743 (28 January 1889).

19 Letter 735 (9 January 1889).

20 Letter 764 (28 April–2 May 1889).

21 The photograph, probably from the Rey family, was acquired by the museum.

22 Published annually in Paris, by Raspail.

23 The commentary in the 2009 edition of the letters states that the envelope depicts 'the special "Jour de l'An" postmark, used by the post office during the busy period around New Year' (Letter 736, 17 January 1889).

24 Van Gogh probably left the painting at the Café de la Gare and the Ginouxs had sold it by 1896. See Feilchenfeldt, 2006, pp. 302–3 and Feilchenfeldt, 2013, p. 131.

25 Letter 735 (9 January 1889). Vincent's slightly earlier response to Jo does not survive.

26 Letter 736 (17 January 1889).

27 Letter 738 (19 January 1889).

28 His three later self-portraits, all painted in September 1889, depict his intact ear (F525, F626 and F627).

29 This was the first of Van Gogh's self-portraits to be sold by Jo Bonger, in 1897 (to Vollard), so she may well have found the bandaged ear upsetting after Vincent's suicide.

30   Stokvis, 1929, p. 4.

31   Braumann, 1928, p. 452.

32   Doiteau and Leroy, 1939, p. 51.

33   Camoin to Doiteau/Leroy, 22 November 1937 (Doiteau and Leroy, 1939, p. 50).

34   Painted in 1902. Sold at Tajan (Drouot), Paris, 18 April 2002. Reproduced in Daniele Giraudy, *Camoin: Sa Vie, Son Oeuvre*, Savoisienne, Marseille, 1972, p. 178.

35   Interview with author, 19 December 1987.

36   Rey had also handed Camoin five other Van Goghs which he sold in 1901, possibly including F438, F440, F485 and F537 (Molinard to Rey, 15 April 1901, RKD archive, The Hague; Feilchenfeldt, 2005, p. 297; and Feilchenfeldt, 2013, p. 283), as well as perhaps two paintings of the Arles hospital (Braumann, 1928, p. 453 and Molinard to Rey, 15 April 1901).

37   Coquiot manuscript, c.1920, p. 7 (Van Gogh Museum archive, b3348).

38   Interview with author, 19 December 1987.

39   Stokvis, 1929, p. 4 and Rey to Leroy, 14 November 1929 (Doiteau and Leroy, 1936, p. 15).

CHAPTER EIGHTEEN: SPRING (pp. 170–8)

1   Letter 760 (21 April 1889).

2   Letter 743 (28 January 1889).

3   Letter 745 (3 February 1889). Van Gogh may have returned a few weeks after the 2 February visit, since seven weeks later he complained about people meddling in his life when he was 'painting, eating or having a fuck in the brothel (not having a wife)' (Letter 751, 22 March 1889).

4   Salles to Theo, 7 February 1889 (Van Gogh Museum archive, b1046).

5   Dr Delon's report of 7 February 1889 (*Van Gogh à Arles*, 2003, p. 62) and Massebieau, 1946, p.232.

6   Gauguin, 1923, p. 21.

7   *Van Gogh à Arles*, 2003, pp. 60–1.

8   *Van Gogh à Arles*, 2003, p. 64. Joseph Ginoux was also interviewed by the police and signed a brief statement. The other witness was Maria Viany, a tobacconist in Place Lamartine.

9   D'Ornano's report of 27 February 1889 and Mayor Jacques Tardieu's order of 3 March 1889 (*Van Gogh à Arles*, 2003, pp. 63–8).

10   Salles to Theo, 18 March 1889 (Van Gogh Museum archive, b1049).

11   Salles to Theo, 26 February 1889 (Van Gogh Museum archive, b1047).

12   Salles to Theo, 1 March 1889 (Van Gogh Museum archive, b1048).

13   Although it is perhaps surprising that Theo never visited Arles again after his Christmas visit, he was very busy with preparations for his married life. See Letter 749 (16 March 1889) and Theo to Jo, 16 March 1889 (Jansen and Robert, 1999, p. 222).

14   Letters 756 (10 April 1889) and 758 (14–17 April 1889).

15   Letter 753 (29 March 1889).

16   Letter 754 (c.4 April 1889). Seven years earlier Van Gogh had written about having 'the occasional ugly tic' (Letter 221, c.26 April 1882), see also Anna (Mother) to Theo, 15 April 1879 (Van Gogh Museum archive, b2492).

17   Letter 760 (21 April 1889).

18   Letter 765 (30 April 1889).

19   Letter 756 (10 April 1889). Since the 1950s the painting has often been entitled 'Peach Blossom in the Crau', but it was done in the area known as Trébon (the Crau lies further south). *Harvest in Provence* (fig. 37) had been painted from a similar spot a year earlier.

20   Letter 756 (10 April 1889). It rained from 5–9 April 1888. *View of Arles with Irises in the Foreground* (fig. 59) was probably painted from a similar spot a year earlier.

21   The hospital would have been on the left side of the horizon.

22   Van Gogh also completed four other landscapes in April 1889: F511, F517, F520 and F575.

23   Letter 764 (28 April–2 May 1889).

24   There is tantalising evidence that Van Gogh may have painted further paintings at the hospital which are now lost. Rey claimed to have once owned a 'hospital garden' (not fig. 117, which was sent to Theo) and a 'ward with a self-portrait' (Braumann, 1928, p. 453). There may also have been another picture of the ward owned by Nivière (Stokvis, 1929, p. 6). Massebieau refers to having seen a 'view of the hospital garden', possibly one owned by Rey (Massebieau, 1946, p. 232).

25   Letter 760 (21 April 1889).

26   Salles to Theo, 10 May 1889 (Van Gogh Museum archive, b1052).

27   F608.

POSTSCRIPT: VAN GOGH'S BED (pp. 180–7)

1   Letter 856 (19 February 1890).
2   Letter 677 (9 September 1888), see also 664 (19–20 August 1888).
3   Letters 705 (16 October 1888) and 677 (9 September 1888).
4   Letter 706 (17 October 1888).
5   Vincent began a letter to Theo by saying that 'I'll paint [the bed] later', which might appear to refer to plans to simply paint the wood a colour. But further on in the same letter he writes: 'I'm going to paint my own bed, there'll be 3 subjects. Perhaps a naked woman, I haven't decided, perhaps a cradle with a child.' (Letter 677, 9 September 1888). It is unlikely that he intended to paint the actual bed (there are no examples of him painting furniture; the bed is unpainted in *The Bedroom* of mid-October 1888; the slats of the bed-end would represent a very difficult surface for paint; Theo does not appear to have questioned the curious idea of painting the bed and at that time reducing its financial value; and there are no indications after Van Gogh's death that the bed, which survived until the 1940s, was painted). Van Gogh probably intended to refer to his bed*room*, not his bed. For a different view, see Louis van Tilborgh in Groom, 2015, p. 67, note 97.
6   Gauguin, 1923, p. 22.
7   Letter 736 (17 January 1889).
8   Letter 765 (30 April 1889).
9   Letter 865 (c.1 May 1890).
10   Jo to Theo, 1 August 1890 and Theo to Jo, 1 August 1890 (Jansen and Robert, 1999, pp. 277 and 279).
11   Vincent Willem van Gogh to Fernand Benoit, 12 July 1937 (Van Gogh Museum archive, b7141).
12   Instead, in the late 1930s Benoit set up a one-room display in the Museon Arlaten, with reproductions of Van Gogh's works and a head of Van Gogh by local sculptor Gaston de Luppé.
13   Rey to Gustave Coquiot, 17 March 1922 (Van Gogh Museum archive, b3282).
14   Coquiot, 1923, pp. 169–70.
15   The earliest mention of Van Gogh in a tourist guidebook appears to be in Fernand Benoit, *Arles*, Rey, Lyon, 1927, p. 22.
16   There were five further bomb attacks on Arles up to 15 August 1944, causing considerable further destruction and fatalities.
17   Johan van Gogh, 'The History of the Collection' in Evert van Uitert and Michael Hoyle, *The Rijksmuseum Vincent van Gogh*, Meulenhoff, Amsterdam, 1987, p. 5.
18   Kardas (text and photographs), 'Les sujets de Van Gogh aujourd'hui', *L'Art Vivant*, September 1933, pp. 394–5. See also 'The Subjects of Van Gogh as they appear to-day', *The Studio*, August 1934, p. 92. The photographs were taken in April 1933.
19   Interview with author, 6 August 2015.
20   Theodoor van Gogh was shot in Amsterdam on 8 March 1945. He was among more than 250 people who were executed in retaliation for a Dutch resistance attack on a top Nazi official, Hanns Rauter.
21   Teun Koetsier, 'Laren en Boxmeer, 70 jaar geleden', 2015 (paper available on the web). Koetsier subsequently found that the photograph we are reproducing was taken on 6 September 1945.
22   Letters 628 (c.19 June 1888) and 687 (25 September 1888).
23   Reproduced in *Résister en Pays d'Arles*, Actes Sud, Arles, 2014, pp. 122–3 (US Army photograph, collection Ville d'Arles).
24   Postcard captioned 'La Maison de Van Gogh après le Bombardement du 25 Juin 1944', photographed by Emilien Barral, no publisher given.

ON THE TRAIL OF VAN GOGH (pp. 188–91)

1   In the past, Van Gogh exhibitions were held in Arles at the Musée Réattu in 1951 and 1961, the Espace Van Gogh (the former hospital) in 1989 and the Fondation Vincent van Gogh Arles in Rond-Point des Arènes in 2003. In 2014 the Fondation Vincent van Gogh Arles opened new premises in Rue du Dr Fanton and since then has regularly held displays of loans of the artist's work.
2   F398 and F480.
3   Van Gogh's other embankment views are F426, F437 and F438.
4   Letter 739 (21 January 1889).
5   F550.
6   The other landscape is F565.
7   F1496.
8   F657 and F658.

SELECT BIBLIOGRAPHY

Arles newspapers: *L'Homme de Bronze, Le Forum Républicain* and *L'Etoile du Midi*, 1888–89 (available at the Bibliothèque Municipale d'Arles)

Martin Bailey, 'Drama at Arles: New light on Van Gogh's self-mutilation', *Apollo*, September 2005, pp. 31–41

Martin Bailey, 'How Van Gogh saw Arles', in Klaus Albrecht Schröder and others, *Van Gogh: Heartfelt Lines*, Albertina, Vienna, 2008, pp. 68–81

Martin Bailey, *The Sunflowers are Mine: The Story of Van Gogh's Masterpiece*, Frances Lincoln, London, 2013

Max Braumann, 'Bei Freunden Van Goghs in Arles', *Kunst und Künstler*, September 1928, pp. 451–4

Bulletin des Amis du Vieil Arles, Arles (various issues, particularly articles by René Garagnon)

Bernhard Bürgi and others, *Vincent van Gogh: Between Earth and Heaven, the Landscapes*, Kunstmuseum Basel, 2009

Jean-Paul Clébert and Pierre Richard, *La Provence de van Gogh*, Edisud, Aix-en-Provence, 1981

Gustave Coquiot, *Vincent van Gogh*, Ollendorff, Paris, 1923

Victor Doiteau and Edgar Leroy, *La Folie de Vincent van Gogh*, Aesculape, Paris, 1928

Victor Doiteau and Edgar Leroy, *Van Gogh et le Drame de l'Oreille coupée*, Aesculape, Paris, July 1936

Victor Doiteau and Edgar Leroy, 'Van Gogh et le Portrait du Dr Rey', *Aesculape*, February 1939, pp. 42–7 and March 1939, pp. 50-5

Roland Dorn, *Décoration: Vincent van Goghs Werkreihe für das Gelbe Haus in Arles*, Olms, Hildesheim, 1990

Douglas W. Druick and Peter Kort Zegers, *Van Gogh and Gauguin: The Studio of the South*, Art Institute of Chicago, 2001

Michel Duplessy, *L'Indicateur Arlésien*, Arles, 1887

Jacob-Baart de la Faille, *The Works of Vincent van Gogh: His Paintings and Drawings*, Meulenhoff, Amsterdam, 1970

Walter Feilchenfeldt, *By Appointment Only: Cézanne, Van Gogh and some secrets of art dealing*, Thames & Hudson, London, 2006

Walter Feilchenfeldt, *Vincent van Gogh: The Years in France, Complete Paintings*, Wilson, London, 2013

Anne-Birgitte Fonsmark, *Van Gogh, Gauguin, Bernard: Friction of Ideas*, Ordrupgaard, Copenhagen, 2014

Paul Gauguin, *Avant et Après*, Crès, Paris, 1923 (originally partly published in Charles Morice, 'Paul Gauguin', *Mercure de France*, October 1903, pp. 100–35)

Martin Gayford, *The Yellow House: Van Gogh, Gauguin and nine turbulent weeks in Arles*, Fig Tree, London, 2006

Judit Geskó, *Van Gogh in Budapest*, Museum of Fine Arts, Budapest, 2006

Gloria Groom (ed), *Van Gogh's Bedrooms*, Art Institute of Chicago, 2016

Ella Hendriks and Louis van Tilborgh, *Vincent van Gogh Paintings: Antwerp & Paris 1885–1888*, Van Gogh Museum, Amsterdam, 2011, vol. ii

Sjraar van Heugten, *Van Gogh: Colours of the North, Colours of the South*, Fondation Vincent van Gogh Arles/Actes Sud, 2014

Sjraar van Heugten, *Van Gogh Drawings: Influences & Innovations*, Fondation Vincent van Gogh Arles/ Actes Sud, 2015

Sjraar van Heugten, *Van Gogh in Provence: Modernizing Tradition*, Fondation Vincent van Gogh Arles/Actes Sud, 2016

Cornelia Homburg, *Vincent van Gogh and the Painters of the Petit Boulevard*, Saint Louis Art Museum, 2001

Cornelia Homburg, *Vincent van Gogh: Timeless Country – Modern City*, Skira, Milan, 2010

Jan Hulsker, *Vincent and Theo van Gogh: A dual biography*, Fuller, Ann Arbor, 1990

Jan Hulsker, *The New Complete Van Gogh: Paintings, Drawings, Sketches*, Meulenhoff, Amsterdam, 1996

L'Indicateur Marseillais, Allard and Bertrand, Marseille, 1887, 1888 and 1889

Colta Ives, Susan Alyson Stein, Sjraar van Heugten and Marije Vellekoop, *Vincent van Gogh: The*

Drawings, Metropolitan Museum of Art, New York, 2005

Leo Jansen and Jan Robert (eds), *Brief Happiness: The correspondence of Theo van Gogh and Jo Bonger*, Van Gogh Museum, Amsterdam, 1999

Leo Jansen, Hans Luijten, Nienke Bakker, *Vincent van Gogh – The Letters: The Complete Illustrated and Annotated Edition*, Thames & Hudson, London, 2009, 6 vols (www.vangoghletters.org)

Vojtěch Jirat-Wasiutyński, 'A Dutchman in the south of France: Van Gogh's "romance" of Arles', *Van Gogh Museum Journal*, 2002, pp. 79–89

Stefan Koldehoff, *Van Gogh: Mythos und Wirklichkeit*, Dumont, Cologne, 2003

Edgar Leroy, see under Doiteau

La Lettre de Vincent (newsletter), Association des Amis de Vincent van Gogh, Arles, 1987–91

Sylvie Malige, 'La Postérité de Vincent van Gogh en Arles', Université Paul Valéry, Montpellier, 2001 (unpublished thesis, available at the Bibliothèque Municipale d'Arles)

Alfred Massebieau, *Mercure de France*, 1 December 1946, pp. 231–2

Julius Meier-Graefe, *Vincent van Gogh: A Biographical Study*, Medici, London, 1922, 2 vols

Victor Merlhès, *Correspondance de Paul Gauguin 1873–1888*, Singer-Polignac, Paris, 1984

Victor Merlhès, *Paul Gauguin et Vincent van Gogh 1887–1888: Lettres retrouvées, sources ignorées*, Avant et Après, Papeete, 1989

Victor Merlhès, *De Bretagne en Polynésie: Paul Gauguin, pages inédites*, Avant et Après, Papeete, 1995

Steven Naifeh and Gregory White Smith, *Van Gogh: The Life*, Profile, London, 2011

Ronald Pickvance, *Van Gogh in Arles*, Metropolitan Museum of Art, New York, 1984

Louis Piérard, *La Vie Tragique de Vincent van Gogh*, Crès, Paris, 1924

Louis Piérard, *The Tragic Life of Vincent van Gogh*, Castle, London, 1925

John Rewald, 'Van Gogh en Provence', *L'Amour de L'Art*, October 1936, pp. 289–98

John Rewald, 'Van Gogh vs. Nature: Did Vincent or the Camera Lie?', *Artnews*, 1 April 1942

John Rewald, *Post-Impressionism: From Van Gogh to Gauguin*, Museum of Modern Art, New York, 1978 (3rd ed)

Mark Roskill, *Van Gogh, Gauguin and the Impressionist Circle*, Thames & Hudson, London, 1970

Jean-Maurice Rouquette (ed), *Arles: Histoire, Territoires et Cultures*, Nationale, Paris, 2008

Klaus Albrecht Schröder and others, *Van Gogh: Heartfelt Lines*, Albertina, Vienna, 2008

Debora Silverman, 'Framing art and sacred realism: Van Gogh's ways of seeing Arles', *Van Gogh Museum Journal*, 2001, pp. 45–61

Timothy Standring and Louis van Tilborgh, *Becoming Van Gogh*, Denver Art Museum, 2012

Susan Alyson Stein, *Van Gogh: A Retrospective*, Park Lane, New York, 1986

Benno Stokvis, 'Vincent van Gogh à Arles', *Gand Artistique*, January 1929, pp. 1–9

Marc Tralbaut, *Vincent van Gogh*, Viking, New York, 1969

Van Gogh à Arles: Dessins 1888–1889, Fondation Vincent van Gogh Arles, 2003

Van Gogh et Arles: Exposition du Centenaire, Musées d'Arles, 1989

Marije Vellekoop and Roelie Zwikker, *Vincent van Gogh Drawings: Arles, Saint-Rémy & Auvers-sur-Oise 1888–1890*, Van Gogh Museum, Amsterdam, 2007, vol. iv

Daniel Wildenstein, *Gauguin: A Savage in the Making, Catalogue Raisonné of the Paintings (1873–1888)*, Wildenstein Institute, Paris, 2002, 2 vols

A NOTE TO THE READER

Van Gogh's letters are numbered from the definitive 2009 edition, *Vincent van Gogh – The Letters: The Complete Illustrated and Annotated Edition*, edited by Leo Jansen, Hans Luijten and Nienke Bakker (www.vangoghletters.org). Where, occasionally, I have modified their translation, this is noted. Van Gogh's paintings are identified by the 'F' numbers from the 1970 catalogue raisonné by Jacob-Baart de la Faille, *The Works of Vincent van Gogh: His Paintings and Drawings*. Gauguin's letters up to 1888 are from Victor Merlhès, *Correspondance de Paul Gauguin 1873–1888*, 1984. His paintings are identified by 'W' numbers in Daniel Wildenstein, *Gauguin: A Savage in the Making, Catalogue Raisonné of the Paintings (1873–1888)*, 2002. Unless otherwise specified, illustrated works in this book are by Van Gogh. For illustrations, height is given before width (in centimetres). Artworks and the archive at the Van Gogh Museum in Amsterdam are mainly owned by the Vincent van Gogh Foundation, set up by the family. Frequently cited sources in the notes have abbreviated references, with the full references in the Bibliography.

INDEX

Page numbers in *italic* refer to illustrations.
Page numbers containing a 'n' refer to the page on
which the note is found, followed by the number
of the note on that page (only the more important
notes are indexed).

A

Alpilles 21, 43, 64, 174, 189, 191
Amsterdam 159, 173, 183, 194, 195
Annuaire Reirum 12, 123, *124*, 126, 197n20, 203n8, 206n21
Arles 7, 20–7, 188–91
    Alpilles 21
    Alyscamps 22, 26, 112–21, *112*, *114*, *115*, *116*, *117*, *118*, *119*, 188, 190, 194
    arena 21, 22, 27, 74, 137, 138, *138*, *139*, 188, 189, 190
    Avenue de Montmajour 8, *9*, 36, 189
    Boulevard des Lices 190
    butcher's shop 26
    Café Civette Arlésienne 184
    Café de la Gare 36, 99, *101*, 110, 145, 177, 182, 185, 189, 192
    Café du Forum 100, 189, 202n5, 202n6
    Chapel of St Accurse 113
    Church of Notre Dame de la Major 174
    Church of St Anne 23, 190
    Church of St Honorat 113, 118
    Church of St Julien 27, 74
    Church of St Trophime 23, 174, 190
    commemorative plaque, Yellow House 184
    Convent of the Cordeliers 27
    Convent of the Récollets 68, 123
    Craponne Canal 115
    Crevoulin grocery shop 36, 185
    Espace Van Gogh 190
    Folies Arlésiennes 137
    Fondation Vincent Van Gogh Arles 188, 189, 209n1
    hospital, *see main entry* hospital
    Hotel Carrel 21, *22*, 26, 27, 36, 124, 191, 192

    Hôtel-Dieu St Esprit 194
    Hotel Terminus 185
    Jardin de la Cavalerie 21
    Jonquet mill 200n3, 201n7
    Langlois Bridge 72, 73–5, *74*, 167, 190
    Mas de Griffeuille 66, 191
    Moines bridge 199n4
    Musée Lapidaire 23, 163
    Musée Réattu 22, 189
    Museon Arlaten 183, 190
    Place de la République 23, 190
    Place du Forum 100, 188, 189–90
    Place Lamartine 7, 21, 22, 35, 36, 38, 40, 43, 74, 103, 105, 156, 158, 159, 165, 167, 172, 183, 184, *184*, 185, 188, 189, 190, 192, 194, 199n7, 202n11, 208n8
    Pont Van Gogh 190
    Port-de-Bouc Canal 73
    Porte de la Cavalerie 21
    public gardens 38, 189, 190
    Rampe du Pont 173
    Réginel Bridge 190
    Rhône, *see main entry* Rhône
    Roman buildings and sites 21, 22, 73, 100, *see also* Arles, arena; Arles, Alyscamps; Arles, theatre
    Roubine du Roi canal 209n12
    Route de Tarascon 37, 44, *51*, 189, 199n4
    Rue Amédée Pichot 21, 191, 192
    Rue Anatole France 189
    Rue de la Cavalerie 197n4
    Rue des Ecoles 129
    Rue du Bout d'Arles 12, 123–4, 126, 129, 156, 157, 171, 191, 192, 197n19, 203n3
    Rue J.F. Kennedy 191
    Rue Léon Blum 191
    Rue Mireille 191
    Rue des Récollets 124, 206n22
    Salon du Forum 100
    Souchon mill 200n3, 201n7

PICTURE CREDITS

The Publishers would like to thank those listed here for permission to reproduce artworks illustrated in this book and for supplying photographs. Every care has been taken to trace copyright holders. Any we have been unable to reach are invited to contact the publishers so that a full acknowledgement may be given in subsequent editions.

akg-images: 44, 59, 66 (Erich Lessing), 78, 87 below, 96, 106, 111, 116, 117, 118 (MPortfolio/Electa), 121, 135, 147, 150 (André Held), 178 (André Held)

Archives Van Gogh Museum, Amsterdam: 164 right (T-331)

Collection of the Museon Arlaten, musée départemental d'ethnographie, cliché J.L. Maby: 115 left

The Art Archive: 28 (Mondadori Portfolio/Electa), 30 (Mondadori Portfolio/Electa), 55 (DeA Picture Library), 69 (DeA Picture Library), 72 (DeA Picture Library), 74 left (DeA Picture Library), 85 (Musée d'Orsay Paris/Collection Dagli Orti), 120 (Musée d'Orsay, Paris/Mondadori Portfolio/Electa), 132 (Musée d'Orsay, Paris/Collection Dagli Orti), 133 (Pushkin Museum, Moscow/Superstock), 138 (Hermitage Museum, Saint Petersburg/Superstock), 140 (Musée d'Orsay, Paris/Collection Dagli Orti), 166 (DeA Picture Library)

Courtesy of Association pour un Musée de la Résistance et de la Déportation en Arles et Pays d'Arles collège Frédéric Mistral, photo by the US Army: 186 above

© The Barnes Foundation: 88, 93, 122, 129

Courtesy of Mairie de Bordeaux: 128

Bridgeman Art Library, London: 20 (Musee Rodin, Paris, France/Flammarion), 38 (Photo © Lefevre Fine Art Ltd., London), 39, 42, 46, 67 (Musee Rodin, Paris/Flammarion), 68 (Kunstmuseum, Winterthur/De Agostini Picture Library), 86 (Photo © Christie's Images), 97 (National Gallery, London), 102 (Rijksmuseum Kröller-Müller, Otterlo), 130 (National Gallery, London), 134 (Pushkin Museum, Moscow), 141 (Photo © Christie's Images), 143 (National Gallery, London), 144 (Museum of Fine Arts, Boston, Massachusetts/Gift of Robert Treat Paine, 2nd), 146 (Museum of Fine Arts, Boston, Massachusetts/Gift of Robert Treat Paine, 2nd), 148 (Saint Louis Art Museum, Missouri/Funds given by Mrs Mark C. Steinberg), 151 (Museum of Fine Arts, Boston, Massachusetts/Bequest of John T. Spaulding), 160 (Pushkin Museum, Moscow), 164 left (Pushkin Museum, Moscow), 168 (© Samuel Courtauld Trust, The Courtauld Gallery, London), 169, 170 (Neue Pinakothek, Munich), 177 (Neue Pinakothek, Munich), 175 (© Samuel Courtauld Trust, The Courtauld Gallery, London)

© The Trustees of the British Museum: 48

Courtesty of Musée Calvet, Avignon: 47 below

Foundation E.G. Bührle Collection, Zurich: 136

Harvard Art Museums/Fogg Museum: 108 (Bequest from the Collection of Maurice Wertheim, Class of 1906)

The Hirschsprung Collection, Copenhagen: 31, 81

Courtesy Kimbell Art Museum, Fort Worth: 61

Kunsthalle Bremen (Der Kunstverein in Bremen, department of prints and drawings, photo Karen Blindow): 19

Courtesy of La Médiathèque d'Arles: 24–5

Mushakoji Saneatsu Memorial Museum, Chofu,
Tokyo: 95

Nasjonalmuseet for kunst, arkitektur og design,
Oslo: 45

National Gallery of Art, Washington, DC: 65
(Collection of Mr and Mrs Paul Mellon, 1992.51.10),
80 (Chester Dale Collection, 1963.10.151)

Courtesy of NIOD Institute for War, Holocaust and
Genocide Studies, Netherlands: 187

Collection Oskar Reinhart, Am Römerholz,
Winterhur: 149, 162

Rijksmuseum, Amsterdam: 48

Scala Archives: 76 (bpk, Bildagentur fuer Kunst,
Kultur und Geschichte, Berlin), 98, 104, 112
(DeAgostini Picture Library), 119 (DeAgostini
Picture Library)

Van Gogh Museum, Amsterdam (Vincent van Gogh
Foundation): Cover (s30V1962), back cover
(s32V1962), 6 (s32V1962), 8 (s32V1962),
14 (s22V1962), 16 above (s22V1962),
16 below (b4780cV1962), 17 (s157V1962),
22 (T-723), 23 (s119V1962), 33 (s24V1962),
34 (s32V1962), 37 above (d193V1962), 37 below
(b520aV1962), 40 (d311V1970), 41 (s47V1962),
52 (s117V1962), 56 (s117V1962), 62 (s30V1962),
64 (s30V1962), 87 above (b4767V1962),
90 (s37V1962), 110 (b1994V1982), 127
(d636V1962), 142 (s257V1962), 152 (s47V1962),
155 (b4822-0001V1962), 176 (s36V1962),
180 (s47V1962)

ACKNOWLEDGEMENTS

My deepest thanks go to the three editors of the magnificent 2009 edition of Van Gogh's 902 letters: Leo Jansen, Hans Luijten and Nienke Bakker. I am extremely grateful to my other colleagues (past and present) at the Van Gogh Museum in Amsterdam, particularly Isolde Cael, Maite van Dijk, Ella Hendriks, Monique Hageman, Anita Homan, Chris Stolwijk, Sjraar van Heugten, Fieke Pabst, Teio Meedendorp, Axel Rüger, Louis van Tilborgh, Lucinda Timmermans, Marije Vellekoop and Anita Vriend. It is a privilege to work in the museum's library, which includes early publications on Van Gogh assembled by Vincent Willem, Theo's son. Sylvie Rebuttini, Michel Baudat and their colleagues at the Archives Communales in Arles have always been very helpful. So too have Fabienne Martin and her staff at the Bibliothèque Municipale d'Arles. I am grateful to the London Library. Others who have kindly assisted in various ways include David Brooks, Barbara Buckley, Anne-Laure Charrier-Ranoux, Roland Courtot, Bice Curiger, Victor Doiteau, Douglas Druick, Walter Feilchenfeldt, Martin Gayford, Pierre Gazanhes, Gloria Groom, Tine van Houts, Marion Jeux, Teun Koetsier, Stefan Koldehoff, Margje Leeuwestein, Jacqueline Leroy, Bernadette Murphy, Steven Naifeh, Henry Travers Newton, James Roundell, Daniel Rouvier, Ashok Roy, Dominique Séréna-Allier, Gregory Smith, Ben Solms, Susan Stein, Anders Toftgaard, Janine Wookey and Peter Zegers. As always, my Provençal and Amsterdam friends Onelia Cardettini and Jaap Woldendorp assisted greatly with research and the intricacies of the French and Dutch languages. At Frances Lincoln, I would like to thank Andrew Dunn, the publisher, and Anna Watson, who was an excellent picture researcher. Above all I would like to thank Nicki Davis, who I worked with on *The Sunflowers are Mine: The Story of Van Gogh's Masterpiece*. She was the perfect editor and designed the elegant layout. Once again, I am deeply grateful to Alison, my wife, for her companionship in exploring Arles and her editorial assistance.